50 STATES 5000 IDEAS

50 STATES 5000 IDEAS

WHERE TO GO · WHEN TO GO · WHAT TO SEE · WHAT TO DO

TEXT BY JOE YOGERST

NATIONAL GEOGRAPHIC

WASHINGTON, D.C.

Contents

Introduction 7

United States 8

Canada 224

Illustrations Credits 282

Index 283

Opposite: Navajo Loop Trail, Bryce Canyon National Park, Utah; pages 2–3: Albuquerque International Balloon Fiesta, New Mexico

INTRODUCTION

Once in a long while, a project comes along that seems ready-made for your skills. That's exactly how I felt when National Geographic asked me to write *50 States, 5,000 Ideas*. To quote Yogi Berra, it was like déjà vu all over again, because one of my ambitions as a kid was to see as much of America as possible.

Blame it on my Uncle Emile. Visiting his home in San Diego was always a great adventure, especially digging through the drawer in his living room that was filled with greasy old gas station highway maps. Spreading them across the floor, I spent countless hours tracing my index finger along the blue highways that my uncle had followed across Texas, Louisiana, Florida, and other states, imagining what the cities, parks, and landmarks were like in each place.

Along the way, my curiosity blossomed into a full-blown love of travel and a determination to explore the continent from sea to shining sea.

My parents cultivated my passion—of both maps and geography—with road trips and vacations that found us roaming the wilds of the western United States and Canada. But my wanderlust didn't hit a fever pitch until college. I chose geography as my major, history as a minor. And rather than spend the summers sunning and surfing like so many of my friends in Southern California, I ventured inland with my own collection of highway maps.

Gas was cheap (less than 60 cents a gallon), roads were uncrowded, and if there weren't any vacancies at a motel or inn, I would simply crash in the back of my Dodge Dart. I didn't get to see the entire continent, but the summer wanderings of my college days certainly checked off a huge portion of my bucket list.

It wasn't until many years later—when I started writing *50 States, 5,000 Ideas*—that my quest to see all of America resumed. Out on the road again, in places as far-flung as the California redwoods, Georgia's Civil War battlefields, lobster shacks on the coast of Maine, Route 66 through rural Oklahoma, and the badlands of North Dakota, I came across lands both pleasingly familiar and radically different from the ones I had discovered earlier.

And just as I'd done as a kid, I started by spreading maps across my own living room floor and scouting out many of the places that appear in these pages. I may have driven my parents mad by insisting that we stop at every landmark on a given map, but it was a trait ready-made for writing this book—an obsession to leave no stone unturned in searching for the best places, experiences, and adventures in each state. Interstate highways whisked me from Point A to Point B, but it was back roads that provided many of the ideas that appear in the pages that follow.

And while it might have been more efficient to concentrate on the highlights of a given metropolis, it was marathon walkabouts—aimless wandering on foot—that unveiled many of the gems in cities big and small, from Dallas, Boston, and Virginia Beach, to Jefferson City, Missouri; Northampton, Massachusetts; and Hilo, Hawaii.

While the main text constitutes the heart of each chapter, and the bulk of the 5,000 ideas, I have to confess that the sidebars were the most fun to write. Even if it weren't my job, I could easily spend hours looking up quirky geographical facts, making mental lists of the best movies or books set in a given place, or mapping out road trips for both myself and friends. Blame it on my Uncle Emile. He's the one who started me down this long and winding road across America, and hopefully all of you who read this book will see it as an invitation to venture out on your own to explore each and every state.

—Joe Yogerst

A Black-tailed fawn (opposite) welcomes spring at Olympic National Park, Washington.

United States

New York Harbor, New York

Alabama

Sweet home to a variety of celebrated Americans—from Rosa Parks and Hank Williams, Sr., to Helen Keller and Hank Aaron—Alabama has transitioned from heart of the Cotton Belt to a well-rounded state with a diverse economy and tourist attractions. The Yellowhammer State has civil rights landmarks, Gulf Coast beaches, charming small towns, and wilderness areas at the bottom end of the Appalachian chain.

TOURISM INFORMATION

The Alabama Tourism Department maintains eight welcome centers around the state adjacent to major highway gateways. Visit alabama.travel.

● **Montgomery Visitor Information Center**
300 Water St.
Montgomery, AL 36104
Tel 334/261-1100
visitingmontgomery.com

● **Greater Birmingham CVB**
2200 Ninth Ave. N (at 22nd)
Birmingham, AL 35203
Tel 205/458-8000
inbirmingham.com

● **Fort Conde Welcome Center**
150 S Royal St.
Mobile, AL 36602
Tel 251/208-7304 or 251/208-2000
mobile.org

CITIES

Set on the banks of the Alabama River, **Montgomery** is at the center of state politics and the American civil rights movement. It was in the basement of Dexter Avenue King Memorial Baptist Church that Dr. Martin Luther King, Jr., helped organize the Montgomery Bus Boycott. Nearby, a black granite civil rights memorial commemorates all who died in the struggle. Also of interest are the Dexter Parsonage Museum, Dr. King's home from 1954 to 1960, and the Freedom Rides Museum, located in an old Greyhound Bus Station, along with the Rosa Parks Library and Museum.

Founded as a trading post in 1785 by a Sephardic Jew from Philadelphia, Montgomery's past is recalled in Old Alabama Town, an assemblage of old homes and buildings gathered from around the state. The First White House of the Confederacy, Jefferson Davis's official residence after his 1861 inauguration, displays personal items, period furniture, and war relics. The nearby Alabama Department of Archives and History was the first state-funded archives in the nation. The complex includes the Museum of Alabama. Country music lovers appreciate how the Hank Williams Museum illustrates the ill-fated superstar's influence on American music. Literary stars Scott and Zelda Fitzgerald lived in the Cloverdale district in the early 1930s; their house is now a museum dedicated to the author, his Alabama-born wife, the Jazz Age, and the Great Depression. Out on the east side of town, the Carolyn Blount Theatre in Woodmere hosts a year-round Shakespeare Festival. The surrounding Wynton M. Blount Cultural Park is also home to the Montgomery Museum of Fine Arts, with a collection that runs heavy on Southern regional art and European Old Masters.

The state's largest city, **Birmingham,** was founded after the Civil

A sign commemorates Montgomery's role in the American civil rights movement.

Downtown Birmingham has a jazz heritage, vibrant businesses, and thriving universities.

War as a steel town, mining center, and transportation hub that would grow into the industrial star of the South. One of the few remnants of those early days is the Sloss Furnaces National Historic Landmark, which produced pig iron for nearly 90 years and is now used for metal arts exhibits and other special events. The downtown Civil Rights District includes the 16th Street Baptist Church, Kelly Ingram Park, and the Birmingham Civil Rights Institute. The **Alabama Jazz Hall of Fame** in the historic Carver Theatre (one of the few theaters in the state that allowed black patrons before desegregation) honors greats of the genre who have ties to Alabama, such as Ella Fitzgerald and Duke Ellington.

A few blocks away the McWane Science Center waits with interactive exhibits, an aquarium, and an IMAX theater. Or step onto the "Heaviest Corner on Earth"—an intersection where four classic skyscrapers arose in the early 20th century. West of downtown, the Arlington Antebellum Home and Gardens is the only pre–Civil War mansion left in Birmingham, spared through its use as a Union headquarters and today fully restored with period furniture and art.

Keeping a close eye on Birmingham from the top of Red Mountain is a statue of **Vulcan,** the Roman god of fire and forge, allegedly the second-largest cast-iron statue in the United States after the Statue of

Liberty. At 56 feet (17 m) high and made entirely from locally produced iron, the statue was originally built

CAPITALISM

The current Greek Revival Alabama State Capitol building in Montgomery was rebuilt in 1850 after the original burned down. Over the years it has been the scene of many landmark events, including the birth of the Confederate States of America in 1861 and the finale of the Selma to Montgomery March in 1965. The inside of the dome is decorated with eight art deco murals each depicting a portion of the history of Alabama from 1540 to 1930.

LOCAL FLAVOR

- **Fried Green Tomatoes:** Southern comfort food doesn't get any better than unripe tomatoes coated in cornmeal and fried in bacon fat. Irondale Cafe has been serving this dish since 1928. *1906 First Ave. N, Irondale*

- **Black Bottom Pie:** A delicious mélange of custard, bourbon, and chocolate is one of the specialties at the Gaines Ridge Dinner Club in south-central Alabama. *933 Hwy 10 E, Camden*

- **Gulf Shrimp:** Forrest Gump taught the world that Alabamans cherish their shrimp, especially along the Gulf Coast at joints like LuLu's at Homeport. *200 E 25th Ave., Gulf Shores*

to represent the city's iron and steel heritage in the 1904 World's Fair in St. Louis. Adjacent to the airport, the **Southern Museum of Flight and Alabama Aviation Hall of Fame** detail the history of civilian and military aviation along with those who made it possible, from the Red Baron to Amelia Earhart. For more speedy transportation, head east to the **Barber Motorsports Museum,** which displays around 600 vintage motorcycles and race cars at any given time.

Neighboring Barber Motorsports Park is home to the Honda Indy Grand Prix of Alabama.

Sultry **Mobile,** Alabama's Gulf Coast metropolis, has a long and rich maritime history. The U.S.S. *Alabama* Battleship Memorial Park includes the decommissioned World War II battleship and the U.S.S. *Drum* submarine as well as aircraft and military memorabilia from various wars. On a lighter note, the Mobile Carnival Museum celebrates the local Mardi Gras, first celebrated

in 1703, which includes 35 parades that wend their way through city streets during the three weeks leading up to Lent. Other Mobile venues to visit include the rebuilt 18th-century Fort Conde, Church Street Historic District, Oakleigh Plantation, and the Gulf Coast Exploreum Science Center.

LANDSCAPES

Thirty-two miles (51 km) of white-sand beaches and crystal clear water are the hallmark of

Little River Canyon begins with a waterfall atop Lookout Mountain.

Alabama's Gulf Coast and host a full gamut of shoreline activities, including water sports, guided boat trips, golf, birding, deep-sea fishing, and adventure zip lines. Other attractions include the Alabama Gulf Coast Zoo, Waterville USA water park, and Gulf State Park, with its talcum-powder-fine beach, backwoods trails, copious wildlife, and freshwater lake.

On the Alabama-Florida border, 140 miles (225 km) east of Mobile, beautiful **Florala City Park** offers plenty of water sports on Lake Jackson as well as a rich stretch of Alabama's Wiregrass birding trail with the possibility of spotting bald eagles, osprey, and waterfowl. Another hour to the north, the Hank Williams, Sr., Boyhood Home in little **Georgiana** shows the country-and-western music legend's humble beginnings.

Tuskegee Institute in the eponymous town was founded in 1881 by former slave Booker T. Washington for the education of blacks. Among those who left their mark here were author George Ellison (*The Invisible Man*) and inventor and scientist George Washington Carver. The self-guided campus tour includes the University Chapel with its "singing windows," the Booker T. Washington Monument, the George Washington Carver Museum, and the graves of both great men. Moton Field on the north side of town is where the first African-American combat pilots were trained during World War II. The Tuskegee Airmen National Historic Site honors their valuable contribution to the war effort.

Set on the banks of the Black Warrior River, **Tuscaloosa** is home to the University of Alabama. Campus attractions include the Alabama Museum of Natural History and

NASA aircraft are on display at Marshall Space Flight Center in Huntsville.

Bryant-Denny Stadium, where the Crimson Tide play their home football games before 100,000 fans. In nearby **Vance,** the Mercedes-Benz U.S. International Visitor Center tenders 90-minute factory tours and a small collection of vintage vehicles.

Parts of three states (Alabama, Georgia, and Tennessee) can be seen from Lookout Mountain in northeastern Alabama. **Little River Canyon National Preserve** hugs the summit, a mosaic of woods and waterfalls, cliffs and canyons, where hiking, kayaking, and rock climbing are among the many outdoor activities. To the west, Frank Lloyd Wright's Rosenbaum House in **Florence** is considered one of his top four masterpieces. Between the two lies **Huntsville,** home to NASA's Marshall Space Flight Center and its U.S. Space & Rocket Center, one of the world's largest collections of rockets and space-related items. Nearby sights include Huntsville Botanical Garden, the EarlyWorks Children's Museum, and the

Weeden House Museum and Garden, home of poet and artist Maria Howard Weeden. ∎

FESTIVALS

• **Mobile Mardi Gras:** Even older than its New Orleans cousin, Mobile's pre-Lent bash includes bands, booze, and loads of beads; February–March.

• **Mule Day (Winfield):** The role of the humble mule in Alabama's rural development is the focus of a wingding that includes a parade, mule judging, country dance and song, and a tractor pull; September.

• **Moundville Native American Festival:** Moundville Archaeological Park hosts this celebration of Southeastern Indian history and culture; October.

• **National Shrimp Festival (Gulf Shores):** A quarter million seafood fanatics flock to local beaches for music, art, sand sculptures, and lots of tasty crustaceans; October.

Alaska

America's Last Frontier clings to its pioneer past. This land of rugged individuals, off-the-grid attitudes, and remote communities sits on the edge of the Arctic. With more than 200 parks and preserves, Alaska also safeguards more nature than any other state. Humans might be sparse in this northern territory, but animals are abundant, from grizzlies and wolves to caribou, polar bears, moose, and bald eagles.

TOURISM INFORMATION

For more information on visiting the Last Frontier, check out the TravelAlaska website: travelalaska.com.

● **Visit Anchorage Tourist Information Center**
Historic City Hall
524 W Fourth Ave.
Anchorage, AK 99501
Tel 907/276-4118
anchorage.net

● **Explore Fairbanks Visitor Center**
101 Dunkel St., Suite 111
Fairbanks, AK 99701
Tel 907/456-5774 or
800/327-5774
explorefairbanks.com

● **Ketchikan Visitors Bureau**
131 Front St.
Ketchikan, AK 99901
Tel 907/225-6166
visit-ketchikan.com

● **National Park Service**
nps.gov/state/ak

● **Alaska State Parks**
dnr.alaska.gov/parks

CITIES

One of the nation's youngest major cities, **Anchorage** didn't really get started until 1920, after being chosen as a seaport for the Alaska Railroad. It grew quickly into the state's biggest city and economic engine. Built in 1942, the art deco–style Anchorage Depot is still the starting point for journeys into the Alaskan wilds on trains such as the *Denali Star, Aurora, Coastal Classic,* and others. Downtown waits the Alaska Center for the Performing Arts, the indoor Fifth Avenue Mall, and the excellent Anchorage Museum at Rasmuson Center. The waterfront Oscar Anderson House, the town's first wood-frame home (1915), depicts life in early Anchorage. From here, the Tony Knowles Coastal Trail hugs the shoreline for 11 miles (18 km) and gives visitors the possibility of spotting moose, wolves, bald eagles, and beluga whales. The trail also passes through Earthquake Park, which commemorates the 1964 quake (9.2 magnitude) that destroyed much of coastal Alaska. The **Alaska Native Heritage Center** near Fort Richardson showcases the state's 11 major indigenous groups with storytelling, song and dance, artist demonstrations, games, and more. Northern and native plants are the focus at the Alaska Botanical Garden in **Baxter Heights,** while the Alaska Aviation Museum at **Lake Hood** has vintage aircraft and bush pilot memorabilia. Lake Hood Seaplane Base is the world's largest and busiest floatplane base.

The state's largest inland city, **Fairbanks,** lies on the banks of the Tanana River 360 miles (579 km) north of Anchorage. The wavy, white Museum of the North on the campus of the University of Alaska at Fairbanks, designed to resemble the Alaskan landscape, safeguards

A male caribou roams the tundra of the Alaska Range.

Serenity Lake mirrors the mountainous landscape of Denali National Park.

more than 1.4 million artifacts and specimens. Browse exhibits on interior and Arctic Alaska at the Morris Thompson Cultural & Visitors Center, and then get up close and personal with Alaska's tundra-dwelling deer at Running Reindeer Ranch. Ply the Chena River on the stern-wheeler *Discovery*, or partake of the many outdoor adventures available in and around Fairbanks—dogsledding, gold panning, river rafting, fly-fishing, aurora borealis viewing, and more. Fairbanks is also the northern terminus of the Alaska Highway, which runs up from British Columbia and the Yukon.

Juneau, the state capital, straddles the Alaska Panhandle and has road connections with the rest of the state. Rather than a fancy domed building, the Alaska State Capitol is boxy and nondescript (with free half-hour guided tours in the summer). However, the nearby State Library, Archives, and Museum (SLAM) is a spectacular modern structure that houses many of the state's intellectual and scientific treasures.

The bright red gondolas of the Goldbelt Mount Roberts Tramway offer panoramic views of Juneau, the Gastineau Channel, and Douglas Island on the far shore. Recall the city's gold rush origins with the Last Chance Mining Museum and the Alaska Gastineau Mill and Gold Mine Tour, and then glimpse the life of James Wickersham,

CAPITALISM

Rather than being named after a Russian explorer, Native American leader, or American pioneer, Alaska's capital city honors a French-Canadian prospector. Born in Quebec, Joe Juneau and his partner Richard Harris struck gold in 1880 and founded a settlement on the site of a nearby Auk fishing camp. Originally named Harrisburg, the name was later changed to Juneau. After Juneau died in the Yukon in 1899, his remains were returned to his namesake town and buried in Evergreen Cemetery. Seven years later (1906), Juneau became Alaska's territorial capital.

HIDDEN TREASURES

Masters of the Alaska coast from 1733 to 1867, the Russians left behind many relics:

- **Three Saints Bay (Kodiak Island):** first Russian settlement in North America; a small archaeological site reached by boat or long overland trek

- **Church of the Holy Ascension (Unalaska):** with distinctive onion domes and red roof, founded by Russian-American Company to attract native Alaskans to the Russian Orthodox faith

- **Russian Bishop's House (Sitka):** built by Finnish laborers in the 1840s, a museum and part of Sitka National Historical Park

- **Russian-American Magazin (Kodiak):** constructed in 1808 to warehouse seal and sea otter pelts, now the Baranov Museum

Alaska's "Pioneer Judge," at the 1904 Wickersham House in the historic Chicken Ridge neighborhood. The great Alaska wilderness begins on the edge of town with Mendenhall Glacier and Nugget Creek Falls, which tumbles 377 feet (115 m) into iceberg-filled Mendenhall Lake. Framing the south side of Juneau are Taku Inlet and the tidewater glaciers of the Tracy Arm Fjords.

LANDSCAPES

Alaska's Highway One runs south from Anchorage across the scenic **Kenai Peninsula.** Along the way is Chugach State Park with its diverse terrain, wildlife, and year-round recreational opportunities. Park highlights include Portage Glacier, Eklutna Lake, the Historic Iditarod Trail, and the climb up Flattop Mountain. The highway continues past Girdwood and the Alyeska winter sports resort before passing Portage Glacier. At the end of the road is **Homer**—the self-proclaimed "cosmic hamlet by the sea"—a funky old town that includes the Pratt Museum of culture and natural history, Wynn Nature Center, and the Alaska Islands and Ocean Visitor Center. Named for the man who negotiated the American purchase of Alaska from the Russians, **Seward** hosts the Alaska SeaLife Center, an education, research, and rehabilitation center for marine mammals. Seward is also the main staging point for fishing, kayaking, backpacking, and sightseeing trips into nearby Kenai Fjords National Park and its 38 tidewater glaciers.

North of Anchorage, the mighty **Alaska Range** throws up a rugged 400-mile-long (644 km) barrier across the middle of the state. The world's highest mountain range other than the Himalaya and the Andes includes 20,310-foot (6,190 m) Denali (Mount McKinley)—the tallest peak in both the U.S. and all

The Alaskan northern lights paint the sky over Denali National Park.

Some 30,000 grizzly bears live in Alaska, and they are normally solitary.

of North America. The monster peak and its hinterland are protected within the confines of **Denali National Park & Preserve,** six million acres (2.4 million ha) of subarctic wilderness that includes boreal forest and tundra, glaciers, and wild rivers. Private vehicles are restricted beyond Mile 15 of Park Road, leaving tour buses and shuttles the best ways to explore Denali's interior. This is the only U.S. national park in which sled dogs are used to patrol the wildlife and wilderness; the kennels are open to the public.

At the western extreme of the Alaska Range are two other spectacular national parks and preserves: Lake Clark and Katmai (the best place in Alaska to view grizzly bears in the wild). Offshore, **Kodiak National Wildlife Refuge** protects the homeland of the giant Kodiak bear and 117 salmon-bearing streams.

Much of southeastern Alaska falls within the boundaries of **Wrangell–Saint Elias,** the nation's largest national park, which extends all the way from the Alaska Range to the Gulf of Alaska. The park protects a

massive mosaic of beaches, fjords, glaciers, active volcanoes, woodlands, tundra, wild rivers, and nine of the 16 highest mountains peaks in the United States. Alaska's portion of the **Inside Passage** starts south of Wrangell–Saint Elias, 500 miles (805 km) of watery wilderness that embraces more than a thousand islands as well as Glacier Bay National Park and Tongass National Forest (the nation's largest national forest). This busy cruise ship route is

also the site of several historic towns.

Ketchikan's Totem Heritage Center boasts the world's largest collection of unrestored Tlingit and Haida totem piles, while Totem Bight State Historic Park offers 14 totem poles and a replica clanhouse. Sitka, the onetime capital of Russian Alaska, features a national historical park with Russian relics and the Southeast Alaska Indian Cultural Center. Skagway, gateway to the 1890s Klondike gold rush, preserves many gold rush–era buildings. Visitors tracing the route of the more than 30,000 who braved arctic conditions to reach the gold fields have three choices: hiking the 33-mile (53 km) Chilkoot Trail, riding the White Pass & Yukon Route Railway, or driving the South Klondike Highway across the mountains into Canada.

The sparsely populated northern half of Alaska above Fairbanks boasts many impressive national parks, including Gates of the Arctic, Kobuk Valley, Cape Krusenstern National Monument, Bering Land Bridge National Preserve, Noatak National Preserve, and the vast Arctic National Wildlife Refuge. ■

ROAD TRIPS

Great drives across the Last Frontier:

• Alaska Highway (Route 2) between the Yukon-Alaska border and Fairbanks (285 miles/459 km)

• The largely unpaved Dalton Highway (Route 11) between Fairbanks and Prudhoe Bay on the Arctic Ocean (500 miles/805 km)

• Highway One between Anchorage and Homer (220 miles/354 km)

• Richardson Highway (Route 4) between Valdez and Delta Junction (268 miles/431 km)

• The unpaved McCarthy Road between Chitina and McCarthy through the heart of Wrangell–St. Elias National Park (60 miles/97 km)

• George Parks Highway (Routes 3 and 1) between Anchorage and Fairbanks via Denali National Park (358 miles/576 km)

Arizona

Outsiders often imagine Arizona as endless desert, but the state comprises a range of natural and man-made landscapes. Scattered between the Grand Canyon and the saguaro forests are snowcapped volcanoes, richly wooded river valleys, and alpine meadows that are flush with wildflowers come spring. From old frontier towns and secluded Native American villages to modern urban sprawl, human Arizona is just as diverse.

CITIES

One of the largest and most energetic cities in the Southwest, **Phoenix,** with its 4.3 million inhabits, sprawls across the Valley of the Sun in the upper Salt River region of central Arizona. Founded in 1867, the city rose from the metaphorical ashes of the ancient Hohokam Indian civilization that once thrived here, and thus earned the name "Phoenix." Given the region's stark geography, it's a bit of a miracle the city survived long enough to become the territorial capital in 1889. With its endless suburbs and jam-packed freeways, modern-day Phoenix is sometimes a hard city to love. But like the Salt River soil, scratch a little beneath the surface and the pickings are rich. Visitors can overlook the city from the crest of saguaro-studded South Mountain or one of the desert trails that crawls across Camelback Mountain. More nature awaits in Papago Park, with its trademark buttes, and Desert Botanical Garden. The native peoples of the Southwest are the focus of the highly regarded Heard Museum, dedicated to the art, culture, and history of American Indians. Among its key collections are Hopi *katsina* (kachina) dolls, Zuni jewelry, Navajo textiles, and Southwestern ceramics. An unexpected gem, the Musical Instrument Museum in north Phoenix showcases musicmakers (and music) from around the globe.

Tucked in the valley's northeast corner, well-heeled **Scottsdale** offers resort hotels, golf courses, leafy urban hiking trails, and more than a hundred art galleries. Guided tours are available at Taliesin West, the Frank Lloyd Wright masterpiece that overlooks Scottsdale.

About a quarter of the size of the state capital, **Tucson** lies in a

Mission San Xavier del Bac was established in 1692 near present-day Tucson.

Changing light in the Grand Canyon, which was carved by wind, rain, and the Colorado River

natural bowl surrounded by the saguaro forests and dramatic desert mountains of southern Arizona. A stark contrast to helter-skelter Phoenix, laid-back Tucson is renowned for its outdoor lifestyle, health and beauty retreats, a college-town vibe that revolves around the University of Arizona campus, and a tasty regional cuisine that blends American and south-of-the-border flavors (such as the city's beloved Sonoran hot dog). Tucson's three historic districts—El Presidio, Barrio Histórico, and Armory Park—flaunt restored buildings and businesses. The Tucson Museum of Art shows off its excellent American West, Spanish colonial, pre-Columbian, and Hispanic folk art collections that are spread through five historic adobes. Pima Air &

Space Museum has more than 300 historic flying machines and offers bus tours of the nearby "boneyard" where some 4,000 aircraft are mothballed. Saguaro National Park bookends the city on the east and west, a vast expanse of desert where hiking trails meander through stands of towering cacti. Right outside the park entrance, the Arizona–Sonora Desert Museum is a combined zoo and botanical garden dedicated to Southwest flora and fauna. On the south side of town, Mission San Xavier del Bac is both the oldest Roman Catholic church in the U.S. and the oldest intact European structure in Arizona. Although founded in 1692, the current church, with its whitewashed Spanish colonial baroque facade, was finished in the 1790s.

LANDSCAPES

Much of the Arizona countryside still carries a wild and untamed mien, especially up north where the Colorado River and the **Grand Canyon** make a very deep impression on the landscape and all

STATE OF THE ART

- **Best movies:** *Stagecoach* (1939) and *Psycho* (1960)

- **Best books:** *The Bean Trees* by Barbara Kingsolver and *The Monkey Wrench Gang* by Edward Abbey

- **Best song:** "The Painted Desert" by 10,000 Maniacs

- **Best art:** Hopi *katsina* figures

HIDDEN TREASURES

- **Pipe Spring National Monument:** evokes the solitary life of a 19th-century frontier military outpost

- **Bearizona Wildlife Park (Williams):** drive-through wildlife park showcases native Arizona mammals, including bears, wolves, bison, sheep, elk, and bobcats

- **Lowell Observatory (Flagstaff):** evening stargazing and telescope viewing

- **Prescott:** old-fashioned Fourth of July parade and World's Oldest Rodeo

- **Musical Instrument Museum (Phoenix):** showcases music and musicmakers from around the globe

- **Cabeza Prieta National Wildlife Refuge:** pristine wilderness protecting the desert bighorn sheep, Sonoran pronghorn, desert tortoises, and other rare species

- **The Wave:** psychedelic rock formation amid the multicolored wilderness of Vermillion Cliffs National Monument

who view it. One of the true wonders of the world, the canyon is a staple on the bucket list of nearly every globetrotter for good reason. The busy South Rim can seem as crowded as a shopping mall at times, but just a few steps can bring visitors to solitude and quiet. In addition to hiking and mule trips, the canyon can also be explored on white-water rafting trips down the roller coaster–like Colorado River. In the Grand Canyon West area, within the Hualupai Indian Reservation, the vertigo-inducing Skywalk is a horseshoe-shaped balcony with a glass floor that sticks out 70 feet (21 m) from the canyon rim.

Given its proximity to the Grand Canyon and the San Francisco Peaks, **Flagstaff** has emerged in recent years as the recreational hub of northern Arizona. Perched at 6,900 feet (2,103 m), the city rotates between warm blue-sky summers and brisk winters that often bring enough snow for skiing, snowboarding, and other cold-weather pursuits. Scattered around Flagstaff are such geological gems as Meteor Crater (caused by an asteroid that hit Earth 50,000 years ago) and the lava beds of Sunset Crater Volcano National Monument.

The aptly named **Painted Desert** sprawls eastward from the Grand Canyon into the Navajo Indian Reservation and Petrified Forest National Park, which safeguards the

A giant saguaro cactus overlooks the city of Tucson.

fossilized remnants of Triassic woodlands that thrived about 225 million years ago, when dinosaurs walked the Earth. Highways lead across the **Navajo Nation** to the cliff dwellings of **Canyon de Chelly** and the spectacular sandstone buttes of Monument Valley and the Four Corners area, the only place in the U.S. where four states come together in one spot.

With water, forest, and red-rock cliffs, central Arizona is the state's most picturesque region. Scenic Oak Creek flows through leafy state parks on either side of **Sedona,** a town renowned for mountain biking and rock climbing, as well as posh resorts and New Age sensibilities. The road west from Sedona crosses the Verde River Valley before starting a steep climb up to **Jerome,** a meticulously preserved old mining town with a mixed bag of craft shops, antique stores, and funky eateries. On the other side of Mingus Mountain, **Prescott** offers another Wild West–flavored historic downtown as well as the World's Oldest Rodeo.

The **Sonoran Desert** spreads across the entire southwest corner of Arizona, from the lower Colorado River all the way to Tucson and beyond. Although well known for its iconic saguaro cacti, the Sonoran has several signature looks, from sand dunes and rocky flats to palm-filled oases and mesquite-shaded creeks. There's also plenty of human variety, ranging from remote Native American settlements to modern resort communities, such as Lake Havasu City. The latter earned its 15 minutes of fame in 1968 when city fathers purchased the fairy-tale London Bridge, had it shipped across the Atlantic, and reassembled on the edge of Lake Havasu. Nowadays the desert community is a thriving

Canyon de Chelly National Monument

water-sports hub and college town. Farther down the Colorado, **Yuma** is home to a historic territorial prison and an annual lettuce festival that celebrates its well-irrigated bounty.

Perched along the Mexican border, **Organ Pipe Cactus National Monument** and UNESCO Biosphere Reserve protect a pristine patch of Sonoran Desert for hikers, birders, night sky enthusiasts, and artists who crave stark beauty. One of the state's best preserved frontier towns, Tombstone's historic district

embraces many structures that date from the late-19th-century silver boom, as well as Boothill Cemetery and the site of the O.K. Corral. Rising high above the desert, the **Chiricahua Mountains** of southeast Arizona were once a remote hideout for Geronimo, Cochise, and other Apaches. Today the mountains and their weird rock formations offer refuge to hikers, campers, and researchers studying the last remaining jaguar habitat in the U.S. ■

LOCAL FLAVOR

• **Sonoran hot dogs:** El Güero Canelo makes a classic version of this alternative dog—a thick bun stuffed with wiener, bacon, pinto beans, chopped onions, tomatoes, and jalapeño sauce. *5201 S 12th Ave. and three other Tucson locations*

• **Dates:** The energy-packed fruit has been an Arizona staple since the 1920s when the first Medjool palms

were imported from Morocco to Dateland Farm near Yuma. *1737 S Ave. 64 E (Milepost 67 on I-8), Dateland*

• **Chimichanga:** Apparently invented by a 1920s Arizona chef, this deep-fried burrito is the house specialty at Macayo's Mexican Kitchen in Phoenix. *4001 N Central Ave. at Indian School Rd.*

Arkansas

From the Ozarks and Ouachitas to steamy Hot Springs and the slow-moving Mississippi, the Natural State is richly endowed with earthly delights, making it a must-see for those who love the great outdoors. But Arkansas has also produced more than its fair share of great Americans, a lineup that includes President Bill Clinton, entrepreneur Sam Walton, country crooner Johnny Cash, and statesman J. William Fulbright.

CITIES

Just about dead center in the state, the city of **Little Rock** sprawls along the south bank of the Arkansas River. Although it was founded in 1831, most of the state capital's sights are fairly new. The William J. Clinton Presidential Library and Museum has the largest collection of presidential papers and memorabilia in the nation and includes a replica of the Oval Office and Cabinet Room. The adjacent Heifer Village is a futuristic, hands-on educational facility that shows ways that poverty and hunger can be alleviated around the world. Visitors can travel the Arkansas River Trail upriver from the Clinton Library to the Witt Stephens Jr. Central Arkansas Nature Center and its six living habitat exhibits, the Museum of Discovery, the whitewashed Old State House (constructed 1833–1842), and the revamped River Market District. The waterfront neighborhood hosts the Ottenheimer Market Hall, antique electric trolleys, and an outdoor amphitheater. At the limestone-and-marble state capitol—the oldest surviving capitol west of the Mississippi—be sure to note the six Tiffany brass doors. Farther south, Little Rock Central High School National Historic Site is both a functioning school and a monument to the American civil rights movement. It was here in 1957 that the governor tried to block nine black students from entering the previously all-white campus. President Eisenhower sent federal troops to intervene, helping pave the way for nationwide school desegregation. Across the road in a renovated Mobil service station, the Central High Museum and Visitor Center details those events. The West 28th Street home of civil rights activist Daisy Lee Gatson Bates, an adviser to the "Little Rock Nine," is also a registered national historic landmark. MacArthur Park invites visitors to stroll the serene contemplation gardens, pay their respects at the AIDS Memorial and the Arkansas Korean War Veterans Memorial, and experience the Arkansas Arts Center and MacArthur Museum of Arkansas Military History. For something more eclectic, visit the nearby ESSE Purse Museum, a collection of

TOURISM INFORMATION

The Arkansas Department of Parks & Tourism has created welcome centers in Little Rock and 12 strategic entry points around the outer edge of the state. Visit the website at arkansas.com.

• **Little Rock Welcome Center**
1 Capitol Mall
Little Rock, AR 72201
Tel 501/682-1511

• **Hot Springs Visitor Center**
629 Central Ave.
Hot Springs, AR 71901
Tel 501/321-2835
hotsprings.org

Little Rock honors its past with the Arkansas Korean War Veteran's Memorial.

Garvan Woodland Gardens, the botanical gardens of the University of Arkansas

more than 3,000 handbags that sets out to describe the 20th-century woman through her handbag and its contents.

Rightfully called "The American Spa," **Hot Springs** lies 55 miles (89 km) west of the state capital in the heavily wooded foothills of the Ouachita Mountains. The city's 47 natural springs gush around a million gallons (3.78 milliliter) of water per day, a thermal bounty discovered thousands of years ago by Native Americans and then again by American pioneers shortly after the Louisiana Purchase. Set aside for federal protection in 1832, the reserve that protects the springs is the oldest participant in the National Park System, designated a full 40 years before Yellowstone. Besides the hiking trails, the therapeutic and de-stressing effects of hot springs are still the major draw at Hot Springs National Park. The park's "Bathhouse Row" protects nine historic bathing pavilions. Fordyce Bathhouse features a

museum of the thermal bathing industry, while the Buckstaff Bathhouse is a working facility still offering a traditional private bathtub experience. Towering above the city, the 216-foot (66 m) Hot Springs Mountain Tower provides amazing views of the Ouachita Mountains.

Around 160 miles (257 km) upriver from Little Rock, **Fort Smith** is the state's second-largest city and gateway to the Great Plains. Founded as a river port and military garrison, Fort Smith was once considered the last outpost of civilization before the lawless Oklahoma Territory. The city's frontier heritage comes alive at Fort Smith National Historic Site, where the fort museum, housed in an original 19th-century brick structure, includes exhibits on the Trail of Tears and the building's long tenure as the courthouse for "Hanging Judge" Isaac Parker, who sent more men to the gallows than any other

federal judge. A Victorian-era mansion called Miss Laura's Social Club—the only brothel on the

ROAD TRIPS

Great drives in the Natural State:

• Highway 7 from El Dorado to Harrison via Hot Springs (275 miles/443 km)

• Crowley's Ridge Parkway from Helena–West Helena to St. Francis (164 miles/264 km)

• Ozark Highlands Trail from Oak Grove to Clarksville (98 miles/158 km)

• Highway 27 from Ben Lomond to Harriet through the heart of the Ouachita (242 miles/389 km)

• Boston Mountains Scenic Loop between Fayetteville and Alma (80 miles/129 km)

National Register of Historic Places—now serves as the city visitor center.

LANDSCAPES

Spreading out in three different directions from Little Rock, the state's three national forests—Ozark, Saint Francis, and Ouachita—encompass almost three million acres (1.2 million ha) of land. In addition to handsome scenery, the parks boast numerous hiking and horseback trails, campgrounds, shooting ranges, and a multitude of lakes and streams that are perfect for fishing, boating, and other water sports. **Ozark National Forest** is also home to the state's highest point, the easily climbable Mount Magazine (2,700 feet/823 m), as well as Blanchard Springs Caverns, where lighted walkways grant visitors access to stunning limestone formations during guided tours led by U.S. Forest Service rangers.

Secluded deep in the Ozarks of northwest Arkansas, **Eureka Springs** was founded as a mountain health resort in the 1880s. The town retains much of its distinctive Victorian and alpine architecture and is considered one of the nation's best preserved 19th-century villages. With diversity weekends and other alternative lifestyle events, Eureka Springs is also renowned as an island of LGBT rights and tourism in an otherwise very conservative state. The town's diverse attractions include the exotic animals of Turpentine Creek Wildlife Refuge and the 66-foot (20 m) Christ of the Ozarks statue crowning the summit of Magnetic Mountain.

Nearby **Bentonville** is known for Sam Walton's original 1950 five-and-dime store overlooking the town square, now the Walmart Visitor Center & Museum. The Alice Walton–endowed Crystal Bridges Museum of American Art—which features the works of American artists from colonial to contemporary—occupies a stunning modern campus designed by Moshe Safdie.

Over on the west side, the Museum of Native American History offers a fascinating glimpse into the life and times of the continent's first inhabitants with artifacts including an elegant Mississippian head effigy pot and complete woolly mammoth skeleton. Fifteen miles (24 km) away, Pea Ridge National Military Park marks the site of a pivotal 1862 clash that kept Missouri from falling into Confederate hands. **Crater of Diamonds State Park** near Murfreesboro is the world's

A cliff of Petit Jean Mountain at the eponymous state park in Arkansas

The Old Grist Mill in North Little Rock was featured in the classic 1939 film *Gone With the Wind*.

only public diamond mine. The sparkly stones are not plentiful, but if you're lucky enough to find one, you can keep it. A gentleman did just that in February 2015 when he unearthed a two-carat diamond here—one of more than 30,000 diamonds discovered by visitors since the crater became a state park in 1972. Forty minutes farther south, **Historic Washington State Park** preserves a pioneer settlement where Davy Crockett and Sam Houston stopped on their way to the Alamo.

The state's eastern boundary is delineated by the Mississippi River and a region called the **Arkansas Delta.** Among the area's landmarks are Lake Chicot, the largest oxbow lake in the U.S., and the very old town of Arkansas Post. Founded in 1686, the waterfront burg was the first permanent French colony in the Mississippi River Valley. Today it's a venue for riparian wildlife viewing and an annual Civil War battle reenactment. ∎

LITTLE-KNOWN FACTS

• The Old Grist Mill in North Little Rock was featured in the opening credits of *Gone With the Wind* and is thought to be the only set from the movie still in existence.

• Arkansas Post is the only place in the state that saw battle during both the American Revolution and Civil War.

• The U.S.S. *Razorback* submarine, centerpiece of the Arkansas Inland Maritime Museum in North Little Rock, actually served longer in the Turkish navy (30 years) than the U.S. fleet (24 years).

• According to carbon dating, the water that bubbles up from beneath the ground in Hot Springs originated as rainwater around 4,400 years ago.

• Based on the *Li'l Abner* comic strip, Dogpatch USA near Marble Falls was a hillbilly-themed amusement park that operated from 1968 to 1993. Instead of garbage cans, large, mechanized pig and goat heads "ate" trash fed to them by the park's visitors. After it closed, Dogpatch was left to decay and today sits overgrown and derelict.

California

The Golden State shines in many ways, from the splendor of the redwoods and the High Sierra to Hollywood's movie magic and the high-tech wonders of Silicon Valley. America's most populous state (est. 38 million) offers something for every style and taste: world-class museums and cutting-edge theme parks; gourmet wining and dining, or fish tacos on the beach; vibrant urban enclaves and remote backcountry trails.

CITIES

A heady blend of bridges and bays, hills and high-rise towers, ethnic enclaves and eccentric history make **San Francisco** one of the world's most alluring cities. A classic tour starts with a cable car ride from Market Street to Chinatown and over the crest of Nob Hill to Fisherman's Wharf with its seafood restaurants, historic ships, and ferries to notorious Alcatraz Island. Drive the waterfront through the posh Marina District to the Golden Gate Bridge and then south through the leafy Presidio to sprawling Golden Gate Park, whose myriad attractions include the de Young Museum of fine art, the California Academy of Sciences museum, and the Japanese Tea Garden. On the park's eastern flank, the Haight-Ashbury district still carries a counterculture vibe that gradually fades into the "painted lady" Victorian splendor of nearby Alamo Square. Other "city by the bay" highlights include twisty Lombard Street, the Exploratorium science center, old Mission Dolores, the Italian eateries of North Beach, and the Impressionist art of the Legion of Honor museum.

TOURISM INFORMATION

Visit California has 19 welcome centers scattered around the state, most of them near interstate highway gateways. Find them at visitcalifornia.com.

● **San Francisco Visitor Information Center**
900 Market St.
San Francisco, CA 94102
Tel 415/391-2000
sanfrancisco.travel

● **Los Angeles Visitor Information Center**
Hollywood & Highland Center
6801 Hollywood Blvd.
Hollywood, CA 90028
Tel 323/467-6412
discoverlosangeles.com

● **San Diego Visitor Information Center**
2688 E Mission Bay Dr.
San Diego, CA 92109
Tel 619/276-8200
sandiego.org

● **National Park Service**
nps.gov/state/ca

● **California State Parks**
Tel 916/653-6995 or
800/777-0369
parks.ca.gov

San Francisco is a small part of the Greater Bay Area that includes edgy **Berkeley,** home of the University of California, Berkeley, campus and funky Telegraph Avenue. Beyond the north side of the Golden Gate Bridge is the colorful waterfront town of **Sausalito** with its houseboats and water's-edge restaurants. An hour's drive down the peninsula, a cluster of cutting-edge cities such as Palo Alto, Sunnyvale, Mountain View, and Redwood City comprise **Silicon Valley.** Here you can informally tour the Googleplex, stroll the Stanford University campus, or play vintage cyber games at the Computer History Museum.

Surfing at sunset at La Jolla's famed Windansea Beach

Lettuce is a thriving crop in California's fertile Salinas Valley.

If you know the way to **San Jose,** visit that city's Winchester Mystery House or Rosicrucian Egyptian Museum.

Los Angeles lies 380 miles (612 km) to the south, a sprawling megalopolis of close to 20 million people and a seemingly equal number of cars. While today's movie studios are located in Burbank and Culver City, cinematic history spangles Hollywood Boulevard with its sidewalk stars and Chinese Theater, and nearby Sunset Strip endures as a musical hotbed. The Fairfax District hosts the bubbling La Brea Tar Pits and Museum of paleontology, the eclectic Los Angeles County Museum of Art (LACMA), and the historic Farmers Market—a foodie's paradise. Sunset Boulevard meanders through Beverly Hills, past the UCLA campus and the artsy Getty Center, on its way to the Pacific Ocean, where a right turn leads to Malibu's beaches and a left to Santa Monica and the vibrant Venice

Beach boardwalk. Downtown Los Angeles is in the midst of a renaissance that includes the L.A. Live entertainment complex, Grammy Museum, futuristic Walt Disney Concert Hall, the recently revived Grand Central Market, and the Museum of Contemporary Art (MOCA). Among the lively neighborhoods clustered around downtown are Little Tokyo, Chinatown, and hipster-heavy Silver Lake. Perched in the hills above it is Griffith Park and its celebrated observatory, where many a movie scene has played out.

L.A.'s satellite cities sprawl down the coast and inland. **Long Beach** is home port to the *Queen Mary* and the Aquarium of the Pacific. The global theme park craze started in and around **Anaheim,** where Disneyland, Disney's California Adventure Park, and Knott's Berry Farm offer fantasy lands and white-knuckle thrills. **Pasadena** is renowned for the Rose Bowl football stadium (which

also hosts a giant flea market once a month) and the Tournament of Roses Parade, as well as the diverse Norton Simon Museum of art. Railroad money funded the nearby Huntington Library with its priceless books, artworks, and botanical gardens.

Over the past 50 years, **San Diego** has morphed from a die-hard

CAPITALISM

California may hold the record for most state capitals. Monterey served as the seat of government during the Spanish, Mexican, and early American periods (1777–1849). But it moved afterward through a quick succession of other towns—San Jose, Vallejo, Benicia, Sacramento, and San Francisco—before the powers that be decided to permanently base the capital in Sacramento starting in 1869. The imposing neoclassical state capitol building was completed in 1874.

ROAD TRIPS

Great drives across the Golden State:

• Santa Monica to Fort Bragg on Highway One (625 miles/1,006 km)

• Highway 49 through the Gold Country (175 miles/282 km)

• Tioga Road over the crest of the Sierras (39 miles/63 km)

• Volcanic Legacy Scenic Byway from Lassen Volcanic National Park to Lava Beds National Monument (196 miles/315 km)

• Olancha to Indio via Death Valley, Mojave National Preserve, and Joshua Tree (407 miles/655 km)

Shops on Fourth Street, West Berkeley; opposite: redwoods' grandeur

"navy town" into a laid-back burg, where the sea, sun, and sand are the major attractions. The nation's largest man-made aquatic park, Mission Bay revolves around water sports and SeaWorld. A former site of two world's fairs, Balboa Park is home to the San Diego Zoo, Old Globe Theatre, and a dozen noteworthy museums. The park overlooks downtown San Diego, where revitalized neighborhoods such as the Gaslamp District, East Village, and Little Italy have turned a once drowsy central city into a thriving dining and entertainment zone. The U.S.S. *Midway* aircraft carrier museum and *Star of India* clipper ship anchor San Diego's waterfront. Across the bay are **Coronado,** with its legendary Hotel Del Coronado, and the giant thumb of **Point Loma** extending into the Pacific as part of Cabrillo National Monument. San Diego's Spanish heritage endures in Old

Town San Diego State Historic Park and Mission San Diego de Alcala.

COASTS

California's coastline stretches 840 miles (1,352 km) between Oregon and Mexico, third longest of any state and remarkably diverse from top to bottom. The northernmost shore is **Redwood Country**, a string of state and federal parklands in Del Norte and Humboldt Counties that embrace the world's highest trees. The northern stretch of Highway One connects such charming coastal towns such as Fort Bragg,

Mendocino, and Bodega Bay. Along the way are Point Reyes National Seashore and the old Russian settlement at Fort Ross, as well as the secluded beaches and hiking trails of Golden Gate National Recreation Area in Marin County.

South of San Francisco, Highway One continues along the **Central Coast,** meandering through bucolic Half Moon Bay and surfer-dude Santa Cruz to the Monterey Peninsula. The towns of Monterey, Carmel, and Pacific Grove are connected by a scenic route known as the 17-Mile Drive past weathered

---

LOCAL FLAVOR

• **Fish tacos:** The original Rubio's restaurant in San Diego is where the California version of the Mexican maritime specialty was born in the 1970s. *4504 E Mission Bay Dr., Pacific Beach*

• **Artichokes:** True to its name, the Giant Artichoke Restaurant in Castroville serves the green spiky vegetable several dozen different ways—in

salads, ice cream, and burgers, deep fried, steamed, and even French fried. *11241 Merritt St., Castroville*

• **California cuisine:** Alice Waters pioneered the state's distinctive combination of artistic presentation and farm-fresh ingredients at her legendary Chez Panisse restaurant. *1517 Shattuck Ave., Berkeley*

LITTLE-KNOWN FACTS

California is the bee's knees when it comes to trees:

• A bristlecone pine in the White Mountains of eastern California is the world's oldest tree (more than 5,000 years old).

• The Torrey pine, America's rarest pine tree, grows naturally in only two places: Santa Rosa Island and San Diego's north shore.

• General Sherman in Sequoia National Park is the world's largest tree (52,508 cubic feet/1,487 cu m total wood volume).

• Hyperion in Redwood National and State Parks is the world's tallest tree (380 feet/116 m).

• California fan palms, which give Palms Springs its name, are the state's only native palm tree.

LANDSCAPES

Blessed with rich soil and abundant microclimates, the valleys running north from the Bay Area produce some of the world's finest wines. **Napa Valley** burst onto the world scene in the 1970s when its wines began beating the best of France in international tasting competitions. Mondavi, Beringer, and Chateau Montelena are among the more established wineries, but upstarts such as Coppola and CADE also produce exceptional vintages. Yountville is the hub of a Napa Valley gastronomic scene that features some of the state's most celebrated restaurants. **Sonoma Valley** is a throwback to the Napa of half a century ago, a mosaic of small wineries, bed-and-breakfast inns, and sidewalk cafés. Sonoma town was once the northernmost extension of Spanish civilization on the West Coast; its 1823 mission is the last of 21 established by the Franciscan padres. Less explored vine lands, such as the Russian River and Alexander Valley, lie farther west.

California's storied **Gold Country** hugs the foothills between Sacramento and the Sierra, a string of towns along aptly named Highway 49 that lured "49er" prospectors from around the world starting in 1849. John Marshall discovered the first nuggets at Sutter's Mill near Coloma, now a state park devoted to the gold rush era. Among other towns that retain their Wild West edge are Nevada City, Murphys, and Columbia. A different sort of gold pours forth from the Gold Country these days—the white wines produced by another up-and-coming wine area. And rather than glistening flakes, the region's rivers are now better known for white-water rafting and tubing. Any Sacramento

cypress trees, fabled golf links, and coves where sea otters frolic. The highway continues through **Big Sur** with its New Age lifestyles and precipitous Pacific vistas to San Simeon and Hearst Castle. The lower portion of the Central Coast revolves around the wine-rich **Santa Ynez Valley,** picturesque **Santa Barbara,** and breezy **Ventura** just north of L.A., jumping-off point for Channel Islands National Park.

The **Orange County** coast on the south side of L.A. is full of affluent enclaves, including Newport Beach and Laguna Beach. Luxury homes and hotels hug the cliff tops all the way down to Dana Point, where the Ocean Institute offers whale-watching cruises and other marine activities. San Diego's **North County** offers a string of famous surf breaks; sleepy beach towns such as Carlsbad, Encinitas, and Solana Beach; as well as Legoland California Resort and Thoroughbred horse racing at Del Mar.

A row of San Francisco's picturesque "painted ladies" glows at sunset.

FESTIVALS

- **Tournament of Roses Parade (Pasadena):** floats festooned with real flowers followed by a classic college football game; New Year's Day

- **Mendocino Crab, Wine, and Beer Festival (Mendocino County):** feast on crustaceans, cabernet, and craft brews; January

- **Chinese New Year Parade (San Francisco):** the nation's largest, loudest, and most flamboyant lunar New Year celebration; January or February

- **Coachella Music Festival (Indio):** Headline acts gather in the desert; April

- **U.S. Open of Surfing (Huntington Beach):** world's largest professional surfing competition; July–August

- **Festival of Arts Pageant of the Masters (Laguna Beach):** Famous artworks come alive; July–August

- **December Nights (San Diego):** Balboa Park transforms into a winter wonderland.

The San Francisco–Oakland Bay Bridge at sunset

sojourn should include a visit to the state capitol, as well as gold rush–era Old Sacramento with its excellent California State Railroad Museum and *Delta King* riverboat, now a hotel and restaurant.

Those raging rivers tumble down from the **Sierra Nevada,** a monumental mountain range that includes the highest point in the lower 48 states (Mount Whitney, at 14,505 feet/4,421 m) as well as Yosemite and King's Canyon National Parks and Sequoia National Forest. The Mammoth Lakes area, a mecca for both winter and summer recreation, lies in the eastern side of the Sierra. Farther north is dark blue (and awfully deep) Lake Tahoe, another year-round outdoor sports hub that California shares with Nevada. North of pioneer-era Truckee—with its transcontinental railroad and Donner Party legacy—the Sierra gently fades into the **Cascade Range** and tectonic hot spots including Mount Shasta and Lassen Volcanic National Park.

California is blessed with two very different arid landscapes. The **Mojave Desert,** which sprawls across a massive area between Los Angeles and Las Vegas, is also called a "high desert" because much of it sits above 2,000 feet (610 m). But ironically it also contains North America's lowest elevation in Death Valley (282 feet/86 m below sea level). The desert's iconic Joshua trees are preserved in a national park of the same name, while other desert wonders unfold in Mojave National Preserve. The **Colorado Desert** (aka low desert) offers much starker scenery, often devoid of vege-

tation and scorched by triple-digit temperatures for much of the year. Irrigation from the Colorado River has transformed Palm Springs and the rest of the Coachella Valley into an oasis of golf courses, spa resorts, and palm-shaded swimming pools. Anza-Borrego, the largest state park in the contiguous U.S., safeguards a desert wilderness roughly the size of Rhode Island. ■

STATE OF THE ART

- **Best movies:** *Citizen Kane* (1941) and *Chinatown* (1974)

- **Best books:** *Cannery Row* by John Steinbeck and *L.A. Confidential* by James Ellroy

- **Best songs:** "California" by Joni Mitchell and "California Girls" by the Beach Boys

- **Best art:** David Hockney's "Swimming Pool" series

- **Best plays:** *Zoot Suit* by Luis Valdez and *The Time of Your Life* by William Saroyan

Colorado

"Transitional" is an apt word for Colorado, a state that marks the geographic changeover from the Great Plains to the Rocky Mountains. It has residents that are among the nation's most conservative and most progressive and is home to communities ranging from massive cities to windswept ghost towns. Numerous national parks, wild rivers, red-rock canyons, and winter sports attractions add to the allure of the Centennial State.

CITIES

Founded in 1858 in what was then the Kansas Territory, **Denver** has grown from a small gold mining settlement into a dynamic metropolis that is both the capital of Colorado and largest city of the intermountain West. With its trademark golden dome, the state capitol building anchors the Capitol Hill district, home to such leading cultural institutions as the Denver Art Museum, the Kirkland Museum of Fine & Decorative Art, and the History Colorado Center. The spirit of Margaret "Unsinkable Molly" Brown—who championed the women's suffragette movement, promoted social reform for Colorado's mining communities, and survived the *Titanic* sinking—lives on at her home, now the Molly Brown House Museum. Also of note is the Clyfford Still Museum, where more than 3,000 pieces represent the lifetime work of abstract expressionist painter Clyfford Still (1904–1980).

On a more mercenary note, the Denver Mint offers free tours of the American moneymaking process. Spend your stash at Union Station, reopened in 2014 after a makeover transformed the 1881 building into a combined hotel, retail, restaurant, and transportation hub. Arrayed along the South Platte River are the Downtown Aquarium, Children's Museum of Denver, and Elitch Gardens theme and water park with its roller coasters and other thrill rides. The River North Art District (RiNo) is home to numerous galleries, furnituremakers, and photographers. Nearby are the Forney Museum of Transportation (heavy on cars, trains, and tractors), the National Western Stock Show grounds, and the Black American West Museum, which honors African Americans who pioneered the West. Parks on the east side hold the Denver Zoo,

TOURISM INFORMATION

Colorado Tourism staffs 10 welcome centers around the state, most of them at interstate or U.S. Highway gateways. For more information, check colorado.com.

• **Visit Denver Tourist Information Center**
1575 California St.
(at 16th Street Mall)
Denver, CO 80202
Tel 303/892-1112 or
800/233-6837
denver.org

• **Fort Collins Welcome Center**
3745 E Prospect Rd.
Fort Collins, CO 80525
Tel 970/491-3583 or
800/274-3678
visitftcollins.com

• **Colorado Springs Visitor Center**
515 S Cascade Ave.
Colorado Springs, CO 80903
Tel 719/635-7506
visitcos.com

• **National Park Service**
nps.gov/state/co

• **Colorado State Parks**
cpw.state.co.us

The state capitol building in Denver has extensive formal gardens.

Autumn meets winter at the Maroon Bells near Aspen.

the Denver Museum of Nature & Science, and the Denver Botanic Gardens with its emphasis on high-altitude and western U.S. vegetation. On Denver's southwest edge, Red Rocks Park and Amphitheatre hosts big-name music acts in awesome natural surroundings.

Colorado's other major cities also lie along the Front Range, both north and south of Denver. **Fort Collins** is a boisterous college town with one of the nation's most vibrant craft beer cultures, with beer tasting tours via bus or bike. Take in the highly interactive Fort Collins Museum of Discovery, the Center for Fine Art Photography, the offbeat Swetsville Zoo (where the animals are metal sculptures), or hop on the vintage trams of the Fort Collins Municipal Railway.

Much farther down the Front Range, **Colorado Springs** flaunts a Southwestern vibe complemented by red-rock surroundings. Garden of the Gods and its massive sandstone formations offer rock climbing, Jeep and Segway tours, and a Native American dance program. Old Colorado City Historic District preserves dozens of buildings erected during the region's late 19th-century gold rush. Suffused with an artsy, counterculture lifestyle, Manitou Springs proffers a large historic district, cliff dwellings, Miramont Castle Museum, Cave of the Winds, and the Pikes Peak Cog Railway. Colorado Springs' other icons include the U.S. Air Force Academy, National Museum of World War II Aviation, the U.S. Olympic Training Center, and the spectacular waterfalls of North Cheyenne Cañon Park.

LANDSCAPES

Colorado is almost equally divided between the Great Plains and the Rocky Mountains, unremittingly flat in the east and ruggedly high in the west. The Colorado Rockies embrace some of the highest peaks in the continental U.S.

CAPITALISM

Denver is renowned as the Mile High City. But over the years there's been some controversy as to where it is exactly one mile (1.6 km) above sea level. The west steps of the state capitol building boast no less than three plaques marking the supposed spot. The earliest marker (dating from the 19th century) is affixed to the 15th step. After a 1969 measurement by Colorado State University students, another mile-high marker was attached to the 18th step. Finally in 2003, modern GPS identified the exact spot as the 13th step and a third plaque was added.

including 14,440-foot (4,401 m) Mount Elbert. **Rocky Mountain National Park** offers an excellent introduction to the Colorado highlands, home to a wide array of wildlife and landscapes ranging from thick woods to alpine meadows and high-altitude tundra, with more than 350 miles (563 km) of trails plus Trail Ridge Road, the nation's highest paved roadway. In the shadow of the Rockies, **Boulder** mixes college life and counterculture, a left-leaning town that hosts the University of Colorado, Fiske Planetarium, the Pearl Street pedestrian shopping zone, and plenty of microbreweries.

On the other side of the Front Range from Denver, **Vail Ski Resort** has evolved into one of the world's premier winter sports venues. Founded in the 1960s, Vail's combination of groomed slopes and backcountry pistes makes it the third largest ski area in the nation. In summer, the nearby Holy Cross Wilderness Area offers 164 miles (264 km) of trails. Other Vail attractions include the Colorado Ski and Snowboard Museum and the Betty Ford Alpine Gardens.

Vail is often mentioned in the same breath with **Aspen,** another primo Colorado ski resort on the far side of the Holy Cross mountains, renowned as a refuge for the rich and famous. Even if you can't afford to buy (or ski), visit for the avant-garde Aspen Art Museum, performances at the 1889 Wheeler Opera House, and such annual events as the Aspen Music Festival & School, Jazz at Aspen Snowmass, and the Food & Wine Classic in Aspen. Much of the area around Aspen falls within **White River National Forest,** with

ROAD TRIPS

Great drives across the Centennial State:

- San Juan Skyway loop (Highways 160, 145, 62, and 550) from Durango or Cortez (236 miles/380 km)

- Highway 34 over the crest of the Rockies on the Trail Ridge Road between Loveland and Granby (93 miles/150 km)

- Silver Thread route (Highway 149) between South Fork and Gunnison (128 miles/206 km)

- Unaweep Tabeguache route (Highways 141 and 145) between Whitewater and Placerville (131 miles/211 km)

- Santa Fe Trail (Highways 350 and 50) between Trinidad and Lamar (136 miles/219 km)

A skier takes advantage of powder-covered ridges in Aspen.

eight wilderness areas filled with trails, lakes, rivers, and a host of campsites.

Reaching western Colorado, the Rockies gradually fade into an arid, semidesert wilderness of mesas, buttes, and deeply eroded canyons. Among the region's landmarks are Dinosaur National Monument, the red-rock landscapes of Colorado National Monument, and the white-water adventure found in Black Canyon of the Gunnison National Park.

Pikes Peak is named after early 19th-century American explorer Zebulon Pike, who tried but failed to reach its 14,110-foot (4,301 m) summit. (Nowadays there's a road all the way to the top.) **Royal Gorge,** on the Arkansas River near Cañon City, is Colorado's answer to the Grand Canyon, a massive gouge in the earth that measures 10 miles (16 km) long and more than 1,000 feet (305 m) deep: The vertigo-inducing Royal Gorge Bridge leaps across the canyon. Nearby attractions include adventure zip lines, gondola rides, and the Royal Gorge, a narrow-gauge heritage railroad (built in 1884) that operates between Georgetown and Silver Plume.

Great Sand Dunes National Park & Preserve in southern Colorado shelters the highest sand dunes in North America including the 750-foot (229 m) Star Dune. Beyond the park's 30-square-mile (78 sq km) dune field, the park's topography gradually rises to woodlands, meadows, alpine lakes, and even tundra in the Sangre de Cristo mountain range.

Dominating Colorado's southwest corner, the San Juan Mountains are ripe for hiking, fly-fishing, or soaking in hot springs. **Durango**

Winds sculpt the changeable hills of Great Sand Dunes National Park & Preserve.

and **Silverton**—connected by a 45-mile (72 km) historic narrow-gauge railroad—are the region's major tourism hubs. The ancient high-rise homes of **Mesa Verde National Park** were built by the ancestral Puebloans between A.D. 600 and 1300. The park protects more than 5,000 known archaeological sites, including 600 cliff dwellings.

Telluride, another old mining town, is a popular summer festival location and winter resort. With around 300 inches (762 cm) of snow and 300 days of sunshine each year, Telluride can almost guarantee that you'll be skiing or snowboarding under blue skies. A gondola ascends to Mountain Village, starting point for both ski pistes and mountain bike trails. Other trails lead to Bear Creek Falls and Bridal Veil Falls. The Telluride Historical Museum recounts the town's history from mining to ski resort. ■

HIDDEN TREASURES

Colorado's copious mining booms are recalled in the state's numerous ghost towns, including:

• **Ashcroft (near Aspen):** another well-preserved relic; gained fame in the 1950s as the location for the popular TV series *Sergeant Preston of the Yukon*

• **Independence (near Aspen):** flourished in the 1880s after silver was discovered in nearby Independence Pass

• **Carson (near Lake City):** was one of Colorado's highest mining camps, perched at 12,000 feet (3,658 m) on the Continental Divide; hard to reach but worth the effort for the dozens of structures from its late 19th-century heyday

• **Saint Elmo (near Buena Vista):** boasts a number of carefully restored wooden buildings, including a guesthouse for overnight stays, and a prospector cemetery at nearby Tincup Pass

Connecticut

The so-called Land of Steady Habits was founded in the 1630s by Puritans from neighboring Massachusetts and later became a bedrock of colonial rebellion and American creativity that nurtured the likes of Mark Twain, Noah Webster, and P. T. Barnum. Today the state draws visitors from all over with its colonial heritage, lengthy shoreline, and an abundance of cultural institutions.

TOURISM INFORMATION

The Connecticut Office of Tourism has established six welcome centers at interstate and major highway gateways around the state. Visit the website at ctvisit .com.

• **Hartford Visitor Information Center**
Old State House
800 Main St.
Hartford, CT 06103
Tel 860/522-6766
hartford.com

• **Info New Haven Visitor Center**
1000 Chapel St.
(at College St.)
New Haven, CT 06510
Tel 203/773-9494
visitnewhaven.com

• **Connecticut State Parks & Forests**
ct.gov./deep

CITIES

Almost dead center in the middle of Connecticut, **Hartford** is the state capital, fulcrum of the American insurance industry, and hub of the largest metro area completely within the state. It also has quite a literary heritage. The Mark Twain House & Museum, where the celebrated author lived for 17 years and penned *The Adventures of Tom Sawyer,* offers insight into his personal and professional life. The nearby Harriet Beecher Stowe House is where the esteemed author of *Uncle Tom's Cabin* lived during the last 23 years of her life. With its lily pond and rolling lawns flanking the state capitol, Bushnell Park—America's first municipal park—offers a green escape in central Hartford. Corning Fountain, the Soldiers & Sailors Memorial Arch, the Spanish-American War Memorial, and an antique carousel are among the park's other attractions. The adjacent Bushnell Performing Arts Center presents a wide array of talent. Near the park's eastern extreme, Wadsworth Atheneum (founded in 1842) is one of the nation's oldest art museums. Reopened in 2015 after an extensive renovation, the collection of nearly 50,000 works spans 32 galleries and 15 public spaces.

Forty miles (64 km) south of the capital on Long Island Sound, **New Haven** is best known for Yale University, founded in 1701 as the third higher education institution in the nation's original 13 Colonies. Highlights of the campus include the Peabody Museum of Natural History, the Yale Art Gallery, Beinecke Rare Book & Manuscript Library (with its Gutenberg Bible), and the Yale Center for British Art. Packed with Italian eateries, New Haven's "little Italy" along Wooster Street is one of the country's oldest intact Italian neighborhoods. The nearby Knights of Columbus Museum features Roman Catholic history and artifacts in the city where the fraternal order was founded in 1882. Centerpiece of heavily wooded East Rock Park is a 200-million-year-old monolith that rises more that 350 feet (107 m) above the Mill River Valley.

Newly minted graduates of Yale University in New Haven

The pedestrian thoroughfare of Founders Bridge in downtown Hartford

Farther west along the shore, **Bridgeport** was the birthplace of the Frisbee and Subway restaurants, as well as the longtime residence of showman supreme P. T. Barnum. The Barnum Museum tenders an extensive collection on the circus legend and the history of Bridgeport. Housatonic Museum of Art offers an extensive collection that spans ancient African and Asian art to works by Chagall and Ansel Adams. Seaside Park and Fayerweather Island form a recreation area on Long Island Sound established in the 19th century largely through the efforts of P. T. Barnum, who envisioned that "a most lovely park might be, and ought to be, opened along the whole waterfront." Anchoring the end of the island is the historic 1823 Black Rock Harbor Lighthouse.

LANDSCAPES

Connecticut offers a host of small towns and main streets. Tucked down in the state's southwest corner is **Greenwich,** its swank main avenue considered by many to be the Rodeo Drive of the Northeast. The tony town also flaunts the Bruce Museum of Arts and Science, Putnam Cottage, and Byram Beach with its public freshwater swimming pool. In summer, ferries travel to offshore Great Captain Island and Island Beach.

Architect Philip Johnson's Glass House in **New Canaan** is considered one of the landmark structures of the 20th century. Completely transparent, the building's wall-less interior is surrounded by quarter-inch-thick (0.63 mm) glass with no curtains or blinds. Aldrich Contemporary Art Museum in **Ridgefield** showcases rotating pieces based on common contemporary themes. The country retreat of painter J. Alden Weir for 40 years, Weir Farm National Historic Site in **Wilton** includes his studio and home as well as the gardens that inspired many of his works.

On Long Island Sound not far from New Haven, **Guilford** offers a large and leafy town green, a significant number of pre-1800 houses, and five historic homes to explore including the Henry Whitfield State Museum, the state's oldest stone house. The Florence Griswold Museum in **Old Lyme** highlights the Lyme Art Colony, where many renowned artists spent their summer during the early years of the 20th century. In **Mystic,** Mystic Seaport comprises a reproduction

19th-century seafaring town and maritime museum. Among its fleet of historic ships are the whaler *Charles W. Morgan,* three-master *Joseph Conrad,* and steamboat *Sabino.* Five minutes up the road, Mystic Aquarium & Sea Research Foundation harbors beluga whales, African penguins, jellyfish, and other denizens of the deep. Located on the Thames River in **Groton,** the U.S. Navy's Submarine Force Library and Museum offers tours of the U.S.S. *Nautilus,* one of the world's first nuclear-powered submarines.

Ten miles (16 km) up the Thames River is **Mohegan Sun,** one of several Native American casinos in Connecticut with a massive (364,000 square feet/33,817 sq m) gambling floor spread over three areas dubbed Earth, Wind, and Sky. The nearby **Foxwoods Resort** in Mashantucket offers another massive casino in addition to five hotels and 30 restaurants. The Mashantucket Pequot Museum & Research Center illuminates the history and culture of the tribal

nation through such exhibits as a re-created 16th-century Pequot village and *The Witness,* a 30-minute film about the Pequot War of 1637, when 600 members of the tribe were killed by English colonists.

Near the state's northeast extreme, the Gothic Revival–style Roseland Cottage in **Woodstock** was built in

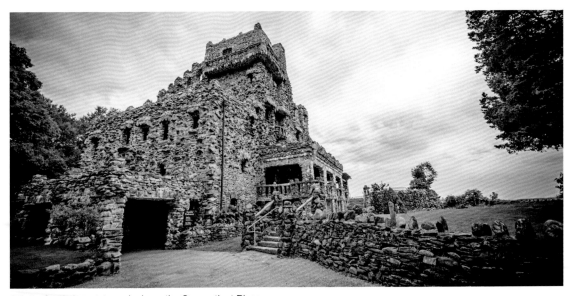

Gillette Castle in a state park above the Connecticut River

Five Mile Point Light marks the harbor entrance to Connecticut's Long Island Sound.

1846 as the summer home of Henry and Lucy Bowen. The estate is now a national historic landmark and features an icehouse, aviary, carriage barn, and the nation's oldest surviving indoor bowling alley. The New England Air Museum in **Windsor Locks** houses more than 80 historic aircraft (including helicopters, amphibious craft, and modern jets) in two large hangars as well as a flight simulator, pedal-pusher airplanes, and other hands-on exhibits. **Talcott Mountain State Park** near Bloomfield offers outstanding hiking and biking, cross-country skiing and snowshoeing, plus panoramic views from the summit and historic Heublein Tower. Rising 700 feet (213 m) above the surrounding terrain, the 13-mile-long (21 km) mountain is large enough to spawn its own microclimates, small ecosystems, and rare plant communities.

Founded in 1846, **Lake Compounce** is the country's oldest continually operating amusement park. Among its main attractions are the wooden Boulder Dash coaster, the 1927 vintage Wildcat coaster, and the new Phobia Phear coaster with its 180-degree vertical twist, as well as the Crocodile Cove water park.

Quirky Gillette Castle, high on a hill in **East Haddam,** was built in 1919 as the home of William Hooker Gillette, the actor who first played Sherlock Holmes on stage and silent film. Inside, no two doors are the same, hidden mirrors allow for surveillance of guests, and there's a movable table set on tracks. Built in the 1870s on the banks of the Connecticut River in East Haddam, Goodspeed Opera House remains a hotbed for musical theater; its Tony Award–winning troupe has staged more than 250 musicals over the past 50 years, including nearly two dozen productions exported to Broadway. ■

HIDDEN TREASURES

Quaff your way along the Connecticut wine and beer trails:

• **Haight-Brown Vineyard (Litchfield):** combines wine, cheese, and chocolate tastings

• **DiGrazia Vineyards (Brookfield):** encourages picnics

• **McLaughlin Vineyards (Sandy Hook):** wine and maple syrup on a farm that includes a hiking trail and a wildlife/bald eagle sanctuary

• **Willimantic Brewing Company (Willimantic):** set within a renovated 1909 U.S. post office with art deco murals and a 60-foot (18 m) mahogany bar

• **Cambridge House Brew Pub (Granby):** blends microbrewery and family-style community tavern with regular live entertainment

• **Ordinem Ecentrici Coctores (OEC) Brewing (Oxford):** tours of the malt house and hop fields, tasting room, food trucks, and special events

Delaware

Colonial history and coastal fun are the twin anchors of Delaware's travel allure. It was the first state to ratify the U.S. Constitution, and it makes up for its small size with a variety of attractions: an urbane big city, charming small towns, one of the eastern seaboard's best beach resorts, and a surprising array of state parks, wildlife refuges, and other parklands.

CITIES

Named for an 18th-century British prime minister, **Wilmington** is strategically perched on Delaware River and the mid-Atlantic transportation corridor. The city makes its living from banking, finance, and multiple entities bearing the DuPont name. Riverfront Wilmington is a good area to stroll and sample local wares. This onetime industrial wasteland on the banks of the Christina River is also home to the Delaware Children's Museum, the Delaware Sports Museum & Hall of Fame, the offbeat City Theatre Company, and the Delaware Center for the Contemporary Arts (the state's only modern art museum). Upstream are the Russell Peterson Wildlife Refuge and the DuPont Environmental Education Center. The Old Swedes Church near downtown recalls Delaware's origins as a Swedish colony. A variety of plays, comedy, and concerts are staged at the historic 1871 Grand Opera House with its imposing Second Empire–style design. Located in leafy Brandywine Hills, the Delaware Art Museum boasts a good pre-Raphaelite collection as well as 19th- and 20th-century American art.

Dover was the hub of the state's patriotic efforts during the Revolutionary War and declared the state capital before the end of the conflict. Described as an urban "park without boundaries," the city's First State Heritage Park links various

The Delaware Legislative Hall, where the state's general assembly gathers

Restaurants and outdoor dining are part of the attraction at Rehoboth Beach.

historic and cultural landmarks and highlights Delaware's role as the First State. Among the park's attractions are the Biggs Museum of American Art with its permanent collection of American fine and decorative arts, the Delaware Public Archives, and the John Bell House, the oldest wooden structure in Dover. The Johnson Victrola Museum highlights the sound recording industry and was named to honor Delaware-born Eldridge Reeves Johnson, who developed the Victrola. The park also holds Woodburn, the official residence of Delaware's governor since 1965; its neighbor, Hall House; and the Old State House, which served as the capitol from 1791 to 1932. Many of the city's historic structures also cluster around The Green, including

the early 18th-century courthouse where Delaware's delegates voted to ratify the U.S. Constitution. DuPont Highway heads north from downtown to Dover Downs Hotel and Casino and the "monster mile" of Dover International Speedway, a NASCAR fixture famous for its 46-foot-high (14 m) Miles the Monster scrunching a full-size stock car in his left hand. On the south side of town, the Air Mobility Command Museum, housed in historic Hangar 1301 at Dover Air Force Base, is dedicated to the history of airlifting and air refueling. The collection includes more than 30 aircraft from a giant C-5A Galaxy cargo hauler and KC Stratotankers to a B-17 Flying Fortress and a VC-9C Air Force Two. Just beyond the base, John Dickinson Plantation

transports visitors back to 18th-century America via living-history tours and events at the home of a

CAPITALISM

Delaware is one of the few states that doesn't have a capitol building per se. Instead, the General Assembly meets in the Delaware Legislative Hall in The Green in Dover. Even though it may look 300 years old, the structure is actually a 20th-century creation, a Colonial Revival–style building erected in the 1930s. Guided tours include visits to both chambers, loads of local history, and portraits of the many celebrated Delawareans, from Founding Father Thomas McKean through to Admiral William F. Halsey.

Founding Father and signer of the Constitution.

LANDSCAPES

Home to many generations of the du Pont family and their grand homes, Delaware's **Chateau Country** luxuriates in the leafy countryside just north of Wilmington. One, Nemours Mansion & Gardens, is the sprawling French-style country estate that Alfred I. du Pont built for his wife, Alicia, in 1910. The nearby Hagley Museum & Library on the banks of the Brandywine Creek includes the original du Pont gunpowder mills, another palatial family home (built by E. I. du Pont in 1803), French-styled gardens, and a collection of antique vehicles. The library has amassed materials on business, technology, and innovation from the 18th century onward.

The fabulous **Winterthur Museum** of American decorative arts was the brainchild of Henry Francis du Pont. Its 175 rooms hold nearly 90,000 objects, including the Campbell Collection of Soup Tureens. Extensive grounds also harbor a research library and 60-acre (24 ha) naturalistic garden with tram rides. Yet another du Pont legacy is the Delaware Museum of Natural History in suburban Winterthur. Founded in 1972 by John Eleuthère du Pont, the state's only natural history collection is still sponsored by the DuPont Company.

Prior to 1965, when the state purchased the land, the du Pont family also owned the area that now contains **Brandywine Creek State Park.** In addition to the nature preserves Tulip Tree Woods and Freshwater Marsh, the park offers a nature center and abundant recreation opportunities. Delaware's newest state park, **Auburn Heights Preserve,** gives visitors a chance to see what life was like when automobiles were first introduced via the Marshall Steam Museum, the

world's largest collection of operating steam cars. Auburn Heights Mansion is furnished as it would have been in the 1890s, with tours by appointment. The Marshall family donated the property to the state in 2008.

Sixteen miles (26 km) south of Wilmington, historic **New Castle** features cobblestone streets and colonial, Dutch, and federal architecture arrayed along a waterfront that looks much as it did 200 years ago. Erected in 1732, the New Castle Court House is one of the oldest surviving courthouses in the U.S.; it also served as Delaware's first state capitol building. Also arrayed around the village green are the 17th-century Dutch House, 18th-century Amstel House, Immanuel Episcopal Church on the Green (1703), New Castle Presbyterian Church (1707), and Jessop's Tavern (1674).

Delaware Bay meets the Atlantic at **Cape Henlopen State Park,** featuring a lighthouse, the Seaside Nature Center, and a World War II observation tower as well as basic

The historic Nemours Mansion & Gardens in Wilmington

The unspoiled beaches of Fenwick Island

campsites. Just outside the park, the **Junction and Breakwater Trail** (5 miles/8 km, one way), a crushed-stone rail trail, leads through wetlands and farmland along the old Penn Central route between Lewes and Rehoboth Beach, on either side of the cape.

Delaware's most popular coastal resort, **Rehoboth Beach** renders good weather practically year-round, as well as a mile-long (1.6 km) boardwalk, wide white-sand beaches, and numerous seaside distractions. Among the latter are Funland amusement park, the musical theater of the Clear Space Theatre Company, and the thirst-quenching brews at Dogfish Head, one of the oldest craft breweries on the East Coast. On the south end of Rehoboth, Dewey Beach offers Atlantic sands on one side and a broad bay on the other, ideal for kayaking, paddleboarding, and windsurfing. Away from the water, the isthmus is packed with

clubs and bars. Farther south, elongated **Delaware Shores State Park** flaunts six miles (10 km) of shoreline with surf fishing, horse-back riding, beach volleyball, clamming, and pretty good board surfing. In addition, the park's Indian River Marina facilitates all sorts of boating.

At the bottom end of the Delaware coast, **Fenwick Island** offers a string of often uncrowded strands for swimming, fishing, and beach-

combing. On the island's leeward side, Assawoman Bay is the place for jet skiing, sailing, windsurfing, boating, and other water sports. Fenwick Island State Park, a three-mile (5 km) stretch of barrier island, is one of the few beaches in Delaware with a designated board surfing area. Inland from the coast and housed in an old schoolhouse, the Nanticoke Indian Museum in Millsboro has artifacts dating back to 8000 B.C. ■

HIDDEN TREASURES

Despite its diminutive size, Delaware is unexpectedly rich in nature areas:

• **Bombay Hook Wildlife Refuge (Smyrna):** Observe migratory birds and other animals along a 12-mile (19 km) driving route and five hiking trails.

• **Trap Pond State Park (Laurel):** This park protects one of the last remaining freshwater wetlands.

• **The Great Marsh (Lewes):** Canoe or kayak this mosaic of wetlands, mudflats, and Atlantic white cedar swamp.

• **Woodlawn Tract (Brandywine):** The northernmost unit of the new First State National Historic Park embraces more than 1,100 acres (445 ha) of rolling hills and woodland in the Beaver Valley.

District of Columbia

At just 68 square miles (176 sq km), the U.S. capital proves that great things come in small packages. In addition to the three branches of the federal government, Washington, D.C., manages to accommodate dozens of museums, monuments, and other attractions, several sizable parks, and a number of intriguing neighborhoods. Founded in 1790, the district set an example for purpose-built national capitals.

THE MALL

District of Columbia designer Pierre l'Enfant envisioned a grand avenue running east–west through the city of Washington, from the young nation's capitol building to the slight rise where the Washington Monument now stands. Over the next half century, that dream gradually transformed into the reality of a long, leafy park-land stretching from Capitol Hill to the Lincoln Memorial. This **National Mall** is today flanked by many of the nation's most import-ant political and cultural institu-tions. Seat of the U.S. Senate and House of Representatives, the colos-sal white-domed U.S. Capitol is perhaps the most recognizable building in the entire nation. The Senate wing was completed in 1800, with the remainder of the original structure built over the next

11 years—just in time to be torched by British troops during the War of 1812. The Capitol's resurrection was completed in 1866 when its distinctive dome was finally fin-ished. Popular tours throughout the inside of the ornately decorated building can be reserved online. Rising behind the Capitol are the U.S. Supreme Court Building and the ornate Thomas Jefferson Build-ing of the Library of Congress, the world's second largest collection of books, documents, and maps after the British Library.

TOURISM INFORMATION

Destination DC is the official visitor's bureau for the city of Washington. Visit the website at washington.org.

- **Washington Welcome Center**
1001 E St. NW
Washington, D.C. 20004
Tel 202/347-6609
downtowndc.org

- **White House Visitor Center**
1450 Pennsylvania Ave. NW
U.S. Dept. of Commerce Building
Washington, D.C. 20230
Tel 202/208-1631
nps.gov/whho

- **U.S. Capitol Visitor Center Capitol Hill**
E Capitol St. NE
(at First St. NE)
Washington, D.C. 20004
Tel 202/226-8000
visitthecapitol.gov

- **Smithsonian Office of Visitor Services**
The Castle
1000 Jefferson Dr. SW
Washington, D.C. 20013
Tel 202/633-1000
si.edu/visit

- **National Park Service**
nps.gov/state/dc

Washington, D.C.'s Chinatown, marked by the Friendship Archway

Cherry trees in spring bloom frame the Thomas Jefferson Memorial by the Tidal Basin.

Near the base of Capitol Hill awaits the National Gallery of Art, originally built around the private collection of financier and Treasury Secretary Andrew Mellon and other philanthropists seeking to create one of the world's great art museums. Today the collection spans most of the great masters of the past 500 years including the only Leonardo da Vinci painting ("Ginevra de' Benci") in any U.S. museum. The Smithsonian Institution, headquartered in a distinctive "castle," along with many of its museums, sprawls along both sides of the Mall and beyond. The National Air and Space Museum, its most popular branch, houses the 1903 Wright Brothers Flyer, Charles Lindbergh's *Spirit of Saint Louis,* the Apollo 11 command module, and many other famous flying machines. Among the Smithsonian's 17 other area collections are the National Museum of American History, the National Museum of Natural History, the National Museum of African Art, the Asian-oriented Freer and Sackler Galleries, the National Museum of the American Indian, the Hirshhorn Museum and Sculpture Garden, and the new National Museum of African American History and Culture.

In the center of the Mall stands the stark stone obelisk of the 555-foot-tall (169 m) Washington Monument, built to honor the nation's first president. The three stages of its construction can be seen in the changing colors of the facing stones. An elevator whisks visitors to the top for bird's-eye views across Washington and northern Virginia. South of the monument, the United States Holocaust Memorial Museum documents Holocaust history and provides interactive opportunities to learn more about it.

North of the monument stretches the oval green space known as the **Ellipse** (annual home of the National Christmas Tree), beyond which stands 1600 Pennsylvania Avenue, the nations' best known address. Home and office to the president of the United States, the White House was built in 1792 and rebuilt in 1818 after being set on fire by the British. While tours are hard to snag and must be reserved through a congressional office or embassy, the adjacent White House Visitor Center offers exhibits on historic occasions and presidential families. Across the North Lawn are historic Blair House (the presidential

guesthouse) and Lafayette Square, with its monuments to the Marquis de Lafayette and Andrew Jackson.

West of the Washington Monument, the Mall takes on a somber mien, with a reflecting pool flanked by the National World War II Memorial, Korean War Veterans Memorial, Vietnam Veterans Memorial, the Vietnam Women's Memorial, and others dedicated to American servicemen and servicewomen. Constitution Gardens provides a shady area to sit or stroll as well as a tribute to the 56 signers of the Declaration of Independence. The Lincoln Memorial anchors the western end of the Reflecting Pool, with a 19-foot (6 m) statue of a seated Abraham Lincoln and 36 columns representing each of the states that existed at the time of his death. The steps in front of the memorial have hosted many historic events, including Martin Luther King, Jr.'s "I Have a Dream" speech in 1963.

URBAN LANDSCAPES

Washington's riverfront is spangled with parks, gardens, and other national monuments. **West Potomac Park** harbors a memorial to Martin Luther King, Jr., and a walk around the edge of the Tidal Basin lined with cherry trees that burst into white bloom each spring inspiring the annual Cherry Blossom Festival. Along the way are the Franklin Delano Roosevelt Memorial (with four outdoor rooms devoted to each of his four terms in office) and the domed Thomas Jefferson Memorial, with a 19-foot (6 m) statue of the third president surrounded by engraved excerpts from the Declaration of Independence and other writings. North along the waterfront are the John F. Kennedy Center for the Performing Arts, the infamous Watergate complex, and the Thompson Boat Center, where canoes, kayaks, rowing sculls, and bikes can be rented by the hour. Old and elegant **Georgetown** hugs the palisades above the

Giant pandas are a favorite at the Smithsonian National Zoo.

river, home to hip shops, trendy restaurants, and the hallowed university of the same name. Upstream from Georgetown, the **Capital Crescent Trail** leads 11 miles (18 km) to Silver Spring, Maryland, while the **Chesapeake and Ohio Canal towpath** eventually meanders 184 miles (296 km) to Cumberland, Maryland.

The revitalized **Penn Quarter** east of the White House has evolved into a lively arts and entertainment district clustered around the Verizon Center (home to the NHL Capitals, NBA Wizards, and WNBA Mystics). Here, too, is Ford's Theatre, where President Abraham Lincoln was shot on April 14, 1865; he was then carried to the redbrick Petersen House across the road, where he died several hours later. Several blocks away are the Smithsonian American Art Museum and the highly acclaimed International Spy Museum. Exhibits at the latter include an Enigma cipher machine instrumental in breaking Nazi codes in World War II, one of James Bond's Aston Martins, and a range of espionage paraphernalia. Along the southern edge of Penn Quarter, the innovative Newseum takes visitors on a journey through the history of American news and journalism. A block away, the

The Martin Luther King, Jr. Memorial

National Archives offers visitors the chance to eyeball original copies of the Declaration of Independence, Constitution, and Bill of Rights, as well as the Emancipation Proclamation and the Louisiana Purchase Treaty.

Northwest Washington quickly morphs from residential streets into the bucolic confines of **Rock Creek Park,** the nation's third national park and the capital's major green space, established in 1890 by an act

of Congress. Perched at the park's southern end, the Smithsonian National Zoological Park (National Zoo) offers one of the country's oldest and finest creature collections. A mile (1.6 km) west rises Washington National Cathedral, one of the world's largest places of worship. Its Gothic architecture, stained-glass windows, gargoyles, and other features can be explored on your own or via expert-led tours. ■

HIDDEN TREASURES

• **United States Botanic Garden:** an outdoor garden and marvelous 1933 glass-enclosed conservatory in the shadow of the Capitol building

• **The Phillips Collection:** the private collection of Duncan Phillips, who helped bring modern art to America's shores

• **Basilica of the National Shrine of the Immaculate Conception:** the nation's foremost Roman Catholic shrine, an immense Byzantine-Romanesque structure with more than 70 chapels and oratories

• **Civil War Defenses of Washington:** a necklace of 17 forts around the outer

edge of D.C., now tranquil confines for outdoor pursuits

• **Hillwood Estate, Museum, and Gardens:** in the former home of cereal heiress Marjorie Merriweather Post; a glittering showcase of Russian imperial and French rococo treasures wrapped inside 25 acres (10 ha) of gardens and forest

Florida

In many respects, the Sunshine State invented modern tourism with its early beach resorts, wacky tourist traps, and sprawling theme parks. And it continues to push the envelope in developing new attractions and luring even more visitors to see them. If Florida were an independent nation, it would welcome more tourists each year (nearly 100 million) than any other country on Earth.

CITIES

Heart of the nation's fourth largest urban area, **Miami** is both a popular vacation destination (with the world's busiest cruise port) and a dynamic business hub, home to many international banks and corporations. Downtown, Baywalk Path meanders along the waterfront past a sculpture honoring the space shuttle *Challenger,* American Airlines Arena (home of the NBA Miami Heat), and the dramatic Pérez Art Museum Miami. Little Havana, just west of downtown, is the best place in Florida to sample salsa, cigars, and Cuban sandwiches.

The celebrated Cuban-American neighborhood's landmarks—such as Domino Park and Versailles Restaurant—are found along Calle Ocho (8th Street). Just offshore on Watson Island are the Miami Children's Museum and Jungle Island, a vintage wildlife attraction (opened 1936). MacArthur Causeway continues across Biscayne Bay, past the Miami Cruise Ship Terminal to Miami Beach. Sprawling across a dozen barrier islands, **Miami Beach** is actually a separate city from big brother Miami, a tableau of beautiful beaches, classic art deco buildings decorated with neon, posh

waterfront hotels, and rowdy nightclubs. The hip South Beach neighborhood comprises everything south of Dade Boulevard. Tucked inside of this über-trendy area is the Art Deco District, many of its pastel-colored treasures set along Ocean Drive.

South of Miami Beach is a string of other barrier islands. **Virginia Key** is home to a very nice beach, mountain bike park, and another vintage attraction, the Miami Seaquarium marine theme park. Home to many celebrities over the years, **Key Biscayne** is known for ritzy hotels and more white-sand strands. **Biscayne National Park** protects coral reefs, mangrove swamps, and limestone keys along Miami's south

Miami's Little Havana pulses with Afro-Caribbean rhythms.

Mickey Mouse is the emblem of Walt Disney's Magic Kingdom.

shore. The park facilitates diving, boating, fishing, kayaking, snorkeling, camping, and wildlife-watching. Suburban **Homestead** provides a venue for the excellent Zoo Miami, with its many cage-less natural habitats, and the Gold Coast Railroad Museum, whose collection of 30 antique railway cars includes the *Ferdinand Magellan,* the official U.S. presidential railcar for FDR, Truman, and Eisenhower.

Prior to 1965, **Orlando** was a small mild-mannered city surrounded by lakes and citrus groves. But in that year, Walt Disney decided that its inland location (away from hurricanes) would be ideal for a Florida version of his wildly popular California theme park. He was right: Orlando hosted 62 million visitors in 2014. Walt Disney World now encompasses four distinct theme parks (Magic

Kingdom, Animal Kingdom, Epcot, Hollywood Studios), two water parks, a permanent Cirque du Soleil theater, the ESPN Wide World of Sports Complex, and more. Following Disney's lead, Universal has its own dazzling complex here, including Universal Studios, Islands of Adventure, and the Wizarding World of Harry Potter–Hogsmeade, as well as a water park, retail zone, and five resort hotels. Rounding out the city's theme park roster are SeaWorld Orlando, Legoland Florida, and the vintage (1949) Gatorland. The Greater Orlando area also offers a world-renowned Tiffany collection at the Charles Hosmer Morse Museum of American Art (Winter Park), The Nature Conservancy's Disney Wilderness Preserve (Poinciana), the Orlando Science Center complete with planetarium, and the

CAPITALISM

Rather than choose from the Spanish capitals of West Florida (Pensacola) and East Florida (Saint Augustine), the Americans who assumed control of Florida in the early 1820s decided to center their territorial government somewhere in between. They selected the site of a former Apalachee Indian village and began legislating in the wilderness. The first capitol was basically a glorified log cabin, but in the 1840s came a handsome domed structure that would host the state government for more than 130 years. Deemed obsolete by the 1970s, the Classical Revival–style "Old Capitol" was replaced by a 22-story cement monolith; they now stand side by side in central Tallahassee.

nearby Mennello Museum of American Art.

Arrayed around a huge bay on Florida's Gulf Coast, the **Tampa–Saint Petersburg** metro area embraces 44 communities and more than 2.4 million people. Snatch a panoramic overview from the landmark Sunshine Skyway bridge, built on stilts and two gigantic pylons. The Tampa Bay History Center has permanent exhibits tracing the history of the area over 12,000 years. Farther east along the Tampa waterfront are the Florida Aquarium and the S.S. *American Victory* cargo ship museum. In the opposite direction, Tampa Riverwalk meanders along the shoreline to the Florida Museum of Photographic Arts, the Glazer Children's Museum, and the Tampa Museum of Art. Northeast of downtown, Ybor City is a national historic landmark district named for its founder, 19th-century cigar baron Vicente Martinez Ybor. Latin flavor runs throughout the neighborhood's shops, galleries, and restaurants, many of them housed in historic structures. Busch Gardens, an enormous Africa-themed park, features thrill rides and animal encounters.

On the Atlantic coast north of Miami, **Fort Lauderdale** is best known for beaches and boating canals. The city has worked hard to eclipse its notorious spring break reputation and now offers a range of upscale hotels, restaurants, nightspots, and shopping. Once the winter retreat of artists Frederic Clay Bartlett and Evelyn Fortune, the Bonnet House Museum & Gardens includes a lovely plantation-style estate situated within five different barrier-island ecosystems. The oldest surviving structure in Broward County, Stranahan House was built by Ohio businessman Frank

Beachside in Fort Lauderdale; opposite: after hours in Miami's South Beach

Stranahan, generally credited as being the city's founding father. Broward Center for the Performing Arts presents a year-round slate of drama, dance, comedy, concerts, and more.

Jacksonville is both the largest city in Florida and the largest city by area in the entire continental U.S. Often overshadowed by the state's tourism heavyweights, Jacksonville offers an enticing blend of outdoor recreation and cultural sights on the Saint Johns River. These include the Cummer Museum of Art and Gardens, the remains of a 16th-century French outpost called Fort Caroline, Catty Shack Ranch Wildlife Sanctuary, the 18th-century Kingsley Plantation, and the art deco Florida Theatre.

COASTS

Everglades National Park protects the southern extreme of the nation's largest tropical wetlands, a vast expanse of grasslands, mangrove swamp, pine and cypress woodland, and inland waterways

ROAD TRIPS

Great drives across the Sunshine State:

- U.S. Highway One between Homestead and Key West via the Florida Keys (127 miles/ 204 km)

- Florida Black Bear Scenic Byway (Highway 40) between Silver Springs and Ormond Beach (65 miles/105 km)

- A1A Scenic and Historic Coastal Byway between Miami and Fernandina Beach (338 miles/544 km)

- Tamiami Trail (Highway 41) between Miami and Tampa through the Everglades and along the southern Gulf Coast (275 miles/443 km)

- Highway 98 along the Florida Panhandle coast between Medart and Pensacola (215 miles/346 km)

that are home to an incredible array of wildlife, including alligators, dolphins, manatees, Florida panthers, black bears, and 360 bird species. The various habitats can be explored via walking trails, boardwalks, and boat. Airboat tours are available outside the park.

On the other side of Florida Bay, the **Florida Keys** stretch 110 miles (177 km) into the wild blue yonder. The fabled archipelago comprises more than 1,700 islands, the main ones connected by causeways and 42 bridges. Key Largo, nearest to the mainland, is host to John Pennekamp Coral Reef State Park, protecting coral reefs and shipwrecks spread across 70 nautical square miles (240 sq km). Islamorada is renowned for sportfishing, while Marathon is a family-friendly boating haven that actually traverses seven isles. Perched at the very end, funky Key West has been home to the likes of Ernest Hemingway, Tennessee Williams, Robert Frost, and Jimmy Buffett. In addition to

loads of history and culture, Key West also boasts its fair share of beautiful beaches.

North of Fort Lauderdale, Florida's Atlantic coast is dotted with hundred of beach towns large and small. **Cape Canaveral** is famously home to the Kennedy Space Center, host to all of NASA's manned space flights since the early 1960s. It spreads across 219 square miles (567 sq km) on Merritt Island and offers a range of exhibits, simulations, and films, as well as bus tours of the complex. **Daytona International Speedway** in Daytona Beach is the location of the most prestigious race in NASCAR: the Daytona 500. The track's museum includes one of the planet's largest collections of motor-racing trophies, vehicles, driver memorabilia, and other racing artifacts. Guided tours include pit road and victory lane.

Founded in 1565 by Spanish conquistadors and the first capital of American Florida, **Saint Augustine** is the state's historical gem. It

STATE OF THE ART

- **Best movies:** *Key Largo* (1948) and *The Right Stuff* (1983)

- **Best books:** *Hoot* by Carl Hiaasen and *The Yearling* by Marjorie Kinnan Rawlings

- **Best songs:** "Margaritaville" by Jimmy Buffett and the *Let It Loose* album by Gloria Estefan and Miami Sound Machine

- **Best art:** the pioneering pop art of James Rosenquist

- **Best TV shows:** *Dexter, Miami Vice,* and the original *Flipper*

safeguards a remarkable inventory of structures from different ages such as the Castillo de San Marcos (1672–1695) and the flamboyant Ponce de León Hotel (1888), now part of Flagler College. Saint Augustine's leading museum is the Lightner, with its excellent collection of 19th-century decorative and fine art housed within a remarkable Spanish Renaissance–style building. Other landmarks include the Oldest Wooden Schoolhouse, Potter's Wax Museum (the nation's first), the Ximenez-Fatio House Museum, the Old Jail, the Spanish Military Hospital and Museum, and Saint Augustine Lighthouse. Among the modern attractions are the World Golf Hall of Fame and the Pirate & Treasure Museum, and ghost and vampire tours are now after-dark staples.

Florida's lengthy **west coast** starts just north of the Everglades with a string of laid-back Gulf resorts—Marco Island, Naples, Fort Myers, and Sanibel Island. One of Florida's early high-society

Ernest Hemingway's Key West home retains many of the author's belongings.

The statue "Christ of the Abyss" at John Pennekamp Coral Reef State Park off Key Largo

hubs, **Sarasota** retains its touch of class with the rambling oceanfront estate of John and Mable Ringling. Their mansion, the Venetian Gothic–style Ca' d'Zan, is now open to the public as part of The Ringling art museum and showcases the work of old masters and includes a circus museum, theater, and extensive gardens. Farther up the coast, **Tarpon Springs** boasts the nation's largest percentage of Greek Americans, whose ancestors immigrated to the area to work in the then-booming sponge industry. Today's visitors come for the Greek food and festivals, historic architecture, and a chance to mingle with the last of the spongers.

The **Florida Panhandle** stretches off the northwest corner of the state, a 200-mile (322 km) strip beneath Georgia and Alabama. Variously called the Emerald Coast or the Redneck Riviera, Panama City Beach tenders 27 miles (43 km) of sugar-white beaches and warm Gulf of Mexico water. Campers can pitch their tents along the shore at Saint Andrew's State Park and Camp Helen State Park. At the panhandle's western end is Pensacola, a hard-core navy outpost where the National Naval Aviation Museum offers a viewing platform to watch the Blue Angels practice (mid-March to mid-November). Offshore, Perdido Key and Gulf Islands National Seashore feature beaches, wetlands, estuaries, and wildlife. ■

LITTLE-KNOWN FACTS

• The Indian Temple Mound Museum in Fort Walton Beach safeguards American Indian artifacts dating back 12,000 years, as well as relics of European explorers, pirates, and early pioneers.

• Fort Jefferson in Dry Tortugas National Park was built over 30 years (1846–1875) with 16 million bricks. It is the largest masonry structure in the Western Hemisphere.

• Siesta Key Beach near Sarasota is made up of 99 percent quartz sand and has been deemed the "whitest beach in the world."

• Fort Mose in Saint Augustine was founded in 1738 and became the first free black settlement in North America. It played a significant role in the 18th-century War of Jenkins' Ear between the Spanish and British.

Georgia

The heart of the New South, Georgia has morphed into a dynamic 21st-century state where innovation, creativity, and entrepreneurial savvy trump the farming and fishing that sustained Georgians in the past. Atlanta leads the way with its high-rise skyline and hip neighborhoods, while moody Savannah continues to thrive on the good old days and its many ghosts, and outdoor recreation abounds in the Sea Islands and Appalachians.

CITIES

Slowly rising from the ashes of Civil War destruction, **Atlanta** became the dynamic capital of the New South and a sprawling metropolis that is now home to more than 5.5 million people. Flanked by modern high-rise towers, Peachtree Street cuts an impressive path through downtown Atlanta and the famous Five Points intersection. In addition to the Georgia State University campus, downtown is renowned for Underground Atlanta, a subterranean redevelopment area that blends shopping, dining, and historical structures. On the other side of Steve Polk Plaza, the Georgia Capitol closely resembles the U.S. Capitol in Washington, D.C. Self-guided tours include a museum with an array of Georgia natural and historical artifacts. On the northwestern edge of downtown lies Centennial Olympic Park and its varied attractions, including the excellent Georgia Aquarium, the National Center of Civil and Human Rights, and the College Football Hall of Fame. East of downtown, the Sweet

TOURISM INFORMATION

Georgia maintains 11 visitor information centers, most of them adjacent to interstate gateways around the edge of the state. Find out more at exploregeorgia.org.

● **Atlanta Centennial Olympic Park Visitor Center**
265 Park Avenue NW
Atlanta, GA 30313
Tel 404/222-7275

● **ACVB Visitor Center**
Underground Atlanta
65 Upper Alabama St.
Atlanta, GA 30303
Tel 404/577-2148
atlanta.net

● **Savannah Visitors Information Center**
301 Martin Luther King, Jr., Blvd.
Savannah, GA 31401
Tel 912/944-0455
visitsavannah.com

● **National Park Service**
nps.gov/state/ga

Auburn Historic District is a storied African-American neighborhood with many of its landmarks now within the confines of the Martin Luther King, Jr., National Historic Site. These include his birth home at 501 Auburn Avenue, Ebenezer Baptist Church, his grave in the Freedom Hall Complex, and the King Center for Nonviolent Social Change. The nearby Jimmy Carter Presidential Library and Museum houses papers, artifacts, and personal memorabilia relating to the 39th president. Midtown's worthy sights include the High Museum of Art, Atlanta Symphony Hall, the offbeat Center for Puppetry Arts, Museum of Design Atlanta, historic Fox Theater, and the Margaret Mitchell House,

Liberty Plaza in front of the Georgia Capitol with Atlanta's skyline beyond

The Forsyth Park fountain in Savannah

where the author wrote *Gone With the Wind*. Located near the Georgia Tech University campus, The Varsity claims to be the world's largest drive-in restaurant, serving Ramblin' Wreck football fans since 1928. The posh Buckhead district includes the Atlanta History Center, 33 acres (13 ha) of gardens and trails that connect the Atlanta History Museum, Centennial Olympic Games Museum, and historic Swan House (1928).

A city rich in both history and legends, larger-than-life personalities, and more than its fair share of ghosts, **Savannah** simmers on the banks of its eponymous river

in the fabled Low Country along the Atlantic coast. Founded in 1733 as the capital of recently established British Georgia, the sultry metropolis has evolved into the stereotype of what we think a southern city should be: grand mansions sprinkled between stately squares spangled with heroic statues and moss-covered trees, the sweet smell of magnolia blending with earthy aromas wafting up from a mighty river. America's largest national historic landmark district, old Savannah covers more than a hundred city blocks and two dozen green spaces. Among its many landmarks are City Hall, the old U.S. Customs House, Christ Church, the birth home of

Girl Scouts founder Juliette Gordon Low, and the Mercer Williams House of *Midnight in the Garden of Good and Evil* fame.

The historic core is best explored on foot, walking down Bull Street and then peeling off along the various side streets; however, trolley, Segway, and horse-drawn carriage tours are also available. The old roundhouse of the Central of Georgia Railway now holds the Georgia State Railroad Museum. Hub of the city's entertainment district, Chippewa Square hums with music from the Historic Savannah Theatre, the nation's oldest continuously operated professional stage. Forsyth Park is a popular venue for recreation, concerts, and a Saturday farmers market. Savannah's other great green space is Bonaventure Cemetery, where John Muir camped amid the tombs in 1867. It is the last resting place of many local luminaries including singer Johnny Mercer and author Conrad Aiken. Savannah's redbrick Riverwalk runs more

than a mile (1.6 km) along the waterfront, backed by the old cotton warehouses along River Street, now home to popular bars, restaurants, and souvenir shops. Factors Row derives its name from the cotton "factors" or merchants who lined the cobblestone street in bygone days. Iron steps and pedestrian bridges link the old redbrick cotton warehouses with the antique shops and historic inns on bluff-top Bay Street.

LANDSCAPES

Stone Mountain Park north of Atlanta honors Confederate soldiers who served in the Civil War. The 863-foot-high (263 m) granite face is carved with giant images of Jefferson Davis, Stonewall Jackson, and Robert E. Lee. A vintage steam railway runs around the mountain while a cable car climbs to the summit. **Kennesaw Mountain National Battlefield Park** preserves the site of a bloody 1864 Rebel victory that temporarily

halted Sherman's famous March to the Sea.

At the north end of Georgia, **Blue Ridge** and **McCaysville** are pleasant

ROAD TRIPS

Great drives across the Peach State:

• Highway 76 through Chattahoochee-Oconee National Forest between Clayton and Ellijay (81 miles/130 km)

• Historic Dixie Highway (Route 19) between Thomasville and Albany (60 miles/97 km)

• Highway 16 between Newnan and Warrenton (141 miles/227 km)

• Ridge and Valley Scenic Byway loop between Armuchee and Villanow (51 miles/82 km)

• Dixie Overland Highway (Route 80) via Macon between Columbus and Savannah (284 miles/457 km)

Heroes of the Confederate Army are commemorated at Stone Mountain Park.

mountain towns on the edge of Chattahoochee-Oconee National Forest. Their cotton-picking and timber-felling past long faded, the highland burgs are now hubs for hiking, white-water rafting, horseback riding, trout fishing, and family-owned winery visits.

South of Atlanta, the Museum of Aviation in **Warner Robins** displays more than 70 military aircraft in five buildings and outside areas, including the SR-71A Blackbird that set a world speed record in 1976 that still stands. FDR first visited **Warm Springs** in 1924 for polio treatment and found the Georgia resort town so pleasant he built a vacation home here, later known as the Little White House. Now a museum, this is where Roosevelt died in 1945. Seventy miles (113 km) farther south along Highway 41, the Jimmy Carter National Historic Site in **Plains** includes the president's boyhood farm and residence as well as the railroad depot that became his campaign headquarters for the 1976 presidential election. Nearby Andersonville National Historic Site tells the story of the largest Confederate prisoner-of-war camp during the Civil War.

Augusta in eastern Georgia is renowned as the home of the Masters, America's most prestigious golf tournament. The Augusta Museum of History covers 12,000 years of local culture from Native American artifacts and slavery relics to suits worn by Augusta-raised soul singer James Brown. Another local luminary is honored at the Woodrow Wilson Boyhood Home, where the future president lived for 13 years while his father was pastor of the First Presbyterian Church.

The **Sea Islands** along Georgia's Atlantic coast form an eclectic

Tybee Island's lighthouse marks Georgia's easternmost point.

archipelago that includes popular holiday destinations, pristine nature areas, and secluded landfalls seemingly lost in time. Brunswick fancies itself as the world's shrimp capital and home of Brunswick stew. Connoisseurs of sun, sea, and sand flock to Saint Simons and Jekyll Islands for their white-sand strands, waterfront resorts, and outdoor activities. Sapelo Island is one of the last bastions of the Gullah Geechee people—descendants of slaves who created their own coastal microculture, including distinctive food, music, crafts, and language. Reachable only by public ferry or private boat, Cumberland Island National Seashore safeguards the largest of Georgia's barrier islands, a medley of maritime forest, marshes, dunes, and a 16-mile-long (26 km) beach where sea turtles, alligators, bobcats, and feral horses count among the wild inhabitants. ■

HIDDEN TREASURES

- **Chippewa Square (Savannah):** renowned for the "bench scene" in the movie *Forrest Gump*

- **Babyland General Hospital (Cleveland):** birthplace of the Cabbage Patch Kids dolls

- **Tallulah Gorge State Park and the nearby Chattooga River:** setting for the film *Deliverance*

- **World of Coca-Cola museum (Atlanta):** includes everything from historic signs and jingles to tasting stations with more than a hundred Coke products

- **Senoia:** a quaint town south of Atlanta famed for its many *Walking Dead* locations, as well as scenes from *Driving Miss Daisy* and *Fried Green Tomatoes*

Hawaii

All the clichés are true: The waves are gnarly, the volcanoes spew red-hot lava, the coconut palms really do sway in the breeze, and the hula makes you want to linger on the islands forever. Of all the states, Hawaii perhaps feels the most like a foreign country, and for good reason: It once was, before the U.S. annexed it. The tropical archipelago is the northernmost part of Polynesia and basically halfway to Asia.

TOURISM INFORMATION

The State of Hawaii staffs 15 information desks at Honolulu International Airport. Airports at Kahului (Maui), Kona and Hilo (Big Island), and Lihue (Kauai) also offer tourist info kiosks. Find out more at gohawaii.com.

• **Oahu Visitors Bureau**
2270 Kalakaua Ave., #801
Honolulu, HI 96815
Tel 808/524-0722

• **National Park Service**
nps.gov/state/hi

• **Hawaii State Parks**
dlnr.hawaii.gov/dsp

CITIES

Historical evidence suggests there has been some sort of settlement on the site of **Honolulu** since the 11th century. With Diamond Head looming in the background and hundreds of surfers testing the waves, Waikiki is one of the most photographed beaches on the planet. Beyond palm-shaded sands rise the Royal Hawaiian and other iconic hotels, as well as such renowned watering holes as the Mai Tai Bar and Duke's Waikiki. Honolulu Zoo and Waikiki Aquarium inhabit Kapiolani Park at the far end of the beach strip. A steep trail winds to Diamond Head's summit and stunning views along Oahu's south shore.

Downtown Honolulu grew up around the onetime hub of royal Hawaiian power—Iolani Palace—a flamboyant "American Florentine" structure erected in 1879. Across King Street stands Aliiolani Hale, the previous royal palace and now home to the state supreme court. Out in front in gold-leafed glory is a statue of King Kamehameha the Great. Other nearby noteworthy sights include Kawaiahao Church (1842), the Hawaiian Mission Houses Historic Site and Archives, the modern state capitol building (1969), and Washington Place (1847), once the official residence of several Hawaiian monarchs. Moored along the downtown waterfront is the *Falls of Clyde,* launched in 1878 and now the world's only surviving

A sunrise over Waikiki Beach on the island of Oahu

Catching a wave in Maui's Honolua Bay, a favorite spot for surfing contests

iron-hulled four-masted full-rigged ship and sail-driven oil tanker. Chinatown is the city's most distinctive ethnic neighborhood, created by migrants who came to work the island's sugarcane fields. Founded in 1927, the Honolulu Museum of Art offers a rich mix of Japanese woodblock prints, Polynesian textiles, and Pacific Basin works by Gauguin, Dampier, Bartlett, and others. The outstanding collection of the Bernice Pauahi Bishop Museum, the state museum of natural and cultural history, is renowned for its royal Hawaiian regalia, including crowns and feather standards. As part of the museum complex, visitors can also explore the Richard T. Mamiya Science Adventure Center, Na Ulu Kaiwiula native Hawaiian garden, and the Hawaiian Sports Hall of Fame.

December 7, 1941, continues to live in infamy at Pearl Harbor, where the U.S.S. *Arizona* Memorial is the most poignant of numerous wartime sights. World War II Valor in the Pacific National Monument also includes the U.S.S. *Bowfin* submarine and museum and the Pearl Harbor Visitor Center. Shuttles travel to Ford Island to visit the battleship U.S.S. *Missouri*, Pacific Aviation Museum, and U.S.S. *Oklahoma* Memorial. Beyond metro Honolulu, Oahu offers the legendary Banzai

ROAD TRIPS

Despite its insular geography, the Aloha State offers some great drives:

• Kau Scenic Byway (Highway 11) around the south shore of the Big Island between Kona and Hawaii Volcanoes National Park (96 miles/ 154 km)

• Kahekili Highway (Route 340) along Maui's secluded northwest coast between Kapalua and Kahului (30 miles/48 km)

• Highway 83 (also known as Kamehameha Highway) along

Maui's "back way" to Hana (Highways 37 and 31) between Pukalani and Hana (53 miles/85 km)

• Saddle Road (Highway 200) across the volcanic desert in the middle of the Big Island between Hilo and the Route 190 Junction (51 miles/82 km)

• Highway 83 along Oahu's northeast shore between Haleiwa and Kaneohe (40 miles/64 km)

• Kuhio Highway (Route 56) along the northeast edge of Kauai between Lihue and Hanalei (32 miles/51 km)

Pipeline and Waimea Bay surfing spots, the Polynesian Cultural Center in Laie, and Byodo-In Temple in Kahaluu.

Compared to Honolulu, **Hilo** seems languid and laid-back. The biggest city on the Big Island is mostly bypassed by tourists driving between the Kona coast and the national park volcanoes. Among its many historic structures are the Palace Theater, the S. Hata Building, and the Lyman Museum and Mission House. Other attractions include the Pacific Tsunami Museum, Mokupapapa Discovery Center, Panaewa Rainforest Zoo, Liliuokalani Gardens, Kaumana Caves, and Banyan Drive with its stout trees planted by celebrities including Babe Ruth, Amelia Earhart, Louis Armstrong, and others.

ISLANDS

Maui offers a rich mosaic of beaches, golf courses, and culinary experiences set against a

lush volcanic backdrop. The island's west coast is anchored by old Lahaina town, the onetime royal capital of Maui as well as a 19th-century American whaling port and missionary outpost. Some of the state's best beaches are farther up the coast at Kapalua and Kaanapali. Maui Ocean Center

aquarium includes an underwater habitat where guests can scuba dive with sharks. There's another great stretch of sand along the island's southwest coast between backpacker-friendly Kihei and the posh Wailea-Makena resorts. Hookipa Beach Park on the north shore is pounded by "Jaws"—one of the globe's most famous surf breaks. Not for the faint of heart (or stomach), the sinuous Hana Highway winds 64 miles (103 km) along Maui's north and east coasts to the town of Hana. Up-country Maui is an altogether different world— flower farms, pineapple fields, and ranches arrayed around bygone towns filled with art galleries and restaurants. Towering above all is mighty Haleakala volcano, a 10,000-foot (3,048 m) beast that last erupted in the late 1700s. A switchback-filled road ascends to scenic overlooks that are especially popular at sunrise. Trails lead across the crater's volcanic wasteland to backcountry campsites. The Haleakala downhill bike ride is one of Maui's

The lush cliffs of the Na Pali Coast on the island of Kauai.

favorite outdoor adventures. The park's coastal Kipahulu section, with its waterfalls and rock pools, is accessed from Hana or the "back road" from Pukalani.

Even more so than Maui, **Hawaii** (aka the Big Island) is dominated by volcanic landscapes—the massive bulk of Mauna Loa (13,678 ft/4,169 m) and Mauna Kea (13,803 ft/4,207 m) and the bubbling fire of Hawaii Volcanoes National Park. From ancient lava beds and craters to active lava flows, the park is perhaps the best place on the planet to view the various stages of volcanism. Hike to Mauna Loa's lofty summit or take a winding road up Mauna Kea to a peak crowded with observatories and sunset-watchers. The Kona coast on the island's western flank is renowned for incredible coffee, black-sand beaches, and upscale resorts. Kona is also popular for close encounters of the sea animal kind (whales, dolphins, manta rays, sea turtles) on

Sea turtles are among the varied life in Hawaii's threatened coral reefs.

boating, scuba, or snorkel adventures. Puuhonua o Honaunau National Historical Park preserves an ancient Hawaiian sacred site while nearby Kealakekua Bay State Historical Park marks the spot where Captain James Cook had the first European contact with native Hawaiians and was later killed by those same people in 1779. The lush Kohala Peninsula at the island's north end boast rodeos and ranches with Hawaiian cowboys, called *paniolos,* and secluded hiking spots including the Waipio Valley.

Locals call **Kauai** the "Garden Isle" because of its copious rainfall (among the world's most) and rich vegetation. The rain forest–drenched heights and rust-colored cliffs of the Na Pali Coast lure hikers, kayakers, and moviemakers. Dubbed the "Grand Canyon of the Pacific" by Mark Twain, 10-mile-long (16 km) Waimea Canyon cuts 3,000 feet (914 m)

down into the island's reddish earth. With its tranquil turquoise waters and white-sand strand— and a famed shaved-ice stand— Hanalei Bay might be the single most gorgeous spot in the entire archipelago.

Reached by ferry from Maui, little **Molokai** is the island where Father Damien earned his sainthood by tending to the spiritual and physical needs of late-19th-century lepers. Kalaupapa National Historical Park, reached by foot or guided mule tours, preserves the famed north-shore leper colony. Nearby **Lanai,** once the world's largest pineapple plantation, is almost entirely owned by one man—high-tech tycoon Larry Ellison. Two luxury resorts cater to the overnight crowd while day-trippers can visit the Lanai Culture & Heritage Center, Keomuku ghost town, several excellent beaches, and the island's cat sanctuary. ∎

Idaho

One of the nation's least populated states, Idaho presents a dramatic array of landscapes, from snow-covered peaks and deep evergreen forests to volcanic wastelands and wind-swept high desert. Recreational activities abound no matter what the season, and Idaho's cities present a mixture of frontier-era and modern attractions.

CITIES

Often cited as among the nation's most livable cities, **Boise** straddles the river of the same name in southwest Idaho. Completed in 1920, the state capitol building draws architectural inspiration from Saint Peter's Basilica in Rome, Saint Paul's Cathedral in London, and the U.S. Capitol in Washington, D.C. Boise's large Iberian population is reflected in the

Basque Museum & Cultural Center downtown, while the Idaho Black History Museum, located in the historic Saint Paul Baptist Church in Julia Davis Park, hosts exhibits and events to bring diverse communities together. Wedged between downtown and the Boise River, Julia Davis Park's other attractions include the Boise Art Museum, Zoo Boise, the Idaho Rose Society garden, Pioneer Village (with its

TOURISM INFORMATION

For more information on the Gem State, check out the Idaho tourism website: visitidaho.org.

● **Boise Convention & Visitors Bureau**
250 S Fifth St., #300
Boise, ID 83702
Tel 208/344-7777 or
800/635-5240
boise.org

● **Southern Idaho Tourism**
2015 Nielsen Point Pl.
Twin Falls, ID 83301
Tel 800/255-8946
visitsouthidaho.com

● **Sun Valley Visitor Center**
491 Sun Valley Rd.
Ketchum, ID 83340
Tel 208/726-3423
visitsunvalley.com

● **Gateway Northwest Visitor Center**
105 N First St., Ste 100
Coeur d'Alene, ID 83814
Tel 208/664-3194
cdachamber.com

● **Eastern Idaho Visitor Information Center**
425 N Capitol Ave.
Idaho Falls, ID 83402
Tel 208/523-1010 or 1012
idahofallschamber.com

collection of antique buildings from around the state), and the Discovery Center of Idaho science museum. The park is part of a string of urban green spaces that comprise the Boise River Greenbelt, with miles of hiking and biking trails. Some of Boise's most popular attractions lie on the outskirts of town, including a prison that held some of the West's most notorious criminals between 1872 and 1973. The Old Idaho State Penitentiary is now open as a state historic site, with 30 historic buildings including solitary confinement, cell

Idaho's capitol dome in Boise

A beaver dam on Fishhook Creek in Idaho's Sawtooth National Recreation Area

blocks, and the gallows. Idaho Botanical Garden is right next door. Boise is also home to the World Center for Birds of Prey, headquarters for The Peregrine Fund, an international nonprofit that protects endangered raptors worldwide. The center has indoor exhibits and live bird presentations. Bogus Basin is a popular winter sports area just 20 miles (32 km) north of the city center.

Pocatello anchors the state's deep south, a gateway to Yellowstone country and the Salmon River Mountains. On the campus of Idaho State University, the Idaho Museum of Natural History features dinosaurs, Ice Age mammals, and a hands-on Discovery Room, as well as a Natural History Garden and Tree Walk. The Rotary Rose Garden flaunts hundreds of rose bushes and a 16-foot (5 m) Idaho Travertine stone statue of city namesake Chief Pocatello. Bannock County Historical Museum showcases the area's vast history, while the Pocatello Model Railroad and Historical Society preserves the region's iron horse heritage. The small but excellent Pocatello Zoo specializes in creatures of the intermountain West, with grizzly bears as one of its main attractions. A replica of 19th-century Fort Hall showcases the explorers, fur traders, pioneers, and Native Americans who passed through, many along the nearby Oregon and California Trails. To the north, in the town of Fort Hall, the Shoshone-Bannock Tribal Museum illuminates tribal history via artifacts, beadwork, music, and more.

LANDSCAPES

The Idaho Panhandle is a wondrous land of woods and water,

CAPITALISM

Boise's offbeat name derives from *la rivière boisée,* a phrase used by early-19th-century French trappers to describe the wooded river valley in which Idaho's capital later arose. Lewiston was the first territorial capital, but its difficult geography sparked a move to Boise in 1864. Miffed at the snub, the Idaho Panhandle threatened to break away and join Washington State. Intervention by the U.S. Congress and President Grover Cleveland curtailed the secessionists.

a glacier-carved landscape of deep lakes and lofty mountains. The northland's main tourism draw is its waters, with fishing, boating, and sightseeing on Lake Coeur d'Alene, Lake Pend Oreille, the Kootenay River, and others.

Coeur d'Alene, the metropolis of the panhandle, offers a range of indoor and outdoor activities from nature trails and white-water rafting to health spas and the Museum of North Idaho. To the east, Lookout Pass Ski and Recreation Area includes the amazing Route of the Hiawatha trail, a 15-mile (24 km) path following an old rail line through 10 train tunnels and across seven sky-high trestles. Silverwood Theme Park in Athol offers families an adrenalin-packed respite from all that nature with 70 rides, shows, and attractions.

Although **Nez Perce National Historical Park** encompasses 38 sites in four states, the visitor center

---

LITTLE-KNOWN FACTS

• Idaho is one of the few states that straddles two time zones: Everything north of Salmon River is on Pacific standard time; everything south of the river is on mountain standard time.

• The Museum of Idaho in Idaho Falls holds the first light bulb powered by nuclear energy and graphite from the world's first nuclear reactor.

• Vintage vacuum cleaners, toilets, washing machines, and trash cans are among the artifacts found at the Museum of Clean in Pocatello.

• The only U.S. memorial specifically dedicated to Holocaust victim Anne Frank is in a small park near downtown Boise, designed for visitors to reflect and engage one another on human rights issues.

---

is located in Idaho near Lewiston, on the Nez Perce Indian Reservation. The park revolves around a series of 1877 battles between the U.S. Cavalry and Nez Perce, as Chief Joseph tried to lead his people to exile in Canada rather than submit to life on a reservation. To the south, **Hells Canyon National Recreation Area** boasts the continent's deepest river gorge and more

than 650,000 acres (263,046 ha) of hiking, horseback riding, and white-water river activities.

Central Idaho is dominated by rugged mountains and national forests that harbor wild rivers and copious wildlife. Beyond the ranger stations and organized campgrounds is a vast road-less region that comprises the Frank Church–River of No Return, Gospel-Hump, and Selway-Bitterroot federally protected wilderness areas that can only be accessed by foot.

Sun Valley and nearby Ketchum in the **Smoky Mountains** are popular winter and summer recreation areas with especially good cross-country and downhill skiing. Bald Mountain (aka Baldy), the valley's primary ski and snowboard area, offers long runs of varying degrees of difficulty with constant gradients. Farther up the valley, Sawtooth National Recreation Area hosts a variety of outdoor activities.

A stunning contrast to the rest of the state, south Idaho is a land of lava flows, desert barrens, and dramatic geological features. **Bruneau Dunes State Park** near Mountain Home revolves around a 470-foot-tall (143 m) sand dune—the tallest

Fly-fishing in a spring-fed creek in Idaho

single-structured sand dune in the U.S. There is also a lake in the park with water activities as well as the Bruneau Dunes Observatory.

Farther up the Snake River Valley is **Shoshone Falls,** one of the nation's most spectacular cascades. The "Niagara of the West" is 1,000 feet (305 m) wide and 212 feet (65 m) high—45 feet (14 m) taller than the real Niagara. Just above the falls, Dierkes Lake Park tenders hiking trails, water activities, playgrounds, and picnic areas. Nearby Minidoka National Historic Site in **Jerome** commemorates the 9,000 Japanese Americans interned at the isolated relocation center during World War II, as well as detainees who served and died in the U.S. military.

The Idaho Potato Museum is entirely devoted to the humble potato, the state's renowned potato industry, and the long ties between potato farming and the railroad. It's located inside the old Oregon Short Line Railroad Depot in **Blackfoot.** Forty miles (64 km) northwest of Blackfoot, **Idaho National Laboratory** was founded in 1949 as the nation's premier nuclear research facility. Although most of the top-secret facility is off-limits to the general public, the EBR-I Atomic

Mule deer, named for their large ears, roam the Rocky Mountains.

Museum is open between Memorial Day and Labor Day for those who cherish a close encounter with Experimental Breeder Reactor No. 1, the first power plant to produce electricity using atomic energy.

The rambling black lava flows of the **Craters of the Moon National Monument & Preserve** were formed during eight volcanic eruptions that took place as far back as 15,000 years ago. The lava fields may soon increase in size, as the average time

between eruptive periods is 2,000 years—and it's been more than two millennia since the last eruption. Trails lead to volcanic craters, cinder cones, and lava tube caves as well as backcountry campgrounds.

Lava Hot Springs in southeast Idaho steams with smoke from geothermal pools that simmer between 102° and 112°F (38–44°C). The town boasts indoor and outdoor hot pools, waterslides, diving platforms, and sunken gardens. ∎

LOCAL FLAVOR

There are many ways to savor a genuine Idaho potato:

• **Spuds Waterfront Grill:** eight different types of gourmet baked potato. *102 N First Ave. & Pine St., Sandpoint*

• **Goodwood Barbecue Company:** sides of mom's potato salad, loaded smashed potatoes, and potato skins smothered in cheddar cheese, bacon bits, chives, sour cream, and ranch dressing. *7849 W Spectrum St., Boise*

• **Red Feather Lounge:** hand-cut Idaho potato fries with fresh herbs, Parmesan, and house-made ketchup, plus potato chowder. *246 N Eighth St., Boise*

• **Grand Teton Distillery:** locally grown potatoes provide the raw ingredient for the award-winning premium vodka distilled here. *1755 N Highway 33, Driggs*

• **Westside Drive-In:** Idaho "Ice Cream Potato"—ice cream molded into the shape of a baked potato and topped with whipped cream and chocolate sauce. *1929 W State St., Boise*

Illinois

Illinois has always cast a giant shadow, whether from landmark skyscrapers or the legacy of Abraham Lincoln. More than half of the state's 12 million people crowd into the Chicago metro area, leaving the rest of Illinois relatively uncrowded—a rolling expanse of farmland and forest between Lake Michigan and the Mississippi River.

TOURISM INFORMATION

The Illinois Office of Tourism has established 10 tourist information centers around the state, most of them located near interstate highway gateways. Visit the website at enjoyillinois.com.

• **Choose Chicago** operates two year-round visitor information centers:
Chicago Cultural Center
77 E Randolph St.
Macy's on State Street
111 N State St.
Lower Level
choosechicago.com

• **Springfield Union Station Visitor Center**
500 E Madison St.
Springfield, IL 62701
Tel 217/789-2360 or
800/545-7300
visitspringfieldillinois.com

• **Illinois State Parks**
www.dnr.illinois.gov /recreation

CITIES

"Stormy, husky, brawling, City of the Big Shoulders," is how poet Carl Sandburg described **Chicago** in 1914. And in many respects, the Windy City still feels that way more than a century later. Surrounded by water on three sides—thanks to Lake Michigan and the Chicago River—downtown includes The Loop central business district and many of the city's celebrated skyscrapers. Looming above the other giants is the 110-story Willis Tower (formerly Sears Tower), the world's tallest building from 1973 to 1998, with its vertigo-inducing Skydeck viewing area. North of the river, a 13-block stretch of Michigan Avenue called the Magnificent Mile flaunts high-end shopping, restaurants, hotels, and landmark buildings such as the Gothic Revival–style Tribune Tower. Another panoramic perch is the 360 Chicago observation deck at the top of the John Hancock Building. One of the few structures to survive the Great Chicago Fire of 1871, the Old Chicago Water Tower on Michigan Avenue now exhibits the work of local artists and photographers.

Chicago's Magnificent Mile, a posh 13-block stretch of North Michigan Avenue

Chicago's coastline is spangled with museums, parks, and other outdoor attractions. Hugging the north shore is Lincoln Park with its namesake zoo (one of only three in the nation with no entrance fee) and the Peggy Notebaert Nature Museum. Built during World War I and extending 3,300 feet (1,006 m) into the lake, Navy Pier has slowly transitioned from military to civilian use as home to the Chicago Shakespeare Theater, the Chicago Children's Museum, and various carnival attractions. Millennium Park showcases the much-photographed sculpture "Cloud Gate," as well as the Frank Gehry–designed Jay Pritzker Pavilion band shell, host of concerts and other outdoor events. Neighboring Grant Park hosts the esteemed Art Institute of Chicago and a Museum Campus

The mirrored bean-shaped "Cloud Gate" sculpture in Chicago's Millennium Park

that includes Shedd Aquarium, Adler Planetarium, and the Field Museum of National History. South shore Jackson Park tenders lagoons, marinas, and the Museum of Science and Industry. An 18-mile (29 km) lakefront path leads to all of these man-made icons.

Chicagoans like to think of their city as a collection of neighborhood clusters rather than one big urban sprawl. Among the historic areas worth exploring are the posh Prairie Avenue District—home to some 75 millionaires in the late 19th century—and the Gold Coast neighborhood which arose after the Great Chicago Fire. The metro area includes several intriguing suburbs. **Oak Park** boasts the world's highest concentration of Frank Lloyd Wright–designed houses,

25 structures built between 1889 and 1913. Wright's own home and studio in the neighborhood is now a museum. Another hometown boy is celebrated at the Ernest Hemingway Museum inside the Oak Park Arts Center. A short walk away is the Queen Anne–style Ernest Hemingway Birthplace Home, where the author spent his first six years. On the north shore, **Evanston** is the home of the leafy lakefront campus of Northwestern University, as well as the Mitchell Museum of the American Indian and half a dozen good beaches.

Besides being the state capital, **Springfield** is the land of all things Lincoln. Although he was born in Kentucky and largely raised in Indiana, the 16th president lived in and around Springfield for more than

30 years (1830–1861). Taking pride of place in downtown Springfield, the Abraham Lincoln Presidential Library and Museum comprises life-size dioramas from key moments in the president's life as well as priceless

---

STATE OF THE ART

- **Best movies:** Young Mr. Lincoln (1939) and Ferris Bueller's Day Off (1986)

- **Best books:** The Jungle by Upton Sinclair and The Devil in the White City by Erik Larson

- **Best music:** the Chicago blues of Bo Diddley and Muddy Waters

- **Best art:** the pioneering animation of Chicago-born Walt Disney

Lincoln memorabilia, such as a signed copy of the Emancipation Proclamation and a handwritten draft of the Gettysburg Address. On the other side of the Old State Capitol, Lincoln-Herndon Law Offices State Historic Site preserves the location where Lincoln and partner William H. Herndon honed their legal skills. Sharing a four-block cluster with other restored 19th-century structures, the Lincoln Home National Historic Site commemorates the president's primary residence—the only home he ever owned—from 1844 until he moved into the White House. The Lincoln Memorial Garden and Nature Center on the south shore of Lake Springfield offers plants native to the three states where "Honest Abe" lived prior to the presidency, as well as trails to explore. Lincoln is buried in the city's Oak Ridge Cemetery—the nation's second most visited burial ground after Arlington National Cemetery.

LANDSCAPES

Ninety miles (145 km) west of Chicago in the northern Illinois prairie, **Rockford** is often called the Forest City because of its manifold parks, gardens, and nature areas. Designed by renowned landscape architect Hoichi Kurisu, Anderson Japanese Gardens is a tiny wonderland of waterfalls, rock formations, a traditional teahouse where breakfast and lunch are served, and a year-round slate of Japanese cultural workshops. Nicholas Conservatory & Gardens on the Rock River revolves around a massive glass-enclosed tropical plant house, while Klehm Arboretum & Botanic Garden concentrates on flora native to the temperate regions of Europe and North America.

Galena anchors the northern end of the state's long Mississippi River waterfront. Named after a mineral rich in lead and silver, it became America's first mining boomtown in the 1820s and later a bustling

steamboat port. The flourishing economy attracted an Ohio family called the Grants; their son Ulysses would mature into a Civil War hero and U.S. president. The redbrick Grant Home, restored to its full 1860s splendor, contains many of his personal belongings. Galena's historic district holds many other notable structures including the Elihu B. Washburne House State Historic Site, Old Market House, Post Office and Customs House, and DeSoto House Hotel.

Some 200 miles (322 km) downstream, **Nauvoo** was home to the Mormons (before they migrated to Utah) as well as the utopian socialist Icarians. Among the riverside town's many Mormon landmarks are the rebuilt LDS Temple, the Joseph Smith Homestead, and Smith's little Red Brick Store. **Quincy** also contains a wealth of 19th-century buildings, many in the South Side German Historic District. On the outskirts of East St. Louis, **Cahokia Mounds State Historic Site** preserves the remains of a sprawling pre-Columbian metropolis. Largest city in the Mississippi Basin prior to

Massive amounts of earth were moved—by hand—to create the Cahokia Mounds.

A water-powered machine shop at the Midway Village Museum in Rockford

the arrival of Europeans, Cahokia was inhabited between A.D. 700 and 1400. At its height, the city was larger than London and may have supported more than 20,000 residents. Today the UNESCO World Heritage site contains more than 80 earthen mounds arrayed around a grand plaza and a "woodhenge" timber circle likely used for ancient astronomical observations.

At the south end of Illinois, **Cairo** sits at the confluence of the Mississippi and Ohio Rivers. Fort Defiance State Park marks the site of a Lewis and Clark encampment as well as a Civil War fort commanded by Ulysses S. Grant. Wedged between the two great rivers, **Shawnee National Forest** has more than 400 miles (644 km) of trails for both horses and humans,

paths that meander over hills and bluffs and along rivers, lakes, and waterfalls. Having undergone millions of years of weathering, the sandstone rock formations of

Garden of the Gods offer vast opportunities for exploring, scrambling, and climbing. Other national forest landmarks include Rim Rock and Pounds Hollow. ■

LITTLE-KNOWN FACTS

They make 'em big in the Prairie State:

• The "world's largest catsup bottle" (actually a bottle-shaped water tower) rises 170 feet (52 m) near Collinsville.

• Robert P. Wadlow (1918–1940) holds the Guinness World Record for being the tallest ever human. Born in Alton, he stood 8 feet, 11 inches (2.7 m) and weighed nearly 450 pounds (204 kg).

• The Nabisco factory in Chicago is the world's largest bakery (1.8 million square feet/167,225 sq m).

• Vandalia is home to the Kaskaskia Dragon, a 35-foot-long (11 m) metal reptile statue that actually breathes fire.

• At 27 feet (8 m) long, the "world's largest wagon" basks on the lawn in front of the Radio Flyer headquarters in Chicago.

Indiana

Boot-shaped Indiana floats between the Ohio River and the lower end of Lake Michigan, a hardworking state with deep roots in agriculture and American car culture. Hoosiers are pretty proud of their basketball, as well as a showbiz legacy that gave the world Michael Jackson, James Dean, Steve McQueen, and Cole Porter. From lakeshore dunes to primeval forest, Indiana flaunts plenty of nature, too.

TOURISM INFORMATION

Indiana's Department of Transportation operates eight welcome centers around the periphery of the state, most of them adjacent to interstate gateways. Find out more at visitindianatourism.com.

• **Visit Indy in the Convention Center**
200 S Capitol Ave., Suite 300
Indianapolis, IN 46225
Tel 317/262-3000 or
800/323-4639

• **White River Park Visitor Center**
801 W Washington St. (off Schumacher Way)
Indianapolis, IN 46204
Tel: 317/233-2434
visitindy.com

• **Fort Wayne Visitor Center**
927 S Harrison St.
Fort Wayne, IN 46802
Tel 260/424-3700 or
800/767-7752
visitfortwayne.com

CITIES

Home to a quarter of all Indianans, the Greater **Indianapolis** metro area dominates just about every aspect of life in the Hoosier State. Dubbed the "crossroads of America" because so many major highways traverse the city—plus it's home to the Indianapolis Motor Speedway—vehicles have long been pivotal to the city's economy and image. Yet downtown Indy is decidedly walkable, especially the Lockerbie Square Historic District with its distinctive federal, Italianate, and Queen Anne–style Victorian architecture. Nearby is an elongated green space filled with fountains, lawns, and the imposing Indiana War Memorial. President Benjamin Harrison's redbrick Victorian home lies on the north side of downtown. The city's eclectic "museum row" includes the Eiteljorg Museum of American Indians and Western Art, the NCAA Hall of Champions, and the Indiana State Museum. Across the White River are the Indianapolis Zoo and the White River Wapahani Trail, which meanders through the heart of the city. On the west side of town, the legendary Indianapolis Motor Speedway offers an excellent motor-racing museum, ground tours, and various on-track experiences for amateur drivers. On the city outskirts, Conner Prairie Interactive History Park features five themed historic areas and a nature walk where families can explore history, nature, science, and the arts. One of the nation's largest municipal parks, Eagle Creek Park and Nature Preserve offers hiking, biking, and sundry water sports.

Around 120 miles (193 km) northeast of Indianapolis, **Fort Wayne** is often called the "city of churches" because of its 360 places of worship that cover many denominations and architectural styles. Located at the confluence of the

The University of Notre Dame's landmark golden dome tops the school's main administrative building.

Indianapolis along the banks of the White River

Maumee, Saint Joseph, and Saint Mary's Rivers, the city has family-friendly attractions such as the Fort Wayne Children's Zoo in Franke Park and the aromatic DeBrand Fine Chocolates factory, where tours end with free samples. The Historic Old Fort living-history museum re-creates late-18th- and early-19th-century frontier life in the Old Northwest, while the Chief Richardville House pays tribute to Fort Wayne's rich Native American heritage. The home of Miami Nation chief Jean Baptiste de Richardville was built in 1827 and is the nation's only surviving national treaty house. Located within walking distance of one another in downtown Fort Wayne are the Foellinger-Freimann Botanical Conservatory, the History Center, and Fort Wayne Museum of Art.

Christened "*la belle rivière*" by French explorers for its beauty, **Evansville** graces the north shore of the Ohio River, a onetime riverboat port that reincarnated itself in the 20th century into a thriving college town and manufacturing hub. The Evansville Museum of Arts, History & Science boasts a permanent collection of 30,000 artworks and artifacts, as well as a planetarium and interactive science center. Also along the waterfront, the U.S.S. LST Ship Memorial features a decommissioned U.S. Navy tank landing ship that participated in several operations, including D-Day at Normandy. Tours of the vessel highlight wartime production at the now defunct Evansville Shipyard. Eight miles (13 km) southeast of the city center, **Angel Mounds** is one of the nation's best preserved prehistoric Native American sites:

11 earthen mounds created for ceremonial and residential purposes. A museum tells the story of the Mississippian people who inhabited the area from roughly A.D. 1050 to 1400.

At the opposite end of the state, the city of **South Bend** is almost

CAPITALISM

Indiana's first state capitol building was a two-story limestone structure in Corydon, a town in the far south near the Ohio River. Completed in 1816, the building comprised just three small rooms and saw politicking only until 1825, when the state government relocated to Indianapolis. Today the old building serves as the main focus of Corydon Capitol State Historic Site and National Historic District.

synonymous with the University of Notre Dame, the Roman Catholic university and college football powerhouse. Even if you're not a Fighting Irish sports fan, the campus is worth a stroll for architectural icons such as the Basilica of the Sacred Heart, the Golden Dome, and the "touchdown Jesus" mural outside Hesburgh Library. The city's Studebaker National Museum displays a wide variety of vehicles created by the South Bend automaker between 1852 and 1967. A much different local product is the focus of tours at the South Bend Chocolate Company.

LANDSCAPES

Indiana's 40-mile (64 km) coast comprises less than three percent of Lake Michigan's total lakeshore, but its diversity is astonishing and ranges from die-hard steel towns to waterfront wilderness areas. As early as the 1890s, locals began efforts to save the riches of the Indiana Dunes—wetlands, prairie, oak savanna, and dunes that rise to nearly 200 feet (61 m)—from development. They are now protected within the confines of a state park and **Indiana Dunes National Lakeshore,** which offers swimming, boating, fishing, hiking, camping, and exploring the array of different habitats. Also on offer are such activities as shopping, gambling, and visiting wineries.

Given its proximity to Michigan, it comes as no surprise that northwest Indiana has a strong motoring heritage. The Auburn Cord Duesenberg Automobile Museum displays more than 120 classic cars made by the hometown Auburn Automobile Company and other Indiana carmakers. Another treat for motorheads is the nearby National Automotive and Truck Museum, which flaunts everything from horse-drawn buggies to futuristic concept cars, plus a large collection of toy cars. The RV Hall of Fame, Museum, and Library in Elkhart features recreational vehicles created

by Airstream, Winnebago, and other American makers, as well as memorabilia dating to the 1920s. The region is also home to Amish Acres, a historic farm and heritage resort homesteaded by Moses Stahly in 1873; the property is the only Amish farm listed on the National Register of Historic Places.

An hour's drive south of the capital, **Bloomington** has emerged as the state's other big cultural hub thanks to the presence of Indiana University and its related institutions. Opened in 1941, the on-campus Indiana University Art Museum shows works by Picasso, Pollock, and many other notable artists. Just west of campus, the WonderLab

Locally made vintage cars at the Auburn Cord Duesenberg Automobile Museum

Maple Grove Road outside the city of Bloomington was an important 19th-century transportation route.

Museum of Science, Health, and Technology is an interactive oasis for families located in the heart of the Bloomington Entertainment and Arts District. The heavily wooded hills east of town culminate in Brown County State Park, 16,000 acres (6,475 ha) of rugged terrain laced by trails.

Hoosier National Forest protects another huge tract of native woodland stretching all the way down to the Ohio River. Among the bucolic communities in this region are French Lick (hometown of basketball legend Larry Bird) and Marengo, home to an eponymous cavern that's been a local attraction since the 19th century. About five miles (8 km) in length, **Marengo Cave** was discovered by two local schoolchildren and, in 1984, was named a national natural landmark by the National Park Service. An obscure and key moment in American history is recalled at **George Rogers Clark National Historical Park,** on the banks of the Wabash River in Vincennes. The Greek Revival–style memorial rises near the presumed site of Fort Sackville, a British fort that General Clark and his troops captured in 1779 after a harrowing winter march. Clark's wilderness campaign set the stage for the United States claiming the Ohio Valley at the end of the Revolutionary War. ■

HIDDEN TREASURES

• **Conner Prairie Interactive History Park (Fishers):** Civil War reenactments, farm animals, and blacksmithing workshops are just part of this mash-up of education and entertainment.

• **Holiday World & Splashin' Safari (Santa Claus):** Roller coasters and reindeer feature prominently at this oddball blend of water park and yuletide village.

• **Blue Gate Theater (Shipshewana):** Vintage country-and-western stars and musical theater are the twin fortes of this rural stage in the heart of Indiana Amish country.

• **Miami County Museum (Peru):** More like a sideshow than an ordinary museum, the collection includes all sorts of eclectic items from Cole Porter's 1955 Cadillac Fleetwood to giant roadside signs and the remains of Big Charley the Killer Elephant.

Iowa

Wedged between the Mississippi and Missouri Rivers, Iowa is a giant field of dreams that includes fascinating small cities as well as places for outdoor pursuits. The tricolor state flag conveys Iowa's early French roots, while the state seal portrays its agricultural bounty, riparian heritage, and strong support of the Union cause before and during the Civil War.

TOURISM INFORMATION

Travel Iowa maintains four visitor welcome centers in different parts of the Hawkeye State. For more information, visit traveliowa.com.

• **Greater Des Moines CVB Information Center**
400 Locust St., Suite 265
Capital Square
Des Moines, IA 50309
Tel 515/286-4950 or
800/451-2625
catchdesmoines.com

• **Dubuque Welcome Center**
280 Main St.
Dubuque, IA 52001
Tel 563/556.4372 or
800/798.8844
traveldubuque.com

CITIES

Perhaps the most mispronounced of all state capitals, **Des Moines** straddles a river of the same name in central Iowa and is a metropolis that has carved out a commercial niche in insurance, financial services, and publishing. Hovering above the city on Capitol Hill, the statehouse is crowned by a large, 23-karat gold-leaf main dome that sparkles in the heartland sunshine. Filled with shops, restaurants, and drinking spots, the historic East Village neighborhood is located between the capitol building and the river. Much of the waterfront has been turned into parkland, including the Greater Des Moines Botanical Garden, which celebrates Iowa's four seasons as well as tropical and desert plants inside a geodesic dome. Six bridges (two of them for pedestrians only) leap across the river into downtown Des Moines and its office towers. Among city-center landmarks are the Iowa Hall of Pride, the interactive Science Center of Iowa, and the World Food Prize Hall of Laureates, which recognizes people who have advanced human development by improving the quality, quantity, or availability of food around the globe. Grand Avenue leads west from the river to an outdoor sculpture garden in Western Gateway Park and the *Better Homes & Gardens* magazine test garden (open to the public), a reminder that Des Moines is home to the media giant Meredith. The Iowa Governor's Mansion sits on Terrace Hill, rising above the Raccoon River. Originally built as the family home of Benjamin Franklin Allen, Iowa's first millionaire, the manse is a fine example of Second Empire architecture, including a 90-foot (27 m) tower with great city views. Farther west along Grand Avenue, the Des Moines Art Center showcases contemporary art as well as representative pieces from the Renaissance era and the Impressionism movement, in addition to Japanese woodblock prints. Modeled after the King's House in Salisbury, England, the

Iowa's capitol building in the city of Des Moines

A skylift ride at the 11-day Iowa State Fair in Des Moines

42-room Salisbury House was built in 1928 and is filled with period objets d'art and furnishings.

Cedar Rapids lies about 100 miles (161 km) as the crow flies east of the state capital, a city built on cattle and corn that later evolved into an arts and culture oasis. As the name implies, the National Czech & Slovak Museum and Library offers exhibits on the history of those cultures in the United States. The Cedar Rapids Museum of Art's collection of 7,200 works of art span from antiquity to modern times but is particularly strong in early-20th-century American art. Featured prominently are works by local painter Grant Wood whose studio, where the artist lived and worked for more than a decade, is preserved three blocks from the museum; this is where he painted *American Gothic* in 1930.

Sioux City anchors Iowa's "west coast" along the Missouri River. Front and center on the waterfront, the Lewis & Clark Interpretive Center commemorates historic events before, during, and after their landmark expedition. Just steps away, within a 1932 riverboat, the Sergeant Floyd River Museum highlights the role of the Missouri River in opening up the West as well as the Army Corps of Engineering's task of managing

CAPITALISM

Trappists or rapids? That is the question. Many argue whether tis' nobler to think that Iowa's capital was named for 18th-century French monks *(moines)* or after a Native American term *(moingona)* for the rocky river portage (although some think the latter refers to the burial grounds near the riverbanks). A newer theory claims the name derives from a derogatory term *(mooyiiinkweena)* used by other Native peoples to describe a tribe living along the river. Historians have never been able to agree on the origin and probably never will.

America's rivers. Downtown, the Sioux City Public Museum features local and regional artifacts, while the Sioux City Art Center showcases a variety of artists. Palmer's Olde Tyme Candy Shoppe on Wesley Parkway is the latest iteration of a local sweet business that started in 1878. In the northeast corner of the city, the 30-foot (9 m) "Immaculate Heart of Mary Queen of Peace" stainless steel sculpture towers over Trinity Heights, an inspirational garden with Christian shrines and quiet corners for prayer and reflection.

LANDSCAPES

Beyond the ubiquitous cornfields, eastern Iowa is rich in nature areas. Dedicated in 1920, **Backbone State Park** near Dundee was the state's first reserve. In addition to the Iowa Civilian Conservation Corps Museum, the park offers 21 miles (34 km) of multiuse trails along with rock climbing and swimming, fishing, and boating on Backbone Lake. Spelunkers flock to the 13 underground caverns at **Maquoketa Caves State Park.** About two hours north, a 500-foot (152 m) bluff overlooks the confluence of the Mississippi and Wisconsin Rivers, the main attraction at **Pikes Peak State Park** near Marquette.

Farther down the Mississippi, the **Dubuque Arboretum and Botanical Gardens** spreads across 50 acres (20 ha) of formal and natural gardens. The arboretum is entirely maintained by some 300 community volunteers, the nation's

largest such entity. The National Mississippi River Museum & Aquarium at the **Port of Dubuque** educates and entertains visitors on the historical and cultural significance of "Old Man River" through exhibits as well as otters, gators,

Pikes Peak State Park affords sweeping views of the Mississippi River.

catfish, and other wildlife. Dubuque's 1893 Fenelon Place Elevator, a narrow-gauge funicular opened in1893, claims to be the world's steepest and shortest railroad line. For fans of the 1989 movie of the same name, a visit to the Field of Dreams near Dyersville in Dubuque County is a must.

Housed in a stunning glass structure in **Davenport,** the Figge Art Museum (known locally as The Figge) houses an extensive collection of European, Spanish, American, and Haitian art. History and natural science are the focus of the river city's Putnam Museum, one of the oldest museums west of the Mississippi. Some 15 miles (24 km) northwest of Davenport, the **Iowa 80 Trucking Museum** flaunts a wide variety of vintage haulers, including a 1911 Walker Electric milk delivery truck and a 1910 Avery combination tractor/truck.

Herbert Hoover National Historic Site in West Branch illuminates the life and times of the only Iowan to occupy the Oval Office. In addition to the Hoover Presidential Library and Museum, the park includes the cottage where he was born, a blacksmith shop, Quaker meetinghouse, school house, and the graves of Herbert and his wife, Lou Henry Hoover. Roughly 35 miles (56 km) west of West Branch, the **Amana Colonies** comprise seven villages originally founded in the 1850s by German Pietists fleeing religious persecution in their homeland. Turning their back on the outside world, the Amanians were almost completely self-sufficient until the 1930s, when hardships brought on by the Great Depression forced them into the "Great Change." The villages are best known today

Herbert Hoover National Historic Site in West Branch

for craft shops, family-style restaurants, and quaint country inns.

Lost Island water park near Waterloo offers a refreshing tropical island paradise escape during the sweltering summer months. If that doesn't wet your whistle, **Adventureland Amusement Park** in Altoona offers 100 rides, shows, and attractions—and its own summertime water park. The **Mamie Doud Eisenhower Birthplace** in Boone sheds light on the life and family history of President Eisenhower's wife. Nearby **Ledges State Park** gets its name from sandstone "ledges" that rise nearly 100 feet (30 m) above the Des Moines River Valley. Located near Hamburg, **Waubonsie State Park** safeguards a unique landform created almost entirely by a type of windblown soil found only along the Missouri River in Iowa and Missouri, and in China. Named for Chief Waubonsie of the Pottawattamie tribe, the park provides insight into the unique Loess Hills as well as panoramic vistas, hiking, fishing, and boating. ■

LOCAL FLAVOR

• **Dutch letters:** 19th-century Dutch settlers introduced this S-shaped butter pastry to the Iowa prairies. Munch them at Jaarsma Bakery in Pella, a town founded by Dutch immigrants in 1847. *727 Franklin St., Pella*

• **Loose meat sandwich:** This "unburger" features loose (rather than tightly packed) ground beef, fried and

then steamed before it's slipped into a bun with various fixins at the retro Canteen Lunch in the Alley. *112 Second St. E, Ottumwa*

• **Pork tenderloin sandwich:** Breaded and deep fried pork is the heart of this unofficial state sandwich, a signature dish at B&B Grocery, Meat & Deli. *2001 SE Sixth St., Des Moines*

Kansas

There really is no place like home, especially if you come from Kansas. The birthplace of *Little House on the Prairie* and "Home on the Range," the bucolic Sunflower State epitomizes the Great Plains experience. From nomadic Native American tribes and Spanish conquistadors to the abolitionist battles of Bleeding Kansas, the days of the Wild West, and civil rights, the state boasts a rich history.

CITIES

Wichita has grown from a dusty cow town on the Chisholm Trail into the "Air Capital of the World" thanks to Cessna, Beechcraft, Learjet, and other aircraft companies headquartered here. It's not unusual to be walking down a Wichita street and see one of the world's most advanced aircrafts making a test flight overhead. It follows that one of the city's main attractions is the Kansas Aviation Museum. Housed inside the city's old municipal airport building, the collection features more than 40 historic aircraft, including a B-52 bomber. Wichita's original raison d'être is the focus of the Old Cowtown Museum, which helps visitors imagine life in an 1870s cattle town through artifacts, period buildings, and costumed interpreters. Nearby, the Mid-America All-Indian Center explores the Native American history and culture of the Great Plains. Outside rises "The Keeper of the Plains," a 44-foot-high (13 m) steel sculpture by Kiowa-Comanche artist Blackbear Bosin. The riverside culture cluster also embraces the Wichita Art Museum; Botanica, The Wichita Gardens; and the Kansas Wildlife Exhibit, a mini-zoo focusing on species native to the Great Plains. On the opposite side of the Arkansas River, Exploration Place is a hands-on science center and planetarium. The multiuse Arkansas River Trail runs through town for about 10 miles (16 km). Out in the College Hill area on the east side of town, Frank Lloyd Wright's Allen-Lambe House was built in 1915 and generally considered his last Prairie house.

On the frontline of the Bleeding Kansas border war and a staging place for a western branch of the Underground Railroad, **Topeka** has long been a key player in American race relations. The Brown vs. Board of Education National Historic Site commemorates the landmark 1954

The sculpture "Keeper of the Plains" stands along the Arkansas River in Wichita.

Downtown Topeka lit up in the evening

Supreme Court decision. The case, which originated at Monroe Elementary School, sparked the end of segregation in public education in the U.S. In addition to being the state's first stone building, Constitution Hall downtown is where the Topeka Constitutional Convention famously voted to ban slavery in Kansas. The structure also served as a "quartermaster's depot" on the Underground Railroad and the first territorial capital (1864–1869). Astride the Arkansas River, the city was also a stop on the Oregon Trail and other migrant routes to the West. Old Prairie Town at Ward-Meade Historic Site is an open-air museum located on a portion of the pioneer trail. Among its bygone buildings are a drugstore, general store, train depot, and church. From Carry Nation's saloon-smashing hammer to Custer's Seventh Cavalry riding boots, the expansive Kansas Museum of History contains many notable artifacts. One of the more intriguing exhibits features everyday items popularized during World War I—including the wristwatch, the zipper, and Kleenex tissue.

Overland Park, the state's second largest city, was created by William B. Strang, Jr., in 1905. He sought to develop a self-sustaining "parklike" community on the prairie, and, true to his dream, the city has received many national awards for livability over the years. The 300-acre (121 ha) Overland Park Arboretum and Botanical Gardens is largely dedicated to native Great Plains flora. About 85 percent of the space is reserved for eight natural ecosystems, including prairie, dry oak savanna, oak-hickory forest, and riparian woodland. Deanna Rose Children's Farmstead, named after the first Overland Park police officer who was killed in the line of duty, shelters some 200 animals and birds

---

CAPITALISM

Newly renovated and with free underground parking, the Kansas State Capitol in Topeka is one of the few statehouses where you can still access the top of the dome. But to reach the 304-foot (93 m) summit, visitors need to climb almost 300 steps from the fifth floor. John Steuart Curry's epic, and controversial, murals are scattered through the capitol.

as well as vegetable and flower gardens, a one-room schoolhouse, and fishing pond.

Founded by abolitionists in 1854, **Lawrence** was another important stop on the Underground Railroad. Most of the budding town was destroyed by Quantrill's Raiders in 1863, but the rebuilt area is now a quaint historic district covering much of the downtown, especially the stretch of Massachusetts Street that combines antique buildings and college-town ambience. The nearby Spencer Museum of Art at the University of Kansas offers an extensive collection of medieval, contemporary, modern, and ethnographic works in various media.

LANDSCAPES

About 100 miles (161 km) south of Kansas City, **Fort Scott National Historic Site** tells the story of various events that transpired there between 1842 and 1873, through interpretive exhibits, 20 historic structures, period furnishings, and living-history programs. Originally built to protect the so-called Permanent Indian Frontier, it was abandoned in 1853 but quickly revived as a federal outpost during the Bleeding Kansas border war. In the Civil War it functioned as a supply base, hospital, training ground, and recruitment center for the Union Army. Fort Scott National Cemetery, two

years older than Arlington National Cemetery in Virginia, was the nation's first. Established by President Lincoln in 1862, the prairie

Tallgrass Prairie National Preserve, an undulating expanse of grasslands

graveyard is the final resting place of soldiers who fought in conflicts from the Civil War through the Vietnam War.

Although born in Texas, Dwight Eisenhower was raised in **Abilene,** Kansas, and always considered it his hometown. The town's Eisenhower Center celebrates the life and many accomplishments of the 34th president and Supreme Allied Commander during World War II. The complex includes the home where "Ike" lived from 1898 to 1946, the Eisenhower Presidential Library, and the burial site of the president, First Lady Mamie Eisenhower, and their eldest son, Icky. The nearby Heritage Center of Dickinson County contains three museums as well as a fully functioning 1901 C. W. Parker carousel.

Administered by the National Park Service, **Tallgrass Prairie National Preserve** in the Flint Hills of central Kansas safeguards the remains of a 19th-century cattle ranch and surrounding grasslands. Nationwide, tallgrass prairie has shrunk to less than four percent of its original 170 million acres (68.8 million ha), with the largest remaining patch found within this reserve. Backcountry hiking, tours of the historic ranch buildings, catch-and-release fishing, seasonal wildflowers, and bison-watching are the park's primary activities.

Visitors can venture 650 feet (198 m) belowground at the Kansas Underground Salt Museum (aka Strataca) in **Hutchinson.** Built into one the world's largest rock salt deposits, the mine remains largely as it was since commercial operations ceased in

A bronze longhorn statue recalls the days of cattle drives that ended in Dodge City.

the 1950s. Located in the middle of town, the Cosmosphere highlights the American-Soviet space race with an aerospace collection second only to that of the Smithsonian, including the Apollo 13 command module, Mercury capsule *Liberty Bell 7,* two Soviet Sputnik satellites, the gloves Neil Armstrong wore on the moon, and an exhibit on the "moon diaper" (or fecal management subsystem) used by American astronauts in outer space.

Some two-plus hours due west from Wichita in what is still remote country, **Dodge City** is famous for its Wild West roots and celebrated figures such as Wyatt Earp and Bat Masterson. Boot Hill Museum aims to keep the area's history alive with a mix of history and entertainment that includes a living-history reconstruction of Front Street circa 1876, with gunfights twice daily during the summer. ■

Kentucky

People normally don't think Wild West when someone mentions Kentucky. But the Bluegrass State was the original American frontier, pioneered in the mid-18th century by Daniel Boone and other legendary woodsmen. From the secluded Appalachian hollows to the Thoroughbred horse farms around Lexington and the state's famous bourbon distillers, Kentucky maintains much of its frontier legacy.

CITIES

Founded by Revolutionary War hero George Rogers Clark and named after the king who lost his head in the French Revolution, **Louisville** lingers on the south side of the Ohio River. The state's largest city is best known for the Kentucky Derby horse race, run the first Saturday in May at Churchill Downs. Louisville ushers in the event with a two-week Kentucky Derby Festival that includes a variety of different races, from hot-air balloons to marathons. The city's sporting history is also reflected in other institutions. The Louisville Slugger Museum & Factory offers guided tours to see the legendary wooden bats being made. The Muhammad Ali Center is an interactive museum and cultural center that aims to inspire people through the values and ideals of its namesake boxing champion, who was born and raised in Louisville. Videos include Ali's boxing matches as well as civil rights–era footage.

A pedestrian bridge links the Ali Center to the Belvedere overlook, the Louisville waterfront, and other downtown attractions. Museum Row on Main offers 10 attractions within walking distance of each other, including the Flame Run Glass Studio and Gallery, Kentucky Science Center, 21c Museum Hotel, and the extremely eclectic Kentucky Museum of Art and Craft (KMAC). The nearby Frazier History Museum covers a thousand years of military heritage with armor, weapons, toy soldiers, and other memorabilia, including the bow of Apache leader Geronimo and the ivory-handled Colt pistols of General George Armstrong Custer. East of downtown, the Thomas Edison House in Butchertown is located in the neighborhood where the inventor lived in 1866–1867. More famous names are honored at Cave Hill Cemetery, the final resting place for Colonel Harland Sanders (of KFC fame), Muhammad Ali, George Rogers Clark, Nicola Marshall (designer of the Confederate flag), and sculptors Enid Yandell and Jeptha Barnard Barney Bright IV. Tours are

Thoroughbred racing at Keeneland racecourse in Lexington

Morning mists over the restored Shaker Village of Pleasant Hill

available. Deep beneath the city lies the **Louisville Mega Cavern,** a place earmarked by civil defense gurus as a safe haven in the event of a nuclear attack. There are several ways to explore the 17-mile (27 km) cave, including trams and zip lines.

Located in the heart of Bluegrass Country, **Lexington** proclaims itself "Horse Capital of the World." Thoroughbreds raised on the region's calcium-rich bluegrass develop stronger bones and more endurance, and thus are well-suited for racing. The sprawling Kentucky Horse Park is a working Thoroughbred farm and theme park that includes the Hall of Champions, Smithsonian-affiliated International Museum of the Horse, and the American Saddlebred Museum as well as a twice-daily Breeds Barn Show with horses from around the globe. Created in 1936, the Keeneland complex includes the

world's largest Thoroughbred auction house, an equestrian reference library, and Keeneland racecourse, America's number one Thoroughbred racing facility. Lexington is also celebrated as the home of the University of Kentucky, known for the

storied Wildcats men's basketball team as well as its art museum and arboretum. Established in 1849 during the city's great cholera epidemic, Lexington Cemetery includes many Civil War memorials and a national military burial ground.

HIDDEN TREASURES

True to the song, there are plenty of "old Kentucky homes" worth exploring:

• **Locust Grove (Louisville):** 1790 Georgian mansion where George Rogers Clark resided during Louisville's formative years; Lewis and Clark and presidents Jackson, Monroe, and Taylor all visited here.

• **Conrad-Caldwell House (Louisville):** eccentric Richardsonian Romanesque mansion (check out the

gargoyles) built by Theophilus Conrad, a Frenchman who made his fortune in the hide-tanning business

• **Mary Todd Lincoln House (Lexington):** childhood home of First Lady Mary Todd Lincoln, built in the early 19th century as an inn and tavern and purchased by the Todd family in 1832

• **Ashland, the Henry Clay Estate (Lexington):** Kentucky statesman's mansion with tours, formal gardens, and trails

LANDSCAPES

Southeastern Kentucky extends into the Cumberland Mountains, part of the Appalachian chain. For centuries the dramatic **Cumberland Gap**—plunging 900 feet (274 m) below the pinnacle on its north side, and situated near the convergence of Kentucky, Virginia, and Tennessee—has served as a major gateway through the highlands. Daniel Boone blazed the first trail through the gap in 1775, opening up Kentucky to European settlement. Honoring his legacy, **Daniel Boone National Forest** in eastern Kentucky comprises more than 700,000 acres (283,280 ha) of mostly rugged terrain with 600 miles (966 km) of trails, one of the world's largest concentrations of caves, and a large natural bridge created by wind and water erosion. Surrounded by national forest, **Cumberland Falls State Resort Park** showcases the largest U.S. waterfall south of Niagara, a cascade that measures some 125 feet (38 m) wide and

68 feet (21 m) tall. Under a full moon and clear night sky, visitors can see a "moonbow" (lunar rainbow) at the base of the waterfall, a phenomenon found nowhere else in the Western Hemisphere.

Cumberland towns present a range of attractions. **Pikeville** celebrates local culture with its annual Hillbilly Days in April, as well as Hatfield and McCoy self-guided tours. Farther south, **Corbin** is the

cradle of Kentucky Fried Chicken. The Harland Sanders Café and Museum preserves the restaurant he operated as "the Colonel" between 1940 and 1956, including the kitchen were he concocted the formula for KFC. North of the Cumberland Gap, **Harlan County** is known for coal mines and bloody skirmishes between miners and management in the 1930s and 1970s. Portal 31 in Lynch is the region's first and only coal mine tour, with visitors descending into the earth on a narrow-gauge railroad.

The open-air **Shaker Village of Pleasant Hill** portrays the traditional lifestyle of the Shakers through buildings, furniture, everyday items, displays, and demonstrations. Also known as the United Society of Believers in Christ's Second Appearing, Shakers branched off from the Quakers in 18th-century England. Many migrated to colonial America, including a group that crossed the Appalachians into Kentucky in 1814.

In nearby **Danville,** the Great American Dollhouse Museum

Cavers explore Mammoth Cave

flaunts 200 dollhouses reflecting various eras of American history, as well as an early-20th-century miniature village. **Bardstown** is the midway point of the Kentucky Bourbon Trail, linking 10 major distilleries, including many of the most famous names. The town's Oscar Getz Museum of Whiskey History displays more than 250 years worth of moonshine memorabilia. Some 35 miles (56 km) farther west is the illustrious **Fort Knox.** An active U.S. Army base, the fort's federal gold depository is closed to the public, but visitors can browse the General George Patton Museum and Center of Leadership.

LOCAL FLAVOR

Sample the best Kentucky bourbon at:

• **Evan Williams Bourbon Experience (Louisville):** Established in 1783, the granddad of Kentucky's bourbon distillers features a guided tour through an artisanal distillery and "educational" tastings.

• **Wild Turkey distillery (Lawrenceburg):** The award-winning architecture of the visitor center is inspired by traditional Kentucky tobacco barns.

• **Jim Beam American Stillhouse (Clermont):** The cradle of bourbon's best-selling brand includes a decanter museum, cooperage demonstrations, and special behind-the-scenes tours.

• **Woodford Reserve Distillery (Versailles):** The oldest of Kentucky's nine bourbonmakers traces its roots to 1780. The old stone distillery building is a national historic landmark.

The wooded Cumberland Gap in autumn as seen from Pinnacle Overlook

Mammoth Cave is the world's longest known cave system, with more than 400 miles (644 km) explored. The entry is located in the Caveland Corridor, about 100 miles (161 km) south of Louisville. The subterranean chambers were visited by Native Americans as early as the first millennium B.C. High points include the flowstone formations of the Frozen Niagara, the 200-foot-high (61 m) Mammoth Dome, and the Ruins of Karnak. Mammoth Cave National Park offers a number of ranger-led underground tours, along with kayaking and canoeing, camping, hiking, and more.

Bowling Green was the provisional capital of Confederate Kentucky during the Civil War.

Nowadays the city marches to the beat of the "blue flame" engines found in vintage Stingrays at the National Corvette Museum. Bowling Green's other great resource is the Kentucky Museum on the campus of Western Kentucky University, with rooms dedicated to such diverse topics as slavery, the Civil War, quilts, and locally born food icon Duncan Hines. The museum's Instruments of American Excellence exhibit features everyday objects used by famous people, including Jimmy Carter's house-building hammer, Thomas Kinkade's paintbrush, Helen Keller's braille Bible, Jay Leno's stand-up microphone, Tony Hawk's skateboard, and Charlie Daniels's fiddle. ∎

Louisiana

Exotic Louisiana flaunts distinctive Cajun and Creole cultures and flamboyant anything-goes New Orleans, a city revived since Hurricane Katrina devastated the region in 2005. The Pelican State is dominated by dramatic water features, from the Mississippi River and its legendary Delta to the Gulf of Mexico, the vast bayou country, and the meandering Red River watershed.

CITIES

One of America's most cherished cities, **New Orleans** sprawls along a curving riverfront that gives it the nickname Crescent City. Unabashedly brash and touristy, the 300-year-old **French Quarter** is one of the country's most storied neighborhoods, with jam-packed bars, restaurants, and souvenir shops as well as old French colonial buildings wrapped in distinctive wrought-iron balconies. Utter chaos erupts in the neighborhood 40 days before Easter, when Mardi Gras carnival takes over streets and squares. Across Pere Antoine Alley, the Presbytère, one of nine museums in the Louisiana State Museum system, offers a glimpse into the history of Mardi Gras, including an interactive parade exhibit. Saint Louis Cathedral is among North America's oldest continuously active places of worship. Jackson Square hums with talented buskers and street artists while nearby Preservation Hall sways to the beat of traditional Dixieland jazz. The extravagant mansions of the posh Garden District may be experienced via bus, horse carriage, walking tour, or the Saint Charles Avenue streetcar line (and no, there isn't one named "Desire").

TOURISM INFORMATION

The Louisiana Office of Tourism staffs 13 welcome centers at convenient roadside and urban locations around the state. Find out more at louisianatravel.com.

• **New Orleans Welcome Center**
529 St. Ann St.
French Quarter
New Orleans, LA 70116
Tel 504/568-5661

• **State Capitol Welcome Center**
Inside the State Capitol
900 N Third St.
Baton Rouge, LA 70802
Tel 225/342-7317

Housed in a large modern space downtown, the National WWII Museum is packed with military artifacts, from combat aircraft and battle tanks to an original Enigma code-breaking machine. Mardi Gras World at the Port of New Orleans offers just what its name implies—everything you have always wanted to know about the famous festival, including behind-the-scenes details and flamboyant floats from past events. Metairie Cemetery is a maze of elaborate mausoleums and other tombs where many of the city's political, cultural, and athletic icons are buried. Nearby New Orleans City Park provides plenty of space for golf, horseback riding, boating, biking, and birding, as well as the New Orleans Museum of Art and Sculpture Garden.

Baton Rouge (meaning "red stick" in French) derives its peculiar name from the reddish cypress poles—draped with fish and bear heads—that local tribes used to mark their boundary when French

Musicians at Preservation Hall in the French Quarter of New Orleans

Nightlife on Bourbon Street in New Orleans

explorers trekked through in 1699. The striking Gothic Revival–style Old State Capitol building stands on a bluff overlooking the Mississippi; it is now a museum of Louisiana's political history and houses the Governors' Portrait Gallery and the "Ghost of the Castle" exhibit that portrays the building's riotous history. Downtown Baton Rouge is separated from the river by a large levee with a hiking/biking path that leads about a mile (1.6 km) along the capital waterfront. Along the way are the Louisiana Art & Science Museum, Belle of Baton Rouge Casino and Hotel, and a World War II destroyer turned floating museum, the U.S.S. *Kidd*. In addition to massive Tiger Stadium (nicknamed "Death Valley," describing the fate of LSU opponents), the leafy campus of Louisiana State University also hosts the LSU Rural Life Museum, the LSU Museum of Natural Science, and 1,600-year-old Native American mounds.

LANDSCAPES

The storied **bayou country** spreads south and west from New Orleans along the Gulf Coast, heartland of a Cajun culture derived from the French-speaking Acadian people expelled from eastern Canada after the British conquest of that region in the 1750s. Distinctive food, music, and language are just a few of the things that set the Cajuns—and by extension the Louisiana bayou country—apart from the rest of the nation. The region is rich in both human and natural history.

Jean Lafitte National Historical Park and Preserve covers six sites in southern Louisiana, each with its own focus. Among them are Chalmette Battlefield on the edge of New Orleans, where troops vanquished far superior British forces

CAPITALISM

The house that Huey Long built, Louisiana's art deco–style state capitol building is the tallest in the nation—34 stories and 450 feet (137 m) high. Governor Long mandated construction of the grandiose structure in the early 1930s as a symbol of his rise to power. He was later assassinated on the capitol's front steps and buried on the grounds.

during the 1815 Battle of New Orleans. Another area of the park, Barataria Preserve in Marrero, encompasses wildlife-rich wetlands explored via elevated wooden walkways, canoes, or kayaks.

Located on a barrier island near the mouth of the Mississippi River, **Grand Isle** and its 10 miles (16 km) of coastline flaunt fishing places, beach activities, and excellent seafood. The Wetlands Acadian Cultural Center in Thibodaux gives visitors a closer look at Cajun culture through exhibits, artifacts, films, and stage plays. The McIlhenny family has been making Tabasco sauce on Avery Island since

1868; a factory tour includes a look at how the hot sauce is made as well as the Jungle Gardens, 170 acres (69 ha) of local flora and fauna.

As the unofficial capital of Cajunland, **Lafayette** hosts the Acadiana Symphony Orchestra & Conservatory of Music as well as the Acadian Cultural Center, which offer music, dance, storytelling, and culinary events. On the outskirts of town, Vermilionville is a living-history museum and folklife park with live performances and more than a dozen artisans creating traditional Cajun, Creole, and Native American crafts. To the east, **Breaux Bridge** is famed as the "Crawfish Capital of the World," while nearby **Lake Martin** is the nation's largest nesting area for wading birds as well as a venue for wildlife-focused swamp tours.

Lake Charles anchors the western end of bayou country, a onetime petrochemical hub that has morphed in modern times into the state's primary gambling center and budding tourist destination. Among its attractions are the Mardi Gras Museum of Imperial Calcasieu and the Black Heritage Gallery. Although it's 20 miles (32 km) from the Gulf, the city's North Beach is the only inland white-sand beach between Texas and Florida. For the real deal head south on Highway 27 to **Holly Beach** on the so-called Cajun Riviera.

Upstream from New Orleans, the **Mississippi Valley** presents a chain

Houmas House Plantation and Gardens along Louisiana's famous Great Mississippi River Road

Live oaks, water, and Spanish moss in Louisiana's bayou country

of historic 19th-century plantation homes converted into museums that reflect life in the antebellum South. Destrehan Plantation, the oldest documented plantation home (1787) in the lower Mississippi Valley, preserves among its many

keepsakes a document signed by Thomas Jefferson and folk art depicting an 1811 slave revolt. Guests can sip mint juleps and spend the night in well-equipped cottages on the grounds of Oak Alley Plantation near Vacherie. Rosedown Plantation in Saint Francisville, home to the Turnbull family for more than 120 years, is considered among the best preserved of all southern plantations.

On the other side of Baton Rouge, Myrtles Plantation is said to be one of the most haunted places in Louisiana, partly because it was built atop an ancient Tunica Indian burial ground. At Frogmore Plantation near Ferriday, visitors can compare and contrast a working cotton plantation of the early 1800s with a modern cotton facility. For a complete change of pace, the Angola Museum, just outside the gates of its

namesake Louisiana State Penitentiary, is open to the public. Its most infamous artifact is "Gruesome Gertie"—the electric chair in which 87 men and women were put to death.

Creole culture also thrives in the **Cane River National Heritage Area,** running 35 miles (56 km) along the Cane River between Alexandria and Natchitoches and in central Louisiana. The largely rural area includes old plantations, forts, churches, cemeteries, and other historically important Creole structures. Foremost among these is Melrose Plantation, one of the largest plantations ever owned and operated by freed black slaves. The heritage area includes the national historic landmark district in downtown Natchitoches, the oldest permanent settlement within the borders of the Louisiana Purchase. ∎

Maine

A land of lakes, forests, and rocky shores, Maine sports a much more rugged vibe than its well-groomed New England neighbors. The Pine Tree State's 5,000 miles (8,047 km) of coastline are spangled with bays, islands, and picturesque villages studded with lobster shacks and lighthouses. Inland from the Atlantic, Maine's copious wilderness provides plenty of scope for adventure both summer and winter.

CITIES

By far the state's largest city, **Portland** is populated by a mix of old-timers and newbies drawn by a funky arts-and-culture scene and clean-living outdoor lifestyle. Set at the confluence of the Fore River and Casco Bay, the city boasts a long and deeply indented shoreline. The Old Port district blends cobblestone streets and bygone brick buildings with hip shops, bars, and restaurants. It's also the place to hop ferries over to Nova Scotia and the islands in Casco Bay. Farther along the waterfront, the Maine Narrow Gauge Railroad Co. & Museum features equipment used on the two-foot gauge tracks that connected communities in rural Maine with coastal outposts during the late 19th and early 20th centuries. Between May and October, the museum offers rides on a short section of track along the harbor front. On the west side of downtown, the Arts District draws its creative energy from the Maine College of Art as well as galleries, a theater company, and the city's best museums. The

Portland Museum of Art (PMA) boasts close to 20,000 pieces dating from the 18th century to present day, including a large selection by Maine artists. Right behind the PMA is the historic McLellan-Sweat Mansion, built in the early 19th century and a prime example of a federal-style brick town house. Additionally, the PMA owns the restored Winslow Homer Studio in Prouts Neck, 12 miles (19 km) to the south. It was here that Homer (1836–1910) lived and painted many of his masterpieces. On the other side of downtown Portland, and surrounded by water on three sides, the hilly East End district is known for its Eastern Promenade, with 68 acres (28 ha) of waterfront parkland and the city's only public beach. Towering behind the shore is the Portland Observatory, a maritime signal tower built in 1807 to communicate with ships via telescope and signal flags. Among other historic homes in central Portland is

TOURISM INFORMATION

The Maine Tourism Association maintains visitor information centers at seven different gateways into the state. For more information, visit maine tourism.com.

- **Portland Ocean Gateway Information Center**
14 Maine State Pier
Portland, ME 04101
Tel 207/772-5800
visitportland.com

- **Acadia Welcome Center**
1201 Bar Harbor Rd.
Trenton, ME 04605
Tel 800/345-4617
barharborinfo.com

- **Maine State Parks**
maine.gov/dacf/parks

Fresh-caught lobsters boiled to order, a specialty in coastal Maine

The Portland Head Light has helped sailors navigate Casco Bay for centuries.

the opulent Victoria Mansion, built in 1858–1860 as a summer home for Ruggles Sylvester Morse, who made his fortune on luxury hotels in New Orleans. Also of interest, the Wadsworth-Longfellow House hosted three generations of a family that made important contributions to Portland's political, literary, and cultural life. Restored to its 1850s splendor, the manse displays household items and family artifacts. On the east side of town, Fort Williams Park in Cape Elizabeth offers rolling hills and shoreline trails along with the ruined (and thoroughly spooky) Goddard Mansion as well as historic Portland Head Light. Commissioned in the late 18th century by George Washington, the whitewashed lighthouse was manned until 1989 and still functions automatically. The

former Keeper's Quarters is now a museum.

One of the nation's smallest state capitals, **Augusta** lies 55 miles (89 km) northeast of Portland on the Kennebec River. The towering capitol building dates from 1832; when the copper dome was replaced in 2014, the old dome was converted into souvenirs and scrap metal for artists. The adjacent Maine State Museum holds a number of treasures, including the controversial Maine labor history mural. Augusta's most noteworthy sight is Old Fort Western, a restored wooden stockade originally built in 1754 and the oldest surviving wooden fort in New England.

LANDSCAPES

New England's only national park, **Acadia** offers a stunning

canvas of coastline, lakes, forest, and mountains set against a backdrop of **Mount Desert Island** and the Atlantic Ocean. The park can be

---

STATE OF THE ART

• **Best movies:** *Andre* (1994) and *The Cider House Rules* (1999)

• **Best books:** *The Pearl of Orr's Island* by Harriet Beecher Stowe and *Dolores Claiborne* by Stephen King

• **Best art:** the Maine maritime works of Winslow Homer

• **Best plays:** *Icebound* by Owen Davis and *Carousel* by Rodgers and Hammerstein

• **Best TV shows:** *Murder, She Wrote* and *Dark Shadows*

explored via a popular driving loop, hiking trails, equestrian paths, and bike routes; other activities include rock climbing, camping, and boating. The park is also open in winter. Bar Harbor, the island's largest town and tourism hub, overflows with restaurants, galleries, shops, and docks where boats offer various types of day trips out to the deep-blue sea. Mount Desert Oceanarium includes a lobster hatchery and touch tank as well as guided tours of the nearby Thomas Bay Salt Marsh.

A causeway connects Mount Desert Island to the mainland and more quaint coastal towns. **Trenton** is home to several lobster pound restaurants as well as Timber Tina's Great Maine Lumberjack Show, a brawny burlesque of chain sawing, axe throwing, logrolling, and pole climbing. **Blue Hill** boasts independent book shops, great restaurants, and the Jonathan Fisher House, which preserves the memory of the 18th-century minister who preached in four languages, built clocks, and painted landscapes

that are now highly praised. Nearby **Mount Battie** in Camden Hills State Park affords commanding views of Penobscot Bay and offshore islands.

One of the state's first European settlements, **Boothbay Harbor** is home to the Coastal Maine Botanical Gardens, 270 acres (109 ha) of tidal shoreline with gardens, trails, and ponds. Boothbay Railway Village offers rides on a vintage steam

engine train plus antique autos and exhibits on Down East rural life. Ten miles (16 km) offshore and reached by ferry from Boothbay Harbor, **Monhegan Island** hearkens back to an era when there were no paved roads, streetlights, or motor vehicles. Trails lead through wooded areas to a lighthouse built in 1824.

Slightly inland from the coast, Brunswick's claim to fame is leafy **Bowdoin College,** alma mater of numerous notable Americans, including President Franklin Pierce, poet Henry Wadsworth Longfellow, and polar explorer Robert E. Peary. Campus sights include the Bowdoin College Museum of Art and the Peary-MacMillan Arctic Museum.

The south coast below Portland is marked by dozens of gorgeous white-sand strands, including seven-mile (11 km) Old Orchard Beach and Ogunquit Beach at the mouth of the Ogunquit River. The mile-long (1.6 km) **Marginal Way**—one of the few paved, public shoreline paths in all of New England—meanders between

A wary bull moose sizes up his photographer in Baxter State Park.

A paddler on Churchill Lake in Maine's North Woods

Ogunquit and Perkins Cove. Long Sands Beach offers two miles (3.2 km) of sand and great views of 1879 Cape Neddick Lighthouse, reputedly the nation's most photographed lighthouse. **Kennebunkport** also boasts several good beaches including Gooch's, Mother's, and Middle Beaches, the sandy trio connected by a scenic oceanfront path. The town is renowned for its cute bed-and-breakfast inns and Walker's Point—location of the summer retreat of the presidential Bush family. Other attractions include the Seashore Trolley Museum and several historic buildings.

Maine's vast interior is heavily wooded and largely uninhabited. **Baxter State Park** enables a wide range of wilderness activities including fishing, swimming, boating, snowmobiling, and camping. At 5,270 feet (1,606 m), the park's Mount Katahdin is the state's highest point and one of the major landmarks along the 281 miles (452 km) of Appalachian Trail, which traverses the state and includes what many experts consider the trail's most difficult stretch, framed by the 100-Mile Wilderness south of Baxter. The **Allagash Wilderness Waterway,** a mecca for whitewater enthusiasts, meanders through 92 miles (148 km) of very remote backwoods between Baxter and the Quebec frontier. Maine's top winter resorts include Sugarloaf, the largest ski area east of the Rockies, as well as nearby Saddleback and Sunday River, on the edge of the White Mountains in southern Maine. ■

ROAD TRIPS

Great drives across the Timber State:

• Highway One along the coast between Brunswick and Calais (234 miles/377 km)

• Old Canada Road (Highway 201) between Fairfield and Jackman (88 miles/142 km)

• Pequawket Trail (Highway 113) from Standish to Gilead (62 miles/100 km)

• Fish River Scenic Byway (Highway 11) between Sherman and Fort Kent (106 miles/171 km)

• Mount Desert Island Loop (Highways 3 and 102) from Trenton (55 miles/89 km)

Maryland

Maryland's distinctive state flag betrays its origins: a colony founded by prominent British Catholics as one of the world's first beacons of religious freedom. Despite its petite size (it is the ninth smallest state), Maryland flaunts a wide range of terrain from Atlantic beaches and Chesapeake Bay islands to the rolling Piedmont country and rugged Allegheny Mountains.

CITIES

Founded in the early 18th century as a tobacco port, **Baltimore** grew into an industrial powerhouse and immigration gateway that also played key roles in the American Revolution and War of 1812. With 72 designated historic districts, Baltimore is sometimes called the "City of Neighborhoods," but it might also be called the "City of Architecture," with historic structures representing just about every era of U.S. history. The central city huddles around the Inner Harbor and its many attractions, including the National Aquarium, the U.S.S. *Constellation* and other historic ships, Oriole Park at Camden Yards baseball park, and the Pier Six Pavilion music venue. The Inner Harbor is surrounded by other storied neighborhoods: Directly east are Little Italy and Fell's Point, an old-time shipbuilding hub. On the south side of the harbor, the gentrified Federal Hill district embraces many renovated old homes as well as the Maryland Science Center and the American Visionary Art Museum. The latter features works produced by self-taught "outsider" artists displayed in several adjacent venues, including a main building covered with mirror tiles and an old whiskey warehouse containing artsy cars and

TOURISM INFORMATION

The Maryland Office of Tourism staffs welcome centers at 12 locations around the state including interstate gateways and major urban areas. Find them online at visitmaryland.org.

● **Baltimore Visitor Center**
401 Light St.
Baltimore, MD 21202
Tel 877/225-8466
baltimore.org

● **Annapolis & Anne Arundel County Visitor Center**
26 West St.
Annapolis, MD 21401
Tel 410/280-0445
visitannapolis.org

● **Great Ocean City Visitor Center**
12320 Ocean Gateway
Ocean City, MD 21842
Tel 410/213-0552
oceancity.org

● **National Park Service**
nps.gov/state/md

a re-created block of Baltimore's famous painted window screens. Behind one building, a large sculpture of a hand supports a rolled movie screen lowered in summer to show outdoor films, which are best watched from Federal Hill Park. The waterfront continues east past the Baltimore Museum of Industry to Locust Point and Fort McHenry, where American forces famously foiled a British attack in 1814. The battle helped turn the tide of war in favor of the U.S. and also inspired Francis Scott Key to pen what would evolve into the country's national anthem. On the eastern edge of downtown, in the Barre Circle neighborhood, is the redbrick house on Emory Street where Babe Ruth was born in 1895. On the

Visitors at the National Aquarium in Baltimore's Inner Harbor

The Maryland State House anchors quaint downtown Annapolis along the Chesapeake Bay.

other side of the University of Maryland Medical Center complex lies the grave of another local hero—author Edgar Allen Poe. North of downtown, the Mount Vernon Cultural District is home to a towering monument to George Washington (climb 228 steps to a viewing platform) and the Walters Art Museum, with a collection that spans global creativity from the third millennium B.C. through the early 20th century. The nearby Basilica of the National Shrine of the Assumption of the Blessed Virgin Mary, designed by early American architectural maestro Benjamin Henry Latrobe, was consecrated in 1821 as the first Roman Catholic cathedral in the U.S. Founded in 1876 as the nation's first research university, Johns Hopkins features the splendid federal-era Homewood Museum (1801) and the venerable Baltimore Museum of Art.

Even though it's been the capital of Maryland since 1694, **Annapolis** is probably more renowned as the home to the U.S. Naval Academy. Established in 1845, the second oldest of the nation's five service academies trains officers for the Navy and Marine Corps. The academy museum in Preble Hall offers exhibits on the history of sea power and the evolution of the U.S. Navy. More seafaring history is on display at the Annapolis Maritime Museum, located in the city's last operating oyster-packing plant. Built up over

CAPITALISM

The oldest state capitol building still in continuous legislative use, the Maryland State House was constructed between 1772 and 1797 and for a short time served as the U.S. capitol. Its distinctive crown is the nation's oldest and largest wooden dome (made without nails). The dome's lightning rod was built and grounded according to Benjamin Franklin's specifications. Outside the capitol are memorials honoring Revolutionary War general Baron Johann DeKalb, Spanish-American War admiral Winfield Scott Schley, and Thurgood Marshall, the first African-American justice of the U.S. Supreme Court.

more than 300 years, Annapolis town offers plenty in the way of historic sights and classic American architecture. The Georgian-style Government House has been the official residence of the governors of Maryland since 1870; public tours are given on Tuesdays and Thursdays. The William Paca House and Garden, home of one of Maryland's four signers of the Declaration of Independence, is filled with period antiques and early American memorabilia. Constructed in the 1770s, the Hammond-Harwood House is a masterpiece of the Anglo-Palladian style and one of the nation's most significant examples of colonial residential architecture. In addition to 18th-century fine and decorative arts, the interior harbors stunning period plasterwork and wood carving.

Annapolis also boasts a significant African-American heritage. During the 19th century, blacks comprised one-third of the Annapolis population and it was a major haven for free people of color prior to the Civil War. The Kunta Kinte–Alex Haley Memorial marks the spot where Kunta Kinte arrived in chains aboard a slave ship in *Roots*. The Banneker-Douglass Museum, the state's official museum of African-American heritage, is located in the old Mount Moriah AME Church (1875).

LANDSCAPES

Maryland's jagged panhandle, defined by the Potomac River in the south and the Pennsylvania border (also the Mason-Dixon Line) in the north, includes part of the **Allegheny Mountains.** Near the state's western extreme, Deep Creek Lake offers 69 miles (111 km) of shoreline and a wide array of outdoor activities, as does nearby Savage River State Forest, which protects a huge expanse of northern hardwood forest. One of the easternmost outliers of the Appalachian chain, Catoctin Mountain Park provides venues for hiking, biking, camping, and the like; it is also home to the presidential retreat of Camp David (closed to the public).

Tumbling down from the heights, the state's **Piedmont** region includes

a large section of the Appalachian Trail through several state parks and Antietam National Battlefield. Also called the Battle of Sharpsburg, the 1862 Civil War clash remains the bloodiest single-day battle in American history. Around 23,000 soldiers from both sides were killed, wounded, or went missing during the 12 hours of combat. More wartime history awaits in **Frederick,** including the National Museum of Civil War Medicine and Monocacy National Battlefield. Carroll County Farm Museum features 15 historic buildings and displays on how rural Maryland families lived and worked in the 18th and 19th centuries.

In addition to endless suburbs, the heavily populated **corridor between Baltimore and Washington, D.C.,** includes several worthwhile detours. Brookside Gardens

Catoctin Mountain Park is home to the Camp David presidential retreat.

The Chesapeake Bay, where more than 150 freshwater rivers and streams meet the Atlantic

inside Wheaton Regional Park in Silver Spring proffers formal and informal flora to wander and contemplate, plus a live butterfly garden in summer. Ellicott City, on the banks of the Patapsco River, offers a mixture of offbeat stores, eateries, antique shops, and historic landmarks such as an 18th-century flour-milling complex. Strathmore arts center in Bethesda has a year-round slate of visual and performing arts. On the eastern edge of the D.C. metro area, Six Flags America theme park in Upper Marlboro has more than 100 thrill rides and a summer water park.

Maryland's **Eastern Shore** harbors beautiful beaches and resorts, nature areas, and historic towns. Ocean City, renowned for its vintage 1902 boardwalk, mixes attractions such as the Life-Saving Station Museum, Fisher's Popcorn stand, and Purple Moose Saloon

among the usual souvenir shops, eateries, and amusements.

Just south of Ocean City lies **Assateague Island,** a 37-mile-long (60 km) barrier island that stretches south into Virginia. The entire island is protected within the confines of Assateague Island National Seashore and Assateague State Park,

which is flush with wild ponies. The Atlantic side offers surfing, beach horseback riding, surf fishing, seashore camping, and a long over-sand vehicle (OSV) driving zone, while the bay side has secluded coves and marsh areas that can be explored by foot, canoe, or kayak. ■

HIDDEN TREASURES

Maryland's long and rich transportation heritage is reflected in these sights:

• **Baltimore & Ohio Railroad Museum (Baltimore):** showcases the world's largest collection of 19th-century American railroad locomotives on the site of the nation's first train factory (1829)

• **Chesapeake & Ohio Canal:** carried coal, lumber, and farm products between Cumberland, Maryland, and

Washington, D.C., from 1831 until 1924; today hiking and biking trails run along the original towpath

• **NASA Goddard Space Flight Center (Greenbelt):** mission control for the Hubble Space Telescope, offers a fascinating visitor center

• **Western Maryland Scenic Railroad (Cumberland):** with steam locomotive excursions to Frostburg's historic Main Street and Thrasher Carriage Museum

Massachusetts

When the *Mayflower* first anchored off the New World in 1620, it's unlikely the Pilgrims imagined their colony would evolve into one of North America's most open-minded places. From Benjamin Franklin to Susan B. Anthony and even Timothy Leary, the Bay State has given birth to many who expanded American ideas and ideals, a legacy apparent in the state's artsy communities, cutting-edge colleges, and historical sights.

CITIES

One of the nation's most fabled cities, **Boston** was a cradle of European civilization in North America, a spark plug of the American Revolution, and a fulcrum of American arts and ideas for nearly 400 years. The 2.5-mile (4 km) Freedom Trail links 16 locations in central Boston deemed significant to the history of America, including museums, meetinghouses, churches, monuments, and burial grounds. Boston Common and the U.S.S. *Constitution* lie at either end of the interesting trail, with busy Faneuil Hall Marketplace about

halfway through. A gathering place since 1742, Faneuil Hall was developed as a place for merchants, fishermen, and farmers to hawk their products, but it also served as a venue for public oratory and political discourse. The adjacent Quincy Market, built as an expansion of Faneuil Hall, now bustles with gourmet food stalls and quirky shops. The Old State House is where Samuel Adams, John Hancock, and John Adams debated the future of the British colonies. The Boston Massacre occurred in front of the building, and the Declaration of Independence was announced from

TOURISM INFORMATION

The Massachusetts Department of Transportation staffs 10 tourist information centers at interstate service plazas around the state. For more information on visitor centers and hours, check out the website at visit-massachusetts.com.

• **Greater Boston Convention and Visitors Bureau Information Center**
Center Court
Prudential Center
800 Boylston St.
Boston, MA, 02116
Tel 888/733-2678
bostonusa.com

• **Boston National Historical Park Visitor Center**
First Floor, Faneuil Hall
15 State St.
Boston, MA 02109
Tel 617/242-5642
nps.gov/bost

• **Destination Plymouth Visitor Center**
130 Water St.
Plymouth, MA, 02360
Tel 508/747-7525 or
800/872-1620
seeplymouth.com

• **Salem Armory Visitor Center**
2 New Liberty St.
Salem, MA 01970
Tel 978/740-1650
salem.org

• **Cape Cod Chamber of Commerce Tourist Information Center**
5 Patti Page Way
Centerville, MA 02632
Tel 508/362-3225
capecodchamber.org

• **Berkshire Visitors Bureau**
66 Allen St.
Pittsfield, MA 01201
Tel 413/743-4500
berkshires.org

• **National Park Service**
home.nps.gov/state/ma

A statue of George Washington on the Boston Common

The shops of Boston's Quincy Market at dusk

its balcony in 1776. Nearby North End, a friendly Italian neighborhood, is also rich in American heritage sites including Old North Church, Copp's Hill Burying Ground, and the Paul Revere House. On the waterfront, the New England Aquarium holds a wide array of aquatic creatures, from tropical fish and sea turtles to anacondas, penguins, and sea lions. Farther down the shore, the Boston Tea Party Ships and Museum illuminate how events escalated from a political protest into full-blown rebellion. Ferries make the run to Boston Harbor Islands National Recreation Area, which encompasses historic forts and lighthouses, as well as hiking trails, tide pools, campgrounds, and swimming sites spread across 34 islands and peninsulas. The fascinating John F. Kennedy Presidential Library and Museum overlooks the bayfront in South Boston.

Fifty-acre (20 ha) Boston Common has served many functions since 1634, including as a cattle pasture, public execution spot, and encampment for British troops. In 1830 it became the nation's first public park and remains a focal point in the city to this day. North of the Common, Beacon Hill is renowned for its federal-style row houses, the golden-domed Massachusetts State House, and the Boston African

LOCAL FLAVOR

- **Boston baked beans:** This early staple of the Pilgrim diet remains one of Beantown's favorite foods, eaten by the crock at Durgin-Park. *340 Faneuil Hall Marketplace, Boston*

- **Clam chowder:** Traditional New England chowder is nothing more than clams, potatoes, and onions cooked in a rich, creamy broth and served with oyster crackers. Soak some up at Belle Isle Seafood. *One Main St., Winthrop*

- **Fluffernutter:** Peanut butter and marshmallow fluff sandwiches, one of the state's favorite foods, are reinvented as deep-fried Fluffernutter dessert at Local 149. *149 P Street, South Boston*

- **Cranberries:** Celebrate the state's leading crop at the October Cranberry Harvest Celebration in Wareham, or take a bog tour at Flax Pond Farms. *58 Pond St., Carver*

American National Historic Site. East of the Common, Back Bay is celebrated for its Victorian brownstones, fine dining, and Fenway Park, legendary home of the Boston Red Sox baseball team and famed for its high left-field wall—the Green Monster. The Museum of Fine Arts is one of the nation's largest, housing more than 450,000 works from ancient Egypt through the 21st century. Boston's tallest skyscrapers also inhabit Back Bay, including the 52-story Prudential Center, topped by the Skywalk Observatory.

Several bridges leap the Charles River to old and venerable **Charlestown,** where the 221-foot (67 m) Bunker Hill Monument offers both history and panoramic views. Charlestown Navy Yard harbors the U.S.S. *Constitution,* the three-masted frigate launched in 1797 that served admirably in the Barbary Wars and War of 1812. "Old Ironsides" is still a commissioned U.S. Navy warship, with a crew of naval officers and enlisted personnel. Along the north shore of the Charles River are the Museum of Science with its many interactive exhibits, and the Massachusetts Institute of Technology (MIT) campus. Farther upstream in stately **Cambridge,** Harvard Square provides great people-watching, shopping, and dining. It fronts Harvard University, venue for the Harvard Museum of Natural History, Museum of Comparative Zoology, Peabody Museum of Archaeology and Ethnology, and the renowned Harvard Art Museums (the Fogg, Busch-Reisinger, and Arthur M. Sackler).

With nearly 700,000 people in its metro area, **Springfield** is the state's second largest urban entity and hallowed ground for several popular sports. James Naismith invented

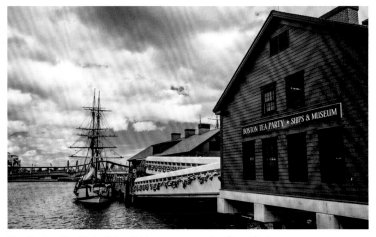

The Boston Tea Party Ships & Museum; opposite: Cape Cod

basketball here in 1891 while teaching at the city's International YMCA Training School, which was also instrumental in the birth of volleyball several years later. Shaped like a giant ball, the Naismith Memorial Basketball Hall of Fame joins Springfield's other landmarks, including the Dr. Seuss National Memorial Sculpture Garden, Springfield Armory National Historic Site, and the D'Amour Museum of Fine Arts, featuring an exemplary collection of Currier and Ives lithographs.

THE COAST

Set on the Atlantic shore nine miles (14 km) south of Boston, **Quincy** nurtured various members of the Adams family to national prominence. Adams National Historical Park examines five generations of family history between 1720 and 1927, including presidents John Adams and John Quincy Adams, U.S. Ambassador to Britain Charles Francis Adams, author Henry Adams, and historian Brooks Adams. The park's three units include a downtown visitor center,

---

HIDDEN TREASURES

• **Walden Pond (near Concord):** appears little changed from the wilderness retreat that inspired Henry David Thoreau

• **Emily Dickinson Museum (Amherst):** comprises two houses important to the poet

• **Crane Estate (Ipswich):** eclectic property encompasses a popular beach, wildlife refuge, and the Great House on Castle Hill

• **Wendell State Forest (near Greenfield):** one of the state's largest and wildest parklands

• **Fitchburg Art Museum (Fitchburg):** showcases work by leading New England contemporary artists; good ancient Egypt and Africa collections

• **Parker River National Wildlife Refuge (Plum Island):** a feeding, resting, and nesting habitat for 300 species of resident and migratory birds

the modest homes where both presidents were born, the Old House at Peacefield, and the Stone Library, believed to be the first presidential library.

Hugging the western shore of Cape Cod Bay, **Plymouth** is where the Pilgrims landed in 1620 onboard the *Mayflower.* Despite its fame, Plymouth Rock is an anticlimax. However, there are about 20 interesting museums in the area as well as historic homes and sites, monuments, memorials, and graveyards. Plimoth Plantation is a living-history museum that tells the story of 17th-century Massachusetts from the perspective of both the new arrivals and the native Wampanoag people. Housed in an 1824 building, Pilgrim Hall Museum features original Pilgrim artifacts and possessions.

Arm-shaped **Cape Cod** is a popular summertime vacation area. Most of the best beaches, hiking, and biking trails are found inside Cape Cod National Seashore. The peninsula is also spangled with quaint waterfront villages such as

Chatham, Truro, and Province-town. Among the cape's many and varied attractions are cranberry bogs, lighthouses, sand dunes, the Wellfleet drive-in movie theater, and the Heritage Museum & Gardens in Sandwich.

Martha's Vineyard, just seven miles (11 km) from Cape Cod, can be reached by ferry from several ports on the Massachusetts mainland. The upscale island gained fame as a summer retreat as well as the place where *Jaws* was filmed in 1974. Nearby **Nantucket** also tenders some of the nation's most expensive coastal real estate; however, all can enjoy the island's beaches, sea cliffs, lighthouses, and gardens.

Once called the "Whaling City," **New Bedford** still revels in its maritime heritage and the New Bedford Whaling Museum spins salty tales from those days. Fans of *Moby-Dick* will want to visit the Seamen's Bethel, immortalized in the book as Whaleman's Chapel. The Rotch-Jones-Duff House and Gardens is the only whaling-era

mansion in New England still on its original site and open to the public. Recently restored to its 1850s splendor, the Nathan and Polly Johnson House played a significant role in the Underground Railroad.

The state's north shore is celebrated for die-hard fishing towns such as **Gloucester,** with its working fleets and memorials to those lost at sea. The past comes alive at the Cape Ann Museum and Maritime Gloucester complex with boatyards, wharves, and a marine railroad, as well as a touch-tank aquarium, scuba diving museum, and cruises on the schooner *Ardelle.* The town is also popular for whale- and dolphin-watching tours.

Just down the coast is infamous **Salem,** location of the 1692 witchcraft trials, today flush with various ghost, witch, and vampire tours. The setting for the novel *The House of the Seven Gables* was inspired by

The *Mayflower* first landed at present-day Provincetown, at the tip of Cape Cod.

a home that belonged to author Nathaniel Hawthorne's ancestors; the 1668 colonial dwelling is now open to the public as a museum. Other Salem landmarks include the modern National Park Service visitor center, the historic ships of Pickering Wharf, the Witch House, Essex Street pedestrian mall, and the cheesy but fun Witch Dungeon Museum. Higher culture rules at the Peabody Essex Museum, with a diverse collection that includes 1.8 million pieces of art.

LANDSCAPES

On April 19, 1775, the "shot heard round the world" was fired about 20 miles (32 km) west of Boston. Visitors can relive the opening battle of the American Revolution at the **Minute Man National Historical Park,** which stretches between the Battle Green in Lexington and the North Bridge in Concord. The informative Battle Road Trail follows the route of the redcoat advance and ignominious retreat.

Once a hotbed of the Industrial Revolution, **Worcester** is now a biotech and health-care hub with a strong arts presence, including the Worcester Art Museum (WAM)

An outdoor concert at Tanglewood in the Berkshires

and the Hanover Theatre for the Performing Arts. **Old Sturbridge Village** is an outdoor living-history museum that offers an insight into New England rural life in the early to mid-1800s. Visitors can explore 40 historic buildings spread across more than 200 acres (81 ha).

Funky **Northampton** is a college town with a liberal vibe that tolerates just about any lifestyle. Among its cultural landmarks are the Smith College Museum of Art (one of the world's top collegiate

galleries), the Calvin Coolidge Presidential Library and Museum, and in nearby Amherst, the Eric Carle Museum of Picture Book Art. Rent bikes from Northampton Bicycle and peddle the Manhan Rail Trail, catch a show at the Academy of Music Theatre before grabbing a cold one at the historic 18th-century Wiggins Tavern in the basement of the old Northampton Hotel.

In western Massachusetts, **the Berkshires** offer plenty of outdoor activities, from hiking to horseback riding to canopy tours and rafting. The heavily wooded mountain region also shelters museums, wineries, a scenic railway, and Hancock Shaker Village. The Boston Symphony Orchestra makes its summer home in these rolling hills at Tanglewood in Stockbridge, a resort town where you can also find the Norman Rockwell Museum and the Berkshire Botanical Garden. In winter, the Jiminy Peak Mountain Resort offers 45 ski and snowboard trails and nine lifts. ∎

LITTLE-KNOWN FACTS

• Whirlwind I, one of the world's first digital computers, was developed at MIT between 1948 and 1951 for the U.S. Navy.

• In 1990, Boston's Isabella Stewart Gardner Museum was the scene of the largest art heist in history.

• Alexander Graham Bell first demonstrated his telephone invention in Boston (1876).

• Tufts University in Medford adopted Jumbo as its official mascot in 1885 when a large monetary bequest to the school from circus showman P. T. Barnum came with a taxidermied elephant. A fire destroyed most of Jumbo in 1975, and the only remaining piece of the pachyderm—his tail—has been kept in a peanut butter jar in the Tufts athletic department since.

Michigan

The Great Lakes State truly relishes water. Flanked by lakes on nearly every side, Michigan boasts more coastline than any state except Alaska—3,000 miles (4,828 km) of lakeshore spangled with bays, beaches, sand dunes, and sandstone cliffs that offer a natural balance to the hustle and bustle of Detroit. Then there is the Upper Peninsula, a rustic throwback to frontier days and a world unto its own.

TOURISM INFORMATION

The Michigan Department of Transportation operates 14 welcome centers along major freeways and roadways for the convenience of the traveling public. Visit michigan.org for more information.

• **Detroit Mexicantown International Welcome Center**
2835 Bagley Ave. (at 21st St.)
Detroit, MI 48216
Tel 800/338-7648
visitdetroit.com

• **National Park Service**
nps.gov/state/mi

• **Michigan State Parks**
michigandnr.com/parksandtrails

CITIES

Renowned for its music and motoring, **Detroit** is far and away the state's largest city—and for much of the early 20th century it was the fourth largest in the entire nation, thanks to the booming auto industry. Downtown Detroit is dominated by the 73-story Renaissance Center, a cluster of seven skyscrapers originally financed by the Ford Motor Company but now the world headquarters of General Motors. To the north, the Cultural Center Historic District is anchored by the Detroit Institute of Arts in a classic art deco building. Modern additions to the artsy enclave include the Charles H. Wright Museum of African American History and the Michigan Science Center. The city's modern music legacy is celebrated at the Motown Museum, housed in the simple two-story suburban building nicknamed "Hitsville U.S.A.," home of the Motown sound from 1959 to 1971.

Born on a farm in 1863 on what was then the city's outskirts, Henry Ford helped transform both Detroit and the United States into an industrial powerhouse. His legacy lives on at Fair Lane, his sprawling estate in **Dearborn,** where Ford and his wife, Clara, lived and entertained for 35 years. The national historic landmark property includes a hydroelectric plant, man-made lake, skating house, and "Santa's workshop." Although the manse is undergoing restoration, the expansive grounds are open to the public. The nearby Henry Ford complex offers five distinct attractions including the Henry Ford Museum, which showcases American ideas, innovations, and life. The collection includes the bus on which Rosa Parks took a stand for civil rights, the Lincoln Continental in which John F. Kennedy was assassinated, the Fokker trimotor airplane that took Admiral Richard E. Byrd on the first flight over the North Pole, and the chair upon which President Lincoln was sitting when he was shot. Also part of the complex, the Ford Rouge Factory Tour offers insights into the birth of the Model A, Mustang,

The University of Michigan Law School in Ann Arbor, built in English Gothic style

An enclosed pedestrian walkway over Jefferson Avenue in Detroit

Thunderbird, and other iconic Ford vehicles. Among the historic structures at neighboring **Greenfield Village** are Henry Ford's childhood home and Thomas Edison's Menlo Park laboratory.

Founded on a stretch of the Grand River renowned for its white water, **Grand Rapids** is the largest city in western Michigan. Although the town earned its first fortune making furniture, its modern forte is craft beer—more than 30 microbreweries (and counting) are located there. Michigan's other famous Ford is remembered at the Gerald R. Ford Presidential Library and Museum, which celebrates the 38th president, who spent most of his childhood in Grand Rapids. He is also buried on the leafy waterfront site. Among the city's other attractions are the Frederik Meijer Gardens

and Sculpture Park and Heritage Hill, a neighborhood southeast of downtown comprised of 1,300 historic buildings collected from around the state.

The University of Michigan moved to **Ann Arbor** in 1837, eventually transforming the once pastoral town into an international center of education, art, and

athletics. With more than 43,000 students and 580 buildings, the university is now one of the nation's largest. Among its many visitor-friendly attractions are the Kelsey Museum of Archaeology, Sindecuse Museum of Dentistry, the expansive Nichols Arboretum, and the Matthaei Botanical Gardens, located just off campus.

ROAD TRIPS

Great drives in the Great Lakes State:

• Highway 31 down the Gold Coast (Lake Michigan) from Mackinaw City to New Buffalo (365 miles/587 km)

• Copper Country Trail (U.S. 41) between Houghton and Copper Harbor (47 miles/76 km)

• River Road National Scenic Byway along the Au Sable River between Alcona Dam in Huron National Forest and Oscoda on Lake Huron (22 miles/35 km)

• Highways 25 and 23 along the Sunrise Coast (Lake Huron) between Mackinaw City and Port Huron (400 miles/644 km)

LANDSCAPES

The most remote national park in the lower 48, **Isle Royale** floats on the north side of Lake Superior, much closer to Canada than the rest of Michigan. Reached by ferry from Houghton and Copper Harbor in Michigan, and Grand Portage in Minnesota, the main island and its 450 islets offer a pristine peek at Great Lakes nature best explored by foot or canoe. Campsites are scattered at secluded coves around the shoreline and beside small interior lakes created by glacial activity eons ago.

Parts of the **Upper Peninsula** (known as the U.P.) are equally unspoiled. Spanning nearly one million acres (0.4 million ha), Ottawa National Forest extends all the way from Lake Superior to the Wisconsin border, a massive expanse of wildlife, water features, and recreational opportunities. Farther east, Hiawatha National Forest features shoreline on three different Great Lakes—Superior, Huron, and Michigan. Forest Service–managed Grand Island National Recreation Area includes six historic lighthouses and a variety of ecosystems explored via hiking, mountain biking, or guided bus tours from the ferry landing. Over on the mainland, Pictured Rocks National Lakeshore stretches 40 miles (64 km) along Lake Superior's southern edge. Among its best known features are the sandstone cliffs from which the park takes its name, long and lonely Twelvemile Beach, and the 300-foot-high (91 m) dunes of the Grand Sable Banks.

But the U.P. is not without its urban sights. The American-Canadian twin town of **Sault Sainte Marie** frames two huge canal locks that ease watercraft through the 21-foot (6 m) drop in elevation between Lakes Superior and Huron. "The Soo" (as locals call it) also tenders the Museum Ship *Valley Camp* (a 1917 Great Lakes cargo vessel) and the bygone buildings of the Water Street Historic Block. Although it's less than four square miles (10 sq km), **Mackinac Island** is the state's most celebrated (and visited) island. Set in the strait that divides the Upper and Lower Peninsulas, as well as Lakes Michigan and Huron, the island featured in two battles in the War of 1812 and became a popular summer resort in Victorian times. Fort Mackinac (1780) affords views over a town crowded with other historic structures. Mackinac Island State Park covers more than 70 percent of the island and includes lakeshore, forest, battlefields, and Michigan's oldest golf course. To the west rises Mackinac Bridge, inaugurated in 1957 and still one of the world's longest suspension spans.

Michigan's **Lower Peninsula** kicks off on the south side of the bridge with Colonial Michilimackinac, a historic state park that is a faithful reconstruction of an 18th-century French trading post and British military bastion. In addition to exhibits in many of the 16 buildings, the lakeside outpost offers living-history tours, military

Wind and water sculpt the shoreline at Pictured Rocks National Lakeshore on the Upper Peninsula

A working windmill and an exuberant crop of tulips in Holland, Michigan

reenactments, and colonial cooking demonstrations.

The **Gold Coast** offers 300 miles (483 km) of bays and beaches along Lake Michigan's eastern edge. Ernest Hemingway spent many a youthful summer in and around Petoskey, where the City Park Grill counts itself among the dozens of places around the world frequented by the famous scribe. Cherry pies and wine produced on the Old Mission Peninsula are the twin culinary pillars of Traverse City. With its clear waters and 45 shipwrecks, Sleeping Bear Dunes National Lakeshore and its Manitou Islands is considered one of the best places for scuba diving in all of the Great Lakes region. Onshore, the park offers more

than 100 miles (161 km) of trails. Farther down the shore, Windmill Island is a heritage park along the Macatawa River in Holland, a coastal town founded by Dutch immigrants in 1847. Highlights include an authentic 18th-century

working windmill and some 175,000 tulips that bloom late spring to early summer. Down at the bottom end of the Gold Coast, New Buffalo is perhaps the only place in Michigan where the waves are high enough for board surfing. ∎

LOCAL FLAVOR

• **Whitefish:** The Cove restaurant in Fishtown serves this Great Lakes treat half a dozen different ways, from smoked and stuffed to garlic-and-Parmesan-flavored to campfire whitefish with roasted peppers and onions. *111 River St., Leland*

• **Cherries:** Half a million people flock to the National Cherry Festival in Traverse City each July to eat

cherry pie, cherry jam, dried cherries, cherry salads, and anything else made with the little red fruits.

• **Pannukakku:** Finnish immigrants introduced these Scandinavian pancakes (topped with fresh berries) to the Upper Peninsula more than a century ago. Cafe Rosetta in the Copper Country offers several varieties. *104 Fifth St., Calumet*

Minnesota

The Land of 10,000 Lakes actually has around 12,000 bodies of water. Toss in 69,000 miles (111,045 km) of rivers and streams and it's easy to understand why the state was named after the Dakota word for "sky-tinted water." Minnesota is the largest of the Great Lakes states and has landscapes that vary from thick northern forest to cornfields and soybean farms. The sophisticated Twin Cities dominate the state's urban scene.

TOURISM INFORMATION

Explore Minnesota Tourism offers 11 travel information centers statewide, most of them near interstate highway gateways. Find out more at exploreminnesota.com.

• **Saint Paul Visitor Information Center**
Landmark Center
75 W Fifth St.
St. Paul, MN 55102
Tel 651/292-3225
visitstpaul.com

• **Visit Duluth**
21 W Superior St.
Duluth, MN 55802
Tel 218/722-4011 or 800/438-5884
visitduluth.com

• **National Park Service**
nps.gov/state/mn

• **Minnesota State Parks**
dnr.state.mn.us/state_parks

CITIES

Although separated by the Mississippi River, the Twin Cities of Minneapolis and Saint Paul blend into the state's largest urban area, home to nearly two-thirds of all Minnesotans. **Minneapolis** is the larger of the two, founded in the 1850s as a sawmill town fueled by the liquid power of Saint Anthony Falls, the only waterfall on the Mississippi. Today tourism rather than timber colors the modern waterfront, with the popular Northeast River District and Mills District both strewn with restaurants, shops, theaters, and riverfront paths, including the Saint Anthony Falls Heritage Trail. Here, too, is The Soap Factory arts center. The stunning stainless-steel-and-brick Weisman Art Museum, designed by Frank Gehry, is a teaching museum for the University of Minnesota focused on contemporary art. Also striking, the Walker Art Center hosts contemporary art exhibits as well as performances. The adjacent Minneapolis Sculpture Garden is known for the iconic "Spoonbridge and Cherry" fountain as well as 40 other works. The city's oldest and largest collection, the Minneapolis Institute of Art (MIA) has amassed more than 83,000 objects spanning ancient to modern with pieces from around the world. On the outskirts of Minneapolis, Minnehaha Falls Regional Park is cleaved by 53-foot-high (16 m) Minnehaha Falls. Located near the confluence of the Mississippi and Minnesota Rivers, Fort Snelling is a living-history museum on the site of a frontier outpost that was established in the early 1820s by Colonel Josiah Snelling, thereby opening the area for homesteaders. Also preserved are the quarters where Dred Scott and his wife stayed in the 1830s while enslaved by a civilian who lived at the fort.

Saint Paul rises on the opposite bank, seat of Minnesota's state government and a thriving business

Whimsical art on a grand scale at the Minneapolis Sculpture Garden

Saint Paul, sister city to Minneapolis

center. Once a scrawny riverfront hamlet dubbed "Pig's Eye," the city was established in the 1830s by a French-Canadian trapper and bootlegger. The frontier-era log chapel that gave the city its permanent name was replaced by the soaring Cathedral of Saint Paul— the third largest in the U.S.— which combines aspects of French Gothic, Renaissance, and classical architecture into a masterpiece of American beaux arts. Down the street and accessible by guided tour stands the equally imposing Hill House, home of Great Northern Railway mogul James J. Hill, who set out to build the largest, grandest, and most expensive home in Minnesota. Completed in 1891, the 36,000-square-foot (3,345 sq m) mansion boasts 13 bathrooms and 22 fireplaces and features the very latest technology of the time, including indoor plumbing, central heating, electricity, and gas lighting.

Downtown Saint Paul sprawls between Cathedral Hill and the river, a mosaic of office towers and cultural institutions including the Ordway Center for the Performing Arts (home base of the Minnesota Opera), Saint Paul Chamber Orchestra, and

ROAD TRIPS

Great drives across the Gopher State:

• North Shore Scenic Drive (Highway 61) between Duluth and Thunder Bay, Ontario, along the north shore of Lake Superior (190 miles/306 km)

• Waters of the Dancing Sky Scenic Byway (Highway 11) from Island View to Karlstad (183 miles/295 km)

• Highway 61 down the Mississippi Valley from Saint Paul to La Crescent (137 miles/220 km)

• Minnesota River Valley Scenic Byway from Belle Plaine to Browns Valley via Mankato (239 miles/385 km)

• Paul Bunyan Expressway (Highway 2) between Duluth and Grand Forks, ND (266 miles/428 km)

touring Broadway productions. Across the street, the flamboyant Landmark Center has evolved from post office to lively arts center with a year-round slate of music, dance, theater, exhibitions, and public forums. The nearby Minnesota Children's Museum has several floors of interactive learning environments and exhibits including Earth World, where kids explore iconic Minnesota habitats such as forest, prairie, and wetlands. The Minnesota History Center offers imaginative and interactive exhibits, as well as a "history players" program during which actors portraying historical figures mingle with guests. Exhibits at the waterfront Science Museum of Minnesota run a broad gamut from dinosaur bones and outer space to "questionable medical instruments" as well as an excellent Mississippi River Gallery. Part of the museum lobby is reserved for the Mississippi National River and Recreation Area visitor center, staffed by rangers who dispense tips on how to hike, bike, or paddle the 72-mile (116 km) corridor that runs right through the heart of the Twin Cities.

Set at the western tip of Lake Superior, **Duluth** does double duty as a brawny seaport for Great Lakes cargo and budding hub for tourists bent on exploring Minnesota's far north. Once a gritty warehouse district, the revitalized Canal Park neighborhood now shelters hotels, restaurants, nightlife spots, and the Lake Superior Maritime Visitor Center, operated by the U.S. Army Corps of Engineers. The scenic Duluth Lakewalk leads to the Duluth Rose Garden and the lakefront Glensheen Historic Estate, while the pedestrian-only Minnesota Slip Bridge hops over to Great Lakes Aquarium and the S.S. *William A. Irvin,* an iron-ore-and-coal carrier that served as flagship of U.S. Steel's Great Lakes Fleet from 1937 to 1978. Canal Park is also a good vantage point to watch the engineering marvels that allow enormous ships to pass beneath the Aerial Lift Bridge into Duluth-Superior Harbor. In

Hollow Rock, off the Grand Portage Reservation in Minnesota's northeastern tip

summer, vacationers head across the bridge to the beaches of Park Point, the world's largest freshwater sandbar. Spirit Mountain Recreation Area offers summer hiking and biking and winter skiing inside the city limits.

LANDSCAPES

North of Duluth, Minnesota truly does become the land of lakes, a vast watery wilderness that seems little changed from the 18th century when French voyageurs were the first Europeans to explore this part of the world. Moose, bear, beaver, wolves, and otter count among the many animals that frequent the region. The boreal forest and its waterways are protected within the confines of Superior and

More than a third of Voyageurs National Park is water with 200-plus campsites accessible only by boat.

Chippewa National Forests, the **Boundary Waters Canoe Area Wilderness** along the U.S.-Canada frontier, and **Voyageurs National Park.** Although the park's Ash River and Rainy Lake visitor centers can be reached by car, most of Voyageurs is only accessible by foot or boat, including the entire Kabetogama Peninsula. During winter, the park transforms into terrain ideal for cross-country skiing, snowshoeing, snowmobiling, and ice fishing.

The International Wolf Center in **Ely** promotes the survival of gray wolves with exhibits, education programs, and close encounters with its resident wolf pack. Located in the Mesabi Range just south of the parklands, the historic iron-mining town of **Hibbing** offers visitors a chance to peer down into the massive (and still active) Hull-Rust-Mahoning Mine, bike the 120-mile (193 km) Mesabi Trail, or snap a selfie in front of the house where Bob Dylan grew up.

Brainerd, another quirky town, embraces the legend of lumberjack Paul Bunyan and Babe the Blue Ox with several attractions, including the old-fashioned Paul Bunyan Land amusement park and newfangled Paul Bunyan Water Park at Brainerd Lakes. Farther south, Munsinger Clemens Gardens in **Saint Cloud** features forest, fountains, water features, and more than 80,000 plants. One of the summer highlights is a garden devoted to white flowers and white flowering shrubs.

Known as the birthplace of Minnesota, historic **Stillwater** lies along the Saint Croix River, across the water from Wisconsin. Many of the old buildings are now occupied by restaurants, galleries, and antique shops, as well as the 1923 Nelson's Ice Cream parlor. Stillwater is a good jumping-off point for activities along the Saint Croix National Scenic Riverway. ∎

LITTLE-KNOWN FACTS

• From blueberries to gooseberries, 30 varieties of edible wild berries can be harvested (by anyone) in the Minnesota countryside.

• Minnesota safeguards the largest bald eagle and wolf populations in the lower 48.

• Come winter, Minnesotans can play on 22,000 miles (35,406 km) of snowmobile trails.

• Said to be more than 300 years old, the Witch Tree on the Lake Superior shore is considered sacred by the local Ojibwe people.

• The Northwest Angle is a tiny slice of Minnesota (596.3 square miles/1,544 sq km) that extends above the 49th parallel, the result of a mistake in the 1783 Treaty of Paris that ended the American Revolution.

Mississippi

Named after the great river that marks its entire western boundary, Mississippi is a real southern charmer, a state that blends blues music with numerous green spaces, Gulf Coast beaches, and Civil War battlefields. With half its population still living in rural areas, the Magnolia State offers a glimpse of Dixie before the rise of the New South.

TOURISM INFORMATION

As joint ventures between Mississippi Tourism and local counties, each of the 13 welcome centers scattered around the state features antebellum-inspired architecture. Visit visitmississippi.org.

- **Jackson Visitor Center**
111 E Capitol St. #102
Jackson, MS 39201
Tel 601/960-1891
visitjackson.com

- **Biloxi Visitors Center**
1050 Beach Blvd.
Biloxi, MS 39530
Tel 228/374-3105 or
800/245-6943
gulfcoast.org

- **Vicksburg Visitor Information**
52 Old Hwy. 27
Vicksburg, MS 39180
Tel 601/636-9421
visitvicksburg.com

CITIES

Known as the "City with Soul," **Jackson** continues to nurture its harmonious heritage with a thriving music scene that features gospel, blues, and R & B. Malaco Records is a living testament of the city's music history, the studio where soul and blues legends such as Johnnie Taylor, Benny Latimore, and Shirley Brown made their records. In 2008, the studio received a historic marker for its contribution to the state's musical reputation. The building was destroyed three years later by a tornado, and many priceless master tapes ruined, but the studio has since been rebuilt on its original site. The nearby Medgar Evers Home details his days as a civil rights activist and his tragic death at the hands of a white supremacist in the home's driveway in 1963.

Three miles (5 km) from downtown Jackson, Fondren and its downtown arts district are listed on the National Register of Historic Places. With its old-fashioned soda fountain and live "howl at the moon" music, Brent's Drugs on Duling Avenue in Fondren was already a local star before it appeared in the film version of *The Help*. In the upscale Greater Belhaven neighborhood, the home and garden of Pulitzer Prize–winning author Eudora Welty is open to visitors. She moved to the Tudor Revival–style house with her family when she was 16, and it remained her primary home until her death in 2001. Mississippi's former state capitol building, erected in the 1830s, has been restored and functions today as the official state historical museum. In 1903, the "new" capitol building opened a few blocks away, a beaux arts structure constructed on the site of a former prison. Its $1 million-plus price tag was funded by a lawsuit settlement with the Illinois Central Railroad. It can now be explored on free guided and self-guided tours. First occupied in 1842, the graceful Mississippi Governor's Mansion is one of the nation's oldest continuously occupied governor's residences

Eight large marble columns support the rotunda of the Mississippi capitol.

LeFleur's Bluff, a lush green state park within the heart of Jackson

where informative and enthusiastic docents lead tours that make the past come alive. Also in Jackson, the Mississippi Museum of Art exhibits a varied collection of local, national, and international works in a variety of media. For a different experience, the Museum of Natural Science in LeFleur's Bluff State Park offers indoor exhibits as well as nature trails aimed at a greater understanding and appreciation of Mississippi's biological diversity. Of particular interest to families are the interactive exhibits at the Mississippi Children's Museum and the living-history farm and re-created 1920s town at the Mississippi Agriculture and Forestry Museum, celebrating the state's rural heritage.

LANDSCAPES

Mississippi's 44 miles (71 km) of coastline are highlighted by **Gulf Islands National Seashore,** which stretches from Cat Island near Gulfport to Santa Rosa Island in the Panhandle of Florida. The elongated archipelago offers various outdoor attractions and activities from white-sand beaches and sea kayaking to hiking and biking trails, camping, and beautiful settings for picnics. Private boats are needed to explore most of the Mississippi islands, but a passenger ferry runs from Gulfport to West Ship Island, where Fort Massachusetts played a small but significant role in the Civil War. The "Vegas of the Gulf Coast," **Biloxi** bustles with waterfront casinos, eateries, and entertainment, as well as deep-sea fishing charters and boat tours. The waterfront Beauvoir estate, postwar home of the president of the Confederate States of America, is now the Jefferson Davis Home and Presidential Library. Across the bridge from Biloxi, **Ocean Springs** offers historic churches, art galleries, crafts shops, and the excellent Walter Anderson Museum of Art (WAMA), dedicated to the works

STATE OF THE ART

- **Best movies:** *O Brother, Where Art Thou?* (2000) and *Mississippi Burning* (1988)

- **Best books:** *Delta Wedding* by Eudora Welty and *As I Lay Dying* by William Faulkner

- **Best songs:** "Cross Road Blues" by Robert Johnson and "My Home Is in the Delta" by Muddy Waters

- **Best art:** the Gulf Coast wildlife and landscape paintings of Walter Inglis Anderson

- **Best play:** *Cat on a Hot Tin Roof* by Tennessee Williams

of the imaginative Gulf Coast painter Walter Inglis Anderson.

The oldest permanent European settlement along the Mississippi River, **Natchez** was founded by the French in 1716. Natchez National Historical Park features three separate units—Melrose Mansion, the William Johnson House, and the site of old Fort Rosalie—that together provide a montage of the effects of European settlement, slavery, the cotton economy, and the civil rights struggle on the lower Mississippi. Natchez boasts more antebellum mansions than anywhere else in the nation, with around a dozen receiving visitors year-round. The four-week Spring Pilgrimage and three-week Fall Pilgrimage are excellent times to visit Natchez, when many historic homes are open to tours guided by costumed owners, friends, and descendants.

Farther up the river, **Vicksburg** is remembered as the place where Ulysses S. Grant broke Confederate power in the west, helping to turn the tide of the Civil War in favor of the Union. Vicksburg National Military Park commemorates the bitter Rebel defeat with numerous monuments and markers, as well as reconstructed trenches and a cemetery with the graves of 17,000 Union soldiers. The park's U.S.S. *Cairo* Gunboat and Museum preserves the remains of a Union ironclad sunk during the war and raised from the muddy depths a hundred years later. Among Vicksburg's other attractions are the Old Depot Museum with its battlefield and railroad miniatures, the U.S. Army Corps of Engineers Lower Mississippi Museum and Riverfront Interpretive Site, and the riverfront murals depicting the town's long and rich history.

The **Delta Blues Highway** (U.S. 61) meanders north along the Mississippi River to Dockery Farms, a 10,000-acre (4,047 ha) former cotton plantation and sawmill widely regarded as the place where Delta blues music was born through cotton workers such as Henry Sloan and Charley Patton. Nearby Clarksdale also has deep musical roots. The town's Rock & Blues Museum features memorabilia from the 1920s through the 1970s, while the nearby Delta Blues Museum in

ROAD TRIPS

Great drives across the Magnolia State:

• Natchez Trace Parkway between Natchez and Tishomingo State Park (310 miles/499 km)

• Delta Blues Highway (U.S. 61) between Vicksburg and Memphis (222 miles/357 km)

• Old Spanish Trail (U.S. 90) along the Gulf Coast between Franklin Creek and Bay Saint Louis (64 miles/103 km)

The antebellum mansion Dunleith in the city of Natchez is now operated as an inn.

A Civil War battle reenactment of the Siege of Vicksburg

the old train depot displays musical instruments, stage costumes, and historic photographs. Here, too, is the log cabin where Muddy Waters grew up, complete with a life-size statue of Waters inside. At the old intersection of Highways 49 and 61 (Desoto Avenue at North State Street) stands a guitar monument marking the crossroads where Robert Johnson is said to have sold his soul to the devil in exchange for his legendary guitar skills.

Home to William Faulkner, John Grisham, Richard Ford, and dozens of other well-known scribes, **Oxford** is the literary capital of the South. Here stands the antebellum Rowan Oak estate—where Faulkner and his family lived for more than 40 years—as well as the Walton-Young Historic House, where playwright and novelist Stark Young lived while attending Ole Miss. The University of Mississippi Museum showcases

everything from American folk art to Roman antiquities. Some 50 miles (80 km) east, **Tupelo** is renowned as the hometown of Elvis Presley. The tiny whitewashed shotgun house in which the "King of Rock and Roll" was born is now the main attraction at the Elvis Presley Birthplace, which also includes a

museum and the Assembly of God church where the Presley family worshipped. On a small lot on Main Street, Tupelo National Battlefield marks the site of an 1864 clash between Union troops and Confederate forces trying to disrupt General Sherman's vital supply lines. ■

LITTLE-KNOWN FACTS

• The freed African-American slaves who founded Liberia in the 1820s came from Prospect Hill Plantation in Jefferson County.

• The Catfish Museum in Belzoni honors Mississippi's role in producing more than half of the nation's pond-raised catfish each year.

• The annual Great Delta Bear Affair in Rolling Fork recalls Teddy Roosevelt's refusal to shoot an already

injured bear during a 1902 hunting trip in Sharkey County—an episode that inspired the Teddy Bear.

• The Biedenharn Coca-Cola Museum in Vicksburg is located where the soft drink was first bottled in 1894.

• Tallahatchie Flats in Greenwood is an old riverside plantation offering overnight accommodations in vintage cotton-picker shacks.

Missouri

The Show Me State definitely has plenty to show. Saint Louis and Kansas City anchor either end of Missouri, two great metro areas with strong urban cultures connected by the state's namesake river. Down south, the landscape rises to a musical, recreational, and geographical crescendo in the fabled Ozarks. German immigrants endowed the state with a tasty beer culture, while Mark Twain created memorable stories.

TOURISM INFORMATION

The Missouri Division of Tourism offers seven welcome centers around the state near key interstate highway gateways. Check out the website at visitmo.com.

● **Saint Louis Visitor Information Center**
Old Courthouse
North Fourth St., between Market and Chestnut
St. Louis, MO 63102
Tel 314/421-1023 or 800/916-0092
explorestlouis.com

● **Kansas City Welcome Center**
1321 Baltimore Ave.
Kansas City, MO 64105
Tel 816/691-3800 or 800/767-7700
visitkc.com

CITIES

The distinctive 630-foot-high (192m) Gateway Arch defines **Saint Louis** as the Gateway to the West. Completed in 1965 to architect Eero Saarinen's 1947 design, the engineering marvel is both the world's tallest arch and the tallest man-made monument in the Western Hemisphere. Clad in stainless steel panels, it offers a lofty viewing platform and the short documentary *Monument to the Dream,* which tells the story of the landmark's creation. It is part of the Jefferson National Expansion Memorial, which also includes a museum and the Old Courthouse, where Dred and Harriet Scott sued for freedom from slavery. The Basilica of Saint Louis, King of France (also called the Old Cathedral) was the first Roman Catholic cathedral west of the Mississippi (1830). North along the waterfront, Laclede's Landing comprises 19th-century warehouses converted into a boisterous dining and entertainment area. Perched on the south side of downtown, Busch Stadium is home to Major League Baseball's Saint Louis Cardinals and also features a team hall of fame and museum. Gateway Mall paints blocks of green space through the middle of downtown between the arch and Union Station. Along the way are the Soldiers Memorial Military Museum and Peabody Opera House.

The Loft District just north of the mall provides a venue for the City Museum, housed in the old International Shoe Factory. Foremost among its many exhibits are a crazy indoor-outdoor playground with caves, slides, and tunnels in which to get lost, as well as random collections devoted to things such as opera posters and doorknobs. The corridor that forms Saint Louis's civic backbone continues to the west with Saint Louis University and Forest Park. Here the campus Museum of Contemporary Religious Art (MOCRA) aims at interfaith understanding, while the Historic Samuel Cupples House

The Missouri History Museum in Saint Louis, built in 1913 to honor Thomas Jefferson

Saint Louis's iconic Gateway Arch on the Mississippi River

and Gallery specializes in late-19th- and early-20th-century fine and decorative arts. Forest Park, one of the nation's largest urban parks, occupies the site of the 1904 Louisiana Purchase Exposition, better known as the Saint Louis World's Fair, and the Summer Olympics staged that same year. Remnants of the fair include the Palace of Fine Arts (now the Saint Louis Art Museum), the Grand Basin lake, and an antique aviary that eventually grew into the modern Saint Louis Zoo, one of the nation's largest with 18,700 animals. The Missouri Botanical Garden offers 80 acres (32 ha) of theme gardens sprinkled with fountains, statues, and historic structures. The park includes the Doris Waters Harris Lichtenstein Victorian District, with its hedge maze and pincushion garden; the Climatron geodesic dome and its tropical rain forest flora; a significant collection of rare and endangered orchids; plus Japanese, German, Chinese, and Ottoman gardens.

On the opposite side of Missouri, **Kansas City** has its own lofty landmark. Erected in 1926, the 217-foot (66 m) Liberty Memorial is dedicated to those who fought and fell in World War I. Designated a national memorial in 2014, the observation deck of the Egyptian

Revival–style tower allows for great city views. It sits atop the National World War I Museum, which tells the story of the war from a soldier's perspective. A double staircase leads from the Liberty Memorial downhill to Union Station, a massive train depot opened in 1914 with a waiting room that could accommodate 10,000 people. After closing in 1980, the impressive building was repurposed into a shopping and restaurant complex, which also includes an Amtrak stop and the interactive museum Science City. Over on the other side of the hill, the Crown Center urban redevelopment district includes the Legoland Discovery Center and Sea Life Aquarium Kansas City. The historic River Market neighborhood along the Missouri features the largest public farmers market in the Midwest as well as the *Arabia* Steamboat Museum. The Southmoreland district is home to many of the city's leading cultural institutions, including the Kemper Museum of Contemporary Art, the Kansas City Art Institute, and the excellent Nelson-Atkins Museum of Art (NAMA) spread across a 1920s beaux arts building and the recent Bloch Building addition. Nearby, the National Museum of Toys and Miniatures on the University of Missouri–Kansas City campus is filled with antique dolls and dollhouses, scale-model trains, and a range of perfectly proportioned miniature artifacts. On the eastern outskirts of Kansas City, the Harry S. Truman Library and Museum in **Independence** illuminates the Missouri native's days as vice president and president. Harry and Bess Truman are both buried in the courtyard. The Victorian house where the Truman family lived from 1919 until his death in 1972 is now preserved as the Harry S. Truman National Historic Site.

LANDSCAPES

Two hours northwest of Saint Louis, **Hannibal** is the riverside

ROAD TRIPS

Great drives in the Show Me State:

• Little Dixie Highway (Route 79) along the Mississippi River between Clarksville and Hannibal (43 miles/69 km)

• U.S. Highway 160 from Poplar Bluff to Branson through the heart of the Ozarks (203 miles/327 km)

• Blue Buck Knob National Forest Scenic Byway through Mark Twain National Forest (24 miles/39 km)

• Missouri Rhineland scenic drive from Weldon Spring to Hermann (57 miles/92 km)

hometown of Samuel Langhorne Clemens (aka Mark Twain). Visitors can walk in the author's footsteps and explore his legacy at places such as the Mark Twain Boyhood Home

Four bronze horsemen in the spray of the J. C. Nichols Memorial Fountain, Kansas City

and Museum (built by Clemens's father in 1843), Jim's Journey: The Huck Finn Freedom Center, and the Mark Twain Cave, which features prominently in *The Adventures of Tom Sawyer*.

On the Missouri River about midway between Kansas City and Saint Louis, **Jefferson City** is the state's small but charming state capital. The riverside state capitol building, built in 1917, houses the chambers of government as well as the Missouri State Museum. Scattered around the capitol grounds are monuments including the "Fountain of the Centaurs" and a bronze relief that depicts the signing of the Louisiana Purchase Treaty. Adjacent to the capitol, Jefferson Landing State Historic Site preserves the Lohman Building (1839) with its restored general store, the Union Hotel (1855), and the lovely redbrick Governor's Mansion (1871). The hotel's Elizabeth Rozier Gallery stages rotating exhibits on Missouri art, history, and culture.

Anchoring the state's southwest region, **Springfield** epitomizes small-town America. Among its hundred-plus parks and gardens is the Nathanael Greene/Close Memorial Park, which harbors a botanical center, butterfly house, walking trails, and playgrounds. Also here is the pretty Mizumoto Japanese Stroll Garden, complete with blossoming cherry trees, a koi lake, moon bridge, and teahouse. Wilson's Creek National Battlefield marks the site of the Confederate victory over the Union troops in August of 1861, the first major engagement of the Civil War west of the Mississippi River.

The wild **Ozarks** start in earnest south of Springfield, a mosaic of rugged plateaus, wooded vales, large lakes, and wild rivers that extends across the border in Arkansas and

Ozark National Scenic Riverways preserves more than 100 historic structures.

Oklahoma. Although the region's distinctive subculture—expressed in language, music, dance, cuisine, religion, and libertarian attitudes—has diluted in recent years, the Ozarks retain a faraway feel and independent streak. Among the area's many recreational assets are the vast man-made Lake of the Ozarks and Ozark National

Scenic Riverways—the first national park unit to protect an entire river system. Since the early 1980s, once sleepy **Branson** has exploded into an entertainment powerhouse on par with Broadway and Las Vegas, with live shows ranging from country, gospel, and pop music to comedy, acrobatics, and mystery dinner theater. ■

LITTLE-KNOWN FACTS

• Missouri was once the second leading wine-producing state in America (after California), but its wineries withered during Prohibition.

• In addition to those giant shuttlecocks, the Donald J. Hall Sculpture Park in Saint Louis boasts the largest collection of Henry Moore sculptures in the U.S.

• Fantastic Caverns near Springfield are billed as the nation's only "no walking required" caves—visitors

are transported underground in Jeep-drawn trams.

• The Missouri State Penitentiary in Jefferson City has morphed from hard cons to hard-core tourists since closing in 2002. The so-called "bloodiest 47 acres in America" now has historical and paranormal tours.

• Leftover materials from the Hallmark greeting card factory are the raw materials for children creating artworks at the Hallmark Kaleidoscope in Kansas City.

Montana

Big Sky Country stretches more than 500 miles (805 km) from east to west, a massive landmass that embraces huge chunks of the Great Plains and Rocky Mountains. The Missouri River makes a broad sweep across the middle of the state, swollen with water from the Yellowstone region and glacier country. Old mining towns, massive ranches, and infamous battlefields color a human palette that makes Montana always seem larger than life.

TOURISM INFORMATION

Partnering with local municipalities, the Montana Office of Tourism helps maintain visitor information centers in cities and towns throughout the state. Find out more at visitmt.com.

• **Bozeman CVB**
2000 Commerce Way
Bozeman, MT 59715
Tel 800/228-4224
bozemancvb.com

• **Helena Tourism Alliance**
105 Reeder's Alley
Helena, MT 59601
Tel 406/449-1270
helenamt.com

• **National Park Service**
nps.gov/state/mt

CITIES

Rather than a single huge metropolis that dominates the state, Montana is endowed with several medium-size cities that each offer a slightly different vibe and visitor experience.

Northern gateway to the Yellowstone country, **Bozeman** is a vibrant university town with loads of outdoor adventure outfitters. The Museum of the Rockies on the Montana State University campus offers an entertaining and interactive overview of the state's natural and human history, including an excellent dinosaur hall, planetarium, living-history farm, and Native American exhibits. On the outskirts of town, Bridger Bowl and Big Sky Resort are laced with snow-sport pistes that morph into mountain biking and hiking trails come spring.

Butte is both an active copper-mining community and a city bent on preserving its past, with plenty of relics of the boom days when the population was three times larger than now. The Butte-Anaconda Historic District contains some 6,000 properties of historic significance, including the opulent Victorian mansion of "Copper King" W. A. Clark (1888), the Asian-oriented Mai Wah Museum (1905–1909), the redbrick Dumas Brothel (1890), and the Rookwood Speakeasy (1912). The World Museum of Mining digs into the history of local copper extraction, including a guided underground tour of the old Orphan Girl Mine. Visitors can also peer into the mouth of the monster—the Berkeley Pit, a former open-pit mine—via a tunnel that leads to a lofty overlook. In addition, daredevil fans will want to visit the grave of Robert "Evel" Knievel in the city's Mountain View Cemetery.

Out on the plains, **Billings** has emerged as the state's cultural capital. The Western Heritage Center spins tales of frontier life in the Yellowstone Valley and Northern Plains through museum displays, a popular lecture series, and walking tours of

Mountain goats frequent the sheer cliffs of Glacier National Park.

Sunset over Saint Mary's Lake in Glacier National Park

historical Billings. On the other side of downtown, the Yellowstone Art Museum specializes in contemporary art of the Rocky Mountains and Northern Plains. **Helena,** the laid-back state capital, is dominated by two towering landmarks, the Gothic Revival Cathedral of Saint Helena (1906) and the Greek Revival–style capitol building (1902). However, the city's most famous sight is probably "Big Medicine"—the rare white bison mounted inside the Montana Historical Society Museum.

ROCKIES

Perhaps the most remarkable thing about **Glacier National Park** (and there are many) is that water melting from the park's glaciers and snowfields makes its way to the Pacific, the Gulf of Mexico, and Hudson Bay. One of the nation's oldest (established 1910) and most beloved parks, Glacier straddles the continental divide in northwestern Montana. A remarkable example of the geological forces that shaped our planet, the park offers a glimpse of North America before the advent of humans. Even though a mere 25 glaciers remain from the 150 counted in 1850, it's still the largest glacier gathering in the lower 48. A variety of animals—grizzly, moose, wolves, mountain goats, cougars, bald eagles, and more—inhabit the park's glacier-carved terrain. The spectacular Going-to-the-Sun Road crosses the park from east to west via 6,646-foot (2,026 m) Logan Pass. More than 700 miles (1,127 km) of trails lead

CAPITALISM

Rarely has so much fuss gone into naming a state capital. It was originally dubbed "Last Chance," but the town fathers decided in 1864 that a less negative name for their budding gold rush settlement would help it prosper. As it was late October, several wags proposed Squashtown and Pumpkinville. Miners from Minnesota put forth the names of towns from back home, including Helena, which eventually won the day. There followed an ongoing feud on how it should be pronounced. A majority that day voted for an accent on the second syllable, but today's first syllable version (HEH-luh-nuh) eventually prevailed.

to remote gems including Iceberg Lake and Grinnell Glacier.

Along the park's western edge is the broad and fertile **Flathead Valley,** home to some of the nation's most delicious cherries as well as the largest natural freshwater lake west of the Mississippi. Easiest access to Flathead Lake for fishermen and boaters is from the marina in Polson, on the south shore. Farther up the valley, Whitefish Mountain Resort offers snow sports in winter and a variety of outdoor pursuits in summer, including a zip line, aerial obstacle course, and forest canopy nature walks. Just south of the valley, **Missoula** spreads across both banks of the Clark Fork River. The city's Smokejumper Visitor Center provides insight into the dangerous missions undertaken by aerial firefighters as they battle blazes in forests around the West. For a more lighthearted outing, head down along the river to the Carousel for Missoula, a modern handcrafted merry-go-round.

Montana's southern Rockies shelter sundry Wild West sights. Vintage mining towns Bannack and Virginia City both served as the territorial capital prior to Helena and today are popular as active "ghost towns." Big Hole National Battlefield marks the site of an 1877 confrontation between the Nez Perce and the U.S. Cavalry. Farther south, Grant-Kohrs Ranch National Historic Site celebrates the role of cattlemen in the American West via historic buildings, ranching demonstrations, and equestrian events. Montana also provides two gateways into Yellowstone National Park. Along with many hotels, restaurants, and nightlife spots, West Yellowstone shelters the Grizzly and Wolf Discovery Center. Over on the park's north side, Gardiner is a hub for fly-fishing and white-water rafting on the Yellowstone River, as well as home to the Yellowstone Association and its

The twin spires of the Cathedral of Saint Helena are a landmark in the city of Helena.

The green rolling landscape of the college town Bozeman

various workshops and field programs inside the park.

GREAT PLAINS

The golden plains of eastern Montana provided a venue for one of the most controversial episodes in U.S. history—the Battle of the Little Bighorn. Also called Custer's Last Stand, the 1876 battle pitted Lieutenant Colonel George Armstrong Custer and his Seventh Cavalry troopers against a much larger force of Sioux, Cheyenne, and Arapaho under legendary Indian leaders Sitting Bull and Crazy Horse. The national battlefield park, located on the **Crow Indian Reservation,** is strewn with markers recalling the battle and those who perished on both sides that day. Roads and footpaths lead to various points where action took place, including Last Stand Hill with its poignant memorial. Farther south on the reservation, Bighorn Canyon National Recreation Area comprises 120,000 acres (48,562 ha) of prairie wilderness on either side of the partially flooded gorge of the Bighorn River. Boating, fishing, hiking, and camping are the main activities in the park's Montana sector.

Tumbling down from the Rockies, the Missouri River meanders across the state's northern plains, a watery route followed by Lewis and Clark between 1804 and 1806. **Great Falls** takes its name from a series of five cascades that mark the upper limit of Missouri navigation for watercraft that could not be carried overland. Lewis and Clark National Historic Trail Interpretive Center, perched on a bluff above the river in Great Falls, outlines Jefferson's grand vision for the expedition and details daily life along the route for both the explorers and the native peoples they encountered. The city's C. M. Russell Museum preserves the home and studio of the renowned Western artist as well as the works of other masters of the frontier genre.

Downstream from Great Falls, America's longest watercourse runs through the **Upper Missouri River Breaks**—a colorful badlands area that inspired many of Russell's paintings—before pouring into massive **Fort Peck Reservoir.** With more than 1,500 miles (457 km) of shorelines, the reservoir is the nation's fifth largest man-made lake. Fort Peck Marina and two other sites provide access for boaters, fishermen, and other recreational users. ∎

Nebraska

They don't call themselves Cornhuskers for nothing: More than nine million acres (3.6 million ha) of Nebraska is planted with maize, nearly twice as much as the next largest crop. A vital link in both the Oregon Trail and the first transcontinental railroad, the state lies close to the geographical center of the lower 48, a vast expanse of Great Plains dissected by the North Platte River.

CITIES

Omaha first took root in 1854, at a crossing called Lone Tree Ferry on the Missouri River. As eastern terminus of the first transcontinental railway, the city became a huge meatpacking center, soon outgrowing Council Bluffs, the city on the other side of the Big Muddy. The past lives on in the city's 30-block Gold Coast Historic District, where the Joslyn Castle and the Spanish Renaissance Revival–style Saint Cecilia's Cathedral are major landmarks. Meanwhile, the Old Market neighborhood has been revitalized into a lively destination. Within walking distance from Old Market, the Omaha Children's Museum is especially strong in science and technology. Kids also dig the Henry Doorly Zoo and Aquarium. Consistently ranked as one of the nation's best, the zoo includes the world's largest indoor swamp and nocturnal habitat, as well as the huge glass Desert Dome. Nearby Lauritzen Gardens blends arboretum, bird sanctuary, conservatory, and a variety of gardens with two great Union Pacific locomotives permanently parked on the south side of the

TOURISM INFORMATION

The Nebraska Tourism Commission offers plenty of information and visitor tips on its website: visitnebraska .com.

• **Omaha Visitors Center**
1001 Farnam St.
Omaha, NE 68102
Tel 402/444-4660
visitomaha.com

• **Lincoln Visitors Center**
Seventh St. and P St.
Lincoln, NE 68508
Tel 402/434-5348
lincoln.org

• **National Park Service**
nps.gov/state/ne

Heartland of America Park on Conagra Lake, with the high rises of Omaha on the horizon

The Nebraska State Capitol building in the city of Lincoln

parking lot. Joslyn Art Museum runs heavy on Impressionist masters displayed inside a handsome art deco building. Housed in the city's former Union Station, the Durham Museum is dedicated to the history of Omaha and the iron horse. Nebraska's past is also the focus of Pioneer Courage Park and the Spirit of Nebraska Wilderness, complementary downtown green spaces with more than a hundred life-size bronze sculptures depicting frontier scenes and wildlife. Bob Kerrey Pedestrian Bridge, a wonder of modern design and engineering, connects Omaha's riverfront with parklands on the Iowa side of the river. Close to the Nebraska end of the bridge is a landing for the *River City Star,* a riverboat with weekend sightseeing cruises along the Missouri.

Out on the plains, **Lincoln** is both the seat of state government and a dynamic college town. The seven-block Centennial Mall connects the capitol building with the

University of Nebraska complex. Many of the city's outstanding attractions are scattered across the huge campus, including the Marx Science Discovery Center and the Mueller Planetarium. The University of Nebraska State Museum at Morrill Hall safeguards the state's largest natural history collection, while the Sheldon Museum of Art (founded in 1888 as the university art club) focuses on American works. Located within the College of Architecture, the Kruger Gallery features four centuries of furniture and decorative arts. With more than 2,000 pieces in its collection, the International Quilt Study Center & Museum reflects the significance of this folk art form throughout the world. Students and townies alike hang out in the historic Haymarket District along the western edge of campus. The area includes Pinnacle Bank Arena with its year-round slate of concerts and sporting events, as well as the new Railyard Lincoln, a

cluster of eating and entertainment venues. On the southwest outskirts of Lincoln, Pioneers Park Nature Center offers eight miles (12 km) of walking trails through tall grass prairie, woodlands, and wetlands. The green space also includes a natural

CAPITALISM

After entering the Union in 1867, Nebraskans struggled to devise a fitting state nickname. Early unofficial sobriquets were anything but appealing—the Great American Desert, the Squatter State, and the catchy Bug Eater State. The latter derives from an 1870s locust plague and was the original moniker of University of Nebraska football teams. It wasn't until 1899 that Lincoln sports editor Cy Sherman decided that "Cornhuskers" was a much better tag for the pigskin boys, a name soon adopted for the entire state.

play area where children are encouraged to dig in the sand or build a fort, as well as a wildlife sanctuary with herds of bison, elk, and white-tailed deer.

LANDSCAPES

Nebraska's premier road trip, the **Lewis and Clark National Historical Trail** driving route traverses the entire eastern edge of Nebraska along the Missouri River. In addition to the trail's National Park Service visitor center in Omaha, the route includes dozens of federal, state, and county parks. Among the best is Ponca State Park in northeastern Nebraska, named for a Native American tribe that once called this region home. The heavily wooded park preserves an array of typical prairie wildlife. Scenic bluffs drop down to a 59-mile (95 km) stretch of the Missouri National Recreational River and its myriad outdoor activities. Farther upstream, the Niobrara National Scenic River boasts more than 200 waterfalls, diverse plant and animal

life, and recreation that ranges from hiking and horseback riding to camping and excellent kayaking.

Covering around a quarter of the state, the **Sandhills** of central Nebraska comprise grass-covered, stabilized dunes formed between 5,000 and 8,000 years ago during the last ice age. One of the best places to access this unique ecosystem is Valentine National Wildlife Refuge. Tucked up in the state's northwest corner, the Museum of the Fur Trade near **Chadron** stands on the site of an American Fur Company post established in 1837 by intrepid trader James "The Bear" Bordeaux. An hour's drive to the south, on the other side of Nebraska National Forest, is one of the state's most bizarre landmarks—"**Carhenge.**" Designed by artist Jim Reinders, the massive metal sculpture park replicates England's Stonehenge with 39 classic American cars.

Looming 800 feet (244 m) above the North Platte River, **Scotts Bluff** served as a major landmark for pioneers and Pony Express riders

making their way along the Oregon, California, and Mormon Trails. The national monument includes a visitor center museum, parts of the original wagon train route, living-history events, and a choice of either driving or hiking to the top of the celebrated bluff. A short distance downriver rises another frontier landmark called "Elk Penis" by Native Americans living in the area—a name changed to **Chimney Rock** by the Anglo newcomers. The rock's visitor center features exhibits on frontier life and western migration.

The former homestead of the state's most famous cowboy has been preserved on the outskirts of **North Platte** as Buffalo Bill Ranch State Historical Park. Visitors are also welcome at the town's Golden Spike Tower overlooking the massive Union Pacific Bailey Yard—the planet's single largest railroad classification yard. In addition to more than a hundred tanks, jeeps, ambulances, and aircraft, the Heartland Museum of Military Vehicles in **Lexington** contains a moving monument to the American evacuation of Saigon titled "Last Helicopter Out." Harold Warp's Pioneer Village near **Minden**

Sandhill cranes on the Platte River near the town of Kearney

Scotts Bluff was a landmark for 19th-century emigrants headed west in covered wagons.

pledges the largest collection of Americana anywhere, more than 50,000 diverse items spread across 28 buildings on 20 acres (8 ha). Bird-watchers flock to the nearby Iain Nicolson Audubon Center at Rowe Sanctuary in **Gibbon,** as well as the Nebraska Bird Observatory at **Crane Meadows** to observe the annual migration of sandhill and whooping cranes along the North Platte corridor. Taking full advantage of the twists and turns of the Cedar River, **Broken Arrow Wilderness** near Fullerton provides plenty of water for paddling, tubing, or running the river in multiperson "tanks." For a more highbrow experience, the Bedient Pipe Organ Company in **Roca** still builds acoustic pipe organs by hand one at a time, and visitors are welcome to watch.

Near **Beatrice,** the Homestead National Monument of America pays homage to the Homestead Act of 1862 and the millions who migrated to the West via wagon, horse, oxcart, and sometimes even on foot. Pioneer life is further brought to life at the Palmer-Epard Cabin and the one-room Freeman School. Trails lead through stands of prairie grass that can reach nine feet (3 m) high in late summer. ■

HIDDEN TREASURES

Anyone who thinks life is slow in Nebraska should reconsider—the Cornhusker State boasts a number of museums devoted to things that go fast including . . .

• **Museum of American Speed (Lincoln):** exotic and vintage vehicles and components as well as toys and memorabilia on motor-racing and car history

• **Pony Express Station and Museum (Gothenburg):** two original stopovers

used by the riders of the legendary western mail service that operated for 18 months in 1860-1861

• **Strategic Air Command & Aerospace Museum (Ashland):** airplanes and spacecraft, including a Lockheed SR-71A Blackbird, the world's fastest manned aircraft

• **National Museum of Roller Skating (Lincoln):** from Roller Derby and hockey to in-line and artistic

Nevada

From the scorching Mojave Desert to the snowcapped Sierra, the Silver State offers extreme contrasts for those who gamble on a Nevada vacation. Las Vegas and Reno bustle night and day, but the desert beyond has more ghost towns than inhabited places. Man-made wonders such as Hoover Dam and The Strip stand in stark contrast to natural attractions like Great Basin National Park and Lake Tahoe.

CITIES

Whether you arrive by land or air, **Las Vegas** is a shock to the system. A million people—and what seem like a billion twinkling lights—huddled in the middle of nowhere. The city was no more than a whistle-stop until mobster Bugsy Siegel unveiled the Flamingo Hotel in 1946. That set off a rash of other casino-hotels that transformed the desert valley into a neon-studded oasis. The modern Vegas scene includes giant resorts and world-class entertainment and restaurants, as well as top-notch museums and theme park attractions. The excellent Mob Museum occupies the downtown courthouse where the Kefauver Committee held hearings to investigate organized crime in the early 1950s. A few blocks away, the equally intriguing Neon Museum is a glass-and-steel fantasyland of signs rescued from old or long-gone hotels. Many of the big casino resorts boast their own museums and wildlife attractions: The Bellagio flaunts an incredible fine art collection. Mandalay Bay features an aquarium with creatures as varied as Komodo dragons, crocodiles, and sharks. The Mirage blends dolphin and big cat habitats, while the Luxor pyramid shelters an exhibit with *Titanic* artifacts. Visitors can snatch bird's-eye views from the thrill rides atop the Stratosphere Tower, the rooftop Big Apple roller coaster, or the new High Roller (the world's tallest observation wheel) on the LINQ Promenade. Thrill seekers can also fly high above the neon on the SlotZilla zip line over Fremont Street.

The "Biggest Little City in the World" has long lived in the shadow of its much larger southern cousin, but that's the charm of **Reno**. While gambling continues, the city has evolved into a well-rounded cultural hub with its own philharmonic, Shakespeare company, and multiple art galleries. The cutting edge

TOURISM INFORMATION

Nevada welcome centers are located at interstate highway gateways around the state including Mesquite, Boulder, and Wendover. For more information, check out the website: travelnevada.com.

● **Las Vegas Visitor Information Center**
3150 Paradise Rd.
Las Vegas, NV 89109
Tel 877/847-4858
lasvegas.com

● **Reno-Sparks Visitor Center**
135 N Sierra St.
Reno, NV 89501
Tel 800/367-7366
visitrenotahoe.com

● **Lake Tahoe Visitors Bureau**
969 Tahoe Blvd.
Incline Village, NV 89450
Tel 775/832-1606
visitrenotahoe.com

● **National Park Service**
nps.gov/state/nv

The Fire Wave rock formation in Valley of Fire State Park

The showy city of Las Vegas draws some 42 million visitors each year.

Nevada Museum of Art, housed inside a dramatic postmodern structure, specializes in contemporary painting, sculpture, photography, and other media arranged by themes rather than period or genre. Design of the vehicular kind is the forte of the city's National Automobile Museum, including celebrity cars once owned by Elvis Presley, Frank Sinatra, and John Wayne. Turning to nature's art, the arboretum at the University of Nevada, Reno, showcases plants from around the globe but is especially strong on the flora of the Great Basin and the Mojave and Sonoran Deserts.

Thirty miles (48 km) south of Reno, **Carson City** is Nevada's mild-mannered capital. Until a recent spate of suburban growth, it was one of the nation's smallest state capitals and, to a large extent, it still bears a small-town vibe. Lodged inside the 1870 U.S. Mint building, the Nevada State Museum offers offbeat treasures such as a huge Columbian mammoth skeleton found in the Black Rock Desert and an intricate silver service from the U.S.S. *Nevada* battleship, fashioned from more than 300 pounds (136 kg) of Tonopah silver. From outside the museum, the Kit Carson Trail may be followed by foot or by car. The route links many of the city's historic buildings, including the State Capitol (1871), the Brewery Arts

ROAD TRIPS

Great drives across the Silver State:

• U.S. 95 from Las Vegas to Fernley with stops at Death Valley, various ghost towns, and historic Fort Churchill (415 miles/668 km)

• U.S. 50 from Carson City to Great Basin National Park, the "Loneliest Road in America" (387 miles/623 km)

• The Extraterrestrial Highway from Las Vegas to Rachel, with stops at Pahranagat National Wildlife Refuge and the Little A'Le'Inn restaurant (148 miles/238 km)

Center within the old Carson Brewery (1865), and the reputedly haunted Saint Charles–Muller's Hotel (1862). The trail peters out at the Nevada State Railroad Museum, where more than 40 of the locomotives and rolling stock date from before the 20th century. Departing from the Eastgate Depot on the east side of Carson City, the Virginia & Truckee Railway uses restored steam engines to chug a 12-mile (19 km) route to nearby **Virginia City.** Between 1859 and 1878, this was the center of the Comstock Lode, the biggest silver boom in American history. A Wild West ambience endures in the Victorian-era brick buildings of the Historic District, especially at old watering holes such as the Bucket of Blood Saloon and Ponderosa.

LANDSCAPES

In 1936, the **Hoover Dam** was completed along the Nevada-Arizona border, and Lake Mead began to form behind the giant concrete barrier. One of the

engineering wonders of the modern world, the 726-foot (221 m) high dam is also an art deco treasure, thoroughly expressive of the era in which it was built. Visitors can view the lake and dam from several dramatic viewpoints, stroll across the dam, or descend deep into its bowels on guided tours. Lake Mead, which extends about 110 miles (177 km) upstream into the lower reaches of the Grand Canyon, is the nation's largest reservoir by water volume. Enclosed within the confines of the first national recreation area, the vast lake is a haven for water sports enthusiasts. Houseboats for multiday lake trips can be rented at marinas on the Nevada shore. Downstream from the dam, **Black Canyon** offers a glimpse of the landscape before Hoover was built, with the Colorado as a wild and rugged river best explored by

The clear waters of Lake Tahoe in the Sierra Nevada

raft or kayak. Farther downstream, **Laughlin** unfolds as a miniature, waterfront version of Las Vegas, with casino-hotels arrayed along the Colorado River.

Spilling over from California, the **Mojave Desert** covers much of southern Nevada. Red Rock Canyon National Conservation Area on the outskirts of Las Vegas presents a range of typical Mojave terrain that often appears in movies and television shows. Hiking and biking trails lead to secluded oasis canyons. The desert beyond Red Rock is riddled with ghost towns, spooky outposts such as Rhyolite and Gold Point that evoke the region's bygone boom and bust cycles. Much of the southern desert is out of bounds on federal military land, including the

The immense Hoover Dam traps the Colorado River in Black Canyon.

Nevada Test Site where nuclear bombs were set off. Here, too, is the supersecretive zone called Area 51, where some say the government shelters captured UFOs, a conspiracy theory that fuels a thriving alien-oriented tourist scene in nearby Rachel.

Lake Tahoe anchors the western side of the state, its dark-blue waters shared with California. Surrounded by thick forest and snowcapped Sierra peaks, Tahoe has long been hailed as one of the world's most beautiful bodies of water. It's also a record breaker as the continent's largest alpine lake and second deepest lake in the U.S. Only the five Great Lakes hold more water. The winter sports hub of Incline Village and casino-heavy Stateline are the largest settlements on the Nevada side, but otherwise the shoreline is a rustic stretch of state parks, campgrounds, rocky beaches, and picnic areas. On the other side of Reno, **Pyramid Lake** is another

huge wilderness watering hole. All that's left of a vast inland sea that once covered most of Nevada, the lake is managed by the Paiute Nation.

Central Nevada is one of the nation's least inhabited areas, a vast expanse of desert basins and mountain ranges where cattle and coyotes easily outnumber human inhabitants. Two highways run east-west across the boondocks. Interstate 80 traces the route of the pioneer-era California Trail and the first Transcontinental Railroad as it meanders between Reno and the Great Salt Lake. One of the few signs of civilization along the route is **Elko**, an old frontier town renowned for its Basque culture and Western Folklife Center that hosts the National Cowboy Poetry Gathering each year. An hour south of Elko, the **Ruby Mountains** offer year-round outdoor fun that ranges from hiking and horseback riding in summer to heli-skiing in the colder months. ∎

New Hampshire

"Live free or die" is New Hampshire's memorable state motto. The phrase originally referred to rebellion against the British, but nowadays "live free" seems to describe a vibe that runs through the entire state. For visitors, it signals the freedom to explore New Hampshire's seacoast, snowy mountains, and sprawling lake district, as well as its archetypal New England villages and small but action-packed cities.

TOURISM INFORMATION

New Hampshire's Division of Travel and Tourism Development offers information at 13 welcome centers and rest areas around the state. Check out the website at visitnh.gov.

● **Discover Portsmouth Center**
10 Middle St.
Portsmouth, NH 03801
Tel 603/436-8433
portsmouthhistory.org

● **Manchester Welcome Center**
Corner of Elm St. and Merrimack St.
Manchester, NH 03101
Tel 603/666-6600
manchester-chamber.org

● **Greater Concord Information Kiosk**
State Capitol Park
Main St.
Concord, NH 03301
Tel 603/224-2508
concordnhchamber.com

● **White Mountains Visitor's Center**
200 Kancamagus Hwy
North Woodstock, NH 03262
Tel 603/745-8720
visitwhitemountains.com

● **New Hampshire State Parks**
nhstateparks.org

CITIES

The state's largest city, **Manchester** was named after its English counterpart in hopes that it too would grow into an industrial powerhouse. While it certainly had its heyday as a mill town, modern Manchester is better known for innovation, cultural institutions, and outstanding livability. The Currier Museum of Art concentrates on works by European and American artists, including pieces by Picasso, Matisse, and John Singer Sargent. The museum also hosts tours of the Frank Lloyd Wright–designed Zimmerman House, a 1950 Usonian-style structure in North Manchester. Opened in 1915, the Palace Theatre has graduated from vaudeville to modern musicals, concerts, movies, and other performing arts. Close by,

The historic town of Portsmouth on New Hampshire's Atlantic coast

the Merrimack River tumbles 50 feet (15 m) over Amoskeag Falls as it rushes through Manchester. The Amoskeag Fishways Learning and Visitors Center is an award-winning environmental facility with interactive exhibits on local ecology. Manchester's other great aquatic landmark is Lake Massabesic, popular for boating, fishing, and hiking through lakeside woods.

Concord, the petite state capital, often feels more like a collection of villages than a city. But that's part of

A statue of John Stark, a major general during the American Revolution, at the New Hampshire State House

its charm. Visitors can tour the New Hampshire State House, unveiled in 1819 and home to the oldest state legislature that still meets in its original chamber. The family-friendly McAuliffe-Shepard Discovery Center offers exhibits on astronomy, aviation, earth science, and space science. Franklin Pierce, the 14th president, lived at the Pierce Manse with his wife, Jane, and their two sons from 1842 to 1848, and their home is open for tours in summer. Nearby, the New Hampshire Historical Society displays objects and archives in an effort to save, preserve, and share the state's long and diverse history.

Down on the shore, **Portsmouth** flaunts plenty of maritime history and several intriguing neighborhoods. Strawbery Banke, a multibuilding outdoor history museum in the South End historic district, aims to inform visitors about the architecture, food, crafts, and everyday life of local families from 1695 through 1954. Among the city's other sights are the Portsmouth Athenaeum historical library in Market Square, the John Paul Jones House (1758), and the U.S.S. *Albacore* submarine museum.

LANDSCAPES

Far and away the state's most prominent geographical feature, the **White Mountains** rise about halfway between the Atlantic Ocean and the Canadian border. Popular with hikers, bikers, skiers, and anyone who cherishes the great outdoors, the highlands are protected within the confines of 800,000-acre (323,749 ha) White Mountain National Forest and several state parks.

Mount Washington, located in the Presidential Range of the White Mountains, soars to a height of 6,288 feet (1,917 m), the most prominent peak east of the Mississippi River. Weather permitting, the Mount Washington Auto Road takes vehicles to the summit via a sinuous eight-mile (13 km) drive. As an alternative, visitors can board

STATE OF THE ART

• **Best movies:** *To Die For* (1995), *The Devil and Daniel Webster* (1941), and *Jumanji* (1995)

• **Best books:** *A Prayer for Owen Meany* by John Irving and *Peyton Place* by Grace Metalious

• **Best art:** Benjamin Champney and other White Mountain Movement artists

• **Best play:** *Our Town* by Thornton Wilder

the Mount Washington Cog Railway for a three-hour guided train tour to the peak. Celebrated for dangerous and erratic weather, the peak is often plagued by subzero temperatures, hurricane-force winds, and serious ice storms. Crowning the summit are historic Tip-Top House (made of rock blasted from the mountain) and the Mount Washington Observatory, which offers overnight tours during the winter months with transportation via snowcat. The observatory also partners with climbing schools on winter mountaineering expeditions. Tours of the summit's weather station are available in season (May–October) by appointment. The visitor center also boasts "Extreme Mount Washington," a hands-on, high-tech exhibit about what it's like on the mountain during winter.

Pastoral landscapes and picturesque villages are scattered through the mountains. Poet Robert Frost lived for many years at The Frost Place, a farmhouse near **Franconia,** which is now a nonprofit education center focused on poetry and the

arts. The farm and its surroundings are mentioned in many of Frost's works. Santa's Village in **Jefferson** is a Christmas-themed amusement park with 16 rides. Several heritage trains operate in the region, including the Hobo Railroad between Lincoln and Woodstock and the Conway Scenic Railroad, which runs between North Conway and the towns of Conway, Crawford Notch, and Fabyan. **North Conway** is also home to the Mount Washington Observatory Weather Discovery Center, an interactive museum that illustrates the science of climate and weather in fun ways. The Remick

Country Doctor Museum & Farm in nearby **Tamworth** highlights the contributions made by country doctors, agricultural practices, and rural pastimes on a 200-year-old farmstead.

South of the mountains, the countryside transitions into a splendid lake district. **Lake Winnipesaukee,** the state's largest, offers 70 square miles (181 sq km) of aquatic recreation and terrestrial activities along 280 miles (451 km) of shoreline and 258 islands. At the lake's eastern extreme, Wolfeboro is home to the Wright Museum of World War II and its exhibits on the American home front during the conflict. In nearby Wolfeboro Falls, the New Hampshire Boat Museum preserves the state's freshwater boating traditions through exhibits and special events. Kimball Castle was conceived in 1897 when Benjamin Kimball, president of the Concord & Montreal Railroad, visited castles along the Rhine River in Germany. Returning home, he hired an architect to duplicate the Gothic Revival architecture on Locke's Hill overlooking Lake Winnipesaukee. The Annalee Doll Museum in Meredith traces the history of these American-made dolls first created by Annalee Thorndike in 1934.

Rocky Gorge along the scenic Kancamagus Highway (Route 112)

At the summit of Mount Washington in New Hampshire's White Mountains

New Hampshire's seacoast may be short (131 miles/211 km) but it's long in interesting detours. The **Isles of Shoals** archipelago astride the New Hampshire-Maine border comprises nine rocky islands, five of them in New Hampshire including Star Island, the only one with a hotel or museum. Once used by Native Americans as spring and summer fishing camps, the isles were given their current name by English explorer John Smith, who passed this way in 1614.

The state's southwest corner offers another mosaic of woods, water, and farmland. **Mount Monadnock** (or Grand Monadnock) was mentioned in the writings of Ralph Waldo Emerson and Henry David Thoreau. **Saint-Gaudens National Historic Site** near Cornish was the favorite atelier of renowned American sculptor Augustus Saint-Gaudens, best known for his colossal public works. The home and its lovely gardens served as Saint-Gaudens's summer retreat from 1885 to 1897, and his permanent home from 1900 until his death in 1907. More than a hundred of his works are on display in galleries and around the grounds.

Formed by glaciers 50,000 years ago, **Polar Caves Park** near Rumney consists of nine granite boulder caves connected by boardwalks and flights of stairs. Squam Lakes Natural Science Center in **Holderness** offers live animal habitats along walking trails through open meadows, mature forests, and marsh boardwalks. Castle in the Clouds, also called the Lucknow Estate, is a 16-room mansion in **Moultonborough** open to the public for tours, murder mystery dinners, wedding ceremonies, and more. ■

FESTIVALS

- **Celebration of Lupine (Franconia):** festival in the White Mountains with wildflowers, fiddle music, photo workshops, and plenty of food; June

- **Hampton Beach Sand Sculpting Competition:** annual battle of sand artists on one of New England's prettiest beaches; June

- **League of New Hampshire Craftsmen's Fair (Newbury):** huge showcase of modern and traditional crafts; August

- **North Country Moose Festival:** classic cars, country fairs, maple syrup, and people clad in moose costumes in Colebrook, Canaan, and Pittsburg villages; August

- **Rochester Fair:** livestock shows, pig races, tractor pulls, demolition derbies, crafts, and more in this celebration of everything country that dates back to the 1860s; September

- **Candlelight Stroll (Portsmouth):** annual holiday event organized by the Strawbery Banke Museum; December

New Jersey

Driving the Jersey Turnpike between Philadelphia and New York, it doesn't seem like there's much "garden" left in the Garden State. But wander a little bit off the state's main drag and New Jersey surprises with its medley of woodlands and beaches, lovely historic sights, and surprising modern wonders.

CITIES

With around 3.5 million people and more than a hundred different communities melted into a continuous urban mass, there's a good argument to be made that much of northern New Jersey constitutes a single, large metropolis. Yet some places do stick out. Across the Hudson River from Manhattan, **Jersey City** is once again (after a 200-year hiatus) the fastest growing city in the state, a polyglot population of African, Arab, Asian, Jewish, and Hispanic Americans plus a large cache of artists who can no longer afford New York. Here, Liberty State Park looks out on New York Bay, the Statue of Liberty, and the Manhattan skyline. Also of note is the interactive Liberty Science Center and the historic Central Railroad Terminal Building, from which ferries run daily to Ellis Island (most of which is part of New Jersey). There, the restored Great Hall has exhibits about the millions of immigrants processed between 1892 and 1954. The Immigration Museum educates visitors on the island's history before, during, and after its days as America's number one gateway. A light-rail line also connects Liberty State Park and downtown, where the Jersey City Museum explores the city's cultural history.

Also part of northern New Jersey, **Newark** is often cited as an example

TOURISM INFORMATION

New Jersey's Division of Travel and Tourism staffs welcome centers off Interstate 80 in Columbia and the Garden State Parkway in Montvale. For more information, check out visitnj.org.

- **Atlantic City Welcome Center**
Atlantic City Expressway
Milepost 3.5
Atlantic City, NJ 08401
Tel 888/AC-VISIT
atlanticcitynj.com

- **Cape May Welcome Center**
609 Lafayette St.
Cape May, NJ 08204
Tel 609/884-5508
capemay.com

- **National Park Service**
nps.gov/state/nj

- **New Jersey State Parks**
www.state.nj.us

The Jersey City skyline across the Hudson River from Lower Manhattan

Fire breathers on the Seaside Heights boardwalk at the Jersey Shore.

of urban decay. However, the state's largest city has several sites of note, including the soaring Cathedral Basilica of the Sacred Heart, which boasts a 37-foot-wide (11 m) rose window—the largest stained-glass portal of any Roman Catholic church in the New World. Home to a large Portuguese-American population, the Ironbound neighborhood offers myriad ethnic shops, restaurants, cultural events, and interesting architecture. In addition, the campus of William Paterson University provides a venue for the Ben Shahn Center for the Visual Arts with its three galleries and ongoing slate of exhibitions in all media. Largest in the state, the strong Newark Museum of art embraces everything from American masters to a world-class Tibetan collection.

LANDSCAPES

Thomas Edison lived and invented in **West Orange** from 1886 until his death in 1931. Thomas Edison National Historical Park includes his expansive laboratories, office, and Black Maria movie stage—all as if nothing had been touched since the 1930s—as well as the celebrated inventor's Glenmont estate. **Morristown** is "where America survived" the dreadful winter of 1779 to 1780, one of the coldest on record. Its national historical park includes three Revolutionary War sites where Washington and his troops hunkered down and prepared for the battles ahead. In addition to the Institute for Advanced Study, where Albert Einstein carried out his final research, the Princeton University campus in Princeton also boasts an excellent

art museum with a concentration on American, European, and Latin American artists.

STATE OF THE ART

- **Best movies:** *Atlantic City* (1980) and *The Station Agent* (2003)

- **Best books:** The Bascombe Trilogy by Richard Ford and *Garden State* by Rick Moody

- **Best music:** *Greetings From Asbury Park, N.J.* album by Bruce Springsteen and *New Jersey* album by Bon Jovi

- **Best art:** the social-realist paintings, prints, and murals of Ben Shahn

- **Best TV shows:** *The Sopranos* and *Boardwalk Empire*

Washington Crossing State Park near **Trenton** enshrines the site where Washington and his troops landed on the night of December 25, 1776, after their epic crossing of the Delaware River to launch a surprise attack on Hessian mercenaries encamped in Trenton. The William Trent House near downtown Trenton played a prominent role in several battles fought here after the crossing. Erected in 1758 to house British troops during the French and Indian War, the Old Barracks near the state capitol also served as a military hospital after Washington's victory.

Grounds for Sculpture in suburban **Hamilton** features more than 270 large-scale works by emerging and established artists set amid lush grounds and roving peacocks. At 11 stories high and nearly three football fields long, the U.S.S. *New Jersey* is one of the largest battleships ever built. The Navy's most decorated vessel is now a museum on the Delaware River in **Camden.** Overnight stays are offered.

THE SHORE

The **Jersey Shore** is much more than the seedy reality television show that introduced the world to Snooki and the Situation. The long coast extends all the way from Perth Amboy on the south side of State Island to Cape May at the mouth of the Delaware River. In picturesque small towns along the way are boardwalks and beaches, casinos and yacht clubs, and wildlife refuges and wild party places.

The long and lean **Sandy Hook** peninsula is the southernmost unit of Gateway National Recreation Area (which also includes parts of Staten Island and Long Island). Its main attraction is the seven-mile (11 km) beach, but Sandy Hook also boasts hiking trails in and around its salt marshes and maritime holly forest, as well as spots for fishing, windsurfing, and other water activities.

In addition to being the hometown of Bruce Springsteen, **Long Branch** is celebrated for the long white sands of Seven Presidents Oceanfront Park, commemorating

the town's role as "summer capital" for seven different presidents (Grant, Hayes, Garfield, Arthur, Harrison, McKinley, and Wilson). It was also a long-time venue for Buffalo Bill's Wild West Show. Nearby **Asbury Park** is home to the Silverball Pinball Museum, a large collection of vintage pinball machines as well as bygone video and arcade games that visitors can actually play. Asbury also hosts popular events along the boardwalk, including its memorable Fourth of July fireworks, Oysterfest (September), and the Asbury Park Zombie Walk (October). Protected by the landmark 1859 Barnegat Lighthouse, **Long Beach Island** is one of the shore's most popular destinations, with close to 100,000 visitors per day in summer.

Casinos and crashing waves at Atlantic City

Airy porches along Beach Avenue in Cape May

Atlantic City, known for its four-mile-long (6 km) Boardwalk, is the stuff of myth and legend. Love it or hate it, "AC" certainly has enough attractions and activities to keep you busy for many days (and nights), roaming up and down the shore on foot or via rolling chair rides. Entrance to the Stars flaunts the handprints of celebrities including Johnny Carson, Cher, Stevie Wonder, and Frank Sinatra. Opened in 1898, the famed Steel Pier offers carnival rides, games, and fast food on a deck stretching 1,000 feet (305 m) into the sea. Other attractions include casinos, beaches, golf courses, shopping malls, the state's tallest lighthouse, and the Atlantic City Historical Museum. Ten miles (16 km) farther south lies **Ocean City** and perhaps the best boardwalk in New Jersey. In addition to thrill rides, water parks, family entertainment, and art galleries, "OC" boasts eight miles (13 km) of sand and surf on the ocean side plus plenty of water activities on the bay side.

At the bottom end of the Jersey Shore, **Cape May** is far and away the most elegant and sophisticated of the Jersey seaside resorts. A retreat for the wealthy and powerful for much of the 19th century, the town is sprinkled with historic Victorian homes including the 1879 Emlen Physick Estate. The cape's 30 miles (48 km) of sand includes popular beaches and quiet stretches. During the summer months, everyone over the age of 12 is required to purchase a beach "tag" from the city; the fees go to pay for lifeguards and cleanup of Cape May's very tidy shores. Away from the sand, attractions include the Naval Air Station Wildwood Aviation Museum and the Cape May County Park & Zoo, as well as whale- and dolphin-watching tours, wineries, and even an alpaca farm. ■

LITTLE-KNOWN FACTS

• The Edison Memorial Tower in Menlo Park is topped by the world's biggest light bulb—an eight-ton (7.25 metric tons) behemoth.

• The Morris Museum in Morristown houses one of the world's largest collection of automata—mechanical dolls, musicians, and other antique robotic figures.

• Navy Lakehurst Historical Society offers guided tours of the site where the German airship *Hindenburg* crashed, historic blimp hangars, and other landmarks at the storied naval air station.

• Holsten's Brookdale Confectionery in Bloomfield is where the famous final scene of *The Sopranos* was filmed.

• Washington won his first victory against British Army regulars in the field in Princeton, in 1777.

New Mexico

The Land of Enchantment lives up to its name with distinctive cultures and unique attractions that make the state seem like another country. New Mexico's Pueblo heritage, Spanish colonial history, and Wild West legacy make it a melting pot set against a varied landscape of red-rock cliffs, towering sand dunes, and the southern extreme of the Rockies.

TOURISM INFORMATION

The New Mexico Tourism Department staffs nine visitor centers around the state, including its main outlet in the state capital of Santa Fe.
491 Old Santa Fe Trail
Santa Fe, NM 87501
Tel 505/827-7336
newmexico.org

● **Albuquerque Visitor Center**
Ground Floor, Plaza Don Luis
303 Romero St.
Albuquerque, NM 87104
Tel 800/284-2282
visitalbuquerque.org

● **Airport Visitor Desk**
Baggage Claim Area
Albuquerque
International Sunport

● **National Park Service**
nps.gov/state/nm

CITIES

In the early 20th century, the exotic ambience of **Santa Fe** attracted scores of painters, writers, and photographers, transforming the sleepy New Mexico capital into an artistic oasis. Life still swirls around the Plaza, the onetime stomping ground for Spanish troops, American frontiersmen, and wagon trains making their way west along the Santa Fe Trail. Nowadays the leafy quad is a venue for festivals, outdoor concerts, and many other special events. The early-17th-century Palace of the Governors dominates the plaza's north side, part of a New Mexico History Museum complex that showcases several thousand years of regional culture and history. Native American artists sell their authentic, high-quality work under the long portal that fronts the museum. Although they look much older, both of Santa Fe's historic churches date from the early American period. The Cathedral Basilica of St. Francis of Assisi (1887) contains relics from Spanish days, including the oldest Madonna on U.S. soil, while the Loretto Chapel is renowned for its "miraculous" wooden staircase, spiraling without obvious support and built, some say, by master carpenter Saint Joseph himself. On the south side of the Santa Fe River, the New Mexico statehouse is the nation's only round state capitol building, a modern structure (1966) that incorporates many Native American symbols. Nearby Canyon Road is flanked by upscale art galleries and restaurants, a product of the well-heeled set who followed the artists to Santa Fe. The Santa Fe Trail shoots south from the state capitol to Museum Hill and its repository of Southwest culture, with huge collections dedicated to international folk art, Spanish colonial art, and the American Indian. Santa Fe Opera House occupies a dramatic red-rock location on the northern outskirts of town, a stunning venue for an eight-week season that runs over summer.

Near Santa Fe, a modern-day cowboy tips his hat.

More than 500 hot-air balloons rise during the annual Albuquerque International Balloon Fiesta.

Albuquerque is a desert metropolis on the rise, one of the fastest growing American cities and one of the new stars of Southwest tourism. Founded by the Spanish in 1706, Albuquerque is another of the continent's oldest urban areas. That Spanish heritage survives in a historic district around Old Town Plaza, with many of the old adobes now occupied by restaurants, art galleries, and curio shops. The neighboring Albuquerque Museum showcases the region's art and history. On the other side of Tiguex Park lies the New Mexico Museum of Natural History and Science, where exhibits run a broad gamut from dinosaur bones to planetarium shows. Paseo del Bosque Trail leads along the Rio Grande riverfront, a convenient pedestrian link between the ABQ BioPark botanic garden and Aquarium and the downstream ABQ BioPark zoo. There are two ways to get a bird's-eye view of the city: taking the historic Tramway to the summit of 10,378-foot (3,163 m) Sandia Peak, or taking to the sky with one of the hot-air-balloon outfitters offering rides from fields within a short drive of the Anderson-Abruzzo Albuquerque International Balloon Museum.

LANDSCAPES

At the foot of the often snow-capped Sangre de Cristo Mountains lies **Taos,** a longtime bastion of Native American culture and 20th-century American art. Taos Pueblo was constructed in multiple phases between A.D. 1000 and 1450. Today some 150 Tiwa-speaking Pueblo Indians call the adobe masterpiece home. Visitors are welcome in the Pueblo during daylight hours except when special ceremonies are taking place. The Spanish founded the adjacent European-style settlement in the late 18th century, which evolved into the modern-day small town of Taos. East Coast artists first became enamored with Taos in the 1890s, viewing its high-mountain air, gorgeous surroundings, and slow-paced lifestyle as the perfect place to paint, sculpt, and write. Many of their homes and studios are now open to visitors, including the creative lairs of Ernest L. Blumenschein, Nicolai Fechin, and D. H. Lawrence. Although created by the Spanish, Taos Plaza is flanked by reminders of the early American period such as the Kit Carson House and Museum and the Governor Bent House and Museum. Hiking and biking trails—as well as skiing and snowboard pistes—lace the mountains to the east. To the west lies the spectacular Rio Grande del Norte gorge, spanned by a 650-high (198 m) bridge with views of white-water rafts running on the mighty river below.

More memories linger along the western edge of the Rio Grande Valley, where artist Georgia O'Keeffe lived and worked in the swooping colors of **Abiquiú** from 1949 to 1984. Her rustic home is now a museum with the largest repository of her work: more than a thousand paintings, drawings, and sculptures. Art of a much different kind (and much older era) is the focus at **Bandelier National Monument,** which safeguards hundreds of petroglyphs and cliff dwellings rendered by people who lived here as long as 11,000 years ago. Just north of the park is **Los Alamos,** a town that changed the world as home to the Manhattan Project from 1943 to 1947, during which the world's first nuclear weapons were developed. The Los Alamos

Saint Jerome Chapel in the desert town of Taos, in northern New Mexico

Historical Museum offers guided walking tours of the town center that include numerous atomic bomb–related relics, such as the Ranch School's Ice House Memorial on the site where the "gadget" was assembled and Robert Oppenheimer's house on Bathtub Row. Los Alamos National Laboratory isn't open to the public, but the super-secret lab offers visitors the Bradbury Science Museum, with galleries dedicated to America's nuclear history, defense, and research.

Native Americans still occupy much of the state's northwest corner, on Navajo, Zuni, and Jicarilla Apache reservations. Here, the massive eroded throat of a volcano called **Shiprock** anchors the landscape, rising 1,583 feet (482 m) from the desert floor. Sacred to the Navajo people, who call it *Tsé Bit'a'í,* or "rock with wings," the dramatic monolith has been off-limits to climbing since 1970. The rock is within sight of **Chaco Culture National Historical Park,** a UNESCO World Heritage site that contains extensive remains of the pre-Columbian peoples who inhabited this region. To the south, Acoma Pueblo's **Sky City** is a living extension of that heritage, a mesa-top village on the Acoma reservation that can be visited on guided

Gypsum crystals form chandeliers at Lechuguilla Cave, Carlsbad Caverns National Park.

walking tours offered by the Sky City Cultural Center and Haakú Museum. Another hulking presence in western New Mexico is **El Morro National Monument,** an impressive sandstone landmark notable for the graffiti rendered by passing travelers over many centuries.

Carlsbad Caverns National Park anchors southern New Mexico, an underground warren of at least 119 limestone caves, with new chambers discovered on a regular basis. Another natural wonder takes place at dusk when hundreds of thousands of Mexican free-tailed bats emerge from the

caverns' main entrance. To the west, **White Sands National Monument** flaunts the world's largest gypsum dune field—275 square miles (712 sq km) of unrelenting desert that includes the Dune Drive through spectacular scenery, as well as hiking trails and backcountry campsites. The adjacent White Sands Missile Range is open to the public just two days each year, when visitors can drive to the Trinity Site where the world's first atom bombs were tested in 1945. Highway 70 leads 132 miles (212 km) northeast from White Sands to **Roswell,** known for the alleged crash of a UFO on the outskirts of town in 1947. ∎

FESTIVALS

• **International Folk Art Market (Santa Fe):** showcases the work of more than 150 artists from 40-plus countries; July

• **Roswell UFO Festival:** celebrates the town's ongoing link to extraterrestrial conspiracies with speakers, entertainment, a light parade, and costumes; July

• **Santa Fe Chamber Music Festival:** global showcase for classical music; July and August

• **Inter-Tribal Indian Ceremonial (Gallup):** Native Americans from around the Southwest gather for four days of rodeos, parades, markets, food stalls, and traditional dance; August.

• **Hatch Chile Festival:** Hot peppers and Hispanic heritage collide at this annual culinary carnival near Las Cruces; September.

• **Albuquerque International Balloon Fiesta:** More than 600 lighter-than-air craft take flight during the world's largest hot-air gathering; October.

New York

The Empire State nurtures two very different worlds: the renascent Rust Belt cities, rife wilderness, and rustic landscapes of Upstate New York and the effusive, nonstop energy of New York City. One of their few common denominators is water—liquid landmarks such as New York Harbor, the Hudson River, the Erie Canal, and Niagara Falls that have helped shape the state for more than 400 years.

CITIES

The nation's most populous city (8.5 million people in 2014), **New York City** spreads across five boroughs on three islands and a mainland peninsula, the heart of a metro area that embraces parts of three states and more than 20 million residents. The Statue of Liberty in New York Harbor symbolizes both American freedom and the millions of immigrants who helped mold New York into such a powerhouse. Another Big Apple icon is Times Square, a chaotic intersection renowned for its giant billboards, neon signs, Broadway shows, and street entertainers. Towering over Midtown is the Empire State Building, a 102-story skyscraper completed in 1931 and for many years the world's tallest building. Rivaling the Empire State in style if not in height, the Chrysler Building is a 77-story art deco masterpiece finished in 1930. Rockefeller Center also arose in the 1930s with the tallest of its 19 buildings, 30 Rockefeller

TOURISM INFORMATION

The New York State Thruway Authority staffs tourism information centers at 15 travel plazas and interchanges around the state, some year-round and others seasonal. Visit iloveny.com for more information.

● **New York City Information Center**
Macy's Herald Square
151 W 34th St. (between Seventh Ave. and Broadway)
New York, NY 10011
Tel 212/484-1222
nycgo.com

● **Finger Lakes Visitor Connection**
25 Gorham St.
Canandaigua, NY 14424
Tel 585/394-3915
visitfingerlakes.com

● **Niagara Visitor Center**
10 Rainbow Blvd.
Niagara Falls, NY 14303
Tel 877/325-5787
niagara-usa.com

● **Thousand Island Welcome Center**
43373 Collins Landing Rd.
Alexandria Bay, NY 13607
Tel 315/482-2520
visit1000islands.com

● **National Park Service**
nps.gov/state/ny

● **New York State Parks**
nysparks.com/parks

Contemplating "Girl Before a Mirror" by Pablo Picasso in Manhattan's Museum of Modern Art

Center (aka 30 Rock), crowned by an outdoor observation terrace above the 70th floor. The complex also includes Radio City Music Hall and Rockefeller Plaza with its outdoor café and winter ice-skating rink. Across Fifth Avenue is Saint Patrick's Cathedral, the neo-Gothic mother church of New York's Roman Catholics. Nearby Grand Central Terminal is one of the world's great train stations, a

Neon, noise, and masses of people in New York City's Times Square

cathedral-like structure with a world-record 44 platforms. Among Midtown's other landmarks are the New York Public Library, Madison Square Garden, and the Museum of Modern Art (MoMA). Another icon perches on the East River: the United Nations Secretariat Building, which offers weekday guided tours of the UN's inner workings.

In Lower Manhattan, One World Trade Center replaces the towers destroyed by the September 11, 2001, terrorist attacks. Soaring up to 104 stories (1,776 feet/541 m), it's the Western Hemisphere's tallest building. The Twin Towers site itself is now occupied by the solemn 9/11 Memorial Plaza and its thoughtful museum. Wall Street runs eight blocks through the heart of Lower

Manhattan, the epicenter of American banking and finance and home to major stock exchanges and financial institutions. Lower Manhattan is also flush with storied

neighborhoods such as Greenwich Village, the Bowery, Chinatown, Tribeca, SoHo, and Little Italy, as well as the legendary Brooklyn and Manhattan Bridges and South Street

LOCAL FLAVOR

- **Buffalo wings:** The tangy chicken was allegedly invented by Teressa Bellissimo at Buffalo's Anchor Bar in 1964, where they still serve them with celery, blue cheese, and a choice of eight different sauces. *1047 Main St., Buffalo*

- **Halfmoon cookies:** An upstate tradition, these two-tone treats have a devil's food base with black-and-white frosting. Hemstrought's Bakery has been making them since the 1920s. *900 Oswego St., Utica*

- **Thin-crust pizza:** A hundred different joints make great New York–style pizza, but only one can claim to be the city's oldest: Lombardi's in SoHo opened its doors in 1902. *32 Spring St., New York City*

- **Cheesecake:** Invented by the ancient Greeks and perfected by 20th-century New Yorkers, including those at Veniero's Pasticceria in the East Village. *342 E 11th St., New York City*

Seaport. The west side of Manhattan along the Hudson River embraces other interesting neighborhoods including Chelsea, the Meatpacking District, and Hell's Kitchen, home of the waterfront Intrepid Sea, Air & Space Museum. Several west side neighborhoods are connected by the High Line, a popular linear park along an old elevated railroad spur. To the north, Central Park offers 843 acres (341 ha) of rolling lawns, woodlands, gardens, paths, lakes, monuments, a small zoo, and more. Flanking the park are some of the city's most significant cultural institutions, including the renowned Metropolitan Museum of Art, the family-friendly American Museum of Natural History and Hayden Planetarium, and the fascinating Frick Collection as well as celebrated music venues Carnegie Hall and Lincoln Center. North of Central Park in Harlem are the famed Apollo Theater, Columbia University, the neo-Gothic splendor of Riverside Church, and The Met

Cloisters museum of medieval art. Farther north, the Bronx hosts Yankee Stadium, the world-renowned Bronx Zoo, and the New York Botanical Garden. Across the East River, the borough of Brooklyn affords great views of the Manhattan skyline from its resurgent waterfront, as well as hip Williamsburg and Coney Island. Flushing Meadows in Queens, former site of two world's fairs, offers its own cluster of

art and science museums as well as the USTA Billie Jean King National Tennis Center and Citi Field, home field of Major League Baseball's New York Mets. Staten Island seems almost rural by comparison, with a mosaic of parkland, suburbs, and colonial remnants such as Historic Richmond Town.

Known for its role as an Erie Canal crossroads and railroad hub, **Syracuse** in upstate New York initially developed around saltworks on the shores of Onondaga Lake. The origins of "Salt City" are explored at the small Salt Museum set on an original boiling block where brine was turned into the valuable commodity. Among other Syracuse attractions are the Everson Museum of Art, the Erie Canal Museum, Rosamond Gifford Zoo, and the historic Landmark Theatre.

Ninety odd miles (145 km) west along the Erie Canal (and modern interstate), **Rochester** grew into an industrial powerhouse on flour and photography. Founded in 1947, the excellent George Eastman Museum within the entrepreneur's 50-room mansion and surrounding estate is very active in photo-and-film preservation. In downtown Rochester, The

The iconic "Charging Bull" in New York City's financial district

Central Park is an oasis of green lawns, lakes, fountains, and gardens in the heart of Manhattan.

Strong (aka the National Museum of Play) is family friendly and includes the National Toy Hall of Fame and World Video Game Hall of Fame. From the end of Clifford Avenue, the Genesee Riverway Trail leads north via the Seneca Park Zoo to the city's Lake Ontario shore and waterfront attractions, including a 1905 Dentzel Carousel.

Buffalo sits on the shores of Lake Erie and the Niagara River just upstream from the famous falls. It hosts several cultural sites, including the six interconnected buildings of the Darwin D. Martin House complex, designed by Frank Lloyd Wright, and a national historic landmark. Also of note is the Albright-Knox Art Gallery, a major center for modern and contemporary art. The Buffalo and Erie County Naval & Military Park offers a large collection of artifacts from the U.S. armed forces.

LANDSCAPES

Long Island stretches nearly 120 miles (193 km) from the East River to Montauk Point. The eastern third—which includes Brooklyn, Queens, and Nassau County—is highly urbanized, but beyond their sprawl are beautiful beaches and bucolic landscapes. At Long Island's eastern tip, Montauk offers a range of public beaches as well as seal colonies and a famous lighthouse. The South Fork's upscale communities, together called The Hamptons, flaunt massive seaside mansions. Tucked among the golden sands is cute little Sag Harbor and its whaling museum. A string of tycoon homes along the island's north shore have been transformed into cultural institutions, including Sagamore Hill, Teddy Roosevelt's private home from 1885 until 1919. The Vanderbilt Museum near Centerport includes the family's Spanish Revival–style mansion plus an art collection and planetarium. The home of Standard Oil heiress Mai Rogers Coe, Coe Hall offers a glimpse into the luxurious lifestyles of the 1920s. It is set within the rolling lawns and formal gardens of Planting Fields Arboretum State Historic Park in Oyster Bay. In addition, the Roslyn estate and Georgian mansion once owned by William Cullen Bryant now hosts the Nassau County Museum of Art.

Scenic **Hudson Valley** extends 150 miles (241 km) from the tip of Manhattan to Albany, a string of historic towns, state parks, wineries, and attractions rising from the mighty Hudson River. America's first homegrown arts movement, known as the Hudson River School, started here in 1825, and landscape paintings in this popular romantic style may be found in major museums worldwide. Upstream from the Big Apple, the Hudson flows through a narrow gap between Bear Mountain State Park and West Point, home of the U.S. Military Academy. FDR's favorite hideaway, **Hyde Park** features his private home, museum, and presidential library as well as the Eleanor Roosevelt National Historic Site. At the north end of town, the grandiose Vanderbilt Mansion National Historic Site showcases a Gilded Age country palace. West of the river, the terrain gradually rises into the eastern **Catskill Mountains,** renowned for their waterfalls, artsy villages, and outdoor music events (including the 1969 Woodstock festival).

New York State's capital city, **Albany** offers a stark contrast in architectural styles—from the 1880s Renaissance-Romanesque capitol building to the modern concrete

canyons of the Governor Nelson A. Rockefeller Empire State Plaza. Nearby **Saratoga Springs** recalls the Victorian age, with period mansions along Broadway that are now home to art galleries, trendy restaurants, and quaint inns. Visitors can still quaff the healing water from fountains in Congress Park or bet on the horses at Saratoga Race Course. Other attractions include the National Museum of Racing and Hall of Fame and the National Museum of Dance and Hall of Fame. On bluffs above the Hudson, Saratoga National Historical Park preserves the site of a pivotal 1777 battle in the American Revolution.

Created in 1892 to conserve the region's water and timber resources, **Adirondack Park** is now the largest publicly protected natural area in the lower 48. Spread across six million acres (2.4 million ha), the park includes more than 10,000 lakes, 2,000 miles (3,219 km) of trails, thousands of campsites, all of the Adirondack Mountains, and the scenic shorelines of Lake

ROAD TRIPS

Great drives across the Empire State:

• Highway 9W between Albany and the George Washington Bridge along the west bank of the Hudson River (141 miles/ 227 km)

• Adirondack Trail (Highway Route 30) between Malone and Fonda (188 miles/303 km)

• Highway 9 between Saratoga Springs and Rouses Point along the western shore of lakes George and Champlain (187 miles/301 km)

• Great Lakes Seaway Trail National Scenic Byway via the Thousand Islands, Lake Ontario, the Niagara River, and Lake Erie (454 miles/731 km)

• Highway 20 between Buffalo and Albany via the Finger Lakes region (283 miles/455 km)

• Highways 25A and 25 across the north side of Long Island between Bayside (Queens) and Orient Point (100 miles/161 km)

George and Lake Champlain. Activities range from white-water rafting and fly-fishing to scrambling up 5,345-foot (1,629 m) Mount Marcy, the state's highest peak. Historical sites include Fort Ticonderoga, an 18th-century citadel that saw action in the American Revolution and French and Indian War. **Lake Placid,** host of the 1932 and the 1980 Winter Olympics, is the official U.S. training center for many winter sports. New York's border with Canada is delineated by the Saint Lawrence River and the **Thousand Islands**

Sailboats on Lake Champlain in New York

The enormous cascades of Niagara Falls set against fall foliage

region, a watery maze of lighthouses, castles, museums, battle sites, vacation homes, resort hotels, and campgrounds.

Set between Rochester and Syracuse, the 11 aptly named **Finger Lakes** may be best known for their local wineries, but craft breweries and artisanal cider mills are increasingly popular. A number of area state parks—such as **Watkins Glen** with its 19 waterfalls—cater to outdoor activities winter and summer. The town of Watkins Glen is also renowned for its racetrack, one of the hubs of U.S. motor sports. **Canandaigua** landmarks include the fascinating Corning Museum of Glass with its glass-blowing demonstrations and the beautiful Sonnenberg Gardens. Sports lovers will want to make the pilgrimage to the

National Baseball Hall of Fame and Museum in **Cooperstown** on the shores of Otsego Lake**.**

Niagara Falls on the New York–Ontario border was "discovered" in 1678 by French explorer Father Louis Hennepin. The three cascades—which have attracted honeymooners and daredevils for more than 200 years—can be viewed from walkways, observation towers, and *Maid of the Mist* boat tours. Niagara Falls State Park, created in 1885, is the nation's oldest state park. ■

HIDDEN TREASURES

• **Huguenot Street (New Paltz):** hosts seven vintage houses, a reconstructed 1717 church, archaeological sites, and a 17th-century burial ground

• **Dryden Theatre (Rochester):** screens rare restored classics and independent movies on the grounds of the historic George Eastman estate

• **Cornell Lab of Ornithology (Ithaca):** offers a chance to learn bird sounds, watch avian videos, and observe feathered friends in the wild

• **Saranac Lake Winter Carnival (Adirondacks):** first held in 1897; has grown into 10 days of winter sports, lumberjack demonstrations, costume balls, and a huge, illuminated ice palace

• **Pomander Walk (Manhattan):** a 1920s town-house complex modeled after a Tudor village

North Carolina

One of the linchpins of the New South, North Carolina has cast aside its cotton-and-tobacco past in favor of science, technology, and world-class universities. Stretching all the way from Cape Hatteras on the Atlantic shore to the Great Smoky Mountains, the Tar Heel State flaunts a wide variety of urban and rural landscapes.

CITIES

One of the nation's fastest growing cities and the center of North Carolina's largest metro area, **Charlotte** is a superstar of the New South. From humble beginnings in 1768, the "Queen City" (named after the wife of King George III) has grown into a vibrant banking and business center, as well as the nucleus of the NASCAR universe. The city's major attraction is the NASCAR Hall of Fame, a massive 150,000-square-foot (13,935 sq m) facility that honors the history, heritage, and people who make stock-car racing one of America's favorite sports. Charlotte Motor Speedway hosts some of the circuit's biggest races while the nearby Hendrick Motorsports complex offers fans a close-up look at their popular racing teams, including cars, trophies, and other memorabilia. Located in what was an original branch of the U.S. Mint, the Mint Museum Randolph opened in 1936 as the state's first fine art museum. Its uptown campus is part of the Levine Center for the Arts, which also includes the Harvey B. Gantt Center for African-American Arts and Culture, the James L. Knight Theater, and the distinctive Bechtler Museum of Modern Art, designed by Swiss architect Mario Botta. Spread across eight leafy acres (3 ha), the sprawling Charlotte Museum of History includes the Hezekiah Alexander House, erected circa 1774. Meanwhile, the Levine Museum of the

Retired race cars help tell the story at the NASCAR Hall of Fame in Charlotte.

TOURISM INFORMATION

North Carolina's Department of Transportation maintains welcome centers and visitor centers at 17 locations around the state. See visitnc.com.

• **Charlotte Visitor Info Center**
Levine Museum of the New South
200 E Seventh St.
Charlotte, NC 28202
Tel 800/231-4636 or
704/333-1887 ext. 235
charlottesgotalot.com

• **Asheville Visitor Center**
36 Montford Ave.
Asheville, NC 28801
Tel 828/258-6101
exploreasheville.com

• **Wilmington & Beaches Convention & Visitors Bureau**
505 Nutt St.
Wilmington, NC 28401
Tel 910/341-4030
wilmingtonandbeaches.com

• **Outer Banks Visitor Bureau**
1 Visitors Center Circle
Manteo, NC 27954
Tel 877/629-4386
outerbanks.org

• **National Park Service**
nps.gov/state/nc

• **North Carolina State Parks**
ncparks.gov

The Biltmore Estate in Asheville gives visitors a glimpse of the Gilded Age.

New South covers post–Civil War southern history from 1865 through the present day.

Marching to the beat of a much different drummer than most southern cities, artsy **Asheville** has a reputation for alternative lifestyles, healthy living, and great beer. Downtown attractions include the Asheville Pinball Museum, the funky River Arts District, Lexington Glassworks, the art deco city hall, and the aSHEville women's museum. Here, too, is the boarding house where author Thomas Wolfe spent much of his youth. Just off the Blue Ridge Parkway on the east side of town, the intriguing Southern Highland Craft Guild Folk Art Center features the traditional and contemporary art of Appalachia, as well as craft demonstrations. Down in Bent Creek on the French Broad River, the 434-acre (176 ha) North Carolina Arboretum offers everything from bonsai trees and botanical gardens to walking and biking trails. On the other side of the river, the Biltmore Estate is the nation's largest and most celebrated private home open to the pubic. Built by George Washington Vanderbilt II between 1889 and 1895, the enormous château-style manse sprawls across 178,000 square feet (16,537 sq m), part of an estate encompassing 8,000 acres (3,237 ha) offering restaurants, a winery, river float trips, horseback riding, clay target–shooting, fly-fishing, a Land Rover off-road driving school, and more. Overnight accommodations are available.

At the opposite end of the state, **Wilmington** basks along the banks of the Cape Fear River around 20 miles (32 km) upstream from the Atlantic. The downtown Historic District offers an intriguing blend of shops and restaurants, classic 19th-century urban architecture, and modern attractions such as the Cape Fear Museum and interactive Children's Museum of Wilmington.

CAPITALISM

North Carolina's British colonial capital shifted throughout the 18th century from Bath (1705) to Edenton (1722) to New Bern (1743), where it remained throughout the American Revolution. It wasn't until after the war (1792) that Raleigh became the fourth capital city, apparently because of its proximity to a tavern popular with Tar Heel politicos. According to North Carolina legend, the state's Constitutional Convention mandated that the new capital be located within 10 miles (16 km) of the pub. It's one of only nine American cities designed from scratch to serve as a state capital.

Across the river, the battleship U.S.S. *North Carolina* hosts a number of World War II–oriented programs, including tours focusing on damage control and firepower. In the heart of downtown, the city's finest antebellum home, graceful Bellamy Mansion, is open for tours. Even older is the Burgwin-Wright House, erected in 1770 and the area's only surviving colonial-era residence. History is also on display at the symmetrical Latimer House and the Poplar Grove Plantation. Close to the Atlantic shore, the 67-acre (27 ha) Airlie Gardens was originally developed in 1886 and today offers formal gardens, trails, lakes, and the famous Airlie Oak, which dates from 1545. Nearby beaches include Wrightsville, Carolina, and Kure, which is home to the North Carolina Aquarium at Fort Fisher.

One of the three tips of North Carolina's vaunted Research Triangle, **Durham** is home to Duke University and a number of cultural institutions, including the Durham Performing Arts Center (DPAC), the Museum of Life and Science, and the extensive Sarah P. Duke Gardens. Here, too, is the Durham Bulls Athletic Park, home to one of the nation's most popular minor league baseball teams. Neighboring **Chapel Hill** is a charming town and host to rival University of North Carolina and campus-related attractions such as the Morehead Planetarium and Science Center, Ackland Art Museum, and the Dean Smith Center, home to the Tar Heels of college basketball fame.

LANDSCAPES

Elongated North Carolina stretches 560 miles (901 km) from east to west and embraces four distinct regions—the Outer Banks, the Atlantic coastal plain, the Piedmont, and the Appalachians.

The **Outer Banks,** a 200-mile-long (322 km) string of narrow barrier islands, divides the mainland from the open ocean. In addition to being one of the graveyards of the Atlantic, the sandy archipelago is celebrated for its lighthouses, wild

ROAD TRIPS

Great drives across the Tar Heel State:

• Blue Ridge Parkway between Cumberland Knob and Great Smoky Mountains National Park (252 miles/406 km)

• Uwharrie Mountains Wine Trail between Salisbury and Stony Mountain Vineyards (42 miles/68 km)

• Highway 12 through the Outer Banks (with connecting ferries) between Sea Level and Corolla (148 miles/238 km)

• Cherohala Skyway (Highways 74 and 143) between Beech Gap, North Carolina, and Tellico Plains, Tennessee (128 miles/206 km)

• Forest Heritage National Scenic Byway between Brevard and Rosman (68 miles/109 km)

horses, and wide beaches. Many of the islands fall within the boundaries of Cape Lookout and Cape Hatteras National Seashores. Fort Raleigh National Historic Site protects remnants of the Roanoke Colony, the ill-fated first English settlement (1587) on American soil. The park also includes an Elizabethan garden, an outdoor theater where a symphonic drama called *The Lost Colony* is performed in summer, and a monument to the ex-slaves who established a Freedmen's Colony here during the Civil War. Nearby Jockey's Ridge State Park flaunts the tallest natural sand dune in the eastern U.S. as well as a boardwalk, museum, and picnic areas. The 60-foot (18 m) Wright Brothers National Memorial at Kill

A strenuous climb to Chimney Rock's summit yields sweeping views.

The sun rises over wide, sandy beaches on North Carolina's Outer Banks.

Devil Hills preserves the windy take-off spot and recounts the story of the first sustained power airplane flight on December 17, 1903.

North Carolina's **Appalachian region** is often rough and rugged, a patchwork quilt of state and national parklands with plentiful outdoor recreation options for both summer and winter. The North Carolina side of **Great Smoky Mountains National Park** includes Oconaluftee Visitor Center and the adjacent Mountain Farm Museum, Clingmans Dome viewpoint, the vertiginous Balsam Mountain Road, and the remote Cataloochee Valley. Just outside the park are the Cataloochee Ski Area, the Wheels Through Time Museum in Maggie Valley, and the Great Smoky Mountain Railroad in Bryson City.

Twenty-five miles (40 km) southeast of Asheville, **Chimney Rock State Park** is named for a 315-foot

(96 m) granite monolith that hovers above Hickory Nut Gorge. Visitors can hike or ride an elevator to the summit for views that often extend for 75 miles (121 km). Trails lead to 404-foot (123 m) Hickory Nut Falls and a narrow rock opening called the Opera Box. **Pisgah National Forest** includes Linville Gorge—the Grand Canyon of North Carolina—and a

federal wilderness area that conserves 12,000 acres (4,856 ha) of pristine forest along a dozen miles (19 km) of the Linville River. The gorge boasts numerous trails, rock formations, waterfalls, fishing spots, and swimming holes. **Grandfather Mountain** in Linville offers trails for all levels of physical fitness, as well as the Mile High Swinging Bridge. ■

LITTLE-KNOWN FACTS

• Moores Creek National Battlefield in Currie marks the spot of a 1776 American victory in the Revolutionary War that ended British rule in North Carolina.

• In 1799, 12-year-old Conrad Reed came across "a yellow substance shining in the water"—the first recorded gold strike in American history—in what became Reed Gold Mine, in Midland.

• "Poet of the People" Carl Sandburg may have been born in Illinois, but he produced more than a third of his works in Flat Rock, North Carolina.

• In 1992, the U.S.S. *Indra,* a World War II landing craft repair ship, sunk off the Beaufort coast. It is now one the state's most popular scuba spots and the site of the annual 4th of July Underwater Bike Race.

North Dakota

Cleaved from its southern cousin in 1889 when both of them became states, North Dakota remains a mystery to many Americans. Closer to Hudson Bay than the Atlantic or Pacific Oceans, the state's extreme winters often draw more press than its landmark sights, including Theodore Roosevelt National Park and the International Peace Garden.

CITIES

Named after the 19th-century politician who united Germany, **Bismarck** has morphed from a sleepy state capital into one of the fastest growing small cities in the U.S. thanks to a 21st-century oil boom that has transformed much of the state. The excellent North Dakota Heritage Center on the state capitol grounds provides a broad overview of the state from the prehistoric era through pioneer times and modern developments. Four blocks south of the capitol park, the Former Governors' Mansion was home to 20 chief executives between 1893 and 1960. The "stick style" Victorian mansion is now fully restored and decorated with period furniture and memorabilia. Camp Hancock State Historic Site offers a 1909 Northern Pacific steam engine and interpretive museum. The latter is set inside the original log headquarters building of a camp established in 1872 to provide a safe haven for the railroad workers who were building the northern transcontinental link. Perched on the banks of the Missouri River, the Dakota Zoo features more than 600 animals from around the world. The wide array of wildlife includes bison, grizzly bears, lynx, elks, and gray wolves—animals that Lewis and Clark would have seen on their epic journey across the continent. Crossing the river, Fort Abraham Lincoln State Park features the reconstruction of an 18th-century Mandan Indian village and 19th-century U.S. Army post that was on the front line of the Indian Wars. Lieutenant Colonel George Armstrong Custer and his Seventh Cavalry were based here prior to the Battle of the Little Big Horn. Living-history tours of the fort's Custer House provide insight into his life and times.

Perhaps more famed for the 1996 cult movie than anything that's actually happened there, **Fargo** anchors the eastern edge of the state, across the Red River from Minnesota. The Plains Art Museum, located in a

Liberty Memorial Bridge spans the Missouri River in Bismarck.

Bison graze at Theodore Roosevelt National Park.

renovated International Harvester warehouse, displays more than 3,000 works by artists such as Andy Warhol, Salvador Dalí, Ellsworth Kelly, and others. Bonanzaville in West Fargo preserves 43 historic buildings and 400,000 artifacts gathered from around the state, with collections including the Eugene Dahl Car Museum, Eagles Air Museum, Tractor Museum, and Law Enforcement Museum. Fargo Air Museum restores, preserves, and displays vintage aircraft from the early days of flight through the Vietnam War, while the city's Red River Zoo specializes in the care and captive breeding of some of the world's rarest cold-climate species, including the red panda, Sichuan takin, Pallas's cat, and white-naped crane.

Eighty miles (129 km) farther up the Red River, **Grand Forks** is home to the University of North Dakota, the state's second largest employer after the U.S. Air Force. Located on campus, the North Dakota Museum of Art features international art in all media from the 1970s onward, with a special emphasis on Native American art. Ralph Engelstad Arena, or "The Ralph," is home to the highly ranked UND men's and women's ice hockey teams.

LANDSCAPES

Located in the western part of the state, **Theodore Roosevelt**

National Park sprawls across 70,000 acres (28,328 ha) of pristine prairie and badlands divided into three sections: the North Unit, South Unit, and Elkhorn Ranch. The park's Medora Visitor Center preserves Teddy Roosevelt's Maltese Cross Cabin, the modest dwelling where the future president stayed during his first sojourn in the Dakotas (1883–1884). Nearby is the start of the 36-mile (58 km) Scenic Loop Drive through the South Unit, meandering past several prairie dog towns, panoramic overlooks, and flatlands along the Little Missouri River, where wild horses and bison often graze. Separated from the rest of the park by Little Missouri National Grassland, the North Unit is reached via an hour-long drive along U.S. Highway 85. This northern section boasts its own scenic drive through glacially carved landscapes that can be further explored on foot along the Achenbach, Buckhorn, and other trails. The remote Elkhorn Ranch is where young Teddy Roosevelt retreated in the 1880s after the deaths of his wife and mother. His wild west adventures were critical in transforming "TR" into an ardent conservationist and world leader. Accessible only via a 35-mile (56 km) gravel road, the ranch buildings have disappeared other than their original foundation stones. The 96-mile (154 km) Maah Daah Hey Trail connects all three park units.

Just outside the park, the town of **Medora** preserves many of its pioneer-era buildings, including the 26-room Chateau de Mores, a rustic hunting lodge built by the French aristocrat Marquis de Mores in 1883. The town is also home to the *Medora Musical,* a melodious historical play staged every summer since 1965 in the Burning Hills Amphitheatre. The Enchanted Highway features six enormous metal sculptures of animals, people, and Teddy Roosevelt by local artist Gary Greff. The sculpture "Geese in Flight" is listed by the *Guinness Book of Records* as the world's largest scrap-metal sculpture. The sculptures are found along 100 1/2 Avenue SW, between Gladstone and Regent (Exit 72 off Interstate 94).

Visitors to the **North Dakota Lewis & Clark Interpretive**

Center in Washburn are greeted by steel statues of explorers Meriwether Lewis and William Clark with Mandan Chief Sheheke by artist Tom Neary. Inside, displays provide an overview of the Lewis and Clark expedition, with special emphasis on the winter of 1804–1805 when the explorers sojourned at Fort Mandan. The reconstructed wooden stockade is three miles (5 km) west of the interpretive center, overlooking the river. North Dakota's Nordic migrants are the focus of Scandinavian Heritage Park in **Minot,** which includes a replica of the medieval Gol Stave Church, a Finnish sauna, and an 18th-century Norwegian home. Located off the highway that leads from downtown to the Strategic Air Command's Minot Air Force Base, the Dakota Territory Air Museum displays vintage and famous military aircraft.

Although in close proximity, Frontier Village and the National Buffalo Museum and bison herd are two separate entities. On the outskirts of **Jamestown,** Frontier

The Fargo Theatre

The Little Missouri River flows through Theodore Roosevelt National Park.

Village features pioneer-era structures arrayed along a dusty main street, including a vintage post office, trading post (now a souvenir shop), the state's oldest grocery store, a saloon, fire department, barber shop, sheriff's office, and a writer's shack dedicated to celebrated Western author Louis L'Amour, who was born and raised in Jamestown. Nearby, the National Buffalo Museum celebrates the pivotal role of bison in plains culture and hosts a bison herd numbering around 30 head, including a very rare albino buffalo named White Cloud. Above their paddock soars the "world's largest bison"—a 26-foot-tall (8 m) cement beast that weighs 60 tons (54 metric tons).

The Cold War heats up at the Ronald Reagan Minuteman Missile State Historic Site in **Cooperstown,** which includes the Oscar-Zero Missile Alert Facility and the November-33 Launch Facility. Ironically, the historic missile silo is only a few hours' drive from the **International Peace Garden** on the border between the U.S. and Canada. The park was established in 1932 as an enduring symbol of peaceful relationships between the two nations. ■

HIDDEN TREASURES

North Dakota's Native American heritage is rich and varied:

• **The Sitting Bull Monument (Fort Yates):** marks where the legendary Sioux leader was originally buried following his controversial death at the hands of Indian Agency police in 1890

• **Knife River Indian Villages National Historic Site (Stanton):** exhibits artifacts recovered from various Plains Indians villages clustered in an area that was an important Native American trade center and marketplace

• **Fort Union (Williston):** the most important trading post on the upper Missouri for much of the 19th century, now reconstructed and hosting Indian arts shows and living-history weekends

• **Chippewa Downs (Belcourt):** Thoroughbred and quarter-horse racing in summer hosted by the Turtle Mountain Band of Chippewa

• **Four Bears Bridge (Fort Berthold Reservation):** decorated with medallions, markers, and storyboards honoring the reservation's Mandan, Hidatsa, and Arikara nations

• **Writing Rock State Historic Site (Grenora):** safeguards two boulders decorated with thunderbirds and other Plains Indians petroglyphs

Ohio

Birthplace of more U.S. presidents than any other state (eight), Ohio has evolved over the past 50 years from Rust Belt poster child into a postindustrial milieu considered among the nation's most livable environments. Stretching between Lake Erie and the Ohio River, the Buckeye State is dominated by three huge cities, but much of the state remains rolling hills, farmland, and forest—true to its bucolic roots.

CITIES

Set on the southern shore of Lake Erie, **Cleveland** has undergone a resurgence from the days when the Cuyahoga River caught on fire and the lakeside metropolis was chastised as the epitome of urban decay. In the 1950s, local disc jockey Alan Freed coined the term "rock and roll," and today the city's Rock and Roll Hall of Fame and Museum has attracted millions to the lakefront. It is part of a North Coast Harbor urban redevelopment that includes the U.S.S. *Cod* submarine museum, the interactive Great Lakes Science Center, the Steamship *William G. Mather* Museum, and FirstEnergy Stadium, home of the National Football League's Cleveland Browns. The many historic buildings of the old Tremont neighborhood include the *A Christmas Story* House & Museum, featured in the classic 1983 movie. The University Circle neighborhood provides a leafy venue for Cleveland Botanical Garden, the Cleveland Museum of Natural History, and the orchestral performances of Severance Hall.

Smack in the middle of the state, **Columbus** is the state's capital and largest city. Downtown attractions include the capitol building, the Columbus Art Museum, and the Kelton House Museum & Garden, showcasing Victorian-era life and its role as a stop on the Underground Railroad. The nearby Thurber House, boyhood home of humorist James Thurber, does double duty as a literary center and museum. Anchoring the north side of downtown, the Arena District is the cornerstone of the state capital's own urban renaissance. The onetime home of the Ohio Penitentiary is now a bustling purpose-built urban environment with sports, entertainment, and residential components. Farther north is the sprawling campus of Ohio State University, one of the nation's largest with some

TOURISM INFORMATION

Ohio tourist information centers can be found at roadside rests at various interstate and U.S. highway gateways around the state. Find more at discoverohio.com.

• **Cleveland Visitor Center**
334 Euclid Ave.
Cleveland, OH 44114
Tel 800/321-1001
thisiscleveland.com

• **Cincinnati USA Visitor Center**
511 Walnut St.
Cincinnati, OH 45202
Tel 513/534-5877
cincinnatiusa.com

• **Experience Columbus Visitor Center**
277 W Nationwide Blvd.
Suite 125
Columbus, OH 43215
Tel 614/221-6623
experiencecolumbus.com

• **National Park Service**
nps.gov/state/oh

Dining alfresco in Cincinnati's Over-the-Rhine district

The John A. Roebling Suspension Bridge links Cincinnati with Covington, Kentucky, across the Ohio River.

60,000 students. In addition to buildings named for Buckeye legends Jesse Owens and Woody Hayes, the university sports complex includes the Jack Nicklaus Museum, which celebrates the achievements of another hometown hero.

Tucked amid rolling hills along the Ohio River, **Cincinnati** was America's first "western" city. Founded in 1788, it soon boomed on riverboat traffic and trade with America's new territories. Cincinnati also provided a major conduit for runaway slaves trying to escape the South, a past recalled at the National Underground Railroad Freedom Center. Steady German immigration created a thriving ethnic enclave called Over-the-Rhine (OTR), now the nation's largest intact 19th-century urban district with close to 1,000 structures on

the National Register of Historic Places. The nation's second oldest public zoological collection, the 75-acre (3 ha) Cincinnati Zoo & Botanical Garden boasts more than 500 animals and a captive breeding program for rare and endangered wildlife.

LAKESHORE

Stretching 262 miles (422 km) from east to west, Ohio's Lake Erie shoreline has transformed over the past century from a water body that largely facilitated trade and industry into a diverse recreational haven. **Ashtabula County** is renowned for covered bridges. A driving tour of the picturesque spans could start with Smolen-Gulf Bridge over the Ashtabula River—the longest covered bridge in the U.S.— and end with the neo-Victorian style

Netcher Road Bridge near Jefferson. Geneva-on-the-Lake village attracts swimmers, fishermen, and boaters to its handsome lakeshore, while nature lovers can explore the area's

CAPITALISM

"Where's the dome?" is a quip heard often in Columbus by those ogling the Ohio state capitol building for the first time. The structure's offbeat architecture is a result of multiple architects and way too many politicians having their say over the design during the 23 years (1838–1861) it took to complete the building. The drum-shaped tower covers an impressive rotunda with a stained-glass skylight featuring the state seal.

freshwater marshes and estuaries. Away from the water, the Grand River Valley provides a Napa-like setting for laid-back, family-owned wineries, many welcoming visitors.

The summer sun and sand continues west of Cleveland, with **Huntington Beach,** the first strand on Lake Erie certified as a Blue Wave beach with a complete eco-coastal experience. **Cedar Point** opened its gates in 1870 as one of the world's first theme parks and today hosts 17 roller coasters—including the tallest, fastest, and steepest coaster ever built—and a world-record 71 total rides.

While Ohio shares the **Lake Erie Archipelago** with Ontario, Canada, the vast majority of the isles are on the American side. In addition to their varied outdoor recreation pursuits and nature areas, the islands are notable for their role in the War of 1812. Towering above South Bass Island, Perry's Victory and International Peace Memorial towers honor those who fought in an 1813 naval engagement called the Battle of Lake Erie. Ferries service the islands from Sandusky, Marblehead, and Catawba.

The self-proclaimed "Water Recreation Capital of the Midwest," **Toledo** sits at the confluence of the Maumee River and Lake Erie. Marinas, boat rides, and waterfront parks cater to the water-loving crowd, but the city also has a cultural bent. The Toledo Museum of Art houses more than 30,000 works from ancient to contemporary in six buildings. These include the stunning Glass Pavilion designed by Frank Gehry, which harbors 5,000 glass works as well as artist studios and classrooms.

LANDSCAPES

Wedged between Cleveland and Akron, **Cuyahoga Valley**

National Park is Ohio's largest and most popular national park unit, a blend of history, nature, and outdoor recreation. It offers 160 miles (257 km) of hiking and biking paths, including the 21-mile (34 km) Ohio & Erie Canal Towpath Trail along the Cuyahoga River. In 1920,

The Marblehead Lighthouse in Marblehead, Ohio, has guided sailors on Lake Erie since 1822.

the National Football League was founded in Canton, home of the **Pro Football Hall of Fame** and its tributes to players, coaches, and journalists.

A much different sort of tough guy is showcased at the **Ohio State Reformatory** in Mansfield, a historic (and no longer active) prison now open to the public for guided tours and "haunted prison" experiences. To the east, **Holmes County** has one of the nation's largest Amish communities. The Amish & Mennonite Heritage Center in Berlin tells their story via museum exhibits and historic buildings, while Amish Heartland Tours arranges dinners in Amish homes as well as artisan tours. In Coshocton, Historic Roscoe Village recalls its days as a boomtown on the Ohio & Erie Canal with living-history events, restored buildings, and plenty of opportunities to relax in its early 19th-century ambience.

Part of the Allegheny Plateau, the rugged **Hocking Hills** of southern Ohio are spangled with cliffs, caves, cascades, and other dramatic geological features. From hiking and camping to a scenic railway, zip-line canopy attraction, and *Tecumseh!* outdoor historical drama, the hills offer plenty of variety. For the serious hiker, the 1,444-mile (2,324 km) Buckeye Trail cuts through the Hocking region on its way to visiting 49 of Ohio's 88 counties. Rare and endangered species from around the world take shelter at The Wilds, a 10,000-acre (4,047 ha) wildlife conservation center in Cumberland with horseback safaris and close-up animal encounters.

Just north of Dayton, the huge **National Museum of the U.S. Air Force** is the world's oldest and largest military aviation museum, with

Cuyahoga Valley National Park

some 300 planes and missiles on display. **Dayton** itself has emerged from its heavy-duty industrial days into a modern cultural hub centered around the Schuster Center, the Dayton Art Institute, the Boonshoft Museum of Discovery, and the Dayton Aviation Heritage National Historical Park.

The National Packard Museum in **Warren** traces the roots of the Packard motorcar and others that have contributed to the advancement of the auto industry. ■

LITTLE-KNOWN FACTS

• Ohio is the only state with a burgee, a triangle-shaped flag.

• Newark, Ohio, is home to the world's largest basket-shaped building, the seven-story headquarters of local basketmakers the Longaberger Company.

• In the 1830s, Ohio and Michigan fought a brief and not-very-bloody war (one injured) for control of the Toledo Strip in northwest Ohio.

• Drivers can still motor down America's first concrete street (1891)—Court Avenue in Bellefontaine.

• Ohio is the birthplace of the first men to fly an airplane (the Wright Brothers) and walk on the moon (Neil Armstrong).

Oklahoma

One of the last states to enter the Union, Oklahoma has a rich history that permeates its landscapes, from the cypress bottoms of the southeast to the high plains of the arid panhandle. Part of the Louisiana Purchase, the rugged region was later Indian Territory and the epitome of the Wild West. Devastated by the Dust Bowl, the Sooner State parlayed the "bubblin' crude" beneath its red soil into modern prosperity.

TOURISM INFORMATION

The Oklahoma Tourism and Recreation Department has 12 tourism information centers around the state, most of them near interstate highway gateways. Check out travelok .com *for more information.*

● **Oklahoma City Visitor Information Center**
Northeast corner of the Cox Convention Center Lobby
58 W Sheridan Ave.
Oklahoma City, OK 73102
Tel 405/602-5141
visitokc.com

● **Tulsa Visitor Information Center**
1 W Third St., Suite 100
Tulsa, OK 74103
Tel 800/558-3311
visittulsa.com

CITIES

One of the most dynamic cities on the Great Plains, **Oklahoma City** unfolds as a sprawling metropolis with nearly 1.5 million people. Its redeveloped downtown and iconic museums are the main attractions, but "OKC" is also an excellent base for exploring the rest of the state. The 50-story Devon Energy Center, visible from just about everywhere in the metro area, is open for views from the top via guided tours or meals at the penthouse restaurant, Vast. Across the street from the blue tower, Myriad Botanical Gardens showcases plants from around the world in outdoor beds and the futuristic Crystal Bridge Tropical Conservatory. Located on the other side of the railroad tracks, Bricktown had become a cluster of derelict factories and warehouses until a 1990s remake morphed it into a lively shopping, eating, and entertainment district with canals and a minor league baseball park. The somber Oklahoma City National Memorial & Museum—on the site of the Alfred P. Murrah Federal Building—anchors the northern end of downtown and recalls the deadly 1995 bombing. The National Cowboy & Western Heritage Museum offers a thorough glimpse of the forces that shaped the American West, with galleries devoted to everything from rodeos and ranchers to Native American culture and the U.S. cavalry. Tucked down in the city's southeast corner, the offbeat Museum of Osteology displays more than 300 skeletons and fascinating exhibits on comparative anatomy and forensic pathology.

Half an hour south of downtown OKC, and an independent city in its own right, **Norman** is famously home to the University of Oklahoma and its massive campus. Big-time college football draws fans to the 82,000-seat Gaylord Family–Oklahoma Memorial Stadium in the fall. Year-round campus attractions include the Sam Noble Museum of natural history and its 10 million specimens and artifacts.

The compact skyline of downtown Oklahoma City

Gardens surround Tulsa's renowned Philbrook Museum of Art.

Also of note is the Fred Jones Jr. Museum of Art, an eclectic compilation that embraces Impressionism, Native American, and contemporary Latin American works, as well as other genres.

About a hundred miles (161 km) up the turnpike from the capital is **Tulsa,** the state's second largest city and very much a product of the early-20th-century oil boom. Local oil barons funded institutions that eventually transformed the city into Oklahoma's cultural, artistic, and architectural capital. Downtown boasts art deco structures including the Philcade Building and Boston Avenue United Methodist Church. The Woody Guthrie Center explores the life and times of the legendary Oklahoma singer-songwriter. Oilman Waite Phillips transformed his 72-room mansion into the Philbrook Museum of Art, one of only five sites in the U.S. that blends historic home, gardens, and art galleries. The globe's most comprehensive collection of art and artifacts on the American West—including an impressive assemblage of Native American objects—is housed inside the Gilcrease Museum. Rounding out the city's art scene, the Sherwin Miller Museum of Jewish Art displays a vast array of Judaica, from fine art and traditional clothing to ritual objects and archaeological relics.

CAPITALISM

Founded in 1887 and called "Queen of the Prairies" by local wags, Guthrie was an obvious choice for state capital when Oklahoma entered the union in 1907. But it didn't last long. In 1910, Oklahoma City businessmen engineered a controversial referendum to move the state capital 30 miles (48 km) south to its present location. Guthrie's city fathers sued, taking the case all the way to the U.S. Supreme Court before losing. While "the Queen" soon faded into a second-tier town, its past is preserved in the excellent Oklahoma Territorial Museum.

LANDSCAPES

Whether you drive old Route 66 or modern Interstate 40, the way west from Oklahoma City offers an intriguing blend of bygone and modern attractions. Established in 1874, **Fort Reno** was a crucial player in the Indian Wars and the late-19th-century Oklahoma land rush. The visitor center museum offers intriguing insights into the U.S. Cavalry and the Buffalo Soldiers stationed here in Wild West days. Quiet and unassuming Weatherford is home to one of the world's best aviation collections—the **Stafford Air & Space Museum.** Named after hometown hero and Apollo astronaut Thomas Stafford, the Smithsonian-affiliated museum houses original space capsules, rockets, fighter jets, and other treasures. America's "Mother Road" comes to life at the **Oklahoma Route 66 Museum** in Clinton, where vintage cars, neon signs, gas station artifacts, and various mementoes are displayed as the classic tunes of Elvis Presley, Woody Guthrie, and others

play. To the west, **Black Kettle National Grassland** preserves a large tract of prairie that includes Washita Battlefield National Historic Site, where Custer and the Seventh Cavalry massacred scores of Cheyenne men, women, and children in the winter of 1868.

Oklahoma's southwest sector is dominated by the **Wichita Mountains,** a welcome contrast to the flat, horizontal topography that marks so much of the Sooner State. Much of the range is preserved within the confines of a national wildlife refuge, protecting a mosaic of red-rock canyons, wilderness trails, heavily wooded vales, and rolling grasslands where herds of bison and feral longhorn cattle graze. Nearby **Medicine Park** was founded in 1907 as a riverside resort town. Today the antique buildings—many built with local rust-colored granite cobblestones—host restaurants, shops, and river adventure outfitters.

Another sudden rise is the **Arbuckle Mountains,** due south of

Oklahoma City along the Interstate 35 corridor. **Turner Falls,** the state's highest cascade, is the centerpiece of a park that includes a stone castle, geological formations, and myriad swimming holes. Water is also the focus of **Chickasaw National Recreation Area,** a warren of lakes, streams, and natural springs on the eastern edge of the mountains. Founded in 1902 as Platt National Park, the reserve enables a wide range of water sports, from fishing and boating to tubing, waterskiing, and kayaking. Hiking and biking trails lead to bird-watching spots, a bison paddock, and the Travertine Nature Center. Just outside the park, the old hot springs resort town of **Sulphur** hosts both the national park visitor center and the Chickasaw Cultural Center. The latter tells the story of the Chickasaw people who, along with other southeastern nations, were forcibly relocated to Oklahoma on a march known as the Trail of Tears. Exhibits are supplemented by an art gallery, theater, and an honor garden dedicated to Chickasaw leaders, elders, and warriors.

Route 66 is memorialized by several Oklahoma museums, including Elk City's National Route 66 & Transportation Museum.

Sunset from Mount Scott within the Wichita Mountains Wildlife Refuge

Native American heritage is also strong in eastern Oklahoma at places such as the Seminole Nation Museum in **Wewoka,** the Cherokee Heritage Center near **Tahlequah,** and the Museum of the Red River in **Idabel,** where the ethnographic collection contains more than 18,000 items. The Jim Thorpe House in tiny **Yale** showcases medals from the Olympic Games, family mementos, and photographs of the Sac-Fox Indian who was once called the world's greatest athlete. Sequoyah's Cabin near Sallisaw pays homage to another great Native American who invented the Cherokee alphabet and written language in the early 1800s. On the south side of the Arkansas River, **Spiro Mounds** is one of the nation's most important pre-Columbian archaeological sites. Built between A.D. 800 and 1450, the 12 mounds are the largest and most distinctive relics of what was once a thriving Native American urban zone. Cherokee actor, humorist, and social commentator Will Rogers was born in a white clapboard house on Dog Iron Ranch near **Oologah,** a home that's now open to the public. More mementoes of the legendary figure are on display at the Will Rogers Memorial Museum in nearby **Claremore,** also celebrated as the town where Rodgers and Hammerstein set the musical *Oklahoma!* ■

LITTLE-KNOWN FACTS

• Oklahoma's original state flag—featuring a white star on a bloodred background—was replaced in the 1925 because it too closely resembled a communist banner.

• Oklahoma is home to 38 federally recognized Indian tribal nations, more than any other state except California.

• The supermarket shopping cart, parking meter, electric guitar, and yield sign were all invented in Oklahoma.

• Hugo, Oklahoma, once served as winter quarters for numerous circus acts; many bygone performers are buried in the town's Showmen's Rest cemetery.

• With more than 200 reservoirs, Oklahoma boasts more man-made lakes than any other state.

• Oklahoma came close to being two separate states in 1905 when the "Five Civilized Tribes" petitioned Congress to form their own state, called Sequoyah after the great Cherokee leader.

Oregon

The pioneer paradise at the end of the Oregon Trail is now one of America's most progressive states, a place where recycling, resource management, and outdoor recreation blend easily with avant-garde culture and alternative lifestyles. Oregon's landscapes are equally diverse, from rocky shorelines and snow-covered volcanic peaks to somber high desert and sophisticated urban areas.

CITIES

Located near the confluence of the Columbia and Willamette Rivers, **Portland** has evolved from a burly frontier town into one of the hippest cities on the continent. Coffeehouses and craft breweries spangle an urban area framed by snowcapped peaks and evergreen forest. The city has grown up around Pioneer Courthouse Square, dubbed "Portland's living room" for hosting more than 300 activities and events each year. Many of the city's cultural institutions—including the Portland Art Museum, Arlene Schnitzer Concert Hall, Oregon Historical Society Museum, Lincoln Recital Hall, and Portland Farmers Market—are arrayed along the 12-block downtown green belt known as the South Park Blocks. Along the west bank of the Willamette River, Tom McCall Waterfront Park harbors the Oregon Maritime Museum within the vintage stern-wheeler *Portland.* Over on the east bank, the Oregon Museum of Science and Industry (OMSI) includes 200 interactive exhibits, a planetarium, and the fast-attack submarine U.S.S. *Blueback* featured in the film *The Hunt for Red October.* North of downtown, the Pearl District, a onetime warehouse area, has morphed into a trendy brewery-and-boutique destination. Nearby Old Town Chinatown boasts some of the city's best Asian food as well as the walled Lan Su Chinese Garden. West of downtown, Washington Park is laced with trails leading to its myriad attractions, including the International Rose Test Garden, the nation's oldest (1917) and site of an annual Rose Festival. Also of note are the serene Portland Japanese Garden, the extensive Hoyt

TOURISM INFORMATION

Travel Oregon offers maps, brochures, and other information on the state at the visitor Information center at Portland International Airport. Find additional information online at traveloregon.com.

• **Portland Visitor Information Center**
701 SW Sixth Ave.
Pioneer Courthouse Square
Portland, OR 97204
Tel 503/275-8355 or
877/678-5263
travelportland.com

• **Newport Oregon Coast 24 Hour Information Center**
555 SW Coast Highway
Newport, OR 97365
Tel 541/574-2679
visittheoregoncoast.com

• **Lane County Eugene, Cascades & Coast Visitor Information**
754 Olive St.
Eugene, OR 97401
Tel 541/484-5307
eugenecascadescoast.org

• **Ashland Chamber of Commerce**
110 E Main St.
Ashland, OR 97520
Tel 541/482-3486
ashlandchamber.com

• **Oregon State Parks**
oregonstateparks.org

Fresh-cooked vegetables at the Portland Farmers Market

Set against a sunrise, snowy Mount Hood looms over Portland's skyline.

Arboretum, the Portland Children's Museum, the Oregon Zoo, and the Pittock Mansion, the palatial home of *Oregonian* newspaper editor Henry L. Pittock. It features a number of early-20th-century conveniences that were cutting edge at the time, including an elevator, a central vacuum cleaning system, diffused lighting, and intercoms in all 46 rooms.

At the southern end of the Willamette Valley, **Eugene** is the state's second largest city, a dynamic college town that largely revolves around the University of Oregon's cultural institutions and sports endeavors. The windowless Jordan Schnitzer Museum of Art concentrates on Asian and American works, both historic and contemporary. Other campus sights include the Museum of Natural and Cultural History and Deady Hall, which was built in the 1870s and

for a decade was the university's only building. Hayward Field hosts many of the nation's premier track-and-field events while Autzen Stadium, in Alton Baker Park, is home to the very successful University of Oregon Ducks football team. The park offers many walking and running trails (including one designed by local long-distance legend Steve Prefontaine), as well as the Science Factory Children's Museum and Exploration Dome, flush with interactive displays. On the outskirts of town the Mount Pisgah Arboretum flourishes on the slopes of its namesake mountain. The 1888 Shelton McMurphey Johnson House on Skinner Butte preserves many pioneer-era artifacts and furnishings. Of particular interest, Cascades Raptor Center has been providing rehabilitation for injured birds of prey and education activities to the general public since 1987.

LANDSCAPES

Demarcating most of the border between Oregon and Washington, the **Columbia River** is the nation's second largest in terms of total water volume. East of Portland,

STATE OF THE ART

- **Best movies:** *National Lampoon's Animal House* (1978) and *One Flew Over the Cuckoo's Nest* (1975)

- **Best book:** *Sometimes a Great Notion* by Ken Kesey

- **Best songs:** "Oregon Trail" by Woody Guthrie and "Portland Town" by Joan Baez

- **Best art:** the Oregon landscapes of Romona Youngquist

- **Best TV show:** *Portlandia*

Columbia River Gorge National Scenic Area offers a wide array of activities from hiking, biking, and bird-watching to skiing, snowboarding, and water sports. The towering cascades along the river's south bank—including 620-foot (189 m) Multnomah Falls—are among the state's most photographed landmarks.

One of the nation's most distinctive peaks, **Mount Hood** rises to 11,239 feet (3,426 m) just 20 miles (32 km) south of the Columbia Gorge. The surrounding Mount Hood National Forest offers ski hills and hiking trails through lush evergreen forest spangled with waterfalls and hot springs.

The snowcapped **Cascade Range** continues south through several national forests. Arrayed along this rugged backbone are other major volcanic peaks including Mount Jefferson, Mount Washington, Three Fingered Jack, Diamond Peak, and the Three Sisters. In addition to 380,000 acres (153,781 ha) of designated wilderness area, high-country attractions include the Dee Wright Observatory at the summit of McKenzie Pass and Salt Creek Falls near Willamette Pass.

At the bottom end of the Oregon Cascades, a collapsed volcanic peak forms the heart of **Crater Lake National Park.** The nation's deepest lake (almost 2,000 feet/ 610 m) is bright blue and surrounded by sheer cliffs with vertigo-inducing viewpoints along 33-mile (53 km) Rim Drive. During summer, boats ferry visitors to Wizard Island for hiking and scuba diving.

Beyond the Cascades, the landscape quickly evolves from peaks and forest into the high desert and rolling plains of eastern Oregon that 19th-century migrants along the Oregon Trail had to endure in order to reach the fertile lands along the coast. The High Desert Museum in **Bend** provides insight into this stark but beautiful region. The National Historic Oregon Trail Interpretive Center, located along a preserved portion of the trail near

ROAD TRIPS

Great drives across the Beaver State:

• Highway 101 along the Pacific Coast between Astoria and Brookings (338 miles/ 544 km)

• Historic Columbia River Highway (U.S. 30 and Interstate 84) between The Dalles and Troutdale (70 miles/113 km)

• Hells Canyon Scenic Byway (Highways 86, 39, and 82) between Baker City and La Grande (197 miles/317 km)

• Highway 97 up the eastern side of the Cascades between Klamath Falls and Biggs Junction (272 miles/438 km)

• Pacific to High Desert drive (Highways 126 and 30) between Florence and Bend (194 miles/312 km)

Baker City, is an interesting stop for Western history junkies. The **Snake River** carves a deep path along the Oregon-Idaho border, including fabled Hells Canyon. The nation's deepest canyon, which drops nearly 8,000 feet (2,438 m) from rim to river, is part of Hells Canyon National Recreation Area.

The Columbia River empties into the sea near **Astoria** and its landmark bridge, a green monster that looms nearly 200 feet (61 m) above the water at high tide. On the other side of Youngs Bay, **Lewis and Clark National Historical Park** includes a replica of Fort Clatsop, the winter encampment for the Corps of Discovery from December 1805 to March 1806. Daily costumed programs and other

A runner jogs past a waterfall near Eugene, Oregon.

Scenic Cannon Beach as viewed from neighboring Ecola State Park

ranger-led activities are staged in summer (the park's interpretive center is located in Cape Disappointment State Park, across the river in Washington State). About 20 miles (32 km) south of Fort Clatsop, **Cannon Beach** is a popular seaside resort, its nine miles (14 km) of uninterrupted sand punctuated with distinctive geological formations including Hay Stack Rock, a favorite puffin hangout.

Perched on **Yaquina Bay** in Newport, the Oregon Coast Aquarium harbors a wide array of Pacific Northwest aquatic creatures while the nearby Hatfield Marine Science Center offers a visitor center with educational exhibits and more live marine animals. Yaquina Head Outstanding Natural Area features tide pools, marine mammals, seabird nesting areas, and Oregon's tallest lighthouse. Due south is the fascinating **Oregon Dunes National**

Recreation Area, which spans 40 miles (64 km) of shore from Florence to Coos Bay. It is the largest expanse of coastal sand dunes in North America, with some dunes ascending to 500 feet (152 m) above sea level.

Oregon Caves National Monument lies beneath the Siskiyou

Mountains in the state's deep south. Ninety-minute guided tours take visitors through the "marble halls of Oregon," a habitat for many unusual plants and animals. Nearby **Ashland** is renowned for its world-famous Oregon Shakespeare Festival that takes place annually from February to October. ■

LOCAL FLAVOR

Oregon was the birthplace of the American craft beer movement and still boasts some of the nation's best microbreweries:

• **BridgePort:** This Portland outfit claims to be the state's oldest craft brewery, founded in 1984 and best known for its India Pale Ale (IPA). *1313 NW Marshall St., Portland*

• **Deschutes Brewery:** a central Oregon sudsmaker offering factory tours, tasting room, and pub. *901 SW Simpson Ave., Bend*

• **Rogue Ales:** a moody brewery and gastropub on Yaquina Bay. *2320 SE Marine Science Dr., Newport*

• **Widmer Brothers Brewing:** Kurt and Rob Widmer's microbrewery is credited with introducing German-style hefeweizen to the U.S. *929 N Russell St., Portland*

Pennsylvania

One of only two states that stretches between the Atlantic coast and the Great Lakes, Pennsylvania offers an amazing variety of landscapes, both rural and urban. Home to both Philadelphia and Pittsburgh, the state boasts two of the nation's most intriguing cities. But the countryside of the Keystone State also dazzles, a scenic mosaic that includes the Allegheny Mountains, Amish Country, and the battlefields of Gettysburg.

TOURISM INFORMATION

The Pennsylvania Tourism Office supports 10 welcome centers located at interstate highway gateways around the edge of the state. Find out more at visitpa.com.

• **Philadelphia Independence Visitor Center**
1 N Independence Mall W
Philadelphia, PA 19106
Tel 800/537-7676
visitphilly.com

• **Visit Pittsburgh Tourist Information Center**
120 Fifth Ave.
Pittsburgh, PA 15222
Tel 877/568-3744
visitpittsburgh.com

• **Discover Lancaster Visitors Center**
501 Greenfield Rd.
Lancaster, PA 17601
Tel 800/723-8824
discoverlancaster.com

• **National Park Service**
nps.gov/state/pa

• **Pennsylvania State Parks**
dcnr.state.pa.us/stateparks

CITIES

More than 240 years since it served as the cradle of American independence, **Philadelphia** still revolves around the cluster of buildings that shaped the nation's future. Independence National Historical Park includes Independence Hall, Congress Hall, Old City Hall and its Supreme Court Chamber, Carpenters' Hall, Franklin Court, the First Bank of the United States, and many more. Originally housed at Independence Hall, the Liberty Bell was moved inside the modern, glass-wrapped Liberty Bell Center in 2003. The park also includes Ben Franklin's grave in Christ Church Burial Ground as well as City Tavern, where 18th-century cuisine is served in a period dining room. The surrounding Old City district is flush with other historical nuggets worth visiting: the National Constitution Center, U.S. Mint, Betsy Ross House, National Museum of American Jewish History, and the 18th-century brick town houses of Elfreth's Alley. Down along the Delaware River waterfront are the Independence Seaport Museum (home of the 1892 cruiser U.S.S. *Olympia*)

Independence Hall in Philadelphia, birthplace of the Declaration of Independence

and modern Penn's Landing with its summer beer garden and concert series, ice- and roller-skating rink, and ferry to Camden, New Jersey. The Philadelphia Museum of Art is renowned for its massive collection of 227,000 works from around the world as well as its monumental steps, featured in the *Rocky* movies. Founded in 1824 and still an active research facility, the Franklin Institute was a pioneer in developing hands-on, interactive museum experiences. The nearby Barnes Foundation boasts one of the world's best collections of Impressionist art. On the other side of the river, the University of Pennsylvania campus offers the splendid Penn Museum

Downtown Pittsburgh, where the Allegheny and Monongahela converge to form the Ohio River

of archaeology and anthropology.

At the opposite end of the state, **Pittsburgh** has morphed from a gritty steel town into one of the nation's most livable cities, an astonishing transformation since its 1970s state of urban decay. The metropolis that steel magnate Andrew Carnegie built is also infused with his philanthropy. The Carnegie Museums of Pittsburgh comprises four distinct units: the Carnegie Museum of Art, the Carnegie Museum of Natural History, the Carnegie Science Center with its planetarium and submarine, and the Andy Warhol Museum. the latter includes the pop artist's personal memorabilia as well as his most famous pieces, including "Campbell Soup Cans" and "Marilyn Monroe". Pittsburgh's other famous family is responsible for the Senator John Heinz History Center, Heinz Hall

(home of the Pittsburgh Symphony), Heinz Memorial Chapel on the University of Pittsburgh campus, and Heinz Field, where the Steelers host other NFL teams. Perched at the confluence of three rivers—the Allegheny, Monongahela, and Ohio—Point State Park offers a blend of nature, recreation, and history, including Fort Pitt blockhouse, the only remnant of Pittsburgh's pivotal role in the 18th-century French and Indian War. Schenley Park, the city's most popular green space, includes the Phipps Conservatory and Botanical Gardens. In the East End district, the Frick Pittsburgh complex of historical buildings and museums allows visitors to experience what it was like to live in Pittsburgh's Gilded Age. Across the Monongahela, the Duquesne Incline funicular

railway whisks passengers to the top of Mount Washington in two original 1877 cable cars.

CAPITALISM

The 600-room Pennsylvania State Capitol in Harrisburg was designed by Philadelphia architect Joseph Miller Huston, who envisioned the building as a "palace of art," blending global motifs that feature the state's historical achievements. His crowning achievement was a 272-foot (83 m) dome based on Saint Peter's Basilica in Rome. President Teddy Roosevelt attended the capitol's dedication in 1906. Part of the capitol complex, the State Museum of Pennsylvania has collected more than five million items spanning from the state's prehistory to the present day.

LANDSCAPES

Pennsylvania's sliver of Lake Erie shoreline (51 miles/82 km) is punctuated by the long, sandy peninsula that embraces **Presque Isle State Park.** Called the Sheltering Arm of the Great Spirit by the Erie Indians who once inhabited the area, the peninsula was later used by Commodore Matthew C. Perry to construct and shelter his fleet during the War of 1812.

The vast **Pennsylvania Wilds** encompasses pristine forest and mountains between Youngsville and Williamsport, an area that includes Allegheny National Forest and four state forests. The region also embraces Pine Creek Gorge (Pennsylvania's answer to the Grand Canyon), Allegheny Reservoir with its myriad water sports, and the Little League baseball complex in Williamsport. Nearby State College is home to **Penn State University** and its Palmer Museum of Art, Matson Museum of Anthropology, The Arboretum, and the Millbrook Marsh Nature Center. Here, too, is Beaver Stadium, home to the Nittany Lions of college football fame.

The star attraction of southwest Pennsylvania is Frank Lloyd Wright's **Fallingwater** house in Mill Run. Built between 1936 and 1939, the home features tiers that extend 30 feet (9 m) over a waterfall and is furnished with pieces designed by the architect. The **Flight 93 National Memorial** near Shanksville honors those who gave their lives to thwart the terrorist hijack of a United Airlines flight on September 11, 2001, while the nearby **Johnstown Flood National Memorial** recalls one of the largest natural disasters in American history, the 1889 deluge that took the lives of more than 2,000 people.

Gettysburg National Military Park marks the site of the most pivotal battle of the Civil War, an epic three-day clash in July of 1863 that ended in 23,000 killed, wounded, and captured on *each* side. The park includes one of the best visitor center museums in the entire National Park System, as well as informative battlefield landmarks. Soldiers' National Cemetery is the final resting place of

George Washington's winter headquarters at Valley Forge National Historical Park

many of the Union dead as well as the place where President Lincoln delivered his immortal Gettysburg Address.

About 15 miles (24 km) east of Harrisburg, the aromatic town of **Hershey** is a mecca for chocolate lovers and headquarters to the nation's largest chocolate factory, founded in 1903 by Milton S. Hershey. The leisure park Hershey created for his factory workers has evolved into the eclectic Hersheypark, with more than 70 rides and shows, a water park, and resort hotels. Allied attractions include ZooAmerica, the interactive

Waterfalls course through old-growth forest in Ricketts Glen State Park in northern Pennsylvania.

Hershey Story museum, the Hershey's Chocolate World factory tour, and Hershey Gardens.

Just beyond Hershey are Lancaster County and the **Pennsylvania Dutch Country,** where farmers and artisans trace their roots to 17th- and 18th-century German immigrants. Called the "plain people" because of their simple, bucolic lifestyles, more than 25 different Amish, Mennonite, and Brethren groups inhabit the region. Buggy tours and farm visits are available across the county. Strasburg is known for both Amish culture and railroad history, with steam train excursions and the Railroad Museum of Pennsylvania boasting an ever expanding collection of vintage locomotives and cars. The Village of Intercourse is famous for its quilt museum and country stores flush with Amish foods and crafts. To the west, the American Music Theatre (AMT) in Lancaster schedules more than 300 events each year.

Created by Pierre S. du Pont on land pioneered by Quaker farmers, **Longwood Gardens** is one of the nation's horticultural showcases, more than a thousand acres (405 ha) of formal gardens, meadows, and woodland in the Brandywine Valley south of Philadelphia. Half an hour north,

Valley Forge National Historical Park is where George Washington and his Continental Army camped during the winter of 1777–1778. The park's 10-mile (16 km) Encampment Tour Route features nine major stops and can be explored by car, foot, bike, or National Park Service trolley. ∎

HIDDEN TREASURES

• **Mütter Museum (Philadelphia):** specializes in such anatomical oddities as the skeleton of the world's tallest man and the death cast of the original Siamese Twins

• **Pittsburgh's North Side:** home to a number of offbeat and unusual attractions including the Randyland art house, Bicycle Heaven museum and bike shop, and the National Aviary with its 200 bird species from around the world

• **National Civil War Museum:** Even though no battles took place in Harrisburg, the city boasts one of the

nation's largest collections of weapons, uniforms, and other artifacts presented without bias toward the North or the South.

• **Eisenhower National Historic Site (Gettysburg):** preserves the house and farm where Ike hosted global leaders Winston Churchill, Nikita Khrushchev, and Charles de Gaulle, and where he later retired

• **Eastern State Penitentiary (Philadelphia):** once home to such infamous inmates as Al Capone and Willie Sutton, now has daytime and spooky night tours

Rhode Island

America's smallest state packs a big punch—a blend of beaches, bays, and bucolic countryside, along with the bright lights of resurgent Providence and the breezy seaside charm of Newport and Block Island. The first of the 13 Colonies to declare independence from the British, Rhode Island revels in its rich past and its intensely creative present.

TOURISM INFORMATION

Rhode Island Tourism offers information on various aspects of visiting the state on its website: visitrhode island.com.

• **Providence-Warwick Visitor Information Center**
Rhode Island Convention Center
One Sabin St.
Providence, RI 02903
Tel 401/751-1177 or 800/233-1636

GTECH Center
10 Memorial Blvd.
Providence, RI 02906
Tel 401/456-0200
goprovidence.com

• **Newport Gateway Visitors Center**
23 America's Cup Ave.
Newport, RI 02840
Tel 401/849-8048
discovernewport.org

• **Bristol Visitors Center**
400 Hope St.
Bristol, RI 02809
Tel 401/410-0040
explorebristolri.com

• **Rhode Island State Parks**
riparks.com

CITIES

The settlement that religious rebel Roger Williams founded in 1636 would be unrecognizable to the Puritan leader today. **Providence** endured the boom-and-bust industrial age before reshaping itself as a 21st-century renaissance city that melds business, culture, and extreme livability. The historic neighborhood of Downcity has three distinct parts: the Financial District, Arts District, and Capital Center. In addition to manifold shops and restaurants, Downcity is home to the Providence Performing Arts Center. On the other side of the Providence River are venerable Brown University and the Rhode Island School of Design (RISD), where the RISD Museum seeks to inspire and educate through a textile collection spanning ancient Egyptian times to present day, as well as painting, sculpture, and other media. Benefit Street, hub of Providence during the colonial and early federal periods, is flanked by a mixture of beautifully restored period buildings and modern structures. The hilltop John Brown House (1786)—built by the merchant and

Perusing artwork in a gallery at the RISD Museum

slave trader who helped endow Brown University—is considered the state's finest example of 18th-century domestic architecture. On the north side of downtown, the Woonasquatucket River waterfront has morphed from urban decay to urbane hangout through a massive renewal project that includes the indoor Providence Place mall and outdoor Riverwalk area. Visitors can cruise the river in Venetian-style gondolas or trek pedestrian bridges to Waterplace Park on the north bank. Riverwalk hosts more than 100 summer WaterFire events, when

Newport Harbor attracts boats of all sizes, from yachts to dinghies.

bonfires illuminate music acts, street performers, and vendors. With its strong Italian-American community, Federal Hill is the place for pasta, pizza, and other Mediterranean eats. Roger Williams Park in south Providence offers various attractions, from a zoo and botanical center to lakes, trails, historic buildings, and a vintage 1890s carousel.

Tucked at the bottom end of Aquidneck Island, **Newport** is celebrated for its seafaring heritage and aristocratic pedigree. The Preservation Society of Newport County manages 10 palatial "summer cottages" of the rich and famous of yesteryear. These include The Elms (1901), modeled after an 18th-century French château and commissioned by Edward J. Berwind, who made his fortune in coal. The

Breakers (1895), an Italian Renaissance manse with 70 rooms, is where railroad tycoon Cornelius Vanderbilt once spent his seaside getaways. Marble House (1892) was the summer home of Mr. and Mrs. William K. Vanderbilt, while Rosecliff (1898–1902) was built for Nevada silver heiress Theresa Fair Oelrichs. The glamorous Doris Duke inherited Rough Point when she was just 12 years old and later led efforts to save dozens of historic structures around Newport. Bowen's Wharf preserves a cluster of 18th-century maritime commercial buildings, many of which are now occupied by shops and restaurants. The waterfront also tenders various types of cruises around the harbor and nearby Narragansett Bay on schooners, speedboats, catamarans, and

America's Cup yachts. Visitors can also explore Newport's rocky shoreline via scenic Ocean Drive or the 3.5-mile (6 km) Cliff Walk National

CAPITALISM

Weekday tours of the Rhode Island State House in Providence include a replica of the Liberty Bell, battle flags from various wars, and Gilbert Stuart's lifelike portrait of George Washington. Its massive top is the world's fourth largest self-supporting marble dome, following Saint Peter's Basilica in Rome, the Minnesota State Capitol, and the Taj Mahal in India. Built over nine years (1894–1905), it's the state's seventh capitol building.

Recreation Trail. The International Tennis Hall of Fame in historic Newport Casino displays a large collection of tennis memorabilia and offers access to the facility's 13 outdoor grass courts. The nation's oldest place of Jewish worship, Touro Synagogue was founded in 1763. Fort Adams State Park, which revolves around an early-19th-century coastal bastion protecting the mouth of Newport Harbor, hosts many annual events from the Great Chowder Cook-Off to the Newport Jazz Festival.

LANDSCAPES

They don't call it the Ocean State for nothing. Rhode Island may be the smallest in land area, but it ranks 22nd in total coastline, a deeply indented shore with numerous coves, bays, and islands that add up to nearly 400 miles (644 km). The tiny state also boasts more than 100 beaches, including **South Shore Beach** in Little Compton, with its long crescent strand, great ocean views, beachfront RV camping, and a hinterland speckled with more than 60 historic cemeteries and buildings, including the 1692 Wilbor House.

Narragansett Bay is ringed by numerous strands including Narragansett Town Beach with its many activities. Roger W. Wheeler State Park, named after the man who created the Rhode Island state life-saving system, offers a relatively quiet beach protected by a breakwater. South Kingstown Town Beach at Matunuck tenders a popular boardwalk, playground, and beach sports. Other fine beaches include the long sandy isthmus at Napatree Point near Watch Hill, and the twin strands on either side of Weekapaug village.

Near the northern end of Narragansett Bay, **Bristol**'s seafaring heritage includes the Herreshoff Marine Museum and America's Cup Hall of Fame on the grounds of the boatyard where U.S. yachts were built for eight America's Cup races. The museum also organizes classic yacht regattas, operates a sailing school, and is dedicated to keeping the art

of yacht design and restoration alive. Overlooking the bay, the 45-room Blithewold Mansion was built in the early 20th century to resemble a 17th-century English country manor. The home's vast garden includes one of the East Coast's largest giant sequoias.

Opened in 1793, **Slater Mill Historic Site** in Pawtucket was the nation's first successful cotton-spinning factory. The riverside complex was restored in the 1920s and transformed into one of the first industrial museums on U.S. soil, hosting exhibits on the birth of the American textile industry, living-history programs, and a variety of workshops. **McCoy Stadium,** home of the Pawtucket Red Sox of the International League, is considered one of the best places in the nation to catch a minor league baseball game.

The **Blackstone River Valley National Heritage Corridor** highlights important industrial revolution sights between Pawtucket and Woonsocket in northern Rhode Island. Along the way are the Great Road

A lively scene at Bannister's Wharf, Newport

Racing in Narragansett Bay aboard champion yachts *Weatherly* and *American Eagle*

Historic District, Blackstone River State Park, the old Albion Bridges, Wright's Dairy Farm and Bakery, and the Museum of Work and Culture, which presents the little-told story of 19th-century French-Canadian farmers who left Quebec to labor in the textile mills of Rhode Island.

Located about 10 miles (16 km) off the Rhode Island mainland and not far from the eastern end of Long Island, **Block Island** boasts 17 miles (27 km) of free public beach and 20 square miles (52 sq km) of bucolic New England countryside. Ferries connect the island to Point Judith, Rhode Island; New London, Connecticut; and Fall River, Massachusetts; and there are flights from Westerly State Airport in Washington County. Crescent Beach on the east shore offers the best facilities, but Mohegan Bluffs on the south

coast flaunts the most spectacular stretch of shore, 151 steps down to the sand from the cliff tops. New Shoreham is home to the ferry docks, restaurants, hotels, art galleries, and the Old Harbor Historic District. Scattered around the island

are the Victorian-era Southeast Lighthouse and Manisses Animal Farm, while there is excellent bird-watching around the Great Salt Pond and Block Island National Wildlife Refuge, at the north end. ■

FESTIVALS

- **Newport Winter Festival:** 10 days of nonstop music, food, and various types of fun; February

- **Great Chowder Cook-Off (Newport):** Clam fans from around New England flock to this outdoor feast at Fort Adams; early June.

- **Gaspee Days (Warwick):** A parade, road races, fireworks, concerts, and colonial living-history encampment commemorate the 1772 burning of the

British revenue schooner H.M.S. *Gaspee* by Rhode Island patriots; June.

- **Newport Jazz Festival:** one of the world's top music fests since 1954; late July or early August

- **Vortex Sci-Fi, Fantasy, and Horror Film Festival (Providence):** Screenings are punctuated by forums with writers, directors, and actors from the three genres; late October.

South Carolina

The only triangular state, South Carolina has always marched to the tune of a different drummer. An early agitator for rebellion against the British, the state also played a crucial role in the South's secession from the Union and the nation's subsequent Civil War. Today the Palmetto State presents a less controversial patchwork quilt of historic sights, beach resorts, and wilderness areas.

TOURISM INFORMATION

*The South Carolina Depart-
ment of Parks, Recreation,
and Tourism has established
nine welcome centers around
the state, most of them
beside interstate and U.S.
highway gateways. Visit*
discoversouthcarolina.com.

- **Charleston Visitor Center**
375 Meeting St.
Charleston, SC 29403
Tel 843/724-7174
charlestoncvb.com

- **Hilton Head Island
Welcome Center**
Independence Blvd.
Hardeeville, SC 29909
Tel 843/784-6333
hhiwelcomecenter.com

- **Myrtle Beach Visitor
Information**
1200 N Oak St.
Myrtle Beach, SC 29577
Tel 843/626-7444
*myrtlebeachareachamber
.com*

- **National Park Service**
nps.gov/state/sc

CITIES

One of the belles of the South, charming **Charleston** hovers on a thumb-shaped peninsula between the Cooper and Ashley Rivers. The city revels in its colonial and antebellum past, its pivotal role in the Civil War, and its modern cultural vigor. The grand homes, magnificent churches, and other old buildings of Charleston's Historic District, French Quarter, and Naval Shipyard bear witness to the city's importance in the history of the U.S. Dating back to the late 18th century, the City Market is one of the nation's oldest public emporiums. Stretching down four city blocks, the continuous series of one-story market sheds shelter more than 300 merchants selling a wide variety of Low Country arts and crafts, including the region's famous sweetgrass basketry. Erected in 1841, the Greek Revival–style Market Hall includes a second-floor Confederate Museum operated by the United Daughters of the Confederacy. Meeting Street leads south from the market into a neighborhood of grand old mansions including the Nathaniel Russell House, built in 1808 by one of Charleston's richest merchants, with an elliptical staircase that spirals, unsupported, up three floors. The nearby Calhoun Mansion was built in 1876 in the Italianate style; a 25-year renovation has brought it back to its former glory. Although a private

The famed Avenue of Oaks at Boone Hall Plantation

Saint Philip's Church at twilight in Charleston's French Quarter

residence, the mansion is open to the public for tours. At the tip of the peninsula, Battery Park and White Point Garden offers views across the bay to Fort Sumter, Castle Pinckney, and Sullivan's Island. North of the market, Meeting Street runs into Wragg Mall and its various landmarks. The Charleston Museum, founded in 1773, is best known for its exhibits on Low Country history, Charleston silver, weaponry, historic textiles, natural history, and ancient Egyptian artifacts. Across the square, the Aiken-Rhett House (1818) retains its original outbuildings, including the kitchens, slave quarters, and animal sheds. On the other side of the Ashley River, Charles Towne Landing State Historic Site marks where

English settlers first arrived in 1670. The park includes archaeological exhibits on the early settlement, a replica 17th-century sailing ship, a natural habitat zoo, and extensive gardens.

Across the Cooper River from downtown Charleston, Patriots Point Naval and Maritime Museum features the aircraft carrier U.S.S. *Yorktown,* the U.S.S. *Clamagore* submarine, and the U.S.S. *Laffey,* a World War II destroyer that also served in the Korean War. Aquarium Wharf is home to both the family-friendly South Carolina Aquarium and the National Park Service visitor center for Fort Sumter National Monument, where the first shots of the Civil War were fired. Ferries to the

island bastion depart from here.

Columbia is the state's capital and largest city. Established in the

---

STATE OF THE ART

- **Best movies:** *The Great Santini* (1979) and *Glory* (1989)

- **Best books:** *The Prince of Tides* by Pat Conroy and *The Secret Life of Bees* by Sue Monk Kidd

- **Best music:** the classic funk of James Brown and the contemporary country of Josh Turner

- **Best art:** the chromatic folk art of William H. Johnson

- **Best play:** *Porgy and Bess* by George Gershwin

mid-18th century at a fall line in the Congaree River, it was one of the cities that Major General William Tecumseh Sherman torched on his destructive March to the Sea. Rising from the ashes of war, the South Carolina State House and its garland of palmetto trees still strike a commanding pose. Located on the Horseshoe of the University of South Carolina campus, the McKissick Museum focuses on the human and natural history of the southeast. Along the river, the South Carolina State Museum offers four floors of local nature, science, technology, art, and culture. Columbia's Riverfront Park provides a shady respite for walkers, cyclists, runners, and people-watchers opposite the Riverbanks Zoo and Garden.

LANDSCAPES

South Carolina's rustic **Low Country** offers a slice of the Old South, historic homes that bring insight into antebellum plantation life as well as the opportunity to appreciate splendid architecture and gardens. Built in 1676 by the Drayton family, Magnolia Plantation and Gardens on the Ashley River is currently on its 13th generation of family ownership. Ten rooms are open for visitors, and a one-hour tram tour takes visitors through the famed gardens, first opened to the public in 1870. Nearby Middleton Place provides a variety of ways to explore the 18th-century rice plantation, including a house tour, horse-drawn carriage tour, garden overview, and nature walks. Its thoughtful African American Focus Tour explores the lives of the plantation's African-American slaves and freedmen. Boone Hall Plantation has been a working plantation for more than 320 years and offers tours of the plantation home, slave cabins, smokehouse, stables, and gardens, and visitors can also pick their own fruits and vegetables.

White-water enthusiasts head for the swift-flowing Broad and Saluda Rivers near Columbia or the Chattooga River to the northwest—all offer some of the best rafting and paddling in the southeastern U.S. Another iconic river forms the nucleus of **Congaree National Park,** which is designated as an international biosphere reserve. A globally significant bird habitat, the park shelters an array of wildlife including alligators, bobcats, coyotes, and deer. Much of the park is floodplain forest—the largest tract

The South Carolina State House and the state tree, the palmetto

of old-growth bottomland hardwoods left in the U.S.—with many world champion trees, including the planet's largest and tallest lob-lolly pines.

The state's unrelenting flatness finally peters out near Cleveland, where the Piedmont rises into a small section of the Blue Ridge Escarpment. **Caesars Head State Park** gets its name from a prominent granite outcrop that rises 3,200 feet (975 m) above sea level: It's only a short hike from the parking lot to the spectacular Caesars Head Overlook. Another popular spot in the park is Raven Cliff Falls, best viewed from a suspension bridge accessed via a two-mile (3 km) trail. Other trails lead to nearby Jones Gap State Park and Mountain Bridge Wilderness Area.

South Carolina's coast transitions from a warren of Sea Islands in the south to long stretches of sandy beach in the north. Developed as a resort island in the 1950s after a new bridge finally connected it with the mainland, **Hilton Head** has evolved into one of the leading holiday destinations along the eastern seaboard. Upscale hotels and golf courses sprawl along the island's 12 miles (19 km) of white-sand beach. The Arts Center of Coastal Carolina offers a year-round slate of exhibits and

Fun, sun, and Ferris wheels await visitors at Myrtle Beach.

performances, while wildlife-watchers head for Pinckney Island National Wildlife Refuge. Boating, tennis, bike trails, fishing charters, and seafood restaurants round out the Hilton Head scene.

Fifteen miles north (24 km) of Hilton Head as the crow flies, **Beaufort** presents a totally different Sea Island experience. Bay Street along the Harbor River is a collage of art galleries, trendy restaurants, and antebellum mansions shaded by moss-covered trees. Built around 1804, the federal-style John Mark Verdier House is decorated with Civil War–era

furnishings and artifacts. Farther north are the resort islands of Edisto, Seabrook, Kiawah, and Folly. South Carolina's north shore is dominated by another huge resort area—**Myrtle Beach.** More than 13 million visitors per year are attracted to Myrtle's 60 miles (97 km) of wide, sandy beach, shopping and dining, and varied recreation opportunities from water sports to carnival rides. Also of note are Ripley's Aquarium, the Wheels of Yesteryear classic car collection, and the Franklin G. Burroughs–Simeon B. Chapin Art Museum. ∎

LOCAL FLAVOR

• **Frogmore stew:** This popular Low Country boil is a blend of shrimp, sausage, and corn on the cob. It's a legendary menu item at Gullah Grub. *877 Sea Island Pkwy, St. Helena Island*

• **She-crab soup:** Meat and roe from a

female crab plus dollops of cream and just a touch of sherry, a specialty at 82 Queen. *82 Queen St., Charleston*

• **Fried okra:** The annual Irmo Okra Strut Festival in September is the best place to try variations of the deep-fried

southern veggie, or pop into a Lizard's Thicket restaurant any time of year. *7569 St. Andrews Rd., Irmo*

• **Shrimp and grits:** Try the Carolina standby at the annual World Grits Festival every April. *St. George*

South Dakota

From the "Coyote State" to the "Land of Infinite Variety," South Dakota has held many nicknames over the years. But this Plains state is perhaps best known for the presidential facade of Mount Rushmore. Split in half by the Missouri River, South Dakota extends from the eastern farmlands that channel Midwestern values to the western Black Hills with their Wild West vibe.

CITIES

Although founded in the 1870s, **Sioux Falls** has been a gathering place of Native Americans for hundreds of years, thanks to the thunderous falls of the Big Sioux River. The cascade tumbles through Falls Park on the north side of downtown, with viewpoints from the city's visitor information center's observation tower as well as the Falls Overlook Cafe in a restored 1908 hydroelectric plant. Downtown Sioux Falls safeguards a number of historic structures, including the Old Courthouse Museum, built with local pink quartzite and offering three floors of regional history exhibits, a restored circuit courtroom, and 16 art deco wall murals. Pettigrew Home and Museum, the 1889 Queen Anne–style home of South Dakota's first senator (Richard Pettigrew), gives a good picture of Sioux Falls in the late 1800s. Great Plains Zoo in Sherman Park houses more than 1,000 animals from around the world, while the adjacent Delbridge Museum of Natural History features some 150 mounted animals, including many endangered species. Good Earth State Park at Blood Run preserves a riparian venue that served as an important trading place and ceremonial spot for Native American peoples from A.D. 1300 to 1700. In addition to its historic features, the park tenders biking, hiking, and birding opportunities along the Big Sioux River.

At the opposite end of the state, **Rapid City** is also named for local white water, in this case the once volatile Rapid Creek, which flows swiftly down from the Black Hills. Called the "City of Presidents" for the parade of visiting U.S. chief executives on their way to Mount Rushmore or the Black Hills, the downtown area features life-size bronze statues of every president, rendered by five local artists. The historic Hotel Alex Johnson (1928) is worth a peek for the richly decorated lobby. Right behind the hotel, funky Art Alley is an outdoor gallery of works by various local artists. The nearby Dahl Arts Center offers a more formal setting, five galleries of contemporary art along with an

TOURISM INFORMATION

For more information on South Dakota and its 13 staffed information centers, visit the state Department of Tourism website: travelsouth dakota.com.

- **Falls Park Visitor Information Center**
900 N Phillips Ave.
Sioux Falls, SD 57105
Tel 605/367-7430
visitsiouxfalls.com

- **Black Hills Visitor Information Center**
1851 Discovery Circle
Rapid City, SD 57701
Tel 605/355-3700
blackhillsbadlands.com

- **National Park Service**
nps.gov/state/sd

A horse and wagon in the restored gold rush town of Deadwood

Washington, Jefferson, T. R. Roosevelt, and Lincoln chiseled in granite at Mount Rushmore

interactive children's gallery. One of the highlights is the 180-foot (55 m) Cyclorama Mural of American economic history painted by Bernard P. Thomas. On the city's southern fringe, the America's Founding Fathers exhibit blends lifelike statues of all 47 men who signed the Declaration of Independence with a 20-minute historical narration inside a scaled-down replica of Independence Hall that also includes a Liberty Bell visitors can ring.

LANDSCAPES

South Dakota's celebrated **Black Hills** derive their name from the Lakota people, who thought the vegetation made the hills look dark from a distance. Locals divide the Black Hills into southern and northern sectors. The best known attraction of the southern hills is **Mount Rushmore National Memorial,** which famously features the 60-foot-high (18 m) sculpted heads of George Washington, Thomas Jefferson, Theodore Roosevelt, and Abraham Lincoln carved into the naked granite. They were chiseled by Danish-American Gutzon Borglum and his son Lincoln Borglum between 1927 and 1941, when a lack of funding forced the project to end before the presidential upper torsos were completed. Located two miles (3.2 km) from Mount Rushmore, the National Presidential Wax Museum imparts an apolitical roundup of each president along with artifacts such as President Bill Clinton's red-white-and-blue saxophone and the controversial "hanging chad" ballot boxes from Florida's 2000 presidential election.

Over on the other side of Harney Peak—by some measurements the highest point in the U.S. east of the Rockies—an even larger sculpture is still in the making. Polish-American artist Korczak Ziolkowski worked on the immense **Crazy Horse Memorial** from 1948 until his death in 1982. Friends and family continue to refine a work that will eventually be 641 feet (195 m) long and 563 feet (172 m) high when completed. From mid-May to mid-October, a laser-light show is projected on the sculpture each night. On the grounds of the memorial, the Indian Museum of North America and the adjoining Native American Educational & Cultural Center feature more than 12,000 modern and historic items, from pre-Columbian to contemporary times.

Another "southern" attraction is **Custer State Park** with its four

lakes, rock-climbing walls, and trail system. A herd of 1,300 bison roam freely throughout the park, as well as pronghorn antelope, elk, deer, wild turkeys, and feral burros. The area also embraces the intriguing hidden worlds of Wind Cave National Park and Jewel Cave National Monument. The Mammoth Site in **Hot Springs** is an active paleontological dig with the largest concentration of mammoth remains in the world. The bones of three woolly mammoths and 58 Columbian mammoths have been discovered here.

The northern hills are anchored by historic **Deadwood,** founded in the 1870s during the Black Hills gold rush and the epitome of a wide-open Wild West town. The Adams Museum and House explores Deadwood's real and storied past, while the Days of '76 Museum

ROAD TRIPS

Great Drives across the Mount Rushmore State:

- Peter Norbeck National Scenic Byway through the Black Hills (68 miles/109 km)

- Wildlife Loop Road in Custer State Park (18 miles/29 km)

- Native American Scenic Byway between Chamberlain, South Dakota, and Cannon Ball, North Dakota (350 miles/ 563 km)

- The Oyate Trail (Highway 18) between Vermillion and Maverick Junction (389 miles/626 km)

honors its first pioneers and prospectors. Other sights include the Broken Boot Gold Mine and the

The enormous annual Sturgis Motorcycle Rally

Homestake Adams Research and Cultural Center (HARCC) with its archival materials, which are available to the public. Deadwood is also home to 30 Vegas-style casinos with slot machines, blackjack, and poker.

East of Deadwood, **Sturgis** is renowned for the world's largest annual gathering of motorcycle enthusiasts. First staged in 1938, the Sturgis Motorcycle Rally has evolved from motorbike stunts and races into an eclectic festival that attracts around a million people each summer. The Sturgis Motorcycle Museum and Hall of Fame displays a variety of motorcycles and memorabilia dating back to 1907.

Hidden amid the prairie east of the Black Hills, **Minuteman Missile National Historic Site** is the only National Park Service unit that honors the significance of the Cold War and the intercontinental ballistic missile that became such an important deterrent. Nearby **Badlands National Park** protects a vast expanse of fantastically eroded geology that also contains some of the world's richest fossil beds. The park's Fossil Preparation Lab is open to the public May to September, and the Badlands can be explored year-round along the 22-mile (35 km) Loop Road with panoramic overlooks. Near the park's northeast entrance, Prairie Homestead comprises an original sod dugout home and farmstead built in 1909 by Badlands pioneers.

Other memories of early Dakota settlers are sprinkled throughout the middle of the state. Scattered around **De Smet** are various locations featured in the life of Laura Ingalls Wilder and her beloved books, including a one-room school, Surveyor's House, and the Discovery Center where visitors can dress up like pioneers, try a treadle sewing

The landscape is crumpled and brightly colored in Badlands National Park.

machine, or experience braille. A self-guided tour leads to 50 sites that Wilder mentioned in her Little House books. Just west of Madison, **Prairie Village** comprises 40 antique-packed historic buildings, plus agricultural displays, a sawmill, a steam carousel,

and an operating railroad. Eight locations in **Wessington Springs** are listed on the National Register of Historic Places including the restored 1905 Opera House, Alpena Bathhouse, Anne Hathaway Cottage replica, and Shakespeare Garden. ∎

HIDDEN TREASURES

Some of South Dakota's lesser known Native American sights:

• **Akta Lakota Museum & Cultural Center (Chamberlain):** This complex on the campus of Saint Joseph's Indian School is dedicated to understanding the past, present, and future of the Northern Plains Indians.

• **Dakota Sunset Museum (Gettysburg):** safeguards the

40-ton (36 metric ton) Medicine Rock, embedded with ancient human footprints and a handprint; it is considered sacred by the Lakota people

• **Bear Butte State Park:** sacred mountain where many Native Americans religious ceremonies are held

• **The Museum at Wounded Knee (Pine Ridge Reservation):** dedicated to those who lost their lives in the 1890 massacre

Tennessee

Tennessee isn't all about music, but with melodious Memphis and Nashville as its biggest cities, the Volunteer State certainly knows how to carry a tune. Wedged between the Appalachians and the Mississippi River, Tennessee tenders a wide variety of landscapes and experiences, from the nation's most visited national park to bloody Civil War battlefields to musical landmarks of country, blues, and rock and roll.

CITIES

Blues and barbecue are the twin trademarks of **Memphis.** Named after an ancient Egyptian city and celebrated as the home of the King of Rock and Roll, the moody western Tennessee metropolis rests on the bluffs above the Mississippi River. Memphis is mentioned in more than a thousand songs—more than any other earthly city—many sung downtown in Beale Street's renowned blues clubs and celebrated at the Memphis Rock 'n' Soul Museum. Elvis Presley's home for more than 20 years,

Graceland offers a multimedia tour leading visitors past the famous green shag–carpeted Jungle Room and the Meditation Garden, where Elvis and other family members are laid to rest. Across the street, satellite museums feature his pink Cadillac, tour bus, and private plane. In 1953, Elvis recorded his first record at Sun Studio on Union Avenue, considered by many as the birthplace of rock and roll. The building that now houses the Stax Museum of American Soul Music was once the recording home of Otis Redding, Isaac Hayes, Booker T. and the

MGs, and other legends of soul. Tucked in among the music industry displays is Hayes's gold-plated Cadillac. The National Civil Rights Museum, dedicated to the struggle for racial equality, is set inside the Lorraine Motel (where Martin Luther King, Jr., was assassinated in 1968) and adjacent buildings including the guesthouse where James Earl Ray fired the fatal shot.

Nashville is synonymous with country music, a tradition that stretches back to the 1920s when the Grand Ole Opry was founded. Since then, everyone from Hank Williams and Johnny Cash to Dolly Parton and Taylor Swift have come here to cut their country music teeth and their first records. The sprawling Country Music Hall of Fame and Museum spans the entire history of country music from the fiddle tunes and folk songs of early

TOURISM INFORMATION

Tennessee's Department of Tourist Development operates 14 welcome centers and maintains brochures in 18 rest areas across the state. Visit tnvacation.com.

- **Nashville Visitor Centers**
501 Broadway
Nashville, TN 37203
Tel 615/259-4747 or
866/830-4440
150 Fourth Ave. N
Nashville, TN 37219
Tel 615/259-4730
visitmusiccity.com

- **Memphis Visitor Center**
3205 Elvis Presley Blvd.
Memphis, TN 38116
Tel 901/543-5333
memphistravel.com

- **National Park Service**
nps.gov/state/tn

Hunter Hayes performing at the Country Music Hall of Fame in Nashville.

Clubs, bars, and restaurants pack three blocks of Beale Street in Memphis.

British settlers to the gospel hymns of African slaves to today's modern stars. The excellent museum's thousands of original items and artifacts include the beat-up Martin D-28 guitar on which Hank Williams, Sr., composed many a tune. Guided bus tours lead to RCA Studio B, which churned out more hits than any other U.S. music studio between 1957 and 1977. Of the 45,000 songs recorded inside this modest brick building on Music Row, around a thousand made it into the Billboard Top 10, including tunes by Elvis Presley, Roy Orbison, Charlie Pride, and Waylon Jennings. All of those artists performed at the redbrick Ryman Auditorium, the "Mother Church of Country Music," which was home to the Grand Ole Opry radio broadcasts and live shows for more than 30 years. Backstage tours are rife with

inside scoops and quirky tales of the stars. In 1974, the Grand Ole Opry moved to the modern Opryland development on the city's outskirts. Nearby attractions include the *General Jackson* paddle wheeler on the Cumberland River and Cooter's Place, a novelty store that doubles as

a *Dukes of Hazzard* museum. Nashville also offers visitors plenty of non-music history, including the Hermitage plantation, the home of President Andrew Jackson from 1804 until his death in 1845. In addition to the two-story Greek Revival manse filled with period

ROAD TRIPS

Great drives across the Volunteer State:

• Pasquo to Cypress Inn on the Tennessee stretch of the historic Natchez Trace Parkway, which follows an ancient trail used by Indians and settlers (100 miles/161 km)

• Cherohala Skyway across the Smoky Mountains between Tellico Plains, Tennessee, and Robbinsville, North Carolina (51 miles/82 km)

• Woodlands Trace through Land Between the Lakes National Recreation Area from Dover, Tennessee, to Grand Rivers, Kentucky (50 miles/80 km)

• Cherokee Warriors Path (aka the East Tennessee Crossing and Thunder Road) between Cumberland Gap and Del Rio (77 miles/124 km)

• Highway 85 between Monoville and Grimsley (80 miles/129 km)

furnishings and personal belongings, slave quarters and the tombs of President Jackson and his wife, Rachel, are preserved. Belle Meade Plantation—a popular spot for weddings, outdoor concerts, and Civil War reenactments—includes another immaculate Greek Revival mansion as well as a dairy, stables, carriage house, mausoleum, gardens, log cabin, and wine-tasting area. Located near the Vanderbilt University campus in Nashville's West End, Centennial Park flaunts walking trails, a sunken garden, and a full-scale replica of the Parthenon, erected in 1897 for the Tennessee Centennial Exposition.

LANDSCAPES

Rising 1,700 feet (518 m) above **Chattanooga** and the Tennessee River, Lookout Mountain in the state's southeastern corner provided a lofty venue for the Last Battle of the Cherokee in 1794 as well as the Battle of Lookout Mountain during the Civil War in 1863. Nowadays its varied attractions include panoramic views from Rock City, Ruby Falls

underground waterfall, and the world's steepest passenger railway. Among Chattanooga's other sights are the freshwater-focused Tennessee Aquarium, the Hunter Museum of American Art, and the Tennessee Valley Railroad Museum, with rides to Missionary Ridge and Chickamauga Battlefield. Also of note are Raccoon Mountain Caverns and the Moccasin Bend National Archeological District, with its copious Native American history.

During World War II, fuel for America's atom bombs was made at the **Oak Ridge National Laboratory.** Nowadays the former top-secret facility is open to visitors with three-hour tours of the rambling facility, including the X-10—the world's oldest nuclear reactor. Located on the campus of Lincoln Memorial University in **Harrogate,** the Abraham Lincoln Library and Museum boasts one of the world's largest collections of Lincolnabilia in a building funded by Colonel Sanders of Kentucky Fried Chicken fame.

Snuggled in the foothills of the Smoky Mountains, **Pigeon Forge** is

a live music hub, car-and-truck-show mecca, and all-around tourist town that attracts around 11 million visitors each year. Its main draw is Dollywood, a 150-acre (61 ha) theme park created by local Dolly Parton. Family-centric and thoroughly down-home, the park features thrill rides and concerts by Parton and others. Built to half scale of the original vessel, Titanic Pigeon Forge is a two-story museum surrounded by water to create the illusion of being at sea. Boarding tickets for the two-hour self-guided tour include the name of a real *Titanic* passenger (at the end you get to find out whether that passenger

Roller coasters at the Dollywood theme park

Sunrise from Oconaluftee Valley Overlook, Great Smoky Mountains National Park

survived). Pigeon Forge is also home to the Southern Gospel Museum and Hall of Fame as well as venues for dinner theater, comedy revues, magic shows, and music concerts.

Straddling the border between Tennessee and North Carolina, **Great Smoky Mountains National Park** is the nation's most visited, thanks to its diverse attractions and proximity to populous eastern states. The park's 850 miles (1,368 km) of trails—including 70 miles (113 km) of the Appalachian Trail—meander through thick woods and dusky mountains to secluded rivers, lakes, and mountaintops. More than 90 historic log buildings in the park have been preserved and rehabilitated. Highlights of the Tennessee side include Roaring Fork Motor Nature Trail, the Sugarlands and Cades Cove visitor centers, the 100-foot-high (30 m) Ramsey Cascades, Alum Cave Trail, and Chimney Tops summit.

Twenty miles (32 km) south of the state capital, charming **Franklin** revolves around a 16-block historic district flush with antique shops, bookstores, fashion boutiques, art galleries, and 19th-century homes. Many of country music's biggest names live here, and the local music scene is second only to nearby Nashville. To the southwest, **Shiloh National Military Park** preserves the place where the bloody 1862 Battle of Shiloh raged during the Civil War. First major battle of the Western Theater, the two-day clash resulted in a Union victory that lifted generals Ulysses S. Grant and William T. Sherman into the national spotlight. ■

LOCAL FLAVOR

• **Memphis barbecue:** Pitmasters slow-cook meats over a low hickory-wood fire in brick or cinder block "pits" at joints such as Payne's Bar-B-Q. Try the signature dish: a chopped pork sandwich with coleslaw. *1762 Lamar Ave., Memphis*

• **Turnip greens with pot liquor:** Loveless Cafe serves this bygone country favorite, a combination of fresh greens and the nutritious liquid they were boiled in. *8400 Tennessee Hwy 100, Nashville*

• **Moon pies:** Found throughout the state, this blend of graham crackers, marshmallow, and chocolate is traditionally washed down with RC Cola, a classic combo celebrated at the annual RC–Moon Pie Festival each June. *Bell Buckle*

• **Jack Daniels:** Although located in a "dry" county, the Jack Daniels distillery still serves up samples at the end of each tour. *182 Lynchburg Hwy, Lynchburg*

Texas

Stretching almost 900 miles (1,448 km) from east to west, Texas really is a massive territory. The Lone Star State terrain ranges from the sandy Gulf Coast and eastern piney woods to the rolling Hill Country, northern prairies, and desert landscapes out west. Scattered among the wide-open spaces, the state's metro areas present dramatic contrasts in urban form and function.

CITIES

The nickname "Big D" just about sums it up—everything is huge in **Dallas,** from its airport and football stadium to its downtown skyline and sprawling suburbs. Although oil fueled much of its growth, Dallas was also built on a bedrock of cotton, cattle, and railroads. Thousands of people each day make the pilgrimage to Dealey Plaza, where a large X marks the spot where President John F. Kennedy was shot. The Sixth Floor Museum in the Texas School Book Depository preserves the window perch where Lee Harvey Oswald

fired the fatal volley and presents exhibits about the assassination and JFK's presidency. Other worthwhile stops near the plaza include the Old Red Museum of Dallas County History and Culture, as well as the West End Historic District, its restored brick buildings now filled with shops and restaurants. The family-friendly Dallas World Aquarium sits beside the Arts District, a 30-block rectangle that includes the highly regarded Dallas Museum of Art and the serene indoor-outdoor Nasher Sculpture Center, where some 300 modern and contemporary pieces are rotated. Meyerson

TOURISM INFORMATION

The Texas Department of Transportation has established tourism visitor centers at a dozen different highway gateways around the state. Find out more at traveltex.com.

- **Dallas Tourist Information Center**
Old Red Courthouse
100 S Houston St.
Dallas TX 75202
Tel 214/571-1316
visitdallas.com

- **Houston Visitors Center**
1300 Avenida de las Americas
Houston, TX 77010
Tel 713/437-5556
visithoustontexas.com

- **San Antonio Visitor Information Center**
317 Alamo Plaza
San Antonio, TX 78205
Tel 210/207-6700 or
800/447-3372
visitsanantonio.com

- **National Park Service**
nps.gov/state/tx

- **Texas State Parks**
tpwd.texas.gov/state-parks

Symphony Center and the AT&T Performing Arts Center provide an epicenter of music, dance, and drama, while the Perot Museum of Nature and Science is a high-tech museum spread over six floors.

Dallas may have gone modern, but twin city **Fort Worth** continues to relish its cow town past. Stockyards National Historic District revolves around a frontier market area that once sold a million head of steer each year. Modern stockyard activities include daily cattle drives down Exchange Avenue, a weekly rodeo, and nightly line dancing at Billy Bob's Texas honky-tonk. More

The distinctive skyline of Dallas at sunset

Restaurants and outdoor dining along San Antonio's popular River Walk

Western lore awaits at the National Cowgirl Museum and Hall of Fame in the Fort Worth Cultural District on the south side of town. Two blocks away, the Amon Carter Museum of American Art boasts more than 300,000 works by American artists. Although much smaller, the Kimbell Art Museum houses an array of treasures ranging from prehistoric Asian pieces to paintings by Rembrandt situated across the street from the Modern Art Museum of Fort Worth. In addition to hosting the Fort Worth Botanic Garden, Trinity Park is a jumping-off point for the expansive Trinity River Trails System.

Houston, the state's largest city, provides a home base for some of the world's largest energy companies along with NASA's Johnson Space Center. Its visitor center expounds on the various aspects of American space exploration, while a tram tour includes both the historical and modern-day Mission Control. Epicenter of the local art scene, the Museum of Fine Arts, Houston (MFAH), has amassed around 65,000 pieces from ancient to modern art in its collection. The sprawling complex includes two gallery buildings, a sculpture garden, and two art schools. The Menil Collection flaunts one of the world's great private art assemblages and is spread across a 30-acre (12 ha) "neighborhood of art" in the city's Montrose district. Houston is also home to the world's largest medical complex—Texas Medical Center—where a fascinating Health Museum educates visitors of all ages about the human body.

With around two-thirds of its residents claiming Hispanic origin, **San Antonio** is now the most Latino of the nation's large cities, an irony not

CAPITALISM

In one of the more obscure conflicts in American history, the Texas Archive War of 1842 involved an audacious middle-of-the-night attempt to hijack the Republic of Texas archives as part of an effort to shift the state capital from Austin to Houston. Coming across the theft in progress, boarding-house owner Angelina Eberly fired a cannon at the hijackers and alerted the town guard, which eventually thwarted the paper snatching.

lost on aficionados of Alamo history. Dwarfed by modern high-rise buildings, the Alamo compound comprises an old Spanish mission church surrounded by shady gardens and historic outbuildings. A few blocks away, the pedestrian-friendly River Walk district offers a mosaic of outdoor cafés, artsy shops, boat rides, and the Briscoe Western Art Museum. Energetic visitors can also trek north along the River Walk to the Tobin Center for the Performing Arts and the San Antonio Museum of Art. The southern branch of the River Walk leads to the four historic Spanish chapels of San Antonio Missions National Historical Park. For a stunning panorama of the south Texas city, visitors can ascend the 750-foot (229 m) Tower of the Americas, centerpiece of the 1968 world's fair.

From the all-encompassing South by Southwest (SXSW) festival to the cries of "hook 'em horns!" that resonate across the University of Texas campus each fall, **Austin** is a capital city full of passion in politics, sports,

and the arts. Reminiscent of the U.S. Capitol building but in red stone, the Texas State Capitol offers free guided tours that bring to life the personalities who have walked its halls. Housed in the late artist's castlelike home and studio, the Elisabet Ney Museum displays examples of her lifelike busts of famous Texans. The Harry Ransom Center on the UT campus holds a copy of the Gutenberg Bible, the Woodward and Bernstein Watergate Papers, plus rare books and more. At the edge of the university, the LBJ Presidential Library and Museum includes a replica of the Oval Office, President Johnson's actual limousine from 1968, and many personal mementoes of the 36th president and his wife, Lady Bird.

LANDSCAPES

The world's largest barrier island, **Padre Island** stretches 115 miles (185 km) along the Gulf of Mexico south of Corpus Christi. While South Padre Island is renowned as a college spring break

ROAD TRIPS

Great drives in the Lone Star State:

• El Camino Real de los Tejas (Highway 21) from San Antonio to Milam (366 miles/589 km)

• U.S. 90 from El Paso (via Alpine) to San Antonio (578 miles/930 km)

• Highway 35 from Houston to Corpus Christi (206 miles/ 332 km)

• Bayous and Backwoods (Highway 87) from Galveston to Center (250 miles/402 km)

• Hill Country Drive (Highways 46, 16, and 470) from New Braunfels to Concan (123 miles/198 km)

destination, the northern part of the island is preserved in a natural wild state as Padre Island National Seashore. In addition to providing a safe nesting ground for sea turtles and numerous bird species, the park is known for excellent birding, boating, and fishing. Farther up the coast, **Galveston** offers 30 miles (48 km) of beaches as well as historic mansions, more than 20 art galleries, and the Lone Star Flight Museum.

Way out west, the mighty Rio Grande divides Texas from Mexico, a watery ribbon that includes recreation havens such as the Amistad Reservoir and **Big Bend National Park.** An incredible desert landscape chiseled with deep canyons and lofty mesas, the park is best explored by foot, on horseback, or via float trips along the muddy river. **Guadalupe Mountains National Park** protects another huge chunk of pristine

Rock climbing at Hueco Tanks State Park

Big Bend National Park is named for the turn the Rio Grande makes along the Mexican border.

terrain on the New Mexico border, as well as the world's best example of a Permian-period fossil reef. Just east of **El Paso,** Hueco Tanks State Park and Historic Site is both a rock-climbing mecca and sanctuary for thousands of Native American pictographs. El Paso itself is the state's most popular gateway into old Mexico and home to three Spanish chapels (San Elizario, Ysleta, and Socorro) that are among the oldest continually active missions in the United States.

Often called the Grand Canyon of Texas, multihued **Palo Duro Canyon** cuts 60 miles (97 km) through the heart of the panhandle just south of Amarillo. Thirty miles (48 km) of hiking, biking, and equestrian trails rise and fall through the canyon's various geologic layers.

During the summer, the state park presents an outdoor musical drama called *Texas* about the trials and triumphs of early pioneers. Almost like a state-within-a-state, **Texas Hill Country** spreads in a broad arc between Austin and San Antonio.

In addition to its karst topography and heavily wooded hills, the region is known for its heady blend of early Mexican and German immigrant cultures, a melting pot that produced many things that are now thought of as typically Texan. ■

HIDDEN TREASURES

• **Longhorn Cavern State Park (Burnet):** includes a Hill Country cave that provided refuge for Ice Age animals, Native Americans, Confederate soldiers, Wild West outlaws, and Prohibition bootleggers

• **Lost Maples State Natural Area (Vanderpool):** Maples left over from the last ice age flash their colors in the fall.

• **Lady Bird Johnson Wildflower Center (near Austin):** preserves native species and educates the public on the benefits of including wildflowers in landscaping

• **Orange Show Center for Visionary Art (Houston):** Postal worker Jeff McKissack spent more than 25 years creating this wacky folk art gallery from scrap collected from junkyards and abandoned buildings.

Utah

Dubbed the Beehive State for its diligent and hardworking Mormon pioneers, Utah could easily be called the Red Rock State or Recreation Wonderland. The state's varied landscapes lend themselves to all sorts of outdoor adventure, from white-water rafting on the Colorado River to scaling Zion canyons to skiing the slopes of Park City or bird-watching on the Great Salt Lake.

CITIES

Founded by Brigham Young and his followers in 1847, **Salt Lake City** has evolved from a Mormon stronghold into a diverse metropolis with an economy built on banking, technology, and tourism. Temple Square, the headquarters of the Church of Jesus Christ of Latter-day Saints (LDS) faith, includes the soaring Salt Lake Temple (1893) topped by a golden statue of the angel Moroni, the oval Tabernacle (1867) where the Mormon Tabernacle Choir performs, the neo-Gothic-style Assembly Hall (1882), and the famed Seagull Monument (1913). Arrayed around the square are other Mormon landmarks including the Church History Museum, the Family History Library, and the Beehive House, an official residence of Brigham Young, which has period furnishings and exhibits. Nearby rises the imposing Utah state capitol building and the Mormon Battalion Monument. Downtown Salt Lake is a more secular place, home to the Utah Museum of Contemporary Art (UMOCA), Abravanel Hall, and Discovery Gateway interactive children's museum in the giant Gateway Mall. On Washington Square, the Leonardo Museum embodies the artist's spirit by exploring the places and ways that science, technology, art, and creativity connect. Over on the city's east side, the University of Utah campus hosts the Utah Museum of Fine Arts, Red Butte Garden, the Natural History Museum of Utah, and the Fort Douglas Military Museum. Just off campus, This Is the Place Heritage Park offers a living-history experience that re-creates 19th-century Utah through pioneer activities, a Native American village,

TOURISM INFORMATION

The Utah Office of Tourism maintains an information center in Council Hall, across the street from the state capitol building in Salt Lake City. Visit utah.com for more info.

- **Utah Valley Convention & Visitors Bureau**
220 Center St., #100
Provo, UT 84601
Tel 801/851-2100
utahvalley.com

- **Park City Visitor Information Center**
1794 Olympic Pkwy.
Park City, UT 84060
Tel 435/658-9616
visitparkcity.com

- **Ogden Tourist Information**
2438 Washington Blvd.
Ogden, UT 84401
Tel 866/867-8824
visitogden.com

- **Zion Canyon Visitors Bureau**
118 Lion Blvd.
Springdale, UT 84767
Tel 435/772-0415
zionpark.com

- **National Park Service**
nps.gov/state/ut

- **Utah State Parks**
stateparks.utah.gov

Delicate Arch at Utah's Arches National Park

A skier exalts in the view above Salt Lake City.

indigenous wildlife, train rides, trail rides, and more. In Liberty Park, Tracy Aviary has grown from a private bird collection to a world-class facility with more than 400 feathered friends from around 140 species.

Forty-five miles (72 km) south of the state capital, **Provo** is another bastion of Mormon culture. In addition to 30,000 students, the sprawling campus of Brigham Young University hosts the BYU Museum of Art with 10 exhibition galleries inside a modern cement-and-glass structure conceived by architect James Langenheim. Among other campus high points are the BYU Museum of Paleontology, the BYU Museum of Peoples and Cultures, and the Monte L. Bean Life Science Museum. Provo Pioneer Village hosts workshops within frontier-era buildings relocated from all across Utah that include a schoolhouse, granary, and blacksmith shop. The scenic drive up Provo Canyon into the foothills of the Wasatch Range leads to white-water rafting and tubing spots as well as 607-foot (185 m) Bridal Veil Falls.

LANDSCAPES

The **Great Salt Lake** lies north-west of the city that bears its name. Its high salinity (variably 6 to 27 percent) makes it the largest salt lake in the Western Hemisphere and the fourth largest terminal lake in the world. It's also a magnet for migratory birds and the focus of legends about lake monsters and inland whales. The easiest access is from Antelope Island State Park, an elongated land mass that fluctuates between island and peninsula depending on the lake level. Here await backcountry trails, salty beaches, a marina with boat rentals, the historic Fielding Garr Ranch (1848), and a surprising array of wildlife. Near the lake's northern shore, Golden Spike National Historic Site at Promontory Summit marks the spot where the last (golden) spike was used to join the Central Pacific Railroad and the Union Pacific Railroad to form the first Transcontinental Railroad on May 10, 1869.

About 30 miles (48 km) south-east of Salt Lake City on the eastern slope of the Wasatch Range, **Park City** is a blend of historic mining town, film festival venue, and outdoor sports destination. Host of the

---

STATE OF THE ART

- **Best movies:** *Butch Cassidy & The Sundance Kid* (1969) and *Footloose* (1984)

- **Best books:** *The Executioner's Song* by Norman Mailer and *Riders of the Purple Sage* by Zane Grey

- **Best song:** "Salt Lake City" by The Beach Boys

- **Best art:** the pioneer-era photography of George Beard

- **Best TV show:** *Big Love*

2002 Winter Games, the town's major snow resorts—Deer Valley and Park City—make up the nation's largest concentration of lifts and skiable terrain. Utah Olympic Park, venue for several Winter Games events, now holds two museums, a zip line, and a bobsled course that visitors can run with a professional driver. Summer activities include lift-facilitated mountain biking and hiking.

Located in the Uinta Mountains on the border between Colorado and Utah, **Dinosaur National Monument** hosts one of the world's richest fossil fields. The remains of nearly 1,500 dinosaurs are embedded in the rocky facades of Carnegie Dinosaur Quarry, accessible from the Quarry Exhibit Hall. The two-state park also offers scenic drives, hiking trails, and river rafting, as well as winter sports.

Much of southern Utah is a red-rock wilderness spangled with national parks that encompass a wide array of geological landmarks. An 18-mile (29 km) scenic drive is one of the best ways to view

spectacular **Arches National Park** and many of the 2,000-plus natural stone arches that give the park its name. Nearby **Moab** on the Colorado River is a hotbed for whitewater rafting, rock climbing, and other outdoor adventure sports.

Many float trips head downriver into **Canyonlands National Park,** a massive expanse of canyons, mesas, natural arches, and cliffs formed by millions of years of wind and water erosion. While paved roads provide

access to the Needles District and Island in the Sky sections of the park, the rest can only be explored by foot, bike, boat, or four-by-four.

Farther downstream, **Glen Canyon National Recreation Area** marks the dramatic confluence of red rock and deep-blue water formed by the Glen Canyon Dam. Five marinas expedite boating and other water sports, as well as day trips to Rainbow Bridge—one of the world's largest and highest natural bridges—on the adjoining Navajo Nation.

The **Navajo Nation** also includes the Monument Valley Navajo Tribal Park with its scenic drives, hikes, and campgrounds set amid an extraordinary red-rock wilderness made famous by John Ford's many Western movies. On the northern outskirts of the reservation, Natural Bridges National Monument features ancient cliff dwellings and three natural bridges named Kachina, Owachomo, and Sipapu in honor of the region's indigenous peoples.

Scenic **Zion National Park** revolves around a deep canyon cut by the Virgin River, 15 miles (24 km) long and flanked by impressive

Hiking within the Narrows, the tightest section of Zion Canyon

A houseboat on Lake Powell in Glen Canyon National Recreation Area

sandstone structures including the Great White Throne, the Sentinel, and Angels Landing. Shuttle buses ferry visitors along the main park road, but hiking is the best way to explore Zion's colorful backcountry. In Springdale, gateway to the park, the Zion Canyon Giant Screen Theatre has IMAX movies about the park. The town's Bumbleberry Theatre and O. C. Tanner Amphitheater host live performances.

Bryce Canyon National Park, perched on the Paunsaugunt Plateau, features a spectacular wind-and-water eroded landscape of stone pillars and natural amphitheaters. Numerous hiking trails meander through this massive rock garden and the pine-studded forests along the rim. Visitors can also drive a scenic road to viewpoints or hop a sightseeing shuttle bus. The main attraction at nearby **Cedar Breaks**

National Monument is a half-mile-deep (0.8 km) natural amphitheater.

One of the nation's premier venues for wilderness mountain biking, **Capitol Reef National Park** preserves 242,000 acres (97,934 ha) of stunning erosion-carved canyons, cliffs, domes, and bridges along the Waterpocket Fold, a warp in the Earth's crust that is almost a hundred miles (161 km) long. ∎

LOCAL FLAVOR

Utah's Mormon menu is flavored with many distinctive dishes more commonly found at homes and potluck suppers than on restaurant menus:

• **Frog's eye salad:** Small acini-de-pepe pasta balls actually do resemble amphibian eyes, especially when

combined with pineapple, mandarin oranges, and marshmallows in this ambrosia-like salad.

• **Hawaiian haystack:** Steamed white rice, pineapple rings, chow mein noodles, and anything else in those Tupperware containers in the fridge make up this highly practical dish.

• **Funeral potatoes:** Created as comfort food for after-funeral meals, this casserole traditionally blends potatoes, chicken soup, and cornflakes.

• **Green Jell-o salad:** Utah's official state snack mixes lime gelatin, pineapple pieces, and cottage cheese, with whipped cream on top.

Vermont

Vermont squeezes between Lake Champlain and the Connecticut River Valley, a mosaic of water, woodlands, and rugged mountains that jealously guards its independent spirit. America's most rural state is dominated by thousands of farms, hundreds of quaint New England villages, and wilderness areas that offer myriad opportunities for summer hiking, winter snow sports, and astounding fall foliage.

CITIES

With just over 42,000 residents, **Burlington** is the least populous biggest city of any state. But small-town charm is what makes the lakeside metropolis so inviting. The city sprawls along Lake Champlain's eastern shore, and many of her institutions and attractions revolve around the water. The ECHO, Leahy Center for Lake Champlain offers habitats for more than 70 species of fish, frogs, and other freshwater creatures from around the world and entices humans with some 100 interactive learning experiences about lake ecology. The Island Line Trail, a 14-mile (23 km) hiking and biking route, follows an old railroad right-of-way that includes a "bike ferry" (summer only) over to Grand Isle. The trail also goes past waterfront parks with spectacular lake views, especially at sunset. Here, too, are docks for the Lake Champlain ferries as well as boat tours on modern sailboats, vintage schooners, or the *Northern Lights*, a replica of a 19th-century lake steamer. Flynn Center for the Performing Arts stages a wide array of music, drama, dance, workshops, and lectures in a magical art deco setting. Perched on the banks of the Winooski River, the Ethan Allen Homestead Museum provides insight into the flamboyant and often controversial patriot who helped found Vermont. The Fleming Museum of Art is located on the leafy campus of the University of Vermont on the east side of Burlington.

Montpelier lies on the other side of Mount Mansfield, about 38 miles (61 km) southeast of Burlington. With fewer than 8,000 people, it's by far the least-populated state capital. Beyond the statehouse, the city boasts several historical attractions

Relaxing on the shores of Lake Champlain

Autumn brings leaf-peepers to New England towns such as Montpelier.

including the Vermont History Museum and the Kellogg-Hubbard Library with its replicas of the Parthenon and Florence Duomo friezes. Montpelier also has a lively arts scene personified by summer stock at the Lost Nation Theater, the Capital City series of classical music concerts, and the T. W. Wood Gallery & Arts Center, which showcases the state's largest permanent art collection and hosts musical performances and lectures. Rock of Ages in neighboring **Barre** is a massive working granite quarry with tours of both the big pit and the cutting and polishing factory work.

LANDSCAPES

Floating about halfway between Burlington and the Quebec border, the **Lake Champlain Islands** offer more than 200 miles (322 km)

of shoreline as well as a variety of outdoor activities ranging from summer swimming and boating to winter ice fishing and cross-country skiing. Living up to its name, Grand Isle is far and away the largest, home to historic Hyde Log Cabin (built in 1783) and the quaint lakeshore village of South Hero with its pretty Snow Farm Vineyard and Winery. Bridges and causeways lead to other parts of the archipelago including North Hero and tiny Isle La Motte. Only three miles (5 km) wide and seven miles (11 km) long, La Motte features a portion of the Chazy Formation, the world's oldest coral reef, sheltered inside the Fisk Quarry Preserve. The reef took shape more than 440 million years ago, during the Ordovician period. The island's working quarry has produced the distinctive dark limestone used for the National Gallery of Art in Washington, D.C., and New York City's Radio City Music Hall, among other places.

Back on the mainland, Lake Champlain Maritime Museum in **Vergennes** presents exhibits on the history and underwater archaeology (aka shipwrecks) of the big blue water body. The museum's replica fleet includes the 1776 gunboat *Philadelphia,* the 1862 canal schooner *Lois McClure,* and the colonial-era bateau *Perseverance.* **Shelburne** is the home port of several interesting attractions, chief among them being the eclectic Shelburne Museum, hosting exhibits on everything from duck decoys, circus posters, and toys to

There's plenty of hiking in the Green Mountains, which run the length of Vermont.

American folk painting, quilts, carriages, and the 1906 lake steamboat *Ticonderoga,* beached on the museum's spacious grounds. Also in town, the Vermont Teddy Bear Company has an annual output of nearly half a million stuffed bruins, making it the largest producer of American-made, hand-crafted teddy bears. The 30-minute factory tour includes a chance to purchase your own mascot.

Moving away from the lake, **Stowe** is a major winter sports hub and home to the Von Trapp family of *Sound of Music* fame. Today, Sam von Trapp, son of Johannes von Trapp (the family's 10th and youngest child) manages the local Trapp Family Lodge. During warmer weather, nearby 4,393-foot (1,339 m) Mount Mansfield and Smugglers' Notch State Park offer wilderness adventure, with winter sports the primary attraction to Stowe and Smugglers' Notch ski resorts. The **Green Mountains** shelter a number of other winter resorts including Killington in Calvin Coolidge State Forest, the largest ski and snowboard area in the eastern U.S. Other winter wonderlands include Sugarbush Resort in the Mad River Valley near Warren, Mount Snow in Green Mountain National Forest, and Okemo Mountain Resort near Ludlow.

Down in the **Connecticut River Valley,** the Montshire Museum of Science in Norwich features more than 125 indoor and outdoor hands-on exhibits covering the natural and physical sciences, ecology, and technology. The Marsh-Billings-Rockefeller National Historical Park in Woodstock preserves the pastoral setting where Frederick Billings established a cutting-edge managed forest and dairy farm starting in 1869. The mansion and gardens are open for guided tours and various events, but the park also offers 20 miles (32 km) of carriage roads and trails for hikers plus a permanent artist-in-residence studio. Calvin Coolidge was born in nearby Plymouth Notch (1872), and the entire tiny village is now a picturesque state historic site ready to transport visitors back in time. Highlights include Coolidge's birthplace and the house where John Coolidge administered the oath of office to his vice president son after

Green Mountain National Forest on a calm autumn morning in Vermont

President Warren G. Harding died.

The pretty Hildene estate near **Manchester** was the summer home of Robert Todd Lincoln and his wife, Mary. The only child of Abraham and Mary Todd Lincoln to survive into adulthood, Robert served as secretary of war, U.S. ambassador to Britain, and chairman of the Pullman Company. The Georgian Revival–style home remained in the family until 1975.

In **Bennington,** a 306-foot-tall (93 m) monument commemorates the 1777 Battle of Bennington,

one of the turning points of the Revolutionary War. The college town's other sights include the Bennington Museum, the Historic Park-McCullough House, and poet Robert Frost's grave beside the Old First Church.

Vermont boasts more than a hundred 19th-century covered bridges, second only to Pennsylvania. Two of the longest cross the West River: the 277-foot (84 m) Scott Bridge in Townshend (1870) and the 267-foot (81 m) West Dummerston Bridge in Dummerston (1872). Halpin Bridge in Middlebury (1824) is the highest, stretching 46 feet (14 m) above the stream it crosses. Gold Brook Bridge in Stowe (1844) is also called Emily's Bridge, as locals claim it is haunted by a ghost named Emily. The A. M. Foster Bridge near Cabot was built in 1988 to replicate the 19th-century Martin Bridge; even though it isn't vintage, the bridge is considered among the most picturesque in the state. ∎

LOCAL FLAVOR

• **Cheese:** Vermont's dairy farms produce the raw material that goes into some of the nation's best artisanal cheeses. Founded in 1892, the Grafton Village Cheese Company makes a range of aged cheddars and specialty cheeses. *400 Linden St., Brattleboro*

• **Maple syrup:** Get up close and personal with all variations of the sticky

stuff at the Vermont Maple Festival, staged every April in Saint Albans.

• **Ben & Jerry's ice cream:** The original 1980 gas station store in Burlington is long gone, but B & J addicts can get their fix with a factory tour that culminates in a full-service scoop shop. *1281 Waterbury-Stowe Rd. (Route 100), Waterbury*

Virginia

Virginia really is for lovers . . . of American history, mid-Atlantic shorelines, Appalachian culture, and rivers that continue to run wild and free. Home to the first English colonists, the state later gave birth to eight presidents and played a crucial part in both the American Revolution and Civil War. Today Virginia offers a fascinating mosaic of battlefields, beaches, museums, and mountains.

CITIES

Among the nation's oldest cities, **Richmond** is where Patrick Henry famously declared "Give me liberty or give me death" at Saint John's Episcopal Church. In addition to the Virginia State Capitol, downtown Richmond also boasts the John Marshall House, where the powerful Chief Justice lived for more than three decades. Another famous son was the orphaned Edgar Allan Poe, who spent much of his youth with a Richmond foster family. The Edgar Allan Poe Museum is located in the Old Stone House, one of the city's few remaining colonial-era structures. On the edge of downtown, Hollywood Cemetery is the last resting place of Virginia-born presidents James Monroe and John Tyler. Northwest of downtown, Richmond's historic districts include Jackson Ward, a traditional African-American neighborhood once dubbed the "Harlem of the South." Among its landmarks are the art deco–style Hippodrome Theater, Leigh Street Armory, and the home of Civil Rights activist and pioneering black businesswoman Maggie L. Walker. The Museum District is graced with the Virginia Museum of Fine Arts, the Science Museum of Virginia, and Richmond Children's Museum. Richmond is also rich in green spaces, with its James River Park System offering hiking, biking, white-water rafting, rock climbing, and many more outdoor activities. As capital of the Confederacy, the city also boasts myriad Civil War relics. Monument Avenue is lined with statues of Robert E. Lee, Stonewall Jackson, and other Rebel leaders, as well as locally born tennis great Arthur Ashe. Richmond National Battlefield Park envelopes the city and encompasses five different units including the visitor center at Tredegar Iron Works, the Chimborazo Medical Museum, Fort Harrison, and Cold Harbor Battlefield. The White House and Museum of

TOURISM INFORMATION

The Virginia Tourism Corporation dispenses information at 12 welcome centers at interstate and other major highway gateways around the state. Visit the website at virginia.org.

- **Richmond Visitors Center**
405 N Third St.
Richmond, VA 23219
Tel 804/783-7450
visitrichmondva.com

- **Visit Norfolk**
232 E Main St.
Norfolk, VA 23510
Tel 800/368-3097
visitnorfolktoday.com

- **Virginia Beach Visitor Information Center**
2100 Parks Ave.
Virginia Beach, VA 23451
Tel 757/437-4888
visitvirginiabeach.com

- **National Park Service**
nps.gov/state/va

- **Virginia State Parks**
dcr.virginia.gov/state-parks

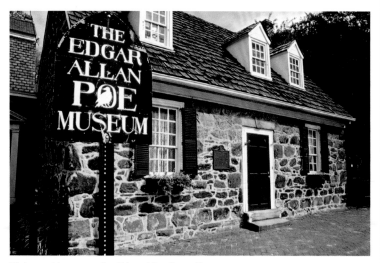

Richmond honors native Edgar Allan Poe with a museum.

The Richmond skyline reflected in the James River

the Confederacy are located in Jefferson Davis's official residence.

Downstream from Richmond, the James River empties into the Chesapeake Bay at **Norfolk,** hub of the huge Hampton Roads metro area that also embraces Virginia Beach, Hampton, Newport News, and Chesapeake. Home to the world's largest naval base, Norfolk boasts many seafaring attractions. Nauticus is an ocean-themed museum and science center that includes aquariums, touch tanks, naval exhibits, and the U.S.S. *Wisconsin,* one of the largest battleships ever built. It's also the launching site for a two-hour harbor cruise that includes a chance to see active submarines, aircraft carriers, and guided-missile destroyers. A narrated bus tour of Naval Station Norfolk takes visitors past buildings constructed for the 1907 Jamestown Exposition as well as ships stationed at the home port of the U.S. Atlantic and Indian Ocean fleets. MacArthur Memorial Museum honors General Douglas MacArthur as well as those who served in both World Wars and Korea. Across the Elizabeth River from downtown Norfolk, Olde Towne Portsmouth is a restored waterfront area with a large collection of period homes and other historic structures. Away from the waterfront, the Chrysler Museum of Art tenders more than 30,000 objects in a permanent collection spanning 5,000 years. Norfolk

Botanical Garden features 52 themed gardens in addition to 95 bird species and 30 kinds of butterflies that dwell in the green space.

Hampton Roads also includes **Virginia Beach,** the state's most populous city and premier seaside resort. The busy beach and boardwalk stretch for 59 blocks, an archipelago of hotels, restaurants, shops, and street performers. Along the

FESTIVALS

• **LakeFest (Clarksville):** More than a 100,000 people gather for water sports, sand castle competitions, hot-air balloon rides, and more; July.

• **Chincoteague Island Pony Swim:** Starting in the 1920s, this annual roundup has horses swimming between Assateague and Chincoteague, followed by a parade and auction; July.

• **Old Fiddlers' Convention (Galax):** Launched in 1935, the fest lures fiddlers and banjo, dulcimer, mandolin, Dobro, and Autoharp players to a week of strumming, dancing, and singing in the mountains; August.

• **Virginia Highlands Festival (Abingdon):** Ten days of events celebrate Appalachian culture and nature; August.

• **Oceana Air Show (Virginia Beach):** The Blue Angels headline this three-day extravaganza of military and civilian flight at Naval Air Station Oceana; September.

way are the Norwegian Lady monument (honoring a Norwegian vessel that wrecked on Virginia Beach in 1891) and a 34-foot-tall (10 m) statue of King Neptune. During the summer months, oceanfront stages present free, live musical acts. First Landing State Park, where the Jamestown settlers arrived in 1607, offers hiking, biking, swimming, and camping on the edge of the city. Virginia Aquarium and Marine Science Center offers underwater animal habitats as well as a 75-minute cruise with educators to collect and examine a variety of local fish and invertebrates before releasing them back into the ocean. The Military Aviation Museum displays one of the largest private collections of World War I and II military aircraft, most restored and flown at air shows. The nearby Back Bay National Wildlife Refuge provides 9,250 acres (3,743 ha) of wildlife habitat and eight miles (13 m) of nature trails. The metro area and its many waterways are also a haven for aqua adventure, from board surfing and paddleboarding to sailing, kayaking, and deep-sea fishing.

The second largest city in the Washington, D.C., metro area, **Arlington** hugs the western bank of the Potomac River in northern Virginia. It is headquarters for many federal agencies, including the Department of Defense in the Pentagon, as well as the Transportation Security Administration (TSA) and Defense Advanced Research Projects Agency (DARPA). Arlington National Cemetery includes the U.S. Marine Corps War Memorial, U.S. Coast Guard Memorial, Tomb of the Unknown Soldier, the graves of President John F. Kennedy and General of

Arlington National Cemetery; opposite: Humpback Rocks on the Blue Ridge Parkway

the Army John J. Pershing, and Robert E. Lee's Arlington House. Also of note in the area are Old Town Alexandria, the Smithsonian National Air and Space Museum's Steven F. Udvar-Hazy Center at Dulles International Airport, Manassas National Battlefield Park, Wolf Trap National Park for the Performing Arts in Vienna, and boulder-strewn Great Falls Park along the Potomac.

LANDSCAPES

The western third of Virginia is dominated by rugged highland terrain including the Cumberland Plateau, the Alleghany Highlands, and the Blue Ridge Mountains. Tucked deep in the mountains, the

ROAD TRIPS

Great drives across the Old Dominion State:

• Colonial Parkway links 200 years of American history between Jamestown, Williamsburg, and Yorktown (23 miles/37 km)

• Highway 13 between Norfolk and Chincoteague Island via the Chesapeake Bay Bridge-Tunnel (105 miles/169 km)

• Skyline Drive through the heart of Shenandoah National Park across the top of the Blue Ridge Mountains (105 miles/169 km)

• Highway 39 through the Alleghany Highlands between Lexington and Warm Springs (44 miles/71 km)

• Highway 17 through the heart of the Virginia Tidelands between Fredericksburg and Yorktown (107 miles/172 km)

• Blue Ridge Parkway between Galax and Waynesboro (213 miles/342 km)

• The Crooked Road musical heritage trail (mostly on Highway 58) between Clintwood and Ferrum College (about 300 miles/483 km)

Heartwood artisan complex in **Abingdon** preserves the traditional arts, crafts, music, and food of Appalachian Virginia. The region's **Mount Rogers National Recreation Area** includes four federal wilderness areas, a long scenic byway, large rock formations, more than 500 miles (805 km) of trails, and numerous outdoor activities.

Popular with travelers since the mid-18th century, **Warm Springs** revolves around the twin Jefferson Pools and their constant 98-degree (37°C) temperature. Thomas Jefferson and Robert E. Lee are among the many famous names who have sampled the waters inside the Gentlemen's Pool House (built in 1761). Nearby **Douthat State Park** features 43 miles (69 km) of hiking, biking, and horse trails through pristine Alleghany scenery, as well as accommodations in historic Civilian Conservation Corps cabins. Home to Washington and Lee University and the Virginia

Military Institute, the Blue Ridge town of **Lexington** sports a lively college atmosphere as well as museums dedicated to Stonewall Jackson, Robert E. Lee, General George C. Marshall, and inventor Cyrus McCormick.

Shenandoah National Park encompasses one of the most stunning stretches of the Blue Ridge Mountains, a mosaic of waterfalls, woods, and wildlife just 75 miles (121 km) from the D.C. metro area. Among the park's varied offerings are scenic Skyline Drive, the hike up Old Rag Mountain, an ambitious EarthCaching program, President Herbert Hoover's Rapidan Camp retreat, and 101 miles (163 km) of the Appalachian Trail. In nearby **Charlottesville,** visitors will find Monticello, Thomas Jefferson's mansion and slave plantation (completed in 1770), and the University of Virginia, which he founded in 1819. Some 60 miles (97 km) southeast, **Appomattox** will forever be remembered as the

place where Lee surrendered to Grant, ending the Civil War.

Starting in Alexandria, George Washington Memorial Parkway meanders 10 miles (16 km) down the Potomac to **Mount Vernon.** Restored to what it would have looked like when the first president lived there, the Palladian-style plantation house and estate is America's second most visited historic home. Even farther down the Potomac (and Interstate 95) in **Quantico,** the National Museum of the Marine Corps traces leatherneck history from the American Revolution to the shores of Tripoli, the halls of Montezuma, Iwo Jima, and the Tet Offensive. Much of the Civil War swirled around **Fredericksburg** and its many battlefields. The city boasts the Mary Washington House (home of the president's mother), the James Monroe Museum and Memorial Library, and early-20th-century artist Gari Melchers's studio.

Wedged between the York and James Rivers, the Virginia Peninsula

King Neptune welcomes visitors to the Virginia Beach boardwalk.

hosts **Jamestown,** the first permanent English settlement in the Western Hemisphere (1607). The waterfront site now includes a National Park visitor center, archaeological digs, and a modern reproduction of the 17th-century Jamestown Settlement. The Colonial Parkway leads to **Colonial Williamsburg,** a living-history town with dozens of redbrick and wooden homes, shops, and other structures—most on their original foundations. The town features artisans in period costume demonstrating traditional crafts and trades. Other Williamsburg attractions include the Abby Aldrich Rockefeller Folk Art Museum, DeWitt Wallace Decorative Arts Museum, and the gorgeous campus of the College of William & Mary. Colonial Parkway continues to **Yorktown,** where Washington and Lafayette defeated Cornwallis in 1781 to end the American Revolution. The peninsula is also home to the Busch Gardens Williamsburg and Water Country U.S.A. theme parks.

Virginia's eastern shore is spangled with sandy strands, swamps, and barrier islands. **Chincoteague Island,** setting for Marguerite Henry's classic children's book *Misty of Chincoteague,* is now a

A fife and drum corps at Colonial Williamsburg

laid-back sea resort that also serves as a gateway for Chincoteague National Wildlife Refuge and the southern (Virginia) portion of Assateague Island National Seashore. In addition to its celebrated wild ponies, the waterfront parks offer a mix of nature and recreation.

Reached by ferry from Reedville, Onancock, and other bay ports,

Tangier Island offers a trip back in time to an era when the Chesapeake Bay islands were extremely isolated from the mainland. With only 700 inhabitants (who speak with a unique accent) and just 1.2 square miles (3.1 sq km) of dry land, the island features a museum, soft-shell crab restaurants, and charming bed-and-breakfasts. ■

LITTLE-KNOWN FACTS

• The Berkeley Plantation in Charles City occupies the site of the first American "thanksgiving"—a 1619 feast between English settlers and local Native Americans.

• The Jackson Ferry Shot Tower in Austinville is a 75-foot-tall (23 m) stone structure that was used in the 18th century for making musket balls. It is one of only three left in the U.S.

• Lake Anna State Park, near Glenora offers gold-panning programs and tours of the Goodwin Gold Mine, a relic of a Virginia gold rush that spanned the mid-19th century.

• Sailor's Creek, near Rice, was the scene of the last major battle of the Civil War, fought 72 hours before Lee's surrender at Appomattox.

• Caledon State Park, located in King George County, is a major summer hangout for bald eagles on the Potomac River.

Washington

A land of mighty waters and towering peaks, Washington State is renowned for stunning geographical features including the Columbia River, Puget Sound, and Mount Rainier. Lumberjacks, fisherman, and wheat farmers may have pioneered the state, but today's aerospace engineers, software wizards, and coffee baristas infuse modern Washington with an enviable vibrancy.

CITIES

Dubbed the "Emerald City" because of its evergreen environs, **Seattle** sits on the eastern shore of Puget Sound, a progressive city renowned for coffee bars and grunge music, megaplanes and microchips. A legacy of the Century 21 Exposition in 1962, the iconic 605-foot (184 m) Space Needle features an observation deck and revolving restaurant, both with jaw-dropping views. Another relic of the world's fair is the 74-acre (30 ha) Seattle Center sprawled around the needle, a venue for many of the city's leading cultural institutions.

Microsoft co-founder Paul Allen funded the Experience Music Project (EMP), a quirky museum designed by Frank Gehry and dedicated to contemporary popular culture, with emphasis on music, science fiction, and fantasy. Pacific Science Center is one of the few global museums with *two* IMAX theaters, as well as a laser dome, living butterfly and insect exhibits, dinosaurs, and more. Among other Seattle Center highlights are the Chihuly Garden and Glass exhibit, the Seattle Repertory Theatre, and the Bill & Melinda Gates Foundation Visitor Center. A vintage

TOURISM INFORMATION

For more information on visiting Washington State visit the Washington Tourism Alliance online at experiencewa.com.

• **Seattle Visitor Center**
Washington State Convention Center
Upper Pike Street Lobby
Seventh Ave. and Pike St.
701 Pike St., #800
Seattle, WA 98101
Tel 206/461-5840
visitseattle.org

• **Pike Place Market Visitor Center**
Pike Place Market
SW corner of First Ave. and Pike St.
Seattle, WA 98101
Tel 206/461-5840
visitseattle.org

• **Visit Spokane**
River Park Square Kiosk
808 W Main Ave.
Spokane, WA 99201
Tel 509/363-0304 or 888/SPOKANE
visitspokane.com

• **Olympia, Lacey, Tumwater Visitor Information**
103 Sid Snyder Ave. SW
Olympia, WA 98501
Tel 360/704-7544
visitolympia.com

• **National Park Service**
nps.gov/state/wa

• **Washington State Parks**
parks.wa.gov

Kayaking Lake Crescent in Olympic National Park

monorail whisks passengers from the center to downtown Seattle and its forest of high-rise buildings. Pike Place Market (1907) blends market stalls and eateries with personable vendors who toss fish and crack jokes. The nearby Seattle Art Museum offers a comprehensive collection of artworks, while Benaroya Hall hosts a wide array of musical events.

The Space Needle, the towering, futuristic icon of the Seattle skyline

Down along the waterfront are the Seattle Aquarium, the Seattle Great Wheel, and ferry terminals for the Puget Sound islands. Discovery Park (the city's largest) offers miles of paths as well as the Daybreak Star Cultural Center, focused on Native American culture. Housed in the massive Naval Reserve Armory on Lake Union, the Museum of History & Industry (MOHAI) preserves the history of Seattle and Puget Sound. After falling on hard times, the neighborhood of Pioneer Square—where Seattle began in the 1850s—has gradually evolved into an eclectic entertainment area that includes the Seattle visitor center of Klondike Gold Rush National Historic Park. Visitors can also take tours beneath the streets and sidewalks for a glimpse of Seattle

Underground, the remains of 19th-century storefronts buried beneath newer construction. Across the railroad tracks, the Chinatown-International District encompasses many different Asian cultures with numerous shops and restaurants.

Looming over both old neighborhoods is CenturyLink Field, home of the National Football League's Seahawks and Major League Soccer's Sounders. At the very southern edge of the city, the excellent Museum of Flight displays historic flying

ROAD TRIPS

Great drives across the Evergreen State:

• Highway 101 around the Olympic Peninsula from Olympia to Aberdeen (284 miles/457 km)

• Lewis and Clark Trail along the north bank of the Columbia River between Clarkston and Cape Disappointment (572 miles/ 921 km)

• Coulee Corridor (Highways 155 and 17) between Othello and Omak (153 miles/246 km)

• North Cascades Scenic Highway (Route 20) between Rockport and Winthrop (95 miles/ 153 km)

• Stevens Pass Greenway (Highway 2) between Monroe and Peshastin (95 miles/153 km)

machines as varied as a Boeing 707 Air Force One that carried four different presidents and World War I biplane fighters.

Down at the bottom of Puget Sound, **Tacoma** is busy morphing its blue-collar roots into a sophisticated modern city. The fine Tacoma Art Museum celebrates the art and artists from the Pacific Northwest, while the intriguing Museum of Glass includes studios where visitors can watch artists create glass art. Linking the latter museum with downtown Tacoma is a 500-foot-long (152 m) pedestrian overpass, Dale Chihuly's "Bridge of Glass." Automobile enthusiasts revel in viewing hundreds of the vintage vehicles that once belonged to Harold LeMay, on display in two Tacoma locations: the LeMay Family Collection Foundation at Marymount and the LeMay America's Car Museum. Foss Waterway Seaport reflects Tacoma's rich maritime heritage with indoor exhibits and

the Working Waterfront Maritime Museum. Fort Nisqually (1833), the first European settlement on Puget Sound, offers a living-history take on pioneer life in the Washington Territory. Nearby is Point Defiance Zoo & Aquarium.

The queen of eastern Washington, **Spokane** is a frontier trading post that prospered on farming and mining. Wedged between the Cascade Range and the Rocky Mountains, the city boasts an arid, Mediterranean-like climate with more than 170 days of sunshine each year. Riverfront Park along the Spokane River—a legacy of the Expo '74 World's Fair—includes the spectacular Spokane Falls, the Great Northern Railroad Depot Clocktower, and the 1909 Looff Carousel. Traversing the park are the Spokane River Centennial Trail as well as the Spokane Falls Sky-Ride, with its signature purple gondolas. On the river's south bank, the INB Performing Arts

Center presents a year-round slate of music, theater, and dance. The Browne's Addition neighborhood is home to the Northwest Museum of Arts and Culture (formerly the Cheney Cowles Museum), a Smithsonian-affiliated collection. On the city's south side, Manito Park and Botanical Gardens offers 90 acres (36 ha) of varied flowers and foliage, including the peaceful Nishinomiya Tsutakawa Japanese Garden. Even farther afield, Mount Spokane State Park in the Selkirk Mountains indulges camping, hiking, skiing, and more.

LANDSCAPES

The Cascade mountain range offers a vast wilderness escape just outside the back door of Seattle, Tacoma, and other Puget Sound towns. Towering above all is

Backpacking in the dense greenery of Olympic National Park

perpetually snowcapped Mount Rainier, centerpiece of one of the country's earliest national parks (1899). The 14,410-foot (4,392 m) peak, an active volcano, has long been a holy grail for climbers, hikers, and backcountry skiers, but the park offers plenty of other activities including scenic drives, fishing, and wildlife-watching.

Mount Saint Helens became a household name when it famously erupted in 1980, creating the spectacular devastation now enshrined within a national volcanic monument. Johnston Ridge Observatory sits in the heart of the blast zone, some five miles (8 km) from the summit. Nineteen miles (31 km) down sinuous Highway 504, Forest Learning Center offers more exhibits on the deadly volcano. The park's Ape Cave is the nation's third longest lava tube.

To the south, along the lower stretches of the Columbia River, **Fort Vancouver** and the **Lewis and Clark National Historical Park** spin tales of early-19th-century frontier life in the Pacific Northwest.

North Cascades National Park safeguards a huge tract of snow-covered peaks and evergreen forest northeast of Seattle, an expanse that also includes Ross Lake and Lake Chelan national recreation areas. The parks tender hundreds of miles of wilderness trails and dozens of backcountry campsites, as well as fishing and boating opportunities, and do-it-yourself winter sports activities. Those with less energy can board the scenic *Lady of the Lake* ferry across Lake Chelan.

Framed by Puget Sound, the Pacific Ocean, and the Strait of Juan de Fuca, the stubby **Olympic**

Mount Rainier rises above the alpine Tipsoo Lake at sunset.

Peninsula offers another massive wilderness expanse. Enormous Olympic National Park is made up of beaches, glaciers, rivers, and a fern-filled temperate rain forest. The peninsula also boasts historic towns including Port Townsend and Port Angeles, where you can hop a ferry across the strait to Victoria, British Columbia.

The **San Juan Islands** in the middle of Puget Sound are divided between Washington State and British Columbia. The three big American isles—Orcas, Lopez, and San Juan—are a time-trip back to the old Northwest, bucolic landscapes that seem little touched by 21st-century life. The archipelago presents one of the world's best opportunities for observing orcas (killer whales) in the wild via sightseeing boats or guided kayak trips. ∎

HIDDEN TREASURES

• **Maryhill Stonehenge (Maryhill):** Erected in 1918 as a memorial to local soldiers lost in World War I, this replica of England's Stonehenge perches on a high bluff above the Columbia River.

• **Whitman Mission National Historic Site (Walla Walla):** The often contentious relationship between American pioneers and Native Americans unfolds at this solemn frontier site, where 13 missionaries were massacred in 1847 after measles devastated a local tribe.

• **Ebey's Landing National Historical Reserve (Whidbey Island):** The reserve maintains a pristine cultural and natural Puget Sound landscape.

• **Ballard Locks (Seattle):** Visitors can watch salmon spawn at an underwater viewing gallery beside a hundred-year-old fish ladder.

West Virginia

They call it the Mountain State for a reason: West Virginia is located entirely within the Appalachian range, within rugged topography that has long defined the state's history, culture, and economic development. In days gone by, West Virginia made a living largely from coal. Today the resurgent state focuses on its wonderland of wild and scenic rivers, gorgeous forests, and abundant outdoor adventures.

TOURISM INFORMATION

The West Virginia Division of Tourism staffs eight welcome centers at interstate gateways around the state. Visit the website: gotowv.com.

• **Charleston Visitor Center**
800 Smith St.
Charleston, WV 25301
Tel 304/344-5075
charlestonwv.com

• **Harpers Ferry Appalachian Trail Visitors Center**
799 Washington St.
Harpers Ferry, WV 25425
Tel 304/535-6331
appalachiantrail.org

• **National Park Service**
nps.gov/state/wv

• **West Virginia State Parks**
www.wvstateparks.com

CITIES

Charleston traces its roots to a frontier fort established by the Virginia Rangers in 1787. The sleepy town at the confluence of the Kanawha and Elk Rivers didn't become the state capital until almost a century later, long after West Virginia had broken away from its mother state during the Civil War. Completed in 1932, the 292-foot-tall (89 m) capitol building with its golden dome remains the tallest building in West Virginia. The capitol complex also includes the West Virginia State Museum, Governor's Mansion, and Veterans Memorial, comprising four limestone monoliths representing the major American conflicts of the 20th century, as well as black granite slabs with the names of the more than 10,000 West Virginians who perished in those wars. Charleston's historic East End district also hosts the farmers-style Capitol Market and Clay Center for the Arts and Sciences. The latter tenders an eclectic array of visual and performing arts, including the well-regarded West Virginia Symphony, as well as the Avampato Discovery Museum and Digital Dome planetarium. The largely undeveloped south bank holds several treasures, including the historic Cox-Morton House, the log cabin of 1840s settler William S. Gilliland, and leafy Kanawha State Forest with its hiking, biking, and cross-country skiing trails.

Anchoring the far western end of the state, **Huntington** sprawls along the south bank of the Ohio River, a linear metropolis hemmed in by water and hillsides. The downtown historic district embraces 59 structures including the 1880s Davis Opera House and the art deco–style Keith-Albee Theatre. Another cultural gem is the Huntington Museum of Art. Located on 52 acres (21 ha) of wooded land looking down on the city, the collection ranges from Appalachian folk art and European masters to American firearms and Islamic prayer rugs. Farther west along the same ridge

Stonewall Jackson is memorialized on the state capitol grounds in Charleston.

Bikers ascend a slope in front of jagged Seneca Rocks.

stands the Museum of Radio and Technology, with exhibits on military and consumer radios and computers through the ages set inside a converted 1920s elementary school. Wedged between the hills and downtown, Ritter Park Historic District includes more than 70 structures reflecting popular architecture between 1913 and 1940 in addition to a popular rose garden and award-winning playground. On the city's southern outskirts, the Smithsonian-affiliated Heritage Farm Museum and Village celebrates Appalachian culture and history in seven separate museums, along with more than 30 log structures and other reconstructed buildings. Visitors can stay overnight in historic inns. Huntington is also home to Marshall University, named after John Marshall, the esteemed fourth Chief Justice of the

U.S. Supreme Court. The school gained notoriety in 1970 when a chartered jet carrying members of the Thundering Herd football team and staff crashed, killing all 75 people on board. Several area monuments honor them, including the Memorial Fountain on campus and a stone column in nearby Spring Hill Cemetery.

LANDSCAPES

Poised on a peninsula between the Potomac and Shenandoah Rivers, **Harpers Ferry** is famed as the place where abolitionist firebrand John Brown staged his ill-fated raid on the federal armory in 1859, and for its pivotal role in the Civil War. Today the town is a living-history museum strewn with dozens of significant structures and sights, including John Brown's Fort,

the Bolivar Heights battlefield, and Jefferson Rock—where Thomas Jefferson famously proclaimed in 1783 that "this scene is worth a voyage across the Atlantic." Harpers Ferry has also evolved into an outdoor adventure hub for white-water rafting, tubing, and kayaking, as well as a convergence point for hiking the Appalachian Trail through three states (West Virginia, Virginia, and Maryland).

Running down the middle of West Virginia, the **Allegheny Mountains** and **Monongahela National Forest** also provide plenty of scope for wilderness contemplation and outdoor recreation. Blackwater Falls State Park near Davis takes its name from the swarthy color of the Blackwater River, a result of tannic acid in the hemlock and red spruce needles that fall into the water. Twenty miles (32 km) of trails carry cross-country skiers in winter and hikers the rest of the year. Once used for Native American ceremonies, Seneca Caverns near Riverton began forming some 460 million years ago. Visitors descend hundreds of feet underground to ogle stalactites, stalagmites, and helictites. Nearby Spruce Knob–Seneca Rocks National Recreation Area is renowned for its gnarly rock

climbing and the summit of Spruce Knob, the highest point in West Virginia and the highest peak in the Allegheny Mountains (4,863 feet/ 1,482 m). Farther south along the range, Snowshoe mountain resort offers great skiing in the winter and hiking, biking, fishing, and swimming in the summer. The vintage steam trains of Cass Scenic State Park take visitors on an 11-mile (18 km) trip that includes the old sawmill town of Cass. On the other side of Back Allegheny Mountain, tiny Green Bank hosts the Green Bank Science Center, with hands-on exhibits and guided tours of the telescopes of the National Radio Astronomy Observatory.

The topography gets even more extreme in the **Cumberland Mountains,** the next great range to the west. Carved by one of the oldest rivers in North America (and a designated American Heritage River), New River Gorge is a mecca for white-water sports and the centerpiece of a 70,000-acre (28,328 ha) park offering hiking, bird-watching, rock climbing, zip-lining, and

camping. Soaring 876 feet (267 m) above the water, New River Gorge Bridge near Fayetteville is one of the holy grails of global BASE jumping. Farther downstream, Hawks Nest State Park is popular for its jet boat rides and the aerial tramway that rises to panoramic bluffs overlooking the river. Just over the hills is another white-water paradise—Gauley River National Recreation Area. Fraught with narrow gorges and several rapids that are Class V and higher, the Gauley River drops an astounding 668 feet (204 m) in just 25 miles (40 km). Along the way, steep gradients, huge waves, massive boulders, and chilly water make this one of the world's most

Appalachian culture is the focus of the Heritage Farm Museum and Village in Huntington.

Blackwater Canyon blanketed by fog in the Allegheny Mountains

challenging white-water runs during a season that runs just six weeks in the fall. The Cumberland's coal mining heritage is the focus of the city of Exhibition Coal Mine in Beckley, Raleigh County, where retired miners lead underground tours of an inactive mine.

Smack-dab in the middle of the state, the Trans-Allegheny Lunatic Asylum near **Weston** is a popular tourist attraction and nationally recognized landmark. One of the nation's largest hand-cut stone masonry buildings, the asylum was designed by well-known architect Richard Andrews in 1964 to provide residents with copious fresh air and sunlight. Daytime historic tours and after-dark ghost tours take visitors through the creepy castlelike facility. Weston's glassblowing heritage is

highlighted in the Museum of American Glass and the Appalachian Glass studio and outlet shop. At the state's northern extreme, the West Virginia State Penitentiary in

Moundsville is open April through November for those who wish to roam buildings that once held more than 1,000 prisoners. Night tours are offered to the especially brave. ■

HIDDEN TREASURES

- **Philippi Covered Bridge:** stretches over the Tygart Valley River; was the fulcrum of the first organized land battle of the Civil War, a Union victory on June 3, 1861

- **Grave Creek Mound (Moundsville):** built between 250 and 150 B.C. by the Adena people

- **Berkeley Springs State Park:** along with the modern mineral spas of Berkeley town forms the nation's oldest destination spa, founded before

the American Revolution and frequented by young George Washington

- **The Greenbrier:** a massive bunker beneath the Greenbrier Resort where the U.S. Congress was supposed to relocate in case of nuclear war during the mid-20th century. Once top secret, it is now open to the public

- **Andrews Methodist Episcopal Church (Grafton):** Mother's Day was first celebrated here in 1908; now it is the International Mother's Day Shrine.

Wisconsin

They call it the Badger State, but not after the little mammal. The nickname comes from the 19th-century lead miners in Wisconsin who worked and lived underground in "badger dens." But this is also the land of dairy, producing 25 percent of the nation's cheese. Especially tasty are artisan varieties made at small, family-owned farms. With water all around and forests galore, Wisconsin is also a great place for exploring the great outdoors.

CITIES

Milwaukee allegedly means "gathering place by the water" in the language of the Native Americans who frequented the area before the arrival of the first Europeans. Located about 90 miles (145 km) north of Chicago, many of Milwaukee's 1.5 million inhabitants claim German roots via a huge influx of Middle Europeans that started in the 1840s. Waterfront shops, restaurants, trendy brewpubs, and Pere Marquette Park line the downtown RiverWalk along the Milwaukee River.

Meanwhile, the Hank Aaron State Trail follows along the south shore of the Menomonee River to sights that include the Harley-Davidson Museum and its collection of vintage "hogs." Near the confluence of Milwaukee's three rivers, the Historic Third Ward is a onetime dock and factory area revamped into a lively arts, entertainment, and design district. Taking pride of place along the city's lakeshore is the *Denis Sullivan,* a replica Great Lakes schooner and the state's official flagship. Farther up the Lake Michigan

coast is the Milwaukee Art Museum with its 30,000-strong collection of works from antiquity to today. Away from the lake, the Milwaukee Public Museum runs a broad gamut from the turn-of-the-20th-century "Streets of Old Milwaukee" walk-through exhibit to the free-flying lepidopterans of the Puelicher Butterfly Wing. The Pabst family played a significant role in Milwaukee's growth into a major city. Captain Frederick Pabst was both a beer baron and a beacon of the city's Victorian era, and his family's heritage lives on at the Pabst Mansion near the Marquette University campus as well as at Pabst Theater (1895), reminiscent of the great opera houses of Europe. Although some think that Frank Lloyd Wright's circular Annunciation Greek Orthodox Church resembles a spaceship, no one can deny the originality of his design. Milwaukee's other nod to modern architecture is the Mitchell

TOURISM INFORMATION

The Wisconsin Department of Tourism staffs welcome centers at eight different locations around the state. Visit travelwisconsin.com.

● **Visit Milwaukee Visitor Information Center**
Wisconsin Center
400 W Wisconsin Ave.
Milwaukee, WI 53203
Tel 414-273-3950 or
800/554-1448
visitmilwaukee.org

● **Downtown Madison Visitor Center**
452 State St.
Madison, WI 53703
Tel 608/512-1342
visitdowntownmadison.com

● **Wisconsin State Parks**
dnr.wi.gov/topic/parks

An upscale Irish pub adds to Madison's eclectic restaurant scene.

Downtown Milwaukee on the water

Park Horticultural Conservatory, a cluster of four giant glass domes featuring tropical, desert, and other exotic plant habitats.

A longtime bastion of environmental ideas and eco-friendly attitudes, **Madison** nurtures one of the nation's best biking networks as well as a cab company that runs on clean propane. The state capital is also renowned for its eclectic cultural scene as well as the educational and athletic endeavors of the University of Wisconsin. The Madison Trust for Historic Preservation sponsors summertime State Street Walking Tours starting from the House of Wisconsin Cheese. The university campus sprawls along the south shore of Lake Mendota just to the west of downtown Madison. Campus landmarks include Memorial Union, often lauded as one of

the most beautiful university student centers in the nation; the globally focused Chazen Museum of Art; and the Geology Museum with its copious collection of rocks, minerals, and fossils. Scattered across the campus are four clusters of Native American burial mounds. South of campus, the 1,260-acre (510 ha) University of Wisconsin Arboretum offers trails winding through a variety of wild terrain and planned gardens along the shore of Lake Wingra. Frank Lloyd Wright spent much of his youth and university years in Madison and later endowed the city with some of his finest work. Among them are the first house he designed for Herbert and Katherine Jacobs (considered to be the first Usonian home) and the innovative Unitarian Meeting House.

LAKESHORES

With more than 800 miles (1,287 km) of shoreline, Wisconsin boasts more Great Lakes frontage than any other state besides Michigan. Both the popular **Lake Michigan** shore and the secluded

---

CAPITALISM

The Madison Farmer's Market takes over Capitol Square every Saturday (6 a.m. to 2 p.m.) between April and November, an alfresco smorgasbord of organic and homemade delights from all over Wisconsin. Munch a selection of gourmet cheeses and artisan breads while lounging on the capitol steps, the building's 187-foot (57 m) dome looming behind.

north shore along **Lake Superior** offer plenty of opportunities for boating, fishing, swimming, or merely staring out at the water.

Thirty miles (42 km) south of Milwaukee, **Racine** offers a lakefront zoo, the historic Wind Point Lighthouse (1880), and North Beach Park, a sandy strand with Blue Wave Beach designation indicating the highest environmental standards. Tranquil **Kohler-Andrae State Park** near Sheboygan encompasses more than a mile of pristine beach backed by towering sand dunes, wetlands, and rare plant habitats.

Outdoor sports junkies flock to Neshotah Beach in **Two Rivers,** which is also an access point for the Ice Age National Scenic Trail, meandering almost 1,200 miles (1,931 km) across Wisconsin from Lake Michigan to the Saint Croix River. The lakeshore town is also home to the Hamilton Wood Type and Printing Museum.

Often cited as one of the most beautiful spots in the Midwest, the bucolic **Door Peninsula** extends nearly 60 miles (97 km) into Lake Michigan. In addition to its renowned cherry and apple orchards, the peninsula features charming villages such as Fish Creek and Egg Harbor, as well as historic lighthouses, five state parks, and the Ahnapee State Trail, a former railroad right-of-way converted into a 48-mile (77 km) multiuse recreational path for summer and winter sports.

The peninsula's western edge is defined by long Green Bay and its namesake city, home to the Green Bay Packers of professional football

Cave Point along the west side of Wisconsin's Door County, which juts into Lake Michigan

and their stadium and hall of fame at Lambeau Field.

At the state's northernmost tip, Madeline Island is the largest of the 21 islands and 12 miles (19 km) of mainland that make up **Apostle Islands National Lakeshore** on Lake Superior. Accessed by private boat or ferry from Bayfield, the park features old-growth forest, sandstone caverns, and historic lighthouses, as well as outdoor activities.

LANDSCAPES

First developed as a tourist destination in the 1850s, **Wisconsin Dells** lies about 55 miles (89 km) north of Madison. Originally built around the dells (rapids) of the Wisconsin River, the resort town now boasts golf courses, health spas, the world's largest concentration of water parks, and offbeat attractions such as the Rick Wilcox Magic Theater, Mr. Marvel's Wondertorium, and an upside-down White House called Top Secret.

About an hour west of Madison, in **Spring Green** on the Wisconsin River, the 600-acre (243 ha) Taliesin complex was architect Frank Lloyd Wright's primary residence and studio from 1911 until his death in 1959. Everything from Shakespeare to Stoppard takes the stage at the American Players Theatre (APT), directly across Highway 23 from Taliesin. Also in Spring Green, and no doubt inspired by Wright's cutting-edge modern style, is House on the Rock. The futuristic structure (built around a stone monolith) contains museum exhibits and the world's largest carousel—replete with 269 wooden animals and 20,000 lights.

An American badger, Wisconsin's state animal

A booming lead and zinc mining town in the early 19th century, **Mineral Point** is flush with historic buildings and an immigrant Cornish miner heritage that includes freshly baked pasties—meat and veggie pies. Nearby Blue Mound State Park attracts mountain bikers to 12 miles (19 km) of challenging single-track trails.

Far less farmed than lower parts of the state, northern Wisconsin is full of forests, streams, and Indian reservations. Those who venture into the wilds of **Copper Falls State Park** can hike 17 miles (27 km) of trails to secluded waterfalls and fishing spots along the scenic Bad River. An hour's drive west, **Brule River State Forest** offers outstanding trout fishing (along with chinook and coho salmon) and canoeing along 44 miles (71 km) of wilderness river that eventually empties into Lake Superior. ∎

ROAD TRIPS	
Great drives across the Badger State:	• Kettle Moraine Scenic Drive between Whitewater Lake and Elkhart Lake (115 miles/185 km)
• The Great River Road (Highway 35) along the Mississippi River from Prescott to Prairie du Chien (178 miles/286 km)	• Wisconsin Lake Superior Byway (Highway 13) between Ashland and Superior (104 miles/167 km)
• Highway 60 along the Wisconsin River from Bridgeport to Sauk City (82 miles/132 km)	• Highway 42 along the Door Peninsula between Two Rivers to Gills Rock (97 miles/156 km)

Wyoming

With fewer people than any other state and towns few and far between, Wyoming's mosaic of prairie, woodland, and snow-clad peaks presents a terrain little changed from the days when Native Americans, French trappers, and American mountain men roamed Yellowstone and the Tetons. Today awestruck tourists visit these landscapes, as well as cowboy towns and hip wilderness resorts.

TOURISM INFORMATION

Wyoming visitor information centers are located along interstate gateways near Cheyenne, Beulah, and Pine Bluff. Check out wyoming tourism.org.

- **Visit Cheyenne**
121 W 15th St.
Cheyenne, WY 82001
Tel 307/778-3133
cheyenne.org

- **Jackson Hole/Greater Yellowstone Visitor Center**
532 Cache Creek Dr.
Jackson, WY 83001
Tel 307/733-3316
jacksonholechamber.com

- **National Park Service**
nps.gov/state/wy

CITIES

Created in 1867 where the under-construction Union Pacific crossed Crow Creek, **Cheyenne** started life as a rough-and-tumble railway town of muddy streets, makeshift saloons, and a transient populous—the epitome of the "hell on wheels" settlements spawned by the transcontinental railroad. But unlike most of the others, Cheyenne endured. By the 1870s wags were calling it the "Magic City of the Plains" because of its rapid growth and prospering business scene. Still the highest building in Cheyenne, the state capitol rises 146 feet (44 m) above the prairie city, hewn from sandstone and crowned by a 24-karat gold-leaf dome. The Historic Governors' Mansion was home to more than six decades of state leaders (from 1905 to 1976), including Nellie Tayloe Ross, the nation's first female governor, who was sworn into office in 1925. The Wyoming State Museum presents a broad overview of local natural and human history, while downtown the Nelson Museum of the West focuses on the heritage of the greater Wild West. A sprawling rodeo ground on the city's north side hosts the annual Cheyenne Frontier Days, the world's largest outdoor rodeo.

Laramie lies 50 miles (80 km) west of the state capital, home to the University of Wyoming and its myriad cultural and sporting activities. A 75-foot-long (23 m) *Apatosaurus* skeleton and a celebrated *Allosaurus* fossil called "Big Al" dominate the on-campus Geological Museum. Shaped like a futuristic teepee, the university's American Heritage Center (AHC) is a repository of books, documents, and artifacts on Wyoming and the American West. Another Union Pacific town that outlasted the railroad, Laramie has 21 structures listed on the National Register of Historic Places, including the Wyoming Territorial Prison and State Historic Site (1872) and the Ivinson Mansion (1892), now home to the Laramie Plains Museum and its vivid depiction of frontier life for the well-heeled set. Railroad Heritage Park is home to both the old train depot and the

Laramie, Wyoming, was once a frontier town; now it's a buzzing college town.

Hardy moose feed on sagebrush during the harsh winters in the Teton Range.

historic Snow Train with its 1903 locomotive and massive snowplow.

The state's second largest city, **Casper** followed a different path to prosperity. Rather than a railroad town, it started life as a stop along the Oregon Trail where migrants had to ferry across the North Platte River. The city's National Historic Trails Interpretive Center spins tales of the Oregon Trail and other routes across the Old West, illuminating their impact on both the migrants and the Native American populations.

NATIONAL PARKS

It all started at **Yellowstone** in 1872—the notion that nations should preserve their natural wonders for the benefit of current and future generations. From here the national park concept spread across the continent and around the globe.

Most of the vast preserve (roughly 50 times larger than the District of Columbia) is located in northwest Wyoming, with small portions spilling across the border into neighboring Idaho and Montana. Its attractions are many and varied. The iconic Old Faithful Geyser is but one manifestation of the world's largest hydrothermal field, revealing the fact that nearly all of the park rests in the caldera of an ancient supervolcano. Indeed, Yellowstone National Park contains more than 1,200 geysers and 10,000 geothermal features. The Grand Canyon of the Yellowstone comes close to rivaling that other big ditch in Arizona, especially with a massive waterfall plunging into the multicolored gorge. Yellowstone Lake is the largest high-altitude lake in North America, a vast liquid asset that's explored by just a fraction of the

3.5 million people who visit the park each year. But Yellowstone's biggest attraction is probably its wildlife. The preserve remains the only place in the lower 48 where the American version of the Big Five—bison, grizzly bear, wolves, moose, and mountain lions—roam within the confines of a single park. Winter in Yellowstone brings a flurry of snow that is ideal for cross-country skiing, snowshoeing, and snowmobiling.

Only eight miles (13 km) of highway separate Yellowstone from Wyoming's other great natural wonder, **Grand Teton National Park.** Cobbled together over 50 years against the strident objection of local ranchers, foresters, and politicians, Grand Teton now encompasses most of the saw-toothed Teton Range, a chain of glacial lakes, and a lengthy stretch of the upper Snake River. With 10 peaks soaring more than 12,000 feet (3,658 m), the Tetons are a magnet for serious mountain climbers. Trails range from gentle lakeshore walks to hard-core hikes, such as the Paintbrush Canyon–Cascade Canyon Loop. But the ultimate Teton experience is probably found by getting out on the water: white-water rafting the Snake River, fly-fishing for native cutthroat trout, sailing across vast Jackson Lake, or kayaking smooth-as-silk Jenny Lake with the snowcapped Tetons as a constant backdrop.

LANDSCAPES

Jackson Hole is both a geographical feature and a frame of mind: a gorgeous valley surrounded by pristine wilderness and celebrated by city slickers who are trying to get in touch with their inner cowboy. The town of Jackson is a hub to a thriving outdoor adventure scene that features snow sports in winter and a variety of land and water pastimes in summer. The town square is renowned for its wacky elk antler arches. Perched on the outskirts of town, the National Elk Refuge provides a winter habitat for the 11,000-strong Jackson elk herd, best viewed from guided sleigh rides. Overlooking the refuge, the National Museum of Wildlife Art embraces all forms of zoological expression including works by artists as diverse as John James Audubon, Picasso, and Rembrandt.

ROAD TRIPS

Great drives across the Cowboy State:

● Highway 89 from Jackson to Mammoth via Grand Teton and Yellowstone (147 miles/237 km)

● Beartooth Highway between Yellowstone and Red Lodge, Montana (68 miles/109 km)

● The Great Skyroad (Route 130) between Laramie and Saratoga (78 miles/126 km)

● Bighorn Scenic Byway between Sheridan and Greybull (94 miles/151 km)

● Highway 287 from Laramie to West Yellowstone, Montana (466 miles/750 km)

From its source in the Wind River Mountains near Jackson, the Green River runs a meandering southward path into **Flaming Gorge National Recreation Area,**

Early morning light catches the peaks and valleys of Grand Teton National Park.

The vibrant hues of Yellowstone's Grand Prismatic Spring are all-natural.

which Wyoming shares with neighboring Utah. With five marinas, the park's namesake Flaming Gorge Reservoir provides plenty of opportunity for water sports.

East of the Rockies and Yellowstone region, Wyoming slowly descends into arid intermontane basins and then the **Great Plains.** Ranges such as the Bighorn and Laramie Mountains break the monotony, but for the most part the country is sagebrush and short-grass prairie. Here and there are isolated towns such as **Cody,** a regional ranching center that celebrates its Wild West roots with a popular night rodeo and the Buffalo Bill Center of the West. The latter includes museums dedicated to various aspects of Western art, history, culture, and nature, including a gallery on William "Buffalo Bill" Cody, who helped found the town in 1895.

On the shores of the Bighorn River, **Thermopolis** is renowned for its mineral hot springs, which can be sampled at a free bathhouse in the state park or commercial pools including the Star Plunge. Tucked up in the state's northeast corner, the huge volcanic plug known as **Devils Tower** rises 1,267 feet (386 m) above the surrounding terrain—equivalent to placing the Empire State Building in the middle of nowhere. The nation's first national monument (1906), it is sacred to several Native American groups and will forever be associated with aliens thanks to the classic Steven Spielberg film *Close Encounters of the Third Kind.* ∎

HIDDEN TREASURES

- **Mountain Man Rendezvous (Fort Bridger):** annual living-history festival

- **Fort Laramie National Historic Site:** old trading post and cavalry garrison where the Oregon Trail crossed the North Platte River in eastern Wyoming

- **King's Saddlery (Sheridan):** cowboy, cowgirl, and equine outfitter with memorabilia museum

- **Dan Miller's Cowboy Music Revue (Cody):** throwback to the country-and-western radio shows of the 1930s, staged at an old cinema

- **Fossil Butte National Monument:** America's "aquarium in stone" preserves scores of ancient creatures.

- **South Pass City:** middle-of-nowhere ghost town with well-preserved remnants of 1860s gold rush

Canada

Banff National Park, Alberta

Alberta

Snowy mountains and golden prairies, evergreen forest and eternal blue sky—the symbols on Alberta's flag reveal a lot of what sets the massive western province apart from the rest of Canada. From dinosaur digs to festival gigs, Alberta also flaunts plenty of man-made attractions. And with an average of more than 300 days of sunshine per year, it promises outdoor adventure every season.

CITIES

Big, brash, and bold, **Calgary** has parlayed its cattle-and-oil boom fortunes into Canada's fastest growing city. The seed that sprouted the modern metropolis, Fort Calgary was created by the red-coated North West Mounted Police (aka Mounties) in 1875 to expedite the fur trade and fend off American whiskey sellers. Today the reconstructed fort buildings and palisades host living-history and education programs. Rising high above the old fort, the city's glimmering high-rise skyline is crowned by the 627-foot-high (191 m) Calgary Tower and its glass-floored observation deck. Down the block, the Glenbow Museum presents a broad overview of western Canada's natural and human history. When the downtown Saddledome arena isn't being used for the famous Calgary Stampede, it hosts home games of the National Hockey League's Flames and other events. The Bow River's ribbon of blue and green through the city center winds past leafy Prince's Island and the Inglewood

TOURISM INFORMATION

Travel Alberta maintains 11 provincial visitor information centers, most of them near major highway entry points. Visit travelalberta.com.

- **Tourism Calgary Visitor Information Centres**
Calgary International Airport and Calgary Tower (downtown)
Tel 403/750-2362 or 403/735-1234
visitcalgary.com

- **Edmonton Welcome Centre**
West Shaw Building
9797 Jasper Ave.
Edmonton, AB T5J 1N9
Tel 780/401-7696
exploreedmonton.com

- **Banff Visitor Information Centre**
224 Banff Ave.
Banff, AB T1L 1C3
Tel 403/762-8421
banfflakelouise.com

- **Parks Canada**
pc.gc.ca

Bird Sanctuary and Nature Centre. The gallantry of Canadian regiments is remembered at the Military Museums complex in Garrison Woods. More history comes alive at nearby Heritage Park Historical Village, where period-clad staff spin tales of frontier life on the Canadian prairies. The park safeguards scores of historic structures transported from all over Alberta, as well as vintage trains, motorcars, and horse-drawn transportation.

Edmonton, 200 miles (322 km) due north, unfolds as an urbane prairie metropolis along the North Saskatchewan River that functions as the province's capital and cultural soul. Many of the city's

Maligne Lake within Jasper National Park in the Canadian Rockies

The bright lights of Calgary, Canada's fastest growing city

artistic icons are arranged around Churchill Square, including the futuristic Art Gallery of Alberta and modern Winspear Centre. For shoppers, the gargantuan West Edmonton Mall also features an indoor ice rink, water park, sea lions, a replica of Christopher Columbus's ship the *Santa Maria,* and more. On the south side of the river, the Old Strathcona neighborhood tenders live music and theater venues, indie fashion boutiques, and student hangouts.

CANADIAN ROCKIES

With peaks soaring to more than 12,000 feet (3,658 m), the Rockies present a 500-mile-long (805 km) natural wall that divides Alberta from British Columbia. Although geographically related to the American Rockies, the Canadian version has a much different geology: Uplifted sedimentary beds have been shaped into jagged peaks and deep valleys by aggressive glaciation over millions of years.

By 1885, a superlative stretch of the Alberta Rockies had been set aside as **Banff National Park**— Canada's first and the world's third national park. The Canadian Pacific Railway delivered early visitors to the doorstep of flamboyant wilderness resorts including the Fairmont Banff Springs Hotel (1887) and the Fairmont Chateau Lake Louise (1890) at either end of the park's Bow Valley. Flanked by snowcapped peaks, alpine lakes, and winter sports resorts, the valley is

CAPITALISM

Why did Edmonton become the provincial capital instead of Calgary? Largely because it was a more established metropolis when Alberta shed its territorial skin in 1905. Eight different towns bid for the capital crown, but the new provincial assembly overwhelming voted in favor of Edmonton during its first-ever session the following year.

the easiest way to access its many splendors. Visitors can ride the gondola to the top of Sulphur Mountain, hike the historic SummitWalk, or cruise Lake Minnewanka. Although the Trans-Canada Highway runs through the middle of the park—connecting Banff to other national parks on the British Colombia side of the continental divide—the best way to explore by car is via the scenic Icefields Parkway and Vermilion Lakes Drive.

Icefields Parkway meanders north through the mountains to neighboring **Jasper National Park,** which protects another huge chunk of the Canadian Rockies. Columbia Icefield is the park's foremost landmark, 125 square miles (324 sq km) of snow and ice that reaches a depth of almost 1,200 feet (366 m). Take a tour onto Athabasca Glacier, one of six major arms that extends from the ice field, or for a vertigo-inducing view, try the glass-floored Glacier Skywalk hovering off a cliff. The

Athabasca River starts as meltwater from the ice field, flowing northward via narrow gorges and the thunderous Athabasca Falls, chilly waters that eventually spill into the Arctic Ocean. The river flows through Jasper village, where most of the park's visitor facilities are located. Arrayed around town are wilderness trails and alpine lakes ripe for canoeing, fishing, and traction kiting. Beyond the Athabasca Valley, more than 90 percent of the national park is wilderness with more than 600 miles (966 km) of hiking, biking, and equestrian trails.

Southeast of Banff, the **Kananaskis Country** unfolds as yet another mosaic of mountains, lakes, and primary forest. Ten different Alberta provincial parks protect its natural wonders, about a 90-minute drive from Calgary. Veterans of the 1988 Winter Olympics, Canmore Nordic Centre and Nakiska Ski Resort provide world-class winter sports facilities. The town of Canmore is the hub of

ROAD TRIPS

Great drives across the Wild Rose Country:

• Icefields Parkway through the Rockies between Lake Louise and Jasper (144 miles/232 km)

• Edmonton to High Level via a boreal forest route called the Deh Cho Trail (567 miles/912 km)

• Kananaskis Trail (Highway 40) from Seebe to Longview (96 miles/154 km)

• Fort McMurray to Fort Smith on the frozen winter "Ice Road" (316 miles/508 km)

• Crowsnest Highway between Medicine Hat and Crowsnest Pass (196 miles/315 km)

outdoor activities such as helicopter "flightseeing" and spelunking.

Bringing up the bottom end of the Canadian Rockies, **Waterton Lakes National Park** combines

Banff National Park has lots of opportunity for outdoor adventure, including dozens of hiking trails.

with neighboring Glacier National Park in Montana to create a trans-national biosphere reserve and UNESCO World Heritage site renowned for deep lakes and glacier-chiseled peaks. But it also boasts a large patch of prairie with wild bison and historic sites such as western Canada's first oil well and the grandiose Prince of Wales Hotel. A guided boat tour cruises Upper Waterton Lake; those with more energy ferry across to the Crypt Lake Trail, a 10-mile (16 km) round-trip to a secluded tarn and Hell-Roaring Falls.

PRAIRIE & BOREAL FOREST

Coming down from the mountains, more than two-thirds of Alberta is covered by golden prairies and evergreen boreal forest. The transition zone between grass and woods starts just north of Edmonton, a sparsely populated band that runs right across the middle of the province. This was once the domain of dinosaurs. More than 50 species have been uncovered in the badlands of **Dinosaur Provincial Park** on the Red Deer River where, in addition to a visitor center, the park offers paleontology lab programs, fossil prospecting, and guided hikes. Farther up the river, the Royal Tyrrell Museum in **Drumheller** showcases such outstanding fossil finds as a complete Triceratops and a ferocious *Albertosaurus*.

Astride the Bow River downstream from Calgary, **Blackfoot Crossing Historical Park** preserves a place where the Blackfoot people and their allies gathered for many centuries. In the days before horses and rifles, the Blackfoot hunted bison by driving them off a high

Bighorn sheep rams in Jasper National Park

cliff now called Head-Smashed-In Buffalo Jump UNESCO World Heritage site. Located near Lethbridge, the park's underground visitor center explores various aspects of Blackfoot culture. **Writing-on-Stone Provincial Park** in the Milk River Valley preserves several thousand years of Aboriginal rock carvings and paintings rendered by the Blackfoot and earlier peoples.

Few visitors venture into the vast boreal forest of northern Alberta, an unspoiled landscape of wild rivers, glacial lakes, and remote parklands including **Wood Buffalo National Park.** Canada's largest national park, it protects the largest free-roaming herd of wood bison as well as the last remaining natural nesting place of the whooping crane. **Fort McMurray,** an old Hudson's Bay trading post, is an excellent place to experience the aurora borealis. ∎

LITTLE-KNOWN FACTS

• Despite its sci-fi sounding moniker, the mission of the Sulphur Mountain Cosmic Ray Station in Banff National Park was to study solar radiation, not UFO weaponry.

• The World Chicken Dance Championship at Blackfoot Crossing replicates the mating dance of the prairie chicken (pinnated grouse).

• Fully embracing the *Star Trek* meme, the town of Vulcan features a Spock Days Festival and statue of the starship *Enterprise* with greetings in English, Vulcan, and Klingon around the base.

• The Outpost at Warden Rock, a remote backcountry lodge near Banff, is accessed via the only authentic working stagecoach in all of North America.

British Columbia

Canada's huge Pacific province has a long and exceedingly handsome shoreline, a medley of islands, bays, and channels commonly called the Inside Passage. In Vancouver and Victoria, it also boasts two of the more intriguing cities on the Pacific Rim. With its heady blend of vineyards, snow resorts, and Canadian Rockies, inland B.C. is just as absorbing.

CITIES

Named for the British captain who explored the British Columbia coast in the 1790s, **Vancouver** is the largest Canadian city west of Toronto. Its forest of skyscrapers stands in stark contrast to the mountains that rise straight up from the water on the far side of Vancouver Harbour. The giant green Lions Gate Bridge, Canada's most renowned span, features a pedestrian walkway with wonderful views. At the bridge's south end is rambling Stanley Park, a thousand acres (405 ha) of woodland and waterfront that includes trails, two popular beaches, the Variety Kids Water Park, and more. Stanley Park Seawall is part of the 17-mile (27 km) Seaside Greenway, which provides an uninterrupted pathway between the Vancouver Convention Centre and Spanish Banks Park. Along the way are Kitsilano (aka Kits) Beach, the Museum of

TOURISM INFORMATION

Destination BC runs visitor centers at five locations around the province including Golden, Merritt, Mount Robson, Osoyoos, and Peace Arch. Find more information online at hellobc.com.

● **Vancouver Visitor Centre**
Plaza Level, 200 Burrard St.
Vancouver, BC V6C 3L6
Tel 604/683-2000
tourismvancouver.com

● **Victoria Visitor Centre**
812 Wharf St.
Victoria, BC V8W 1T3
Tel 250/953-2033
tourismvictoria.com

● **Whistler Visitor Centre**
4230 Gateway Dr.
Whistler, BC V0N 1B4
Tel 604/935-3357
whistler.com

● **Kelowna Okanagan Valley Visitor Center**
544 Harvey Ave.
Kelowna, BC V1Y 6C9
Tel 250/861-1515
tourismkelowna.com

● **National Parks**
cpawsbc.org

● **British Columbia Provincial Parks**
env.gov.bc.ca/bcparks

A visitor peruses an Andy Warhol exhibit in a converted Vancouver warehouse.

Vancouver, Vancouver Maritime Museum, and False Creek, which delineates the south side of Vancouver's Burrard Peninsula. The creek's Granville Island (actually another peninsula) hosts a public market renowned for its food vendors. Farther up False Creek are Edgewater Casino, the Olympic Village from the 2010 Winter Olympics, Rogers Arena (home of the National Hockey League's Vancouver Canucks), and the distinctive geodesic dome of Science World at TELUS World of Science,

Vancouver by night, with the distinctive TELUS World of Science's geodesic dome front and center

an interactive science and technology museum.

Wedged between False Creek and the harbor, downtown Vancouver nourishes several interesting neighborhoods including Yaletown with its trendy restaurants and nightclubs, the Victorian-era architecture of the old Gastown District (named after Vancouver's pioneering pub owner "Gassy Jack" Deighton), and the multicultural tapestry of Chinatown. Beyond excellent Asian eateries, the area's main attraction is the Dr. Sun Yat-Sen Classical Chinese Garden, the first full-size scholar's garden developed outside of China. Downtown's musical high notes include the Jimi Hendrix Shrine on Homer Street and the wonderfully restored Orpheum Theatre (1927), home of the Vancouver Symphony Orchestra.

Way out west at Point Grey, the University of British Columbia (UBC) campus offers the beautiful Foreshore Trail along the Strait of Georgia, clothing-optional Wreck Beach, and the Nitobe Memorial Garden. Campus collections include the Museum of Anthropology with renowned ethnographic objects from around the world and the Beaty Biodiversity Museum.

Plant life also flourishes in the city's South Cambie district, home to VanDusen Botanical Garden and the domed Bloedel Conservatory (with its 200 free-flying birds) in Queen Elizabeth Park. On the opposite side of the harbor, **North Vancouver** segues into B.C. nature. Constructed in 1889, Capilano Suspension Bridge hovers 230 feet (70 m) above the Capilano River.

Originally made of hemp ropes and cedar planks, the bridge was "modernized" with wire cables in 1903

CAPITALISM

Although it seems like a gentle city today, Victoria was a thriving opium entrepôt during much of the 19th century. The raw product was shipped directly from British-ruled Hong Kong and processed in Victoria's dozen opium factories for distribution to Chinese railway workers and other users throughout the Pacific Northwest. The production and sale was totally legal and local government coffers were enriched by duties on the trade until 1908 when opium was finally banned.

and completely rebuilt in 1956. Beside the bridge, Treetops Adventure offers views from seven footbridges suspended 110 feet (34 m) above the rain forest floor as well as a Cliffwalk. The nearby Grouse Mountain Skyride, North America's largest aerial tramway system, takes riders on a one-mile (1.6 km) flight to Alpine Station at 3,700 feet (1,128 m) above sea level. Grouse Mountain Resort offers alpine sports on 26 runs and a range of outdoor activities in summer.

Across the Strait of Georgia, **Victoria** perches at the bottom end of Vancouver Island. Considered one of Canada's most "British" cities, the capital of British Columbia retains many of its Victorian-era buildings and gardens. Many of the city's landmarks are set around the busy Inner Harbour, including the hulking Empress Hotel (1908), the flamboyant neo-baroque British Columbia Legislature Building (1897), and the Royal BC Museum, which highlights the province's natural and human history. Beside the museum, numerous totem poles and other First Nations treasures can be found at Thunderbird Park. Other attractions in the Inner Harbour/downtown area include the Maritime Museum of British Columbia, the Victoria Bug Zoo, and Fisherman's Wharf. The Emily Carr House and Garden (complete with pet cats) is just blocks away from the Inner Harbour. A definitive collection of the trailblazing artist Robert Bateman's copious work is housed at the Robert Bateman Centre.

Most orca- and dolphin-watching tours, as well as kayak adventures, depart from docks in the Inner Harbour area. Beacon Hill Park provides a huge green space in the central city, bordered by Dallas Road

Butchart Gardens, Victoria; opposite: Emerald Lake, Yoho National Park

Waterfront Trail along the strait. East of the city center, Craigdarroch Castle was built between 1887 and 1890 for Robert Dunsmuir, a Scottish immigrant who made a fortune off of Vancouver Island coal, and remains furnished in grand Victorian style. Nearby Government House, the official residence of the province's lieutenant governor, is open for tours one Saturday per month. The grounds feature formal gardens as well as the Cary Castle Mews Interpretive Centre and Tea Room. Half an hour north of the city, Butchart Gardens' amazing array of flowers and plants from around the globe flourishes on the site of a former cement quarry. Over on the east side, Fort Rodd Hill and Fisgard Lighthouse National Historic Sites overlook Esquimalt Harbour in Colwood. The fort offers visitors a glimpse of bunkers and the

HIDDEN TREASURES

B.C., or "Hollywood North," boasts locations used in a number of movies and TV shows including:

• **Riverview Hospital (Coquitlam):** has appeared in *MacGyver*, *The X-Files*, *Stargate*, *Fringe*, *Battlestar Galactica*, and more than 50 other movies and TV shows

• **Cleveland Dam (North Vancouver):** played roles in two different Arnold Schwarzenegger films—*Eraser* and *The 6th Day*—as well as *First Blood* with Sylvester Stallone

• **Langley Township:** provided spooky venues for *Bates Motel*, the *Twilight* films, *The Fog*, and *The Vampire Diaries*

• **Squamish:** screen credits include more than 80 movies and TV shows as varied as *McCabe & Mrs. Miller*, *Happy Gilmore*, *Insomnia*, *Free Willy 3*, and *The Revenant*

• **Vancouver Art Gallery:** stood in for fictional buildings in *The Accused*, *Night at the Museum*, *Scooby-Doo 2*, and *The X-Files*

command post of a military base active from 1895 to 1956, while the 1860 lighthouse is the oldest on the Canadian west coast.

LANDSCAPES

The largest island along the entire Pacific shore of the Western Hemisphere, **Vancouver Island** stretches nearly 300 miles (483 km) from stem to stern and creeps nearly halfway up the B.C. coast. Heavily forested, much of the island is protected within the confines of nature reserves including Strathcona Provincial Park and three units of **Pacific Rim National Park.** The latter includes great (cold water) surfing at Long Beach, the Kwisitis Visitor Centre, the West Coast Trail, and the hundred or so Broken Group Islands in Barkley Sound, a haven for kayaking and camping.

Port Hardy near the island's northern extreme is the southern terminus of the summertime **BC Ferries Discovery Coast Connector** through the myriad islands along the central and northern B.C. shore. Much of the region is protected as part of the **Great Bear Rainforest,** the world's largest coastal temperate rain forest (21 million acres/8.5 million ha) and the only place to see the rare, white Kermode bear (aka spirit bear). Among the stops along the ferry route are Bella Bella, with its strong First Nations culture; Bella Coola, gateway to Tweedsmuir South Provincial Park; and Prince Rupert, the onetime "Halibut Capital of the World" and northernmost port along the B.C. coast.

From Prince Rupert, another B.C. Ferries line makes the run to Canada's version of the Galápagos—the remote and wildlife rich **Haida Gwaii** (Islands of the People). Previously called the Queen Charlotte Islands, this rugged archipelago is overseen jointly by Parks Canada and the Haida Nation. Gwaii Haanas National Park Reserve and Haida Heritage Site, often called simply Gwaii Haanas, is the planet's first area protected all the way from mountaintop to seafloor.

The **Inside Passage** between Vancouver Island and the B.C. mainland is lined by secluded, floating fishing camps and charming towns such as Gibsons, Powell River, Madeira Park, and Sechelt. Johnstone Strait is considered one of the best places to see orcas (killer whales) in the wild.

Tucked into the Coast Mountains 75 miles (121 km) north of

The imposing Fairmont Empress, Victoria's grand dame hotel

Vancouver, **Whistler** is Canada's paramount winter sports resort. Here the Peak 2 Peak Gondola connects ski and snowboard areas on Whistler and Blackcomb Mountains with a combined 200 marked runs, 16 alpine bowls, and three glaciers. It's even possible to ski in summer on Horstman Glacier. Whistler Olympic Park hosted both alpine, Nordic, and sliding events for the 2010 Winter Games. Only pros can use the ski jumps but mere mortals can try their hand at (guided) bobsled and skeleton at the Whistler Sliding Centre. During summer, the region offers a multitude of outdoor adventures as well as the Squamish Lil'wat Cultural Centre and Whistler Museum.

Mount Assiniboine, the "Matterhorn of the Canadian Rockies"

South-central B.C., dominated by the **Okanagan Valley,** contains Canada's premier vineyard and winemaking region. This stretches about 125 miles (200 km) from north to south, much of the massive glacial trough filled by Okanagan Lake. In addition to wine tasting, the valley offers hiking trails, golf courses, sandy beaches, and lakeshore spas. Kettle Valley Steam Railway and its 1912 steam locomotive takes visitors on a 90-minute journey past vineyards and orchards and across the 238-foot-high (73 m) Trout Creek Bridge. Farther south, Keremeos in Similkameen Valley is the self-proclaimed "Fruit Stand Capital of Canada."

East of the Okanagan, B.C.'s immense **Central Plateau** gradually rises into a series of mountain ranges—Monashee, Selkirk, and Purcell—that eventually culminates in the Canadian Rockies. Many of the highland towns have distinct personalities. With trails on old railway beds, prospector trails, and whiskey running routes, Rossland is

one of the Canada's top mountain-biking destinations. Nelson exposes its silver-rush roots with numerous restored buildings that now house restaurants, bars, and shops. Kimberley's Underground Mining Railway takes visitors through Mark Creek Valley and a 2,475-foot (754 m) tunnel to the Underground Interpretive Centre for a brief taste of what it was like to be a miner. The region is also rife with winter resorts including Revelstoke, Panorama, Kicking Horse, and Fernie scattered along the "powder highway" (Route 95).

The B.C. Rockies embrace several awesome nature areas including Kootenay and Yoho National Parks, as well as Hamber, Mount Assiniboine, and Height of the Rockies Provincial Parks. In addition to impressive snowcapped peaks, Kootenay offers a chance to soak in steamy Radium Hot Springs and take guided hikes to

three different fossil beds. The highest peak in the Canadian Rockies—12,972-foot (3,954 m) Mount Robson lurks within a provincial park of the same name. ■

STATE OF THE ART

• **Best movies:** *The Grey Fox* (1982) and *The Grocer's Wife* (1991)

• **Best books:** *Up the Lake: Coastal British Columbia Stories* by Wayne J. Lutz and *The Cure for Death by Lightning* by Gail Anderson-Dargatz

• **Best music:** "The Crawl" by Spirit of the West

• **Best art:** the British Columbia landscapes and portraits of Sophie Pemberton and the sculptures of Bill Reid

• **Best TV shows:** *Continuum* and *The Beachcombers*

Manitoba

Canada's land of lakes stretches from the tundra-trimmed coast of the Hudson Bay south to the golden prairies. In Winnipeg, the province boasts one of the nation's most intriguing cities. Polar bears, great fishing, pioneer-era towns, and a marvelous array of national and provincial parks round out the Manitoba travel experience.

CITIES

Whether you call it the "Chicago of the North" or "Gateway to the West," **Winnipeg** does seem to have several things in common with the Windy City—extreme winter weather and an unrelenting drive to create a metropolis on the prairie. The Forks National Historic Site near downtown traces 6,000 years of local history, from the Aboriginal peoples who once lived here to the coming of the railway and European immigration. The sprawling waterfront complex also includes the Forks Market, the highly interactive Manitoba Children's Museum, and the Manitoba Theatre for Young People, as well as a popular Riverside Walk. Farther north along the waterfront, the Canadian Museum for Human Rights seeks to foster better understanding and spur human rights leadership. The dramatic Esplanade Riel Footbridge leaps across the Red River to Saint Boniface, a French-Canadian neighborhood with roots stretching back to the early 19th century. The area's unique culture is reflected in such institutions as Le Musée de Saint-Boniface, La Maison des Artistes Visuels Francophones, and the imposing facade of Saint Boniface Cathedral—the only thing that remains of the church after a 1906 fire destroyed the original building. Guided tours are available of the Royal Canadian Mint, where all of Canada's coinage is created; the Mint has also made metal currency for 75 other nations. Hidden among the downtown highrises are the intriguing Manitoba Museum and the Centennial Concert Hall. Triangular Old Market Square hosts summer concerts and other special events, while the adjacent Royal Manitoba Theatre Centre is the place to catch big Broadway-style shows. For more entertainment, MTS Centre is home to the National Hockey League's Winnipeg Jets.

The provincial government quarter south of downtown is dominated by the majestic Manitoba

TOURISM INFORMATION

Travel Manitoba maintains a tourist information center at The Forks Market in Winnipeg. Visit travelmanitoba.com for more information.

• **Tourism Winnipeg Information Centre**
259 Portage Ave., #300
Winnipeg, MB R3B 2A8
Tel 204/943-1970
tourismwinnipeg.com

• **Churchill Visitor Centre**
Train Station
1 Mantayo Seepee Meskanow
Churchill, MB R0B 0E0
Tel 204/675-8863
everythingchurchill.com

• **Parks Canada**
pc.gc.ca

• **Manitoba Provincial Parks**
gov.mb.ca/conservation /parks

Winnipeg's Manitoba Museum recalls life some 65 million years ago.

Ice floes near remote Churchill on the Hudson Bay in northern Manitoba

Legislative Building, a neoclassical landmark opened in 1920 with a dome topped by a statue known as Golden Boy. The capitol district also provides a venue for the Winnipeg Art Gallery, the Queen Anne–style Dalnavert Museum and Vistors' Centre, and the Naval Museum of Manitoba. Over on the west side, Assiniboine Park flaunts playgrounds, a sculpture garden, an outdoor theater, a miniature railway, the municipal zoo, and the 700-acre (283 ha) Assiniboine Forest. The Royal Aviation Museum of Western Canada is housed in a 1930s Trans-Canada Airlines hangar at the edge of Winnipeg International Airport. The Living Prairie Museum near Sturgeon Creek safeguards a rare inner-city tract of pristine tall-grass prairie, with more than 160 plant species and a variety of indigenous wildlife. Another huge green space on the edge of the city, FortWhyte Alive mixes environmental education and outdoor recreation center, an eclectic park that features everything from a bison herd to winter sports facilities.

LANDSCAPES

Set along the autumn migration route between polar bear dens and their floe-edge feeding grounds, **Churchill** in northern Manitoba is considered the best place on the planet to get up close (and sometimes personal) with polar bears in the wild. The big white beasts gather along the rocky coast of Hudson Bay to wait for pack ice to form each October and November so they can hunt seals. They wander into town often enough to justify a tranquilizer dart–equipped patrol, polar bear "jail," and helicopter service to airlift them to the wilderness far away from humans. Meanwhile, tundra buggies transport visitors into the wilds around Churchill to view polar bears in their natural habitat, and the unique rolling Tundra Lodge affords an opportunity to spend the night in bear country. Helicopter tours into **Wapusk National Park** include aerial views of the migrating giants and a chance to crawl into an empty (but recently occupied) bear den. Churchill's other natural attractions include spectacular aurora borealis viewing in winter and beluga whale–watching in summer on Hudson Bay. The town's Eskimo Museum offers Inuit art and tools from 1700 B.C. through present day as well as displays on local history.

The star-shaped Prince of Wales Fort at desolate Eskimo Point was built in the 1700s as a Hudson's Bay Company trading post. Train and plane are the only ways to reach Churchill; there is no overland road from southern Manitoba.

Manitoba's other great natural escape, **Lake Winnipeg** is one of the world's dozen largest lakes. It's also one of the globe's best places to fish, well-stocked with more than a dozen game species from whitefish and walleye to sturgeon, sauger, and northern pike. Although the name Winnipeg means "murky waters" in the Cree language, the lake is also a pretty good place to swim come summer, especially at Grand Beach.

Set amid the boreal forest west of Lake Winnipeg, **The Pas** takes its name from an 18th-century French fur-trading post, Fort Paskoyac. Today this edge-of-the-

wilderness town is known as a great place to view the northern lights. Other attractions include the offbeat Sam Waller Museum, Aseneskak Casino, paddling on the Grass

White-sand beaches on vast Lake Winnipeg, which covers an area about the size of New Hampshire

River, and the lucent waters of Clear Lake.

Clear Lake is the hub of **Riding Mountain National Park** in western Manitoba. Water sports, camping, and trekking the park's 250 miles (402 km) of trails are the big thing in summer; ice-skating, snowshoeing, and cross-country skiing prevail in winter. Wildlife is profuse and spread across three distinct habitats: prairie, boreal forest, and deciduous woods. Nearby Asessippi Ski Area, the province's largest winter resort, boasts 26 downhill ski/snowboard runs, two terrain parks, and a snow-tubing park as well as dogsledding.

Sights are few and far between on the province's great plains but well worth the long drives to reach them. **The International Peace Garden** on the Manitoba–North Dakota border features a botanical garden, a huge floral clock, hiking trails, and an interpretive center. The **Canadian Fossil Discovery Centre** in Morden flaunts the nation's largest collection of prehistoric marine reptile remains, many of them found in the surrounding hills. The **Mennonite Heritage Village** in Steinbach re-creates a turn-of-the-century Russian Mennonite settlement. The village's two dozen structures include a classic house barn, fully operational Dutch windmill, historical museum, and Mennonite restaurant.

The **Red River Valley** between Winnipeg and its namesake lake is also rich in pioneer-era history. At Lower Fort Garry National Historic Site, staff in period dress give living-history presentations in buildings dating from the fort's days as a 19th-century Hudson's Bay Company trading post. The Marine Museum of Manitoba in

A polar bear and its cub on the tundra near Churchill

nearby Selkirk showcases Lake Winnipeg and Red River watercraft and other artifacts from about 1850 to the present day. Oak Hammock Marsh is a popular birding destination, with more than 20 miles (31 km) of trails radiating out from an excellent modern interpretive center.

About a 90-minute drive east of Winnipeg, **Whiteshell Provincial Park** flaunts more than a thousand square miles (2,590 sq km) of protected wilderness, including lakes, rivers, waterfalls, rock formations, and forest. Nature-oriented activities abound, and the area also has its man-made attractions: ancient petroforms (rock alignments), the Alfred Hole Goose Sanctuary, the Whiteshell Natural History Museum, and the Museum of Geological History, beside West Hawk crater lake. ■

LITTLE-KNOWN FACTS

• The Narcisse Snake Dens of central Manitoba boast the world's greatest reptile concentration—what's believed to be as many as 10,000 red-sided garter snakes wintering in a single spit.

• Winnipeg hosts the planet's longest skating rink—a natural five-mile (8 km) track that takes shape each winter along the frozen Red and Assiniboine Rivers.

• Winnipeg and Ulaanbaatar (Mongolia) are considered two of the world's coldest big cities. The lowest ever temperature recorded in Manitoba's capital was an ultra-chilly -54°F (-47.8°C) in 1879.

• With around 26,000 people claiming ancestry, Manitoba has the largest Icelandic population other than Iceland.

New Brunswick

Named for the ancestral German home of England's Georgian kings, New Brunswick is the only officially bilingual Canadian province, linguistically blending the nation's French and British heritages. Picturesque coastlines along the Bay of Fundy and Gulf of Saint Lawrence are the province's main attractions, but it also hosts vibrant cities as well as a largely unexplored hinterland of river valleys, mountains, and farmland.

CITIES

Canada's first incorporated city (1785), **Saint John** grew up at the spot where its eponymous river flows into the Bay of Fundy. Saint John City Market is the country's oldest continuously operated farmers market, with a ringing bell marking the start and end of each shopping day. Housed in a block-long, open-air building erected in 1876, it's a great place to browse for edibles, crafts, and souvenirs. Also arrayed around leafy King's Square in the heart of the city are the meticulously restored Imperial Theatre (1913), the Old No. 2 Engine House firefighting museum, Trinity Church (1880), and the Loyalist Burial Ground, where many of those fleeing the 13 Colonies during the American Revolution found their last resting place. The nearby Georgian-style Loyalist House National Historic Site, built in 1817 for Thomas Merritt and his family, is filled with authentic furnishings and memorabilia from that era. It is also one of the few structures that survived the Great Fire of Saint John in 1877. Part of the modern retail and entertainment complex of Market Square, the three-story New Brunswick Museum—Canada's oldest continuing museum (1842)—aims to "collect, preserve, research, and interpret" the natural and cultural heritage of the province. On the opposite side of the harbor from

TOURISM INFORMATION

Tourism New Brunswick operates seven provincial visitor information centers at popular points around the province. For more information, check out tourismnewbrunswick.ca.

- **Saint John Visitor Information Centre**
Shoppes of City Hall
15 Market Square
Saint John, NB E2L 1E8
Tel 506/658-2855 or
866/463-8639
discoversaintjohn.com

- **Tourism Moncton Information Centre**
20 Mountain Rd.
Moncton, NB E1C 2J8
Tel 800-363-4558
tourism.moncton.ca

- **Fredericton Tourism Information Centre**
11 Carleton St.
Fredericton, NB E3B 4Y7
Tel 506/460-2041
tourismfredericton.ca

- **Parks Canada**
pc.gc.ca

- **New Brunswick Provincial Parks**
tourismnewbrunswick.ca

Nicknamed "hub city," Moncton lies at the center of the Maritime Provinces.

Sea grasses under cloudy skies near the fishing village of Cape Pelé

downtown, ferries to Nova Scotia depart from the West Side docks. Overlooking the waterfront, the Carleton Martello Tower National Historic Site includes a restored powder magazine and barracks as well as exhibits on the bastion's role in the War of 1812 through World War II. The region's remarkable hydrology has endowed Saint John with several natural landmarks. Notable are the powerful Reversing Falls rapids formed twice daily when the rising tide from the Bay of Fundy pushes against the flow of the Saint John River, forcing the river to change directions. Reversing Falls Bridge offers a great perspective on this impressive natural phenomenon.

Located in the Petitcodiac River Valley upstream from the Bay of Fundy, **Moncton** is the province's largest Francophone city, founded by Acadians who were not expelled by the British after the French and Indian War. The Musée Acadien de l'Université de Moncton features more than 42,000 artifacts and gives an excellent overview of Acadian religion, politics, business, folklore, and the arts. Le Centre Culturel Aberdeen (Aberdeen Cultural Centre) provides space for local artists and cultural organizations, along with a gallery. Nearby Resurgo Place is home to the Moncton Museum and the Transportation Discovery Centre, as well as historical relics such as the Free Meeting House and Cemetery. Centennial Park

HIDDEN TREASURES

Fundy National Park isn't the only place that showcases the Bay of Fundy, one of the world's most unique waterways:

• **The Hopewell Rocks (Lower Cape):** carved by tidal erosion; stand 40 to 70 feet (12–21 km) tall; walk around them during low tide or kayak around during high tide

• **Cape Enrage (Waterside):** features a small lighthouse (1838), cliffs with panoramic views over the Bay of Fundy, and an outdoor activity center

• **Grand Manan Island:** This onetime haunt of famous painters and writers is accessible by ferry from Blacks Harbour; it's a great place for whale- and bird-watching.

• **Campobello Island:** long-time summer home of U.S. president Franklin Roosevelt and his wife, Eleanor; offers an FDR museum, nature park, and the East Quoddy Lighthouse

• **Saint Andrews Village:** hosts the Huntsman Fundy Discovery Aquarium and whale-watching boat trips out into the open bay waters

encompasses trails, sports fields, playgrounds, the TreeGO zip line, and even an artificial beach on Centennial Lake. On the northern outskirts of town, Magnetic Hill Park offers several distinct attractions—its name derives from the optical illusion based on the rising and descending terrain that make vehicles appear to coast uphill when parked at the base of Magnetic Hill Road. Magnetic Hill Zoo displays more than 400 animals from 90 species, and Butterfly World features hundreds of winged friends. Also of interest, Magic Mountain Waterpark is the largest man-made attraction in Atlantic Canada.

The provincial capital of Fredericton was a British garrison from 1784 to 1869. Remnants of this history live on in the Historic Garrison District, including a daily changing of the guard during summer in Officers' Square, croquet matches in Barracks Square, and heritage walking tours as well as summer theater and concerts. The Fredericton Region Museum mainly concentrates on the heritage of York and Sunbury Counties, while the School Days Museum showcases artifacts and memorabilia from area public schools dating from the mid-19th century. The New Brunswick Sports Hall of Fame offers an interactive virtual sports system where visitors can test their skills. The New Brunswick College of Craft and Design has a gallery as well as courses in art and design. Among the capital's other sights are the Lighthouse on the Green, deeply wooded Odell Park, Beaverbrook Art Gallery, and performances at the restored Fredericton Playhouse.

LANDSCAPES

New Brunswick's southern shore borders the renowned **Bay of Fundy,** one of North America's most storied waterways. Its most remarkable feature is the world's greatest tidal range, as much as 53 feet (16 m) in some places. Each day, 160 billion tons (145 billion metric tons) of seawater flows in and out of the 170-mile-long (274 km) bay, which formed in the ancient rift valley that separates New Brunswick and Nova Scotia.

Fundy Trail Parkway—a combined driving, biking, and hiking route—hugs the coast between Saint John and **Fundy National Park,** where visitors can walk a beach exposed by low tides, watch for whales, kayak the rising tide, and fish or swim the bay. Away from the water, numerous hiking and biking trails lead to waterfalls and pristine forest. Other habitats include a salt march estuary and a bog with birding and other wildlife viewing.

The province's other coast, along the Gulf of Saint Lawrence, is sprinkled with nature areas, bygone

ROAD TRIPS

Great drives across the Picture Province:

• Fundy Coastal Drive (Highways 1, 111 and 114) between Saint Stephen and Moncton (220 miles/354 km)

• Miramichi River Route (Highway 8) between Fredericton and Miramichi (108 miles/ 174 km)

• Acadian Coastal Drive (Highway 11) between Moncton and Dalhousie (260 miles/418 km)

• Appalachian Range Route (Highways 17 and 385) through the mountains between Dalhousie and Perth-Andover (173 miles/278 km)

Tides alternately expose and submerge the sandstone Hopewell Rocks in the Bay of Fundy.

fishing villages, and Acadian historical sites. Parlee Beach Provincial Park near **Shediac** revolves around strands where visitors can swim in what Canadians consider warm coastal waters. One of several burgs along the Atlantic seaboard that claim to be the world's lobster capitals, Shediac offers good French restaurants, art galleries, the Neptune Drive-In movie theater, and that giant lobster statue on Rotary Park.

Farther north along the gulf coast, the Miramichi River offers a mother lode of 18th- and 19th-century history. **Beaubears Island Shipbuilding National Historic Site** focuses on New Brunswick's wooden ship–building heritage, while **Boishébert National Historic Site** preserves the remains of an Acadian refugee camp from the French and Indian War. The area is still covered in old-growth forest, including 200-year-old white pines. Upstream, **Metepenagiag Heritage Park** near Red Bank celebrates the indigenous Mi'kmaq people on ancestral lands where they have lived continuously for more than 30 centuries.

Chaleur Bay harbors a number of small Acadian communities. Caraquet provides a venue for a popular Acadian festival and the Village Historique Acadien, an open-air museum that brings the years between 1780 and 1890 back to life through the reenactment of daily life and "villagers" in period costumes. More than 40 historical buildings are scattered around the site.

At 2,690 feet (820 m), Mount Carleton is the highest peak in the Maritimes. Named after New Brunswick's first lieutenant governor, the peak is a landmark on the

Humpbacks and other whales frequent the Bay of Fundy, a rich marine feeding ground.

Canadian extension of the Appalachian Trail. Mount Carleton Provincial Park protects more than 42,000 acres (16,997 ha) of pristine wilderness, home to 30 mammal species and some 100 kinds of birds.

Hartland Bridge, the world's longest covered wooden bridge, leaps 1,282 feet (391 m) across the Saint John River between Hartland and Somerville. Opened in 1901, it wasn't actually covered until two decades later owing to local moralists who fought against the so-called kissing bridges they alleged corrupted area youth. ∎

FESTIVALS

• **Fiddles on the Tobique (Nictau):** offbeat three-day shindig combining two of the region's favorite pastimes—fiddling and canoeing; June

• **Festival Western (Saint-Quentin):** Acadian cowboys buck broncos, ride bulls, and court Miss Cowgirl Atlantic; July.

• **Provincial Peat Moss Festival (Lamèque Island):** Acadian culture takes the stage with comedy and country music shows, a treasure hunt,

a classic car show, hockey games, and more; July.

• **Larlee Creek Hullabaloo (Perth-Andover):** down-home music from down east; August

• **Winter Warmer Festival (Saint Andrews-by-the-Sea):** month-long homage to the holiday season includes the Fireman's Candlelight Parade, big Boxing Day Dance, and more; late November to early January

Newfoundland & Labrador

A separate British colony until 1949, Newfoundland and Labrador may have come late to Canada but they are now considered vital components of the maple leaf nation. "The Rock" (Newfoundland) flaunts a rich maritime history, intrepid explorers, and fisher folk who founded the island's moody waterfront communities. Meanwhile Labrador, or "the Big Land," brings wilderness to the edge of the sea.

CITIES

The most easterly city in the Americas, **Saint John's** is actually much closer to Ireland than Canada's west coast. Its permanent year-round settlement stretches back to the 1630s, and many of the city's major attractions are found on or near its snug harbor, including George Street with its wall-to-wall pubs, the Railway Coastal Museum, the colorful Jellybean Row houses, and the National War Memorial.

Government House, official residence of the lieutenant governor of Newfoundland and Labrador, offers public tours by appointment. Among the city's other colonial-era landmarks is the hilltop Basilica-Cathedral of Saint John the Baptist (1839–1855) with its skyline-dominating twin towers. Next door, the Provincial Museum, Archives, and Art Gallery are clustered in an unusual cultural hub called The Rooms. Perched high above

TOURISM INFORMATION

Newfoundland & Labrador Tourism maintains nine provincial visitor information centers around the territory. Visit newfoundlandlabrador.com.

- **City of St. John's Visitor Information Centre**
348 Water St.
St. John's, NL A1C 5M2
Tel 709/576-8106
destinationstjohns.com

- **Port aux Basques Provincial Visitor Information Centre**
Route 1 north of Port aux Basques
Tel 709/695-2262

- **Deer Lake Provincial Visitor Information Centre**
South side of Route 1, beside Circle-K Irving Gas Station
Tel 709/635-2202

- **Gateway to Labrador Visitor Centre**
Old Church
38 Main Hwy (Route 510)
L'Anse Au Clair, Labrador
Tel 709/931-2013
labradorcoastaldrive.com

- **Newfoundland & Labrador Provincial Parks**
www.env.gov.nl.ca/parks

the harbor entrance, Signal Hill is where the final battle of the Seven Years' War played out, a 1762 skirmish that ended in French surrender to the British. It's also the spot where Marconi received the first transatlantic wireless signal in 1901. Despite its Gothic mien, the hilltop Cabot Tower was built in 1900 to mark the 400th anniversary of Cabot's discovery of Newfoundland. The park also hosts the Signal Hill Tattoo, a military performance compete with cannon fire and 18th-century uniforms staged during the summer months. At the

The vibrant houses of Jellybean Row in downtown Saint John's

Lighthouse and the ruins of World War II batteries at Fort Amherst on Saint John's Harbor

base of Signal Hill, the innovative Johnson GEO Centre features galleries on outer space and the *Titanic* shipwreck. On the north side of Signal Hill, Quidi Vidi Lake is the venue for North America's oldest annual sporting event, the Royal Saint John's Regatta, first staged in 1816. Suncor Energy Fluvarium, a public environmental education center in Pippy Park, includes underwater windows to view brown trout in their natural environment.

South of Saint John's, **Cape Spear** is the continent's most eastern point, less than 2,000 miles (3,219 km) from Ireland's west coast. The cliffs are a popular vantage point for watching the sunrise as well as icebergs and passing whales. Cape

Spear Lighthouse is the province's oldest surviving coastal light.

THE ISLAND

Saint John's perches on the sea star–shaped **Avalon Peninsula,** the cradle of British settlement in Newfoundland and longtime hub of the island's fishing industry, given its close proximity to the Grand Banks. The 164-mile (264 km) East Coast Trail meanders down the peninsula's Atlantic shore between Cape Saint Francis and Cappahayden. The hiking route is divided into 24 well-marked and rated sections that can each be walked in a single day, perhaps while exploring La Manche Provincial Park or the active archaeological dig at

ROAD TRIPS

Great drives across the Rock and the Big Land:

• Trans-Canada Highway between Channel-Port aux Basques and Saint John's (560 miles/901 km)

• Heritage Run (Route 210) down and around the Burin Peninsula between

Goobies and Grand Bank (164 miles/264 km)

• Viking Trail (Route 430) across the Great Northern Peninsula between Deer Lake and Saint Anthony (258 miles/415 km)

• Southern Shore Highway (Route 10)

along the Atlantic side of the Avalon Peninsula between Saint John's and Saint Vincent's (114 miles/183 km)

• Trans-Labrador Highway (Routes 510 and 500) between Blanc-Sablon and Labrador City (700 miles/1,127 km)

Ferryland, the remains of the Colony of Avalon founded in 1621 by Lord Baltimore. The dig interpretation center features some two million artifacts found thus far.

More history abounds along the shore of the peninsula's Conception Bay. Canada's version of Jamestown, **Cupids** is the oldest English colony in Canada. Founded in 1610 by John Guy, this is thought to be where the continent's first European child was born. The Cupids Legacy Centre illuminates local history through innovative exhibits and artifacts uncovered at Cupids Cove Plantation Provincial Historic Site.

Among the town's other attractions are Saint George's Heritage Church and the John Guy Flag Site.

Isolated from the rest of Newfoundland for centuries, the **Burin Peninsula** developed its own dialect, dances, and architecture—a microculture influenced by English, French, and Basque settlers. The Burin is renowned for great birding, as well as spectacular coastal hikes and classic fishing villages such as Grand Bank and Fortune. The latter is also the gateway to Saint Pierre and Miquelon, the last remaining French territory in North America and the final vestige of New France. Once

dependent on fishing, the twin isles have evolved into a tourist destination that revolves around French colonial architecture, French cuisine, nature walks, and wildlife viewing. High-speed ferries make the crossing in less than an hour.

Cape Bonavista on the north shore is where Italian mariner Giovanni Caboto (aka John Cabot) first sighted the New World in 1497, during an expedition funded by King Henry VII of England. A statue of Cabot looms near the historic 1843 lighthouse at the end of Cape Shore Road. In the nearby town of Bonavista, Ryan Premises National Historic Site and Mockbeggar Plantation showcase the area's rich fishing heritage.

Farther up the north shore, **Terra Nova National Park** sprawls across several rocky fingers that extend into Bonavista Bay. The park terrain varies from islands and inlets to wetlands and boreal forest inhabited by bear, moose, and lynx. Marine mammals are often spotted offshore. Beyond Gander and its famous air base, **Fogo Island** and its rocky coast are home to 11 villages with brightly colored clapboard buildings, many occupied by artists.

Newfoundland's west coast is anchored by imposing **Gros Morne**

Sod houses at L'Anse aux Meadows recall life when Vikings lived here.

National Park, a UNESCO World Heritage site spangled with fjords and forests, bogs and beaches. The park is also celebrated for its intricate geology, the place where scientists finally proved the theory of plate tectonics. From remote hiking trails and rock climbing to camping and kayaking, Gros Morne provides varied adventures. Villages around Boone Bay offer whale-watching and fjord cruises.

At the tip of the Great Northern Peninsula, **L'Anse aux Meadows National Historic Site** preserves the place where Norsemen landed and established a small settlement around A.D. 1000—probably the "Vinland" discovered by Leif Erikson. Rangers in Viking garb lead visitors on a living-history tour of a reproduction Norse longhouse, workshop, and stable with original artifacts. Complete with a full-scale replica of the Viking ship *Snorri,* nearby **Norstead** is another fine living-history museum where costumed interpreters recount Norse tales.

THE MAINLAND

Across the Strait of Belle Isle lies **Labrador,** the province's huge and largely uninhabited mainland portion. Europeans settled the southeast coast around the same time as Newfoundland, leaving the rest of Labrador to the indigenous Inuit and Mother Nature. Ferries cross the strait between Saint Barbe and Blanc-Sablon, Quebec, eastern terminus of the Trans-Labrador Highway.

Fifty miles (80 km) up the shore from Blanc-Sablon, **Red Bay National Historic Site** preserves a bygone Basque whaling station established in the mid-16th

Newfoundland is home to hundreds of Atlantic puffin breeding colonies.

century. The interpretation center displays original Basque whaling boats and other artifacts. Located on a near-shore island, **Battle Harbour** has morphed from a fishing village into a tourism hub with historic homes, hiking trails, fishing charters, and boat trips to watch whales and icebergs.

Torngat Mountains National Park on the northern tip of the Labrador Peninsula sprawls across 3,745 square miles (9,700 sq km)

of pristine nature where visitors can hike, canoe, cross-country ski, and snowmobile through a landscape dominated by tundra, glacial valleys, and the highest mountains in eastern mainland Canada. The park's abundant wildlife includes polar bears and large caribou herds. Tent-style accommodations are available at the park base camp, which also organizes multiday trips into the park led by Parks Canada rangers or Inuit guides. ■

HIDDEN TREASURES

Newfoundland offers many close encounters of the animal kind:

• **Cape Saint Mary's Ecological Reserve (Saint Bride's):** a cliff-side rookery that supports major colonies of seabirds

• **Ocean Quest Adventures (Saint John's):** scuba diving, snorkeling, and kayak encounters with whales, seabirds, creatures on the ocean floor, and other wildlife

• **Newfoundland Insectarium (Deer Lake):** wide variety of mounted insects from around the world organized by geographical region

• **Bay du Nord Wilderness Reserve:** home to the island's largest woodland caribou herd (15,000 strong) as well as moose, bear, beaver, otter, ptarmigan, and more

• **Captain Wayne's Marine Excursions (Bay Bulls):** cruises to view whales, dolphins, and puffins

Northwest Territories

"North of 60" is the motto for this remote and rugged Canadian land that lies completely above 60° north latitude. The liquid wonders of Great Slave Lake and the Mackenzie River beckon visitors to get out on the water, while the tundra barrens along the territory's Arctic coast lure polar bears, caribou, and those who come to see the creatures in their natural habitat.

CITIES

Yellowknife, sprawled along the north shore of Great Slave Lake, is a hardworking city that makes its living from diamond mining, government, and tourism. The unusual name derives from the copper blades once manufactured and traded by the region's Dene people (who were once called the Copper Indians). First Nations influence remains strong in this metropolis of the Canadian north. Almost a quarter of the city's 20,000 residents claim Aboriginal ancestry, and five different languages are spoken around town. Yellowknife first took shape in the 1930s, when gold miners established a small settlement on a narrow peninsula jutting into the lake. Now called Old Town, the bygone neighborhood retains such gold rush relics as the log cabin Wildcat Cafe, the original Weaver and Devore trading post (now Bullock's Bistro), Old Town Warehouse, and the

TOURISM INFORMATION

Discover more about Canada's secluded corner on the Northwest Territories Tourism website: spectacularnwt.com.

• **Northwest Frontier Visitors Centre**
4807 49th St., #4
Yellowknife, NT X1A 3T5
Tel 867/873-4262
visityellowknife.com

• **Western Arctic Regional Visitor Centre**
276 Mackenzie Rd.
Inuvik, NT
Tel 867/873-5007
spectacularnwt.com

• **Fort Simpson Visitor Information Centre**
100th St. at 93rd Ave.
Fort Simpson, NT
Tel 867/695-3182
fortsimpson.com

• **Fort Smith Visitor Centre**
Federal Building
149 McDougal Rd.
Fort Smith, NT X0E 0P0
Tel 867/872-8400
fortsmith.ca/visitors

• **Northwest Territories Parks**
nwtparks.ca

hilltop Bush Pilots Monument with its view over the city and lake. Offshore is a floatplane base and several floating bed-and-breakfasts.

By the 1940s the town had expanded beyond the peninsula into New Town with government buildings, art galleries, and saloons frequented by local miners. Overlooking Frame Lake, the modern Prince of Wales Northern Heritage Centre preserves the history and culture of the Northwest Territories via exhibits and archives. Farther up the shore is the flying saucer–shaped

Trained sled dog teams lead the way across Great Slave Lake.

Aurora borealis, or northern lights, near Yellowknife

Northwest Territories Legislative Building. The city also offers plenty of opportunities for outdoor adventure, from lake and river fishing to hiking the Cameron River Falls Trail and teeing off at the Yellowknife Golf Club (home of the Canadian North Midnight Sun Classic Golf Tournament). Yellowknife is far and away the best place to plan winter and summer forays into the vast territorial wilderness.

LANDSCAPES

The majority of those who drive rather than fly into the Northwest Territories enter via the **Mackenzie Highway** from Alberta. Most of the region's other major towns are scattered along the wilderness thoroughfare as it meanders down the Mackenzie (Deh Cho) River Valley toward the Arctic.

Fort Providence occupies a strategic place where Great Slave Lake pours into the Mackenzie River and where the only highway to Yellowknife leaps across the river on Deh Cho Bridge. Completed in 2012, the bridge was a major feat of engineering, overcoming major climate and hydrological challenges before replacing the old summer ferry and winter "ice bridge." The town's Dene craft shops feature traditional porcupine quill crafts and beaver fur garments. Nearby attractions include Lady Evelyn Falls and the 3,000 buffalo that roam Mackenzie Bison Sanctuary (and sometimes wander into town).

Set on the south shore of Great Slave Lake, **Hay River** is the northern terminus of the railway from Edmonton, as well as a major fishing port. Fishing trips ranging from a couple of hours to a few weeks are easily arranged through local outfitters. When the lake ice finally melts and the summer suns bursts through, locals head to the driftwood-covered beach at Vale Island for a dip in the chilly waters.

Founded in 1791, **Fort Resolution** on the lake's south shore is the territory's oldest continually occupied town. More than 90 percent of the residents claim Aboriginal heritage, mainly Dene and Métis. Summer swimming, boating, and birding are popular at the nearby Slave River Delta. Around 160 miles (257 km) up the Slave River, **Fort Smith** is the gateway to the northern sector of the huge Wood Buffalo National Park. The town's Northern Life Museum & Cultural Centre

showcases one of Canada's best collections of northern Aboriginal and European pioneer artifacts, from birch-bark canoes to a reconstructed trading post and trapper's cabin. Another museum relic is the *Radium King,* a 1937 river tug that hauled barges transporting the uranium used in the Manhattan Project atomic bombs.

One of the world's largest game reserves, **Wood Buffalo National Park** spreads across more than 17,000 square miles (44,030 sq km) of Alberta and the Northwest Territories—an area larger than Denmark. North America's largest free-roaming bison herd—more than 6,000 animals strong—traverses the park's boreal forests and plains. Wood Buffalo is also home to whooping cranes, timber wolves, and peregrine falcons, as well as bear, moose, and lynx. The park's beavers constructed the world's largest known beaver dam (longer than 10 football fields), discovered in 2007 near Lake Claire. A number of sights are scattered along

ROAD TRIPS

Great drives across Canada's last frontier:

• Mackenzie Highway between Grimshaw in northern Alberta and Wrigley (722 miles/1,162 km)

• Dempster Highway between Dawson City in the Yukon to Inuvik in the Mackenzie River Delta (481 miles/774 km)

• Yellowknife Highway between Fort Providence to Yellowknife around the western end of Great Slave Lake (196 miles/ 315 km)

• Liard Highway between Fort Nelson, British Columbia, and Fort Simpson (301 miles/ 484 km)

• Ingraham Trail between Yellowknife and Tibbitt Lake, a route made famous by the TV show *Ice Road Truckers* (43 miles/70 km)

• Tuktoyaktuk Winter Road (over the ice) between Inuvik and Tuktoyaktuk (121 miles/ 195 km)

Highway 5 in the park's northern sector, including the 180-foot-deep (55 m) Angus Sinkhole, the Wetlands Interpretive Trail, and the bizarre Salt Plains, the remains of an ancient sea that covered the region 390 million years ago.

Nahanni National Park Reserve, the territory's other great national park, protects a dramatic stretch of the Mackenzie Mountains along the Yukon frontier. The park's geographical gem is a series of four deep canyons carved by the swift-flowing Naha Dehé (South Nahanni River).

Alexandra Falls on the Hay River close to the MacKenzie Highway

River trips and backpacking are the only way to experience the remote gorge. Beyond the river, Nahanni's terrain varies from snowcapped peaks and tundra plains to sulfurous hot springs and pristine aspen and spruce forests. The Parks Canada visitor center in Fort Simpson is the best place to plan trips into the wilderness. Locally based Simpson Air offers day flights to Glacier Lake and Virginia Falls (twice as high as Niagara).

The Mackenzie Highway finally peters out at Wrigley, a tiny Aboriginal community on the east bank of the **Mackenzie River.** Traveling farther down Canada's longest river (1,080 miles/1,738 km) requires a boat or floatplane in summer, or snowmobiles or dogsleds in winter. Near the spot where the river crosses the Arctic Circle is remote **Norman Wells,** named for the oil wells that once dotted the landscape. The bubbling crude long gone, Norman Wells is better known these days as the eastern terminus of the Canol Heritage Trail, a 221-mile (356 km) hiking route through the boreal forest, tundra, and mountains to the Yukon. Mementoes of the oil boom and exhibits on the area's natural and human history are found at the

A herd of bison graze at the Mackenzie Bison Sanctuary near Fort Providence.

Norman Wells Historical Centre. Canoe North Adventures is the place to organize river trips.

Inuvik lies on the edge of the Mackenzie Delta not far from the Arctic Ocean. The northernmost point that one can drive to in Canada, the town is linked to the Yukon via the Dempster Highway. With the decline of military and mining as the twin foundations of the local economy, Inuvik has refashioned itself as the adventure center of the Northwest Territory's polar wilderness. The Western Arctic Regional

Visitors Centre offers displays on local wildlife and culture, as well as tips on how to explore the region. Local outfitters offer birding boat trips and fishing expeditions in the delta; snowmobile, dogsled, canoe, and camping adventures; and scenic flights. During the winter, visitors can drive the ice roads to Tuktoyaktuk on the Arctic coast and Aklavik on the western side of the delta. The town maintains a network of groomed cross-country skiing and snowshoeing trails, as well as the Roads End Golf Club. ∎

LOCAL FLAVOR

• **Bannock:** A starchy staple of Inuit communities, this flour-and-lard-based flatbread is transformed into a dessert down south, where the Aurora Village restaurant serves it with tart cranberries and Yukon Jack sauce. *Aurora Lake, Yellowknife*

• **Arctic char:** Similar to salmon or trout, this cold-water fish is a favorite throughout the Canadian Arctic.

Trader's Grill serves it grilled with tomato chutney or smoked in seafood salad. *The Explorer Hotel, 4825 49th Ave., Yellowknife*

• **Bison:** The historic Wildcat Cafe serves lean, tasty bison meat several ways including burgers, stew, and mixed with scrambled eggs on a bed of hash browns. *3904 Wiley Rd., Yellowknife*

• **Whitefish:** Freshly caught in Great Slave Lake, whitefish is served as a pan-fried fillet or as beer-battered fish and chips at Keys Dining. *Ptarmigan Inn, 10 J. Gagnier St., Hay River*

• **Musk ox and caribou:** Two other Inuit standbys have morphed into gourmet dishes in the territorial capital and are served as steaks or stew at Bullock's Bistro. *3534 Weaver Dr., Yellowknife*

Nova Scotia

The most populous of Canada's three Maritime Provinces blends gorgeous shorelines, secluded wilderness, and a wide array of historic and cultural sights that reflect the region's mix of French, English, Scottish, and First Nations heritages. Extending far into the Atlantic, Nova Scotia nurtures a long and sometimes tumultuous relationship with the sea as evidenced by the numerous lighthouses, fishing villages, and busy Halifax Harbour.

CITIES

The largest urban center in the Maritimes, **Halifax** was one of the first British beachheads in Canada and later gained fame for its role as the Canadian equivalent of Ellis Island. Halifax Harbour is lined with the 2.5-mile (4 km) Waterfront Boardwalk where visitors can stroll, watch the boats, or explore shops, cafés, museums, and other attractions. The Historic Properties comprise three city blocks of restored heritage buildings, most built during the Napoleonic Wars and the War of 1812 to store the booty captured by British/Canadian privateers from enemy shipping vessels. In modern times, the old timber-and-stone warehouses have been converted into shops and restaurants. In 1948, a group of Royal Canadian Navy officers founded the Maritime Museum of the Atlantic as a means to preserve information and memorabilia from the country's naval past. The Halifax Seaport Farmer's Market tenders more than 250 vendors selling local produce, artisan foods, crafts, and more. At the far end of the boardwalk, the Canadian Museum of Immigration on Pier 21 reminds visitors that one in five families came to Canada via Halifax Harbour.

Halifax Citadel has long watched over the city and harbor from its hilltop location but has yet to engage in battle: Nowadays it provides a venue for historical tours and reenactments. The road up to the Citadel passes the Old Town Clock, allegedly commissioned by Prince Edward, Duke of Kent, to make the Napoleonic-era British garrison more punctual. On the far side of Citadel Hill, Halifax Public Gardens traces its roots to 1841 when part of the Halifax Common was developed into an English-style garden. Fairview Lawn Cemetery in the North End embraces the graves of more than a hundred *Titanic* victims, a reminder of the city's role in recovering the bodies of those who perished

TOURISM INFORMATION

Tourism Nova Scotia staffs visitor information centers at six different spots around the province. Visit their website at novascotia.com.

• **Halifax Visitor Information Centre**
Sackville Landing
1655 Lower Water St.
Halifax, NS B3J 1S3
Tel 902/424-4248
destinationhalifax.com

• **Cape Breton Island Visitor Information Centre**
96 Highway 4
Port Hastings, NS B94 1M4
Tel 902/625-4201
cbisland.com

• **Parks Canada**
pc.gc.ca

• **Nova Scotia Provincial Parks**
parks.gov.ns.ca

A placid waterscape at Fisherman's Cove near Halifax

Peggy's Point Lighthouse at the entrance to Saint Margaret's Bay

from the 1912 disaster. The Old Burial Ground on the south side of downtown is the last resting spot for many famous Haligonians (Halifax residents). Among the city's warm-weather attractions are Shakespeare by the Sea—performed in the ruins of Cambridge Battery in Point Pleasant Park—and the H.M.C.S. *Sackville* warship and museum along the boardwalk. Looking offshore, the national historic site on Georges Island revolves around old Fort Charlotte, named after the wife of King George II. The fort was built during Father Le Loutre's War (1749–1755) between the British and the Mi'kmaq Indians.

CAPE BRETON ISLAND

Nova Scotia's northern extreme, Cape Breton Island floats between the Gulf of Saint Lawrence and the open Atlantic, a mixture of wilderness, rugged shoreline, and historic sites where England and France once clashed over control of Canada. The only land access is a causeway across the Strait of Canso between Mulgrave and Port Hastings.

Located near the island's northern extreme, **Cape Breton Highlands National Park** spreads across 367 square miles (951 sq km) of remote beaches, rivers, deep valleys, a forested plateau, and spectacular sea cliffs. The park also boasts abundant wildlife (bear, moose, lynx, bald eagles, whales) in the sea, sky, and land. The small Acadian fishing community of Chéticamp lies just outside the park boundaries.

Best access to the park is via the 186-mile (299 km) **Cabot Trail,** a scenic drive that rings the entire island. The drive unofficially begins and ends in the small village of Baddeck, home to the father of the telephone, Alexander Graham Bell, from 1885 until his death in 1922.

CAPITALISM

Constructed between 1811 and 1819, Province House in Halifax is the oldest house of government and legislative building in Canada. The three-story Palladian edifice is home to the Nova Scotia House of Assembly, also the oldest of its kind in Canada, having organized its first meeting in 1758. A further historical landmark achieved by both the building and its occupants was the 1848 meeting of the first "responsible government" outside of the Mother Country in the entire British Empire, a huge stepping stone toward Canada's eventual independence.

On the island's east coast, the Cape Breton Miners' Museum in **Glace Bay** traces 250 years of Cape Breton coal mining and offers visitors an underground mine tour. Visitors to the Fortress of Louisbourg National Historic Site can see what life was like inside an 18th-century fortified town in New France, helped by a cast of costumed soldiers, servants, fishermen, maids, and merchants. Likewise, Highland Village Museum, which overlooks Bras d'Or Lake in Iona, is an outdoor living-history museum that tells the story of Gaelic culture and settlement in Cape Breton.

One of the continent's largest saltwater lakes, **Bras d'Or** sprawls across a large portion of the island interior. A UNESCO biosphere reserve, the lake watershed harbors an unusual blend of cold water (Arctic) and warm water (Virginian) aquatic life within close proximity. The coastal portion of the biosphere encompasses a broad range of geography, from barrier beaches and barachois ponds (lagoons) to

wetlands and rocky headlands. The area is just as varied when it comes to human occupants—a blend of English-, French-, Mi'kmaq-, and Cape Breton Gaelic–speaking residents.

THE PENINSULA

The remainder of Nova Scotia occupies a roughly triangular peninsula bound by the Atlantic Ocean, Bay of Fundy, and Saint Lawrence Gulf. Near the top end of the peninsula's eastern shore, **Sherbrooke Village** resurrects 19th-century Nova Scotia via 25 heritage buildings that once belonged to blacksmiths, potters, weavers, and printers.

Nova Scotia boasts 160 historic lighthouses, including the popular **Peggy's Point Lighthouse** in the fishing village of Peggy's Cove at the eastern entrance of Saint Margaret's Bay. **Ross Farm Museum** presents a picture of what a working farm looked like some 150 years ago, with farm animals, heritage buildings, and vintage agrarian equipment. Established in 1753 and known for its brightly painted wooden homes, **Lunenburg** was voted the most beautiful small town in Canada. It is considered the best surviving example of a planned British colonial town in North America.

Located near Nova Scotia's southern tip, **Birchtown** was once the largest free black community in British North America. The town's Black Loyalist Heritage Centre offers exhibits and artifacts from that time, including Carlton's *Book of Negroes,* a document containing the names of all Black Loyalists who escaped from the 13 Colonies to Canada during the American Revolution.

Moving around to the province's Bay of Fundy shore, **Yarmouth**

Shaggy Highland cattle thrive in Nova Scotia, unfazed by its climate or terrain.

Fly-fishing in the Margaree River on Cape Breton Island

offers ferry service to and from Portland, Maine. In addition to very high tides and Acadian fishing villages, the Fundy coast is rich in First Nations sites. Housed in an old schoolhouse, the Bear River Heritage Museum concentrates on Mi'kmaq culture while Kejimkujik National Park and National Historic Site safeguards petroglyphs detailing 10,000 years of Mi'kmaq history.

The first permanent French settlement in North America, **Port-Royal** was founded in 1605. It was later captured by the British, renamed Annapolis, and served as Nova Scotia's capital for a century and a half. Star-shaped Fort Anne offers living-history presentations and a museum inside the restored officers' quarters. Outside of town, Port-Royal National Historic Site is a modern reconstruction of the old French settlement on its original location along the Annapolis Basin shoreline.

Farther north along the Fundy shore, **Grand-Pré National Historic Site** is the centerpiece of a UNESCO World Heritage site showcasing the French-speaking Acadian culture that dominated Nova Scotia between 1682 and 1755. When the Acadians refused to swear allegiance to England in 1755, the British deported about 10,000 people (to Louisiana and elsewhere) and destroyed their farms. Memorials in Grand-Pré and Horton Landing pay homage to those expelled from Nova Scotia during the Great Expulsion. ∎

LOCAL FLAVOR

• **Rappie pie:** a casserole-like concoction of boiled potatoes, onions, and broth made from meat or seafood. Red Cap Restaurant on the Pubnico Peninsula makes theirs with chicken broth. *1034 Route 335 S, Middle West Pubnico*

• **Fricot:** hearty chicken soup with dumplings, vegetables, and a locally grown herb called summer savory (*Satureja hortensis*). Andrè's meat fricot at Le Gabriel Restaurant and Lounge also has chunks of beef. *15424 Cabot Trail, Chéticamp*

• **Nova Scotia chowder:** You'll never go back to the New England variety after tasting Chef Roland's chowder at Charlotte Lane Café, imbued with scallops, shrimp, haddock, maple-smoked salmon, tarragon, parsnip, sweet potato, bacon, and Boxing Rock beer. *13 Charlotte Lane, Shelburne*

• **Fricadelles de poisson:** These tasty fish cakes, another of the province's ancient Acadian dishes, are made with salted pollack at La Cuisine Robicheau on Nova Scotia's southwest coast. *9651 Highway 1, Saulnierville*

Nunavut

Created in 1999 when the Northwest Territories were split in half, Nunavut is Canada's newest and largest political unit. It's also the most indigenous, with Inuit people comprising more than 84 percent of the population of 32,000. Best explored by boat or air, this enormous northern exposure includes most of Canada's Arctic Archipelago as well as a huge chunk of Arctic mainland.

MAINLAND

Framed by the Hudson Bay and the Northwest Passages, mainland Nunavut is one of the planet's least populated regions. The Arctic Circle cuts straight across this vast transition zone between the boreal forest and tundra. Nearly all of its settlements hug the coast, including **Kugluktuk,** meaning "place of moving water," at the mouth of the Coppermine River. The community is renowned for its resident Inuit artists, whose work can be purchased at the Kugluktuk Co-operative. More art is on display at Kugluktuk Heritage Visitor Centre and Museum, which also showcases local history and culture. The hamlet is the

take-out point for float trips down the Coppermine River through a region rich in caribou, musk ox, moose, and various birds of prey. Nine miles (14 km) upstream from the coast, **Bloody Falls Territorial Park** marks the site of a 1771 massacre of Inuit families by Dene guides leading British explorer Samuel Hearne to the Arctic coast.

The north coast is also home to the **Queen Maud Gulf Migratory Bird Sanctuary,** Canada's largest federally protected nature reserve. The sanctuary provides a breeding ground for somewhere between two and three million geese, as well as tundra swans, sandhill cranes, peregrine falcons, and snowy owls.

TOURISM INFORMATION

Learn more about traveling the great northern territory at the Nunavut Tourism website: nunavuttourism.com.

• **Unikkaarvik Visitor Centre**
Sinaa Rd. (near Umiaq Crescent)
Iqaluit, NU X0A 0H0
Tel 867/979-4636

• **Arctic Coast Visitor Centre**
3 Omingmak St.
Cambridge Bay, NU X0B 0C0
Tel 867/983-2224
cambridgebay.ca

• **Nattinak Visitor's Centre**
Pond Inlet, NU, X0A
Tel 867/899-8225

Cambridge Bay on Victoria Island offers the best base for exploring the sanctuary.

By comparison, the mainland's Hudson Bay coast seems downright crowded—three tiny towns that serve as travel and tourism hubs. Celebrated as the starting point for the annual Hudson Bay Quest dogsled race, **Arviat** is also home to the Margaret Aniksak Visitors Centre with its displays on local nature, culture, and history. Nearby Arvia'juaq and Qikiqtaarjuk National Historic Site boasts hundreds of prehistoric archaeological relics. McConnell River Migratory Bird Sanctuary provides a summer home to myriad avian species. Arviat outfitters organize fishing trips and ATV safaris in summer and dogsled and snowmobile safaris during the snowy months, as well as trips to view beluga whales and polar bears.

Repulse Bay is the main gateway to **Ukkusiksalik National Park**

Snowy owls at the Queen Maud Gulf Migratory Bird Sanctuary

A monolithic iceberg dwarfs a visitor on Baffin Bay north of Baffin Island.

and its copious Arctic wildlife. The park also flaunts human history, from old Hudson's Bay Company outposts to thousand-year-old archaeological sites. Reached by boat or seaplane, Sila Lodge on Wager Bay is one of the few places to stay inside the park. Repulse Bay offers its own attractions, including a chance to snap a selfie on the Arctic Circle (which runs right through the middle of town) and sea cliffs where thousands of seabirds nest.

Some 200 miles (322 km) inland from the Hudson Bay, **Baker Lake** is the territory's only landlocked community, founded in 1916 as a Hudson's Bay Company outpost. The hamlet now makes its living from gold mining and tourism; the Vera Akumalik Visitor Centre is a good first stop. The unique culture of inland Inuit groups is preserved and promoted at the Inuit Heritage Centre, and the Jessie Oonark Arts and Crafts Centre showcases the carving, weaving, and paintings of local artists. The lake provides plenty of scope for boating and fishing, as do the nearby Thelon and Kazan wild rivers. Baker Lake is also the gateway to the enormous **Thelon Wildlife Sanctuary,** where grizzly, caribou, and musk oxen count among the many creatures that roam the tundra terrain. Fall Caribou Crossing National Historic Site on the Kazan River is where thousands of migrating caribou forded the river each autumn, to be hunted by the inland Inuit.

FESTIVALS

- **Return of the Sun (Igloolik):** This tiny island settlement celebrates the return of the winter sun with igloo building, traditional foods, and dog-team rides; January.

- **Nattiq Frolics (Kugluktuk):** Usher in the spring with traditional music and foods, races, pond hockey, and other fun; April.

- **Nunavut Day (Iqaluit):** The territorial capital celebrates semiautonomy with traditional games, music, and dance; June.

- **Northwest Passage Marathon (Somerset Island):** Snow, icebergs, rock fields—and the possibility of dodging polar bears and musk ox—are all highlights in this unique race across the tundra; July.

- **Inummarit Music Festival (Arviat):** Throat singing and drum dancing make this annual autumn event one of the most lively; September.

ISLANDS

Separated from the mainland by the Northwest Passages, the Arctic Archipelago embraces hundreds of bits and bobs, from giant landmasses to sandy bars and rocky outcrops. Largest of them all is **Baffin Island,** almost a mirror image of nearby Greenland with its glacial topography and iceberg-filled bays. Baffin's rich history of Arctic exploration and Inuit culture stretches to the Paleolithic era, and there's a good chance that Norsemen made landfall on the island while transiting down the west Atlantic coast.

The huge territory's diminutive capital, **Iqaluit** ("place of many fishes") sits at the southern end of Baffin Island on Frobisher Bay. The Unikkaarvik Visitor Center offers tips on how to explore the island's wild places as well as exhibits on wildlife and culture. The Nunatta Sunakkutaangit Museum tenders a large selection of Inuit art and artifacts. For most travelers, Iqaluit is merely a stopover on the way to natural splendors elsewhere on the giant island. **Auyuittuq National Park** on the east coast is a geological jigsaw puzzle of glaciers, fjords, and granite peaks. Nunavut's most popular national park, the "land that never melts" can be explored by foot, dogsled, snowmobile, or cross-country skis. The 60-mile (97 km) Akshayuk Pass trail follows an ancient Inuit route to Summit Lake. Climbers flock to the park for challenges like Mount Thor and its world record–setting 4,101-foot (1,250 m) vertical wall.

Living up to its name, **Sirmilik National Park** really is a "place of glaciers." Perched at the island's northern tip, the reserve includes the Borden Peninsula and Bylot Island. The park's glacial valleys, iceberg-choked channels, and floe edge of floating sea ice provide a refuge for polar bears, walrus, narwhal, caribou, beluga whales, and other Arctic creatures. On the other side of Eclipse Sound, Pond Inlet expedites exploring Sirmilik via foot, kayak, snowmobile, or dogsled. The town's Tununiq Arsarniit Theatre Group presents plays that mix the Inuit and English language, as well as Arctic and outside themes.

Even more remote, giant **Ellesmere Island** extends above 83° north latitude—just 447 miles (719 km) from the North Pole. Grise Fiord at the island's bottom end is the place to organize trips

An arctic fox kit enjoys the short summer near Cambridge Bay.

A walrus off remote Ellesmere Island near the North Pole

to supersecluded Quttinirpaaq ("top of the world") National Park, a desolate land of rock and ice that blends glaciers and the highest peaks in eastern North America.

Cambridge Bay, the largest town on Victoria Island, earned fame as a Distant Early Warning (DEW) base during the Cold War. Aboard the expedition ship *Maud,* explorer Roald Amundsen sojourned in the bay during his epic first voyage through the Northwest Passage. Later used as a Hudson's Bay Company supply ship, the three-masted schooner sank in Cambridge Bay where its exposed hull still rises above the surface. The town's other sights include the Old Stone Church, the Arctic Coast Visitor Centre, and the new Canadian High Arctic Research Station (CHARS). Just east of town, Ovayok Territorial Park offers five hiking trails across a tundra landscape strewn with ancient Inuit archaeological sites, musk ox herds, and small lakes.

Farther east along the Victoria Strait, **King William Island** also played a key role in Arctic exploration; stories are related on signboards along the Northwest Passage Territorial Trail in Gjoa Haven. These include how for nearly two years (1903–1905) Amundsen and his men were stranded in sea ice near the island's south shore aboard the *Gjøa,* and the discovery in 2014 of the wreck of the H.M.S. *Erebus,* one of Sir John Franklin's twin ships last seen entering Baffin Bay in 1845. The hamlet's other claim to fame is a nine-hole golf course, one of just a few links above the Arctic Circle. ◼

LITTLE-KNOWN FACTS

• Nunavut boasts enough geographical oddities to warrant its own category on *Jeopardy!*

• Nunavut, although roughly the same size as Mexico, has just 0.026 percent of Mexico's population (32,000 vs. 122 million).

• The territory's 26 communities are connected by neither road nor rail; they can only be reached by air, water, or dogsled.

• The territory includes three of the world's 10 largest islands: Baffin, Victoria, and Ellesmere.

• Nunavut has just 20 miles (32 km) of paved highways.

• Alert on Ellesmere Island is the world's northernmost permanently inhabited place (82° 28' N), while Grise Fiord on the same island is Canada's northernmost civilian town (76° 25' N).

Ontario

The linchpin that connects eastern and western Canada, Ontario spreads all the way from the Saint Lawrence River Valley to the prairies, across the top of four different Great Lakes. From Toronto and other world-class cities to iconic landmarks such as Niagara Falls to vast wilderness areas and rolling farmland, the Heartland Province offers a rich tapestry of landscapes and attractions.

CITIES

With some six million people in the metro area, **Toronto** is Canada's largest city and the capital of Ontario province. The city's location along the northern shore of Lake Ontario gave rise to its name—*tkaronto* or "place where trees stand in the water" in the language of the Iroquois people who lived here before the first Europeans arrived in the mid-18th century. Rising 1,815 feet (553 m) above downtown, CN Tower features an observation deck reached via glass-fronted elevators, a glass-floor look-down, an edge walk, and three restaurants, one with revolving views. Families enjoy the nearby Ripley's Aquarium of Canada as well as the Toronto Railway Museum inside the historic C.P.R. John Street Roundhouse. The SkyWalk leaps the modern railroad tracks to downtown Toronto and a 19-mile (31 km) network of underground pedestrian walks known as PATH facilitates weatherproof movement beneath the central city. Downtown highlights include the Hockey Hall of Fame, the Toronto Symphony at Roy Thomson Hall, the Art Gallery of Ontario (AGO), and the 200-year-old Saint Lawrence Market, home to more than 120 food and craft vendors. For stark architectural contrast, stand in the middle of Nathan Phillips Square and contemplate Toronto's Romanesque Revival–style Old City Hall (1899) and the futuristic New City Hall (1965).

East of downtown, the Distillery Historic District today flaunts cafés, shops, microbreweries, and performance spaces inside the largest collection of Victorian-era industrial

Parliament Hill, seat of the Canadian government, along the Ottawa River

The flashy angles of Toronto's Royal Ontario Museum

buildings left in North America—making it a sought-after shooting location for scores of movies and TV shows. North of downtown are the sprawling University of Toronto campus and the posh Yorkville district, home to the Royal Conservatory of Music and the Royal Ontario Museum (ROM). The latter is Canada's largest museum, with more than six million historical, cultural, and natural history artifacts in more than 30 galleries. ROM also features a variety of architectural styles, from Gothic Revival and Byzantine to a modernist extension that appears to explode from the older building. Toronto's lakeshore is lined by parklands and piers with ferries to Toronto Island Park.

Ottawa spreads along the south bank of the Ottawa River about 100 miles (161 km) upstream from Montreal. Ironically, Canada's national capital was actually founded by an American who established an agricultural colony on the river in 1800. Rising above the river, Parliament Hill is dominated by the Gothic Revival–style Centre Block, erected in the 1920s to house Canada's Parliament. Visitors can ascend the building's 180-foot-tall (55 m) Peace Tower for a bird's-eye-view. Nearby are the modern Supreme Court of Canada, Library and Archives Canada, and Confederation Square—home to the National War Memorial and the National Arts Centre. The Rideau Canal,

CAPITALISM

A widespread misconception prevails that Ottawa governs both the nation of Canada and the province of Ontario (Toronto is actually the provincial capital). Nonetheless, Canada's imposing Gothic Revival–style federal government complex crowns Parliament Hill overlooking the Ottawa River. Construction started in the 1850s after Queen Victoria chose the site to govern her dominion, although the distinctive Peace Tower dates from 1927. Ontario's Legislative Building, an 1890s Romanesque-Revival castle, sits in Queen's Park adjacent to the University of Toronto campus.

constructed in the 1830s to link the Ottawa River and Lake Ontario, divides Ottawa into eastern and western halves. Now a UNESCO World Heritage site, the canal is a prime venue for recreational boating. The ByWard Market area on the canal's eastern side hosts scores of food and craft vendors, as well as Notre-Dame Cathedral Basilica (1846), the Royal Canadian Mint (1908), and the National Gallery of Canada. Major's Hill Park is the eastern terminus of the Ottawa River Pathway that meanders 19 miles (31 km) upstream along the river's south bank. Along the way are the expansive Canadian War Museum, several recreational islands, and beautiful Chaudière Falls. Ottawa is blessed with a vast array of other museums including the Canadian Museum of Nature in the castlelike Victoria Memorial Building, the 130-aircraft-strong Canadian Aviation and Space Museum, the interesting Canada Agriculture and Food Museum, and Diefenbunker—Canada's Cold War

museum—which preserves offices, sleeping quarters, and cryptographic areas in a four-story underground bunker.

LANDSCAPES

By far Canada's most popular tourist attraction, **Niagara Falls** comprises three separate cascades that carry water between Lake Erie and Lake Ontario along the Niagara River. Horseshoe Falls, the largest, drops 187 feet (57 m, about 13 stories) and swells to an estimated volume of 100,000 cubic feet (2,832 cu m) per second in summer. The numerous ways to experience the falls include vertigo-inducing walkways, boat tours, and helicopter flights. Man-made viewpoints include the Skylon Tower and the Niagara SkyWheel. A hotbed of action during the War of 1812, the area is also known for historic attractions such as the Niagara Falls History Museum, Lundy's Lane battlefield, Old Fort Erie, and Fort George.

Hamilton, perched at the western extreme of Lake Ontario, revolves around things that float and fly, such as the World War II destroyer H.M.C.S. *Haida* and the Canadian Warplane Heritage Museum, where members can sign up for flights on the rare Fairey Firefly, Westland Lysander, and Avro Lancaster aircraft. The western end of Lake Ontario empties into the Saint Lawrence River and meets the **Thousand Islands,** an archipelago of 1,864 islands along the Canada-U.S. border. **Gananoque,** the main resort town on the Canadian side, offers plenty of opportunities to get out on the river, as well as restaurants, shops, and a casino. The **Frontenac Arch Biosphere Reserve** marks a historic migration route spreading west from the river along an immense granite ridge now strewn with lakes and woodland.

Ontario's long shoreline with **Lake Huron** includes the Stones 'n Bones fossil and dinosaur museum in Sarnia, the Blue Mountain winter

The Hockey Hall of Fame in downtown Toronto celebrates Canada's national winter sport.

The peaceful morning shores of Lake Ontario invite vacationers.

sports resort, and Sainte-Marie among the Hurons, the reconstruction of an early 17th-century Jesuit mission. The 210-mile (338 km) **Trent-Severn Waterway** connects Georgian Bay and Lake Ontario, with many historic sites along the way. Farther north are the **Muskoka District** with its 1,600 lakes and maple forests, and the enormous Algonquin Provincial Park, the nation's oldest provincial park (1893).

Far-off western Ontario is for those who cherish the great outdoors. **Lake of the Woods** near Kenora encompasses more than 14,000 islands and 65,000 miles (104,607 km) of shoreline to explore by canoe, kayak, or motorized boat. **Thunder Bay** on Lake Superior offers Kakabeka Falls Provincial Park and Fort William Historical Park, inland headquarters of the fur-trading North West Company from 1803 to 1821. Lake Superior Provincial Park safeguards 618 square miles (1,601 sq km) of

lakeshore wilderness including the 650-foot (198 m) cliffs of Old Woman Bay and the Agawa Rock Pictographs.

Even more rugged and remote, Ontario's mammoth northern region flows across hundreds of miles of sparsely populated boreal forest, barrens, and tundra to Hudson Bay and James Bay. Towns are few and far between here, where First Nations people comprise a large percentage of the population

and animals far outnumber humans. Among the region's natural attractions are **Polar Bear Provincial Park,** which shelters caribou, moose, walrus, whales, seals, and fox in addition to several hundred white bears. Also of note are the wild and scenic Winisk River and Opasquia Provincial Park, with its glacial geology and renowned wolverines. All of these parks are primitive, without roads or visitor facilities. ∎

ROAD TRIPS

Great drives across the Heartland Province:

• Trans-Canada Highway across Ontario between Ottawa and Kenora, crossing all 10 provinces (1,200 miles/1,931 km)

• Highway 3 along the northern shore of Lake Erie between Windsor and Fort Erie (250 miles/402 km)

• Rideau Heritage Route (Highway 15) between Kingston and Ottawa (111 miles/179 km)

• Heritage Highway (Route 2) along the north bank of the Saint Lawrence River between Kingston and Lancaster (125 miles/201 km)

• Highway 6 between Hamilton and Whitefish Falls via the Georgian Bay ferry (242 miles/389 km)

Prince Edward Island

While Prince Edward Island is still the nation's smallest province in both population and land area, it overflows with historical places and scenic delights, now linked to the mainland via the spectacular Confederation Bridge. Its best ambassador may be a redheaded orphan girl, title character of the novel *Anne of Green Gables,* by P.E.I. native Lucy Maud Montgomery.

CITIES

More like a large town than a true city, **Charlottetown** is Canada's most user-friendly provincial capital, easy to explore on foot and filled with friendly residents who delight in sharing the unique aspects of their hometown and quirky island. Although closed for renovation, Province House National Historic Site preserves the building where, in 1864, delegates from across the British North American territories decided to unite into one nation called Canada. Learn more about Canadian independence at "The Story of Confederation," a new historical program about the birth of the maple leaf nation at the nearby Confederation Centre of the Arts (CCA). Another ongoing production is the popular *Anne of Green Gables* musical, staged each summer during the Charlottetown Festival. Down on the waterfront, Founders' Hall—Canada's

Actors convey Canada's past in "The Story of Confederation" in Charlottetown.

TOURISM INFORMATION

Tourism P.E.I. has created visitor information centers at three strategic points around the island, including the island end of the Confederation Bridge, Woods Island ferry landing, and downtown Charlottetown. For more information, visit tourismpei.com.

• **Charlottetown Visitor Information Centre**
Founders' Hall
6 Prince St.
Charlottetown, PE C1A 4P5
Tel 902/368-4444

• **Borden-Carleton Visitor Information Centre**
100 Abegweit Blvd.
Borden-Carelton, PE C0B 1X0
Tel 800/463-4734

• **Wood Islands Visitor Information Centre**
13054 Shore Rd., Rte 4.
Wood Islands, PE C0A 1B0
Tel 800/463-4734

• **PEI Provincial Parks**
tourismpei.com/
pei-provincial-parks

birthplace pavilion—details Canadian history from 1864 through the present day. The waterfront is also the place to hop aboard a sailing and sightseeing cruise, fishing charter, waterfowl-watching tour, or the *Top Notch* lobster charter to haul up traps and enjoy your fresh catch right on the boat. Among Charlottetown's heritage buildings are the French Gothic–style Saint Dunstan's Basilica and the elegant Beaconsfield Historic House (1877), a superb example of the Victorian homes once occupied by the capital's elite. In the heart of the city, Victoria Park was bequeathed to the people of Charlottetown in 1873 "for the use of all her Majesty's

The small lighthouse at Victoria Harbour in Charlottetown

subjects as a park, promenade, and pleasure ground." Its waterfront walk is especially lovely at dusk and dawn. Multiple layers of island history are revealed at Port-la-Joye— Fort Amherst National Historic Site on the other side of the harbor in Rocky Point, which served as the island's first French (1720) and British (1755) military bases. It was also a major staging ground for expelling French-speaking settlers from P.E.I.

LANDSCAPES

Locally born author Lucy Maud Montgomery put Prince Edward Island on both the literary and tourism map with her book *Anne of Green Gables.* Published in 1908, the story of orphaned farm girl Anne Shirley has sold more than 50 million copies worldwide. During her long and fertile literary career, Montgomery wrote 20 novels and more than a thousand poems and

short stories, many of them set on P.E.I. Fans flock to the island to see the various sites associated with the real-life Montgomery and fictional Anne. From 1876 to 1911, the author lived with her grandparents on a farm in Cavendish, and her cousins resided on a nearby Green Gables Farm, where the author set much of her renowned tome. Besides touring the old farmhouse,

activities at **Green Gables Heritage Place** include the barnyard, ice cream–making demonstrations, sack races, geocaching, carriage rides, nature trails through the Haunted Woods and Balsam Hollow, and interpretive programs led by rangers clad like characters from the books.

Green Gables homestead is part of **Prince Edward Island National Park,** which sprawls along the Gulf

---

LOCAL FLAVOR

How many different ways can you eat lobster on P.E.I.?

• **Lobster roll:** Island Favorites cooks up four different types of lobster roll, served together in the "sailor's sampler." *8989 Cavendish Rd., Cavendish*

• **Lobster burger:** Try chunks of lobster meat stuffed into a grilled kaiser roll at Richard's Fresh Seafood. *9 Coovehead Wharf, Stanhope*

• **Lobster taco:** Dave's Lobster serves them with mayo, lime, cilantro, and a dash of chili pepper in soft corn tortillas topped with coleslaw. *Founders' Hall, 6 Prince St., Charlottetown*

• **Lobster mac & cheese:** Blue Mussel Café makes a wondrous blend of fresh lobster with Gruyère and sharp cheddar cheese. *312 Harbourview Dr., North Rustico Harbour*

of Saint Lawrence about midway on the north coast. The park preserves a number of unique insular ecosystems including coastal cliffs and headlands, barrier islands and sand spits, salt marshes, and forests where red fox, beaver, coyotes, and other creatures roam. Within its 5,440 acres (2,201 ha) are 50 miles (80 km) of hiking and biking trails, as well as campgrounds, a golf course, and seven beaches. The park's newest section is the Greenwich Peninsula, with its parabolic dune system and 10,000-year-old archaeological sites. Among other north coast sights are the Gardens of Hope in New Glasgow, the Haunted Mansion in Kensington, and movies at the vintage Brackley Drive-In.

North Cape is the island's most remote region, a windswept place that seems far removed from Charlottetown's refined charm. Located beside the lighthouse, North Cape Wind Energy Interpretive Centre explains how the area's futuristic wind farm turns gulf breezes into electrical power. The North Cape Nature Trail meanders across the top of ocher cliffs to scrub

woodland and marshes good for bird-watching.

Summerside anchors the island's south-central shore, a seaport huddled around a photogenic waterfront lined with various historic structures better known for its cultural scene than its lobster catch. Aficionados of Celtic music and dance come to Summerside for the outdoor summer concerts staged by groups from the College of Piping and Celtic Performing Arts of Canada. Eptek Art & Culture Centre offers exhibits and events on P.E.I. history, science, and fine art, while the island's French heritage is explored in depth at the Acadian Museum, near Summerside Airport.

When P.E.I. joined the confederation in 1873, the Canadian government promised to build a bridge linking the island with the rest of Canada. That pledge was finally fulfilled in 1997 with the completion of the eight-mile-long (13 km) **Confederation Bridge,** which carries the Trans-Canada Highway from New Brunswick. A dozen miles (19 km) farther along

Northumberland Strait, **Victoria-by-the-Sea** embodies P.E.I. quaintness with seafood cafés, a chocolate shop, a seaport museum, a community theater, fishing wharves, and even a tiny lighthouse. The distinctive pink, orange, and red beaches are tinted thanks to erosion from the area's red sandstone cliffs.

At the eastern end of the isle, **Points East Coastal Drive** meanders along another picture-perfect shoreline past beaches, sand dunes, and more lighthouses. Along the way, the Orwell Corner Historic Village resurrects life in a typical 19th-century island community, including farm, church, general store, and shingle mill. **Basin Head Provincial Park** is renowned for its "singing sands"—a nine-mile

The Anne of Green Gables Museum on Prince Edward Island

Lupines grow wild throughout Prince Edward Island.

(14 km) beach that makes a peculiar sound when you scuff your feet against the sand in a certain way. The park also includes a tidal lagoon with rare Giant Irish Moss *(Chondrus crispus).* Here, too, is the Basin Head Fisheries Museum with its displays on the island's inshore fishing, shipwrecks, and lighthouses. Once the eastern terminus for trains from Charlottetown, the **Elmira Railway Museum** boasts exhibits and artifacts, as well as re-creations of a Victorian-era ladies' waiting room and stationmaster's office. At the end of the drive, the octagonal wooden **East Point Lighthouse** offers an excellent panorama of the coast and Gulf of Saint Lawrence, with views across the water to Cape Breton Island.

Wood Islands on the southeast coast offers a seafaring alternative to accessing P.E.I.: a ferry that crosses the Northumberland Strait from Caribou, Nova Scotia. Even

if you don't hop the boat, climb to the top of the small lighthouse in Wood Islands Provincial Park for the view. If you've finally had your fill of lobster, pop into the Oyster Lovers' Experience in South Pinette to sample another of the island's seafood delights.

One of the best ways to explore Prince Edward Island, especially

for those without a vehicle, is the **Confederation Trail.** Traversing relatively flat terrain, the 270-mile (435 km) path is shared by hikers, bikers, and runners. The route follows an old railroad line between Elmira and Tignish, with spurs shooting off to Charlottetown, Borden-Carleton, Souris, and Georgetown. ■

LITTLE-KNOWN FACTS

• P.E.I. has more curling clubs per capita than any other Canadian province, displaying a passion for the quirky winter sport that may have its roots in the arrival of the first Scottish settlers in 1770.

• The province's official tartan includes four colors: reddish-brown for the iron-rich soil, green for the lush vegetation, white for the waves pounding its shores, and yellow for the sun.

• P.E.I. boasts two lobster harvests and regions: The spring season (May and June) covers the eastern half of the island, while the fall season (August through October) takes place only along the isle's western shore.

• Created by local French-Canadian artist Édouard Arsenault, the Bottle Houses (Maisons de Bouteilles) of P.E.I.'s southwest coast are made from more than 25,000 recycled glass bottles.

Quebec

La Belle Province really is like another country from the rest of the maple leaf nation: the heartland of French-Canadian culture, the cradle of Cirque du Soleil, the birthplace of modern ice hockey, and the creator of poutine. In addition to urbane Quebec City and Montreal, the province flaunts dramatic landscapes such as the Saint Lawrence Valley, the Laurentian Mountains, and the Gaspé Peninsula.

CITIES

Quebec City, the provincial capital, lies around 150 miles (241 km) down the Saint Lawrence River from Montreal. One of the Western Hemisphere's most distinctive cities, Quebec is renowned for its striking bluff-top location and characteristic architecture. Old Quebec in the city center is the only walled town in North America. Split into Upper (Haute-Ville) and Lower (Basse-Ville) Towns, the historic district blends French and British colonial influences into a photogenic urban landscape ready-made for walking, especially along the ramparts. Although the city walls were vastly reinforced by the British during the War of 1812, their construction commenced in 1609 under Samuel de Champlain, just a year after he founded the city. Remnants of the French period—including the Saint-Louis Forts and Châteaux National Historic Site—can be viewed in modern archaeological digs along Dufferin Terrace and the Governors' Promenade. Musée du Fort puts the ramparts and ruins in historical context via meticulous scale models and a sound and light show. Looming nearby, the Gothic bulk of the Basilique-Cathédrale Notre-Dame de Québec traces its roots to 1647 and the continent's first Roman Catholic parish. The adjacent Séminaire de Québec is nearly as old, founded in 1663. Also arrayed around the cathedral square are the Hôtel de ville (City Hall) and Musée de l'Amérique francophone (Museum of French-speaking America), which preserves and promotes the French culture in North America. Artillery Park includes the 18th-century Dauphine Redoubt, early 19th-century British officers quarters, and an early-20th-century arsenal foundry. Living-history guides clad in colonial uniforms or civilian garb lead tours in both French and English. The old town's most prominent structure is the Château Frontenac, a flamboyant

TOURISM INFORMATION

Tourisme Québec staffs tourist information centers at five sites around the province. Visit the website at quebecoriginal.com/en.

- **Centre Infotouriste de Montréal**
1255 Rue Peel
Montreal, QC H3B 4V4
Tel 514/873-2015
tourisme-montreal.org

- **Centre Infotouriste de Québec**
12 Rue Sainte-Anne
Quebec City, QC G1R 3X2
Tel 418/641-6290
regiondequebec.com

- **Parks Canada**
pc.gc.ca

- **Quebec Provincial Parks**
sepaq.com

Whimsical displays at the Montreal Botanical Gardens

The hotel Château Frontenac crowns Quebec City's old town.

18-story hotel erected in 1893. There are several ways of descending to the Basse-Ville, including Côte de la Montagne road, the aptly named Breakneck Steps (L'Escalier Casse-Cou) and the vintage Funiculaire du Vieux Québec (1879). At the bottom are Place-Royale and Quartier Petit Champlain with their posh shops, dining establishments, and theater. The Lower Town is also the place to catch ferries to Lévis, wander the Vieux-Port (Old Port), and visit the Musée de la civilisation (Museum of Civilization).

La Citadelle de Québec, which forms part of the city walls, is an active army base as well as Canada's oldest military installation. The classic star-shaped fortress includes the historic Governor General's mansion and the Royal 22e Régiment

Museum; it also hosts a daily changing of the guard. Spreading south from the citadel, the Plains of Abraham was the scene of a bloody 1759 battle that sealed the British conquest of Canada from the French.

Rising nearby are the majestic provincial Parliament Building (1886) and Musée National des Beaux-Arts du Québec (MNBAQ) with its extensive collection of Quebec art and artists. An observation deck on

HIDDEN TREASURES

While the role of Quebec City in the War of 1812 is well known, other province wartime sites are far more obscure:

• **Châteauguay Battlefield:** The 1813 victory by French-Canadian troops over an invading U.S. army here became a rallying point for Quebec pride.

• **Lacolle Mills Blockhouse (Richelieu River):** Twice during the war, the

combined British, Canadian, and Mohawk garrison at this two-story wooden stronghold repelled American raids into Quebec.

• **Fort Lennox (Île-aux-Noix along the Richelieu River):** helped defend a British naval shipyard against an American gunboat attack in June 1813

• **Coteau-du-Lac (Saint Lawrence River):** protected the vital British-Canadian river trade during the war

the 31st floor of the Marie-Guyart Building affords stunning views. On the outskirts of town the excellent Quebec Aquarium offers polar bears and other Arctic mammals. The beautiful, 272-foot-high (83 m) Montmorency Falls are surrounded by a park featuring viewing platforms, a vertiginous suspension bridge, cable car ride, three Via Ferrata cliff-climbing circuits, and zip-lining.

The province's largest city, **Montreal** is located on a massive island in the Saint Lawrence River and named after the prominent hill that dramatically backdrops the city center. Although also founded by Samuel de Champlain in the early 1600s, it took longer for Montreal to evolve into a proper city than cousin Quebec. Old Montreal and its flock of historic buildings includes the twin-towered Basilique Notre-Dame de Montréal (1656). Anchoring the northern end of the old town, Notre-Dame-de-Bon-Secours chapel dates to 1771. The finger piers of Vieux-Port (Old Port) were revitalized in the early 1990s into a promenade with a variety of activities including riverboat tours, the Centre des Sciences de Montréal, and Plage de l'Horloge (Clock Tower Beach). The conspicuously modern Pointe-à-Callière (Museum of Archaeology and History) exhibits artifacts related to more than a thousand years of local human activity.

Downtown Montreal offers such cultural icons as the Musée des Beaux-Arts de Montréal (MMFA), with more than 40,000 works from antiquity to modern times, and the Quartier des Spectacles entertainment district, venue for many of the city's landmark

The Fontaine de Tourney and Quebec Parliament Building; opposite: Montreal

festivals. Located within the quarter, the Place des Arts cultural complex is composed of multiple performance halls—visitors can catch the opera, ballet, and the symphony here—as well as the Musée d'Art Contemporain de Montréal (MAC). Founded by royal charter in 1821, McGill University offers visitors the McCord Museum of Canadian history. Rising 764 feet (233 m) above the city center, Mont Royal's 494 acres (200 ha) include lawns, woods, trails, panoramic viewpoints, public art, and cemeteries, as well as the Italian Renaissance–style Saint Joseph's Oratory, Canada's largest church. Parc Jean-Drapeau is made up of two islands in the Saint Lawrence—Île Sainte-Hélène and the man-made Île Notre-Dame—which together hosted Expo 67. Remnants of the renowned world's fair include the sphere-shaped Biosphere Environment Museum and Alexander Calder's "L'homme" sculpture, and the Olympic Basin—a legacy of the 1976 Summer Games—is still a hub for paddle and oar sports. Also on the islands are the 1820 Fort de

l'Île Sainte-Hélène and its Stewart Museum, the motor-racing course Circuit Gilles Villeneuve, and an

LITTLE-KNOWN FACTS

• The Appalachian Mountains extend into southern Quebec, including the rugged topography of Mont-Mégantic National Park and Massif du Sud Regional Park.

• l'Île-Bonaventure-et-du-Rocher-Percé National Park safeguards the world's largest colony of northern gannets, an estimated 100,000 birds.

• The Basilica of Sainte-Anne-de-Beaupré attracts about a million pilgrims and visitors each year who come to reflect at the mother church of Quebec's patron saint.

• Lachine Rapids near Montreal were named by explorer Jacques Cartier, who mistakenly believed the mighty rapids were his last barrier to reaching China via the Northwest Passage.

aquatic center. Also remaining from the 1976 Summer Games—staged at the Parc Olympique de Montréal just north of the city center—are the Olympic Stadium, Maurice Richard Arena, the Olympic Pool, and Athletes' Village. The velodrome was later converted into the Biodôme, with walk-through replicas of four North American ecosystems. Looming over the stadium, the 575-foot (175 m) Montréal Tower tilts 45 degrees, the world's tallest leaning tower. A funicular whisks visitors to an observation deck at the summit. Adjoining the Olympic Park, Montreal Botanical Gardens offers flower beds, forests, greenhouses, and an insectarium spread across 185 acres (75 ha).

LANDSCAPES

One of the world's oldest ranges, the **Laurentian Mountains** slash across southern Quebec between the Saguenay and Ottawa Rivers. Although they aren't very tall—reaching a peak of 3,825 feet (1,166 m) at Mont Raoul

Blanchard—the range encompasses some 9,000 lakes, hundreds of rivers, and millions of forested acres. Located within an easy drive from Montreal and Quebec City, the region offers abundant outdoor escapes both for summer and winter. North America's first ski lift was built in the Laurentians in 1931, and today the mountains host dozens of winter sports resorts including Saint-Sauveur, Mont Blanc, Mont Olympia, and Mont Tremblant.

Mont-Tremblant National Park, the most renowned of the Laurentian's many nature reserves, is popular for canoeing and kayaking, Nordic sports, backcountry camping, and wildlife-watching. The cutting-edge park has also introduced new wilderness experiences including Via Ferrata rock climbing, and *rabaska* tours—Algonquin birch-bark canoes. Other national parks in the range include La Mauricie, Jacques-Cartier, Hautes-Gorges-de-la-Rivière-Malbaie, and the spectacular Saguenay Fjord.

Lake Saint-Jean at the head of the Saguenay River harbors several worthwhile sights including the small but interesting Mashteuiatsh Amerindian Museum, the Val-Jalbert historic timber company town and adjacent Ouiatchouan Falls, and the quirky Museum of Cheddar Cheese in Saint-Prime. However, the lake area's main attraction is Zoo Sauvage de Saint-Félicien, a collection of boreal forest animals from around the world housed in large, natural habitats. The cold-climate menagerie includes polar bears, Amur tigers, Siberian ibex, Japanese macaque "snow" monkeys, and even a few Tibetan yaks.

In addition to the province's two big cities, the Saint Lawrence River (and its tributaries) account for many of Quebec's other historic, cultural, and scenic highlights. About halfway between Montreal and Quebec City, Trois-Rivières is home to the notorious **Old Prison,** Canada's longest

Kayaking Lac-Monroe in Mont-Tremblant National Park, below the Laurentians.

serving prison (1822–1986). Now a museum, the joint features a "Sentenced to One Night" program that includes sleeping in an authentic jail cell. **La Cité de l'Énergie** in Shawinigan is an offbeat energy theme park that includes a Cirque du Soleil–like production in an outdoor amphitheater, a 377-foot (115 m) electricity pylon with observation deck, and tours of old power plants.

Downstream from Quebec City, **Le Massif de Charlevoix** tenders ski and snowboard runs that look down on the Saint Lawrence River as well as a 2,500-foot (762 m) vertical drop—highest in eastern Canada. The Marine Mammal Interpretation Centre in **Tadoussac** affords a superb introduction to many of the animals found in nearby **Saguenay–Saint Lawrence Marine Park,** which may be explored via guided boat and Zodiac cruises, kayak, or scuba.

From Forestville, a fast-ferry crosses the 30-mile-wide (48 m) Saint Lawrence Estuary to **Rimouski,** where the Pointe-au-Père maritime museum spins 200 years of seafaring history and includes artifacts from the R.M.S. *Empress of Ireland* (sunk 1914) and H.M.C.S. *Onondaga* submarine. Rimouski is also the

Tiny Percé village perched on the tip of the Gaspé Peninsula

southern terminus of the *Relais Nordik,* an authentic supply ship that transports a limited number of passengers to remote ports along the Gulf of Saint Lawrence coast, including Anticosti Island.

The **Gaspé Peninsula** extends far into the gulf, a place of bygone fishing villages, pounding surf, and massive sea cliffs. Among the peninsula's best nature areas are the rugged mountains of Gaspésie National Park

and Forillon National Park. The latter has impressive, tortuous sea cliffs pocked with caves, and wave-cut coastal benches that have been eroded into low platforms by the sea. Perched near the outer edge of the peninsula, Percé village offers whale-watching cruises, sea kayak adventures, and access to the secluded Île-Bonaventure with its hiking trails, bird-watching, and historic structures. ∎

LOCAL FLAVOR

• **Poutine:** This blend of French fries covered in cheese curds and gravy is Canada's unofficial national dish; it's easy to make at home and often found on menus at popular fast-food joints such as Poutineville. *1365 Ontario Est, Ville-Marie, Montreal*

• **Montreal-style bagels:** The city's large Jewish community has developed a bagel that is smaller and sweeter than

its New York cousin; it is still baked in wood-fired ovens at St-Viateur Bagel. *263 St-Viateur Ouest, Mile End, Montreal*

• **Ragoût de boulettes de porc:** Despite its name, this meatball stew can be made with pork, beef, veal, or any other meat flavored with cloves, nutmeg, and other spices. It's one of several traditional French-Canadian

dishes on the menu at Le Buffet de L'Antiquaire. *95 rue Saint-Paul Vieux-Port, Quebec City*

• **Tourtière:** These savory deep-dish meat pies are made with pork, beef, veal, rabbit, salmon, or wild game. Aux Anciens Canadiens and other Quebec City eateries are reputed to serve the province's best versions. *34, rue Saint-Louis, Quebec City*

Saskatchewan

Wide-open spaces form the overriding vibe of Saskatchewan, the prairie province that calls itself the "Land of Living Skies." Indeed the sky is alive, whether with the aurora borealis that glows overhead in winter, the migrating birds of spring and fall, or summer's big stretches of cloud-crossed blue. The province also boasts plenty of indoor attractions, especially in the vibrant cities of Saskatoon and Regina.

CITIES

The Queen City of the Canadian prairies, **Regina** was founded in 1882 in what was basically the middle of nowhere. The provincial capital managed to thrive in isolation, developing a lively arts scene to complement its government functions. Today Regina revolves around Wascana Lake, a man-made reservoir enveloped by parkland and many of the city's cultural institutions, including the Royal Saskatchewan Museum of natural history, the vital MacKenzie Art Gallery, the interactive exhibits of the

Saskatchewan Science Centre, the Conexus performing arts complex, and the Queen Elizabeth II Gardens. The Devonian Pathway leads along Wascana Creek past the contemporary Art Gallery of Regina and the Royal Canadian Mounted Police Heritage Centre, located on the grounds of the RCMP Academy (Depot Division)—where all cadets undergo initial basic training. The museum stages parades and other tattoo-like activities. Nearby Government House arose in the early 1890s, an Italianate manse that served for many years as the official

residence of the territory's lieutenant governor. Those looking for action find plays at the Globe Theatre in the Old Post Office building, games of chance at Casino Regina, and ice hockey heroes at the Saskatchewan Sports Hall of Fame.

The province's largest city, **Saskatoon** lies astride the South Saskatchewan River on the prairie 160 miles (257 km) northwest of Regina. In addition to downtown, many of the city's landmarks are arrayed along the river's west bank, including the orchid-rich Civic Conservatory, vibrant Ukrainian Museum of Canada, active Meewasin Valley Interpretive Centre and outdoor ice-skating rink, and the theme park PotashCorp Playland in Kinsmen Park. The University of Saskatchewan, which rises on the river's eastern shore, offers the Diefenbaker

A statue of Queen Elizabeth II riding her favorite horse in the city of Regina

The South Saskatchewan River passes the city of Saskatoon.

Canada Centre that's devoted to the life and times of Canada's 13th prime minister. The Gordon Snelgrove Gallery displays works by students and the wider community. On the city's south side, the Exhibition neighborhood holds the Marquis Downs Thoroughbred horse-racing track as well as the Saskatoon chapter of the Western Development Museum. Dedicated to the theme "Boomtown 1910," the latter features a reconstructed prairie town and transportation gallery. The 39-mile (63 km) Meewasin Valley Trail system—popular with hikers, bikers, and runners—runs through the city along both sides of the South Saskatchewan River. On Saskatoon's northern outskirts, Wanuskewin Heritage Park encourages better understanding of the region's indigenous peoples. Part of an active archaeological site, the park displays First Nations artifacts dating as far back as 6,000 years ago and hosts 19 precontact dig sites.

LANDSCAPES

Saskatchewan's unrelenting prairie flows south from Regina all the way to the U.S. border, a massive sea of grass where towns are few and usually far between. Forty-four miles (71 km) from Regina, **Moose Jaw** is decorated by 50 giant murals depicting the town's frontier years. Actors in period costumes give theatrical tours of the tunnels beneath the downtown, while the Western Development Museum–Moose Jaw focuses on early transportation on the prairies. Six miles (10 km) from the international border, the small town of **Coronach** (named after an Epsom Derby–winning horse) relishes its Wild West past. Gateway to the deeply eroded geology of the province's Big Muddy Badlands, the town is also the northern terminus of the Outlaw Trail between Canada

CAPITALISM

One would think that a town named for an English queen (and christened by her own daughter) would have a refined past. But almost from the get-go, Regina recorded a turbulent and often bloody history. It was a fulcrum of the North-West Rebellion that pitted the Métis people against the Canadian government as well as the place where Métis leader Louis Riel was hanged. In 1912, the city endured the deadliest tornado in Canadian history. The streets were bloodied again during the notorious Depression-era Regina Riot between unemployed demonstrators and local police.

and Mexico. The local coal mine and power plant offers guided tours. West of Coronach, **Grasslands National Park** provides opportunities for visitors to backpack the prairies, sleep under the stars, work alongside paleontologists in fossil beds, and view the park's bison herds at closer range.

Farther west, the prairie gradually rises into the wooded **Cypress Hills,** shared by Saskatchewan and Alberta. The Saskatchewan side is divided into two areas: the Centre Block, fully developed with rustic vacation resorts, and the undeveloped West Block. During lawless frontier days, the hills were frequented by American buffalo and wolf hunters as well as whiskey traders whose belligerent attitude toward the region's native Assiniboine people resulted in the 1873 Cypress Hills Massacre. In order to quash the illegal cross-border trade, the Mounties built Fort Walsh, which later became a refuge for

Sioux warriors fleeing the U.S. cavalry. Today the national historic site offers a range of historically-based programs led by costume-clad staff.

Another geographical anomaly, the **Great Sandhills** sprawl across more than 700 square miles (1,813 sq km) of south-central Saskatchewan. The area's semiarid climate has resulted in towering beige and orange dunes that could easily pass as the Sahara rather than central Canada. Great Sandhills Museum & Interpretive Centre in Sceptre features exhibits, historic buildings, and tips on how to explore the sandy wasteland. Accessible by car, bike, or foot, the Beechy Sandcastles and Sunken Hill Trail wanders past wildlife, large sand dunes, teepee rings, and a sunken plateau—likely the result of a collapsing natural gas pocket.

The hardships of early prairie life are revealed at the Addison Sod House in **Oakdale,** built

between 1909 and 1911 by James Addison. Members of the Addison family continued to live here until 2007. The homestead remains privately owned, but tours can be arranged.

North Battleford's colorful past includes French fur trappers, red-coated Mounties, and early Assyrian settlers from the Middle East. An RCMP post from 1876 to 1924, North Battleford National Historic Site explains the role of the Mounties during frontier days. The nearby Western Development Museum–North Battleford is devoted to the province's agriculture heritage.

Batoche was headquarters for the Métis and their legendary leader Louis Riel during the North-West Rebellion of 1884–1885, as well as the scene of their final clash with

The northern hawk-owl at home in Prince Albert National Park

Sunrise at Cypress Hills Interprovincial Park, shared between Saskatchewan and Alberta

Canadian government troops. Today it includes an encampment, church, rectory, and farmhouse occupied by costumed interpreters who spin tales of the Métis, people of mixed European-Indian heritage who are recognized by the Canadian government as an official Aboriginal nation. Nearby Fort Carlton operated as a Hudson's Bay Company fur-trading post between 1810 and 1885. Now a provincial park, it includes reconstructed stockades and buildings as well as a reproduction 19th-century teepee encampment.

Immense **Prince Albert National Park** offers a blend of prairies, spruce bogs, boreal forests, and glacial lakes traversed by such wildlife as free-ranging bison herds, timber wolves, black bears, lynx, and numerous avian species. Beaver Lodge on Ajawaan Lake is where the English writer-naturalist Grey Owl and his two pet beavers lived in the 1930s. Waskesiu is a year-round, lakeside resort town located within the park's borders.

One of the world's most northerly dune fields is found within **Athabasca Sand Dunes Provincial Park,** which stretches more than 60 miles (97 km) along the shore of Lake Athabasca. This unique ecosystem supports many endemic plants. Access is by floatplane; the park has no support facilities and visitors must be fully self-supported for wilderness travel. Activities include fishing and camping. ■

FESTIVALS

- **Prince Albert Winter Festival (Prince Albert):** western Canada's biggest cold-weather bash with ice sculptures, sleigh rides, sled-dog racing, a beard contest, and more; February

- **Shakespeare on the Saskatchewan (Saskatoon):** a feast of stage plays, medieval banquets, and workshops in a makeshift Elizabethan village; July and August

- **Saskatchewan Festival of Words (Moose Jaw):** a four-day homage to literature, verse, lyrics, and anything else that gets written down; July

- **Northern Lights Bluegrass and Old Tyme Festival and Music Camp (Ness Creek):** Acoustic jamming and campfires highlight this outdoor music and camping jamboree near Big River in northern Saskatchewan; August.

Yukon

The Klondike gold rush might be long gone, but the Yukon continues to attract people bent on discovering the heritage and wilderness of this fabled territory. Astride the land route to Alaska, the Yukon offers a heady mix of historic towns, high mountains, and outdoor adventure between the Arctic and the Pacific coast.

CITIES

George Carmack, Tagish Charlie, and Skookum Jim discovered gold near the Klondike River in 1896, setting off the so-called Great Stampede for the mass of people who hastened north. **Dawson City** arose at the confluence of the Klondike and Yukon Rivers to service the goldfields. The ore eventually ran out, but Dawson was rescued from ghost-town fate by the Canadian government, which started preserving historical sites in and around the city as early as the 1950s. Dawson Historical Complex National Historic Site encompasses eight square blocks of downtown, including the Old Territorial Courthouse, the Commissioner's Residence, Red Feather Saloon, Harrington's Store, and the Canadian Bank of Commerce—all built around the turn of the 20th century. Learn more about the gold rush at the excellent Dawson City Museum, housed in the Old Territorial Administration Building. In summer, daily poetry readings are a staple at the Robert Service Cabin, where the namesake "Bard of the Yukon" lived for three years while working at a bank. A replica of Jack London's modest abode features photos and other relics of the American writer's 1897 sojourn in Dawson Creek. The past also comes alive during living-history shows at the Palace Grand Theatre as well as musical reviews at Diamond Tooth Gerties Gambling Hall.

One of the last of the Yukon River steamboats, the S.S. *Keno* is now a floating museum on the waterfront. The remains of other riverboats lie in the "paddlewheel graveyard" on the other side of the river, accessed via the George Black Ferry. *Klondike Spirit*, a reproduction paddle wheeler, offers narrated cruises along the Yukon River in summer. A much different side to the Yukon experience is showcased

TOURISM INFORMATION

Tourism Yukon maintains visitor information centers at six sites around the territory; the Whitehorse center is open year-round, the others from May through September. Visit travelyukon.com *for more information.*

- **Dawson City Visitor Information Centre**
  Front St.
  Dawson, YT Y0B 1G0
  Tel 867/993-5566
  dawsoncity.ca

- **Whitehorse Yukon Visitor Information Centre**
  100 Hanson St.
  Whitehorse, YT Y1A 6C2
  Tel 867/667-3084
  travelyukon.com

- **Carcross Visitor Information Centre**
  Train Station
  Dawson Charlie St.
  Carcross, YT Y0B 1B0
  Tel 867/821-4431
  travelyukon.com

- **National Parks**
  pc.gc.ca

- **Yukon Territorial Parks**
  env.gov.yk.ca

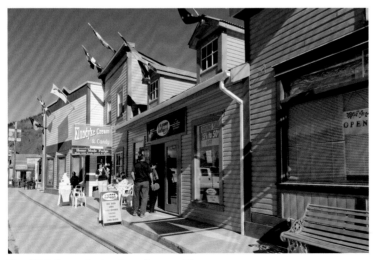

The 1800s live on in downtown Dawson City.

Kluane Lake, part of the enormous Kluane National Park and Reserve

at the Dänojà Zho Cultural Centre, which tells the story of the Tr'ondëk Hwëch'in First Nations people who lived in the region for thousands of years. Visitors can spot the old gold-fields scattered in the countryside around Dawson City. Discovery Claim National Historic Site on Bonanza Creek preserves the spot where it all started in 1896, explored via a self-guided trail with interactive displays and old mining tools. A massive steel beast called Dredge No. 4, which scoured Bonanza Creek between 1912 and 1960, shows how gold mining was later mechanized. About a two-hour drive northeast of Dawson, Tombstone Territorial Park offers hiking, wild-life, and strange permafrost land-forms including pingos and palsas.

Whitehorse, the territorial capital, lies more than 300 miles (483 km) south of Dawson City via the Klondike Highway (Route 2). Whitehorse's past is explored at the MacBride Museum, which concen-trates on frontier and gold rush themes as well as the Yukon Beringia Interpretive Centre, with its focus on prehistoric times. The Kwanlin Dün Cultural Centre celebrates the culture of local First Nations people. Modern development didn't spare many of the city's gold rush relics, but a few endure including the S.S. *Klondike* floating museum, the Old Log Church, and several wooden buildings on Lambert Street. A restored 1925 yellow trolley plies a scenic route along the Whitehorse waterfront. The White Horse Rapids

CAPITALISM

A child of the Great Stampede, Whitehorse was born at the place where the overland route to the goldfields was inter-rupted by the raging White Horse Rapids (named for their resemblance to a flowing horse's mane). When copper was discovered nearby, White-horse exploded into its own Wild West boomtown. The arrival of the White Pass & Yukon Route Railroad in 1900 assured the town's long-term survival and eventual role as the territorial capital; although that didn't happen until the 1950s, when the government moved from Dawson City and the new capital's name was tweaked from White Horse to Whitehorse.

have disappeared, drowned when Schwatka Lake was created in 1958. Beside the dam, an observation deck provides overhead views of Chinook salmon climbing the world's longest wooden fish ladder. South of the reservoir, the Yukon River continues to run wild and free through Miles Canyon with its hiking trails and old Robert Lowe Bridge (1922). Several attractions have taken root on the northern outskirts of Whitehorse, including the Copperbelt Railway & Mining Museum, which offers rides on a tiny narrow-gauge train. The mineral-rich Takhini Hot Springs is a great place to soak weary bones after summer hiking or to view the aurora borealis on winter nights. The Yukon Wildlife Preserve showcases 13 north country creatures—including musk ox, wood buffalo, arctic fox, lynx, and caribou—in natural boreal habitats.

LANDSCAPES

South of Whitehorse, the Klondike Highway rises into the rugged **Coast Range** mountains, a lake-spangled region trekked by would-be prospectors during the Klondike gold rush and wilderness junkies in modern times. Much of the region lies in the remote northwest corner of British Columbia, which can only be accessed by road from the Yukon or the Alaska Panhandle. **Carcross** is the northern terminus of the historic White Pass & Yukon Route Railroad, which provides scenic journeys from Skagway. In addition to food and souvenirs, the town's Caribou Crossing Trading Post offers a wildlife museum, a gold-panning experience, and sled-dog cart rides. Another way to experience the Great Stampede route is by hiking the 33-mile (53 km) Chilkoot Trail between Dyea and Bennett Lake.

STATE OF THE ART

Best movie: *The Call of the Wild* (1935)

Best books: *White Fang* by Jack London and *Steam Laundry* by Nicole Stellon O'Donnell

Best poem: "The Spell of the Yukon" by Robert Service

Best spoken-word album: *Tales of the Yukon* by Hank Snow

Best music: the folk tunes of Northern Tutchone "Keeper of the Songs" Jerry Alfred

Best art: the carvings of Kaska master Dennis Shorty

The region's newest attraction is the Yukon Suspension Bridge, a 200-foot-long (61 m) pedestrian span over the rapids of the Tutshi River Canyon.

Camping beneath the northern lights at Tombstone Territorial Park

Almost a hundred miles (161 km) west of Whitehorse via the Alaska Highway, Haines Junction is the gateway to the great and mighty **Kluane National Park and Reserve.** The massive reserve boasts several claims to fame including Canada's largest ice field, most genetically diverse bear population, and highest peak—19,551-foot (5,959 m) Mount Logan. Kluane is also part of a UNESCO World Heritage site and International Biosphere Reserve that spreads across 50,000 square miles (129,499 sq km), an area about the same size as England. The only ways to explore most of this vast, roadless wilderness is long-distance backpacking or drop-in bush plane camping or mountaineering. However, several short trails are accessible from the Alaska and Haines Highways along the park's eastern edge. Kathleen Lake offers the only drive-in camp-ground, and flightseeing trips are available from Haines Junction.

The Kluane Museum of Natural History in **Burwash Landing** ten-ders displays on local wildlife and Southern Tutchone people. A little farther up the Alaska Highway, the George Johnston Museum in **Tes-lin** showcases Tlingit culture and the photographs of the museum's namesake, a local fur trader and trapper who cataloged early-20th-century life in the Yukon with his Brownie box camera.

The territory's southeast corner is anchored by **Watson Lake** near the spot where the Alaska Highway crosses from British Columbia into the Yukon. Explore the history of the famed route at the Alaska High-way Interpretive Centre and learn more about the aurora borealis at the Northern Lights Space and Sci-ence Centre. The town's most iconic

A female grizzly bear near Carcross along the path of the Klondike gold rush

attraction is the Sign Post Forest, decorated with more than 77,000 town and city signposts from around the globe. The collection started in 1942 when homesick American soldier Carl K. Lindley erected a sign pointing the way to Danville, Illinois, his hometown.

The Yukon's far north boasts sev-eral spectacular but utterly remote nature reserves. **Ivvavik National Park** protects a portion of the

migratory route and calving ground of the 160,000-strong Porcupine caribou herd. The huge park stretches between the Beaufort Sea and the British Mountains, a tundra and taiga landscape that includes the Firth River Valley. Fishing, backpacking, fly-in camp-ing, and rafting trips are staged out of Sheep Creek base camp. Adja-cent Vuntut National Park is even more remote. ■

FESTIVALS

- **Available Light Film Festival (Whitehorse):** billed as the biggest feature-film fest north of 60° north latitude; February

- **Yukon Sourdough Rendezvous (Whitehorse):** Can Can Dancers, Sourdough Sams, Keystone Kops, and Snow Shoe Sufflers are among the regular characters at this rowdy midwinter revival of gold rush days. A Rendezvous Queen is named, among other events; February.

- **Yukon Quest sled-dog race:** cov-ering 1,000 miles (1,609 km) of frozen ground between Fairbanks, Alaska, and Whitehorse; February

- **Adäka Cultural Festival (White-horse):** showcasing First Nations music, dance, drumming, storytelling, art, and even comedy; July

- **Dawson City Music Festival:** world-class grassroots music acts perform under the midnight sun; July

ILLUSTRATIONS CREDITS

Cover (MAIN), Stephen G. Weaver; (UP), Pete Saloutos/GI; (LO LE), Axel Brunst/TandemStock.com; (LO CT), Markus Mainka/SS; (LO RT), lazyllama/SS; spine, fotomak/SS; back cover, AndreyKrav/GI; 2-3, Dave and Les Jacobs/GI; 4, Nico De Pasquale Photography/GI; 6, Danita Delimont/GI; 8-9, Tetra Images/GI; 10, LMspencer/SS; 11, Sean Pavone Photo/Adobe Stock; 12, Rob Hainer/SS; 13, LMspencer/SS; 14, Jeff McGraw/SS; 15, Galyna Andrushko/SS; 16, Daniel A. Leifheit/GI; 17, Adam Van Spronsen/SS; 18, Lane V. Erickson/SS; 19, huci/Adobe Stock; 20, David Sucsy/GI; 21, James Forte/NGC; 22, Mnapoli501/Adobe Stock; 23, Bonita R. Cheshier/SS; 24, Zack Frank/SS; 25, mnapoli/SS; 26, Dobino/SS; 27, Ken Wolter/SS; 28, Lonnie Gorsline/SS; 29, cdrin/SS; 30, ventdusud/SS; 31, IM_photo/SS; 32, f11photo/SS; 33, kan_khampanya/SS; 34, Tetra Images—Shawn O'Connor/GI; 35, Kritti Kolatat/SS; 36, f11photo/SS; 37, Sean Pavone/SS; 38, alexpro9500/SS; 39, Enfi/SS; 40, Nagel Photography/SS; 41, Margie Politzer/GI; 42, John Greim/GI; 43, Matt Propert; 44, Matt Propert; 45, f11photo/SS; 46, Png Studio Photography/SS; 47, Charles Kogod/GI; 48, Matt Propert; 49, Bloomberg/GI; 50, Matt Propert; 51, Panoramic Images/GI; 52, Kay Hankins; 53, Mike Theiss/NGC; 54, Rob Hainer/SS; 55, LMspencer/SS; 56, Paul Brennan/SS; 57, Sean Pavone/SS; 58, Chad Ehlers/GI; 59, Makena Stock Media/GI; 60, Sorin Colac/SS; 61, tropicdreams/SS; 62, Vishwanath Bhat/GI; 63, Charles Knowles/SS; 64, Megan Carley/SS; 65, HES Photography/SS; 66, Richard Nowitz/NGC; 67, Tupungato/SS; 68, Ira Block/NGC; 69, maksymowicz/Adobe Stock; 70, Chuck W. Walker/SS; 71, Alexey Stiop/Adobe Stock; 72, Chad Bontrager/SS; 73, Steve Raymer/NGC; 74, Nagel Photography/SS; 75, Joel Sartore/NGC; 76, Jack Vanden Heuvel/GI; 77, Dennis Macdonald/GI; 78, Ricardo Reitmeyer/SS; 79, digidreamgrafix/Adobe Stock; 80, Jim Richardson/NGC; 81, Walter Bibikow/GI; 82, Amy Nichole Harris/SS; 83, Sam Abell/NGC; 84, Stephen Alvarez/NGC; 85, Willard Clay/GI; 86, Franz Marc Frei/LOOK-foto/GI; 87, f11photo/SS; 88, Richard Nowitz/NGC; 89, Pierre-Jean Durieu/Adobe Stock; 90, David Zentz/GI; 91, Doug Lemke/SS; 92, Scott Suriano/GI; 93, Kennan Harvey/GI; 94, Greg Dale/NGC/ASP; 95, Sean Pavone/SS; 96, zrfphoto/GI; 97, Yvonne Navalaney/SS; 98, holbox/SS; 99, Stephanie Hager—HagerPhoto/GI; 100, CO Leong/SS; 101, Jon Bilous/SS; 102, Rolf_52/SS; 103, T photography/SS; 104, tinyal/Adobe Stock; 105, Mike Kline (notkalvin)/GI; 106, Saddako/GI; 107, Thomas Barrat/SS; 108, photo.ua/SS; 109, Saibal Ghosh/SS; 110, nikitsin.smugmug.com/SS; 111, puwanai/SS; 112, Dosfotos/Design Pics/GI; 113, John J. Miller Photography/GI; 114, HixnHix/SS; 115, James P. Blair/NGC; 116, Tinnaporn Sathapornnanont/SS; 117, amolson7/SS; 118, Sam Kittner/NGC; 119, clearviewstock/Adobe Stock; 120, julielubick/Adobe Stock; 121, Pung/SS; 122, Gonzuller/Adobe Stock; 123, Anna M./Adobe Stock; 124, Eric Francis/SS; 125, Katherine Welles/SS; 126, Danita Delimont/GI; 127, Zack Frank/SS; 128, sumikophoto/Adobe Stock; 129, Sylvain Sonnet/GI; 130, stevedunleavy.com/GI; 131, Bob Stefko/GI; 132, DenisTangneyJr/GI; 133, jiawangkun/SS; 134, Jon Bilous/SS; 135, Jose Azel/GI; 136, Francois Roux/Adobe Stock; 137, Amy Toensing/NGC; 138, f11photo/Adobe Stock; 139, Aneese/GI; 140, Jodi Cobb/NGC; 141, Douglas Knight/Adobe Stock; 142, giumas/Adobe Stock; 143, Michael Nichols/NGC; 144, Christian Kober/GI; 145, Luciano Mortula/SS; 146, Stuart Monk/SS; 147, Sylvain Sonnet/GI; 148, Amy Riley/GI; 149, Orchidpoet/GI; 150, Yury Shchipakin/SS; 151, Fotoluminate LLC/SS; 152, Alexey Rotanov/SS; 153, Rick Sause/GI; 154, Chuck Haney/Danita Delimont/ASP; 155, Tim Fitzharris/Minden Pictures/NGC; 156, Richard Cummins/robertharding/GI; 157, Michael Melford/GI; 158, Melissa Farlow/GI; 159, RuthChoi/SS; 160, Doug Lemke/SS; 161, Michael Shake/Adobe Stock; 162, Katherine Welles/SS; 163, val lawless/SS; 164, Gimas/SS; 165, John Elk/GI; 166, iStock.com/deebrowning; 167, Josemaria Toscano/SS; 168, Jordan Siemens/GI; 169, Anton Foltin/SS; 170, f11photo/SS; 171, Jon Bilous/SS; 172, Delmas Lehman/SS; 173, Mark VanDykePhotography/SS; 174, RosaIreneBetancourt 2/ASP; 175, Steve Dunwell/GI; 176, Richard Cummins/GI; 177, Onne van der Wal/Bluegreen Pictures/ASP; 178, Dave Allen Photography/SS; 179, Sean Pavone/SS; 180, Sean Pavone/SS; 181, Sean Pavone/SS; 182, Vicki L. Miller/SS; 183, wishfaery14/Adobe Stock; 184, Andrew Cullen/GI; 185, Andrew Cullen/GI; 186, Hunter Hayes/GI; 187, Bruce Yuanyue Bi/GI; 188, Oliver Gerhard/imageBROKER/ASP; 189, Dave Allen Photography/SS; 190, mandritoiu/SS; 192, Aaron Black/Aurora Photos/ASP; 193, Inge Johnsson/ASP; 194, Josemaria Toscano/SS; 195, Scott Markewitz/GI; 196, Galyna Andrushko/SS; 197, Danita Delimont/GI; 198, Geoffrey Clifford/GI; 199, DenisTangneyJr/GI; 200, Corey Hendrickson/GI; 201, DenisTangneyJr/GI; 202, Witold Skrypczak/GI; 203, Sean Pavone/SS; 204, Pat & Chuck Blackley/ASP; 205, Orhan Cam/SS; 206, Ritu Manoj Jethani/SS; 207, Steve Heap/SS; 208, Justek16/SS; 209, TinaImages/SS; 210, Jordan Siemens/GI; 211, Aaron Huang/SS; 212, StudioOneNine/SS; 213, Skip Brown/National Geographic/GI; 214, Andre Jenny/ASP; 215, Jon Bilous/SS; 216, Peter Ptschelinzew/GI; 217, kickstand/GI; 218, Kenneth Keifer/GI; 219, critterbiz/SS; 220, John Elk/GI; 221, Chase Dekker Wild-Life Images/GI; 222, Dean Fikar/GI; 223, Lorcel/SS; 224-5, rcfotostock/Adobe Stock; 226, Sekar B/SS; 227, Andrew Zarivny/SS; 228, robertbohrer1/Adobe Stock; 229, Dennis Donohue/Adobe Stock; 230, Sergei Bachlakov/SS; 231, Dan Breckwoldt/SS; 232, Steven Castro/SS; 233, 2009fotofriends/SS; 234, meunierd/SS; 235, Benedikt Juerges/SS; 236, Yvette Cardozo/GI; 237, graphicjackson/GI; 238, Nelepl/SS; 239, Gudkov Andrey/SS; 240, DenisTangneyJr/GI; 241, Barrett & MacKay/GI; 242, Maurizio De Mattei/SS; 243, Ian Crysler/Design Pics/GI; 244, Elena Elisseeva/SS; 245, Orchidpoet/GI; 246, Barrett & MacKay/GI; 247, SeventhDayPhotography/GI; 248, Gordon Wiltsie/GI; 249, Vincent Demers Photography/GI; 250, Henry Georgi/GI; 251, Edmond van Hoorick/Prisma Bildagentur AG/ASP; 252, Joe Regan/GI; 253, Joe Regan/GI; 254, matthewsinger/SS; 255, creighton359/GI; 256, John E Marriott/GI; 257, John E Marriott/GI; 258, drferry/GI; 259, JohnPitcher/GI; 260, DenisTangneyJr/GI; 261, Lissandra Melo/SS; 262, Kiev.Victor/SS; 263, RuthChoi/SS; 264, prosiaczeq/SS; 265, Barrett & MacKay/GI; 266, Barrett & MacKay/GI; 267, Barrett & MacKay/GI; 268, Richard Cavalleri/SS; 269, Yves Marcoux/Design Pics/GI; 270, Chris Cheadle/GI; 271, Maurizio De Mattei/SS; 272, Wolfgang Kaehler/GI; 273, MmeEmil/GI; 274, Scott Prokop/SS; 275, sprokop/GI; 276, Nick Saunders/GI; 277, Mike Grandmaison/GI; 278, Egmont Strigl/imageBROKER/ASP; 279, LaraBelova/GI; 280, Piriya Photography/GI; 281, Murphy_Shewchuk/GI.

INDEX

Boldface indicates illustrations.

A

Alabama 10–13
  Birmingham 10–12, **11**
  festivals 13
  Florala City Park 13
  Gulf Coast 13
  Huntsville 13, **13**
  Little River Canyon Nat. Pres. **12,** 13
  Mobile 12, 13
  Montgomery 10, **10,** 11
  Tuscaloosa 13
  Tuskegee Institute 13
  Vulcan (statue), near Birmingham 11–12

Alaska 14–17
  Alaska Range **14,** 16–17
  Anchorage 14
  Denali NPP **15, 16,** 16–17
  Fairbanks 14–15
  Homer 16
  Inside Passage 17
  Juneau 15–16
  Kenai Peninsula 16
  road trips 17
  Russian history 16
  Seward 16
  Wrangell–Saint Elias NP 17

Alberta, Canada 224–229
  Banff NP **224–225,** 227–228, **228,** 229
  Blackfoot Crossing HP 229
  Calgary 226, **227**
  Dinosaur PP 229
  Edmonton 226–227
  Jasper NP **226,** 228, **229**
  Kananaskis Country 228
  road trips 228
  Waterton Lakes NP 228–229
  Wood Buffalo NP 229
  Writing-on-Stone PP 229

Arizona 18–21
  Canyon de Chelly Nat. Mon. 21, **21**
  Chiricahua Mountains 21
  Flagstaff 20
  Grand Canyon NP **19,** 19–20
  Organ Pipe Cactus Nat. Mon. 21
  Painted Desert 20–21
  Phoenix 18
  Scottsdale 18
  Sonoran Desert 21
  Tucson **18,** 18–19, **20**

Arkansas 22–25
  Bentonville 24
  Crater of Diamonds SP 24–25
  Eureka Springs 24
  festivals 24
  Fort Smith 23–24
  Hot Springs 22, 23
  Little Rock **22,** 22–23, 24
  Ozark NF 24
  road trips 23

B

British Columbia, Canada 230–235
  Capilano Suspension Bridge 231, 233
  Great Bear Rainforest 234
  Haida Gwaii 234
  Inside Passage 234–235
  Mount Assiniboine **235**
  Okanagan Valley 234, 235
  Pacific Rim NP 234
  Rocky Mountains 235
  Vancouver **230,** 230–231, **231,** 233
  Vancouver Island 234
  Victoria 230, 231, **233,** 233–234, **234**
  Whistler 230, 235
  Yoho NP **232**

C

California 26–31
  coasts **26,** 29–30
  festivals 31
  Gold Country 30–31
  Los Angeles 26, 27
  Mojave Desert 31
  Napa Valley 30
  Redwood Country **28,** 29
  road trips 29
  Sacramento 27, 30–31
  San Diego 26, 27–28, 31
  San Francisco 26, **30,** 31, **31**
  Sierra Nevada 31
  Sonoma Valley 30

Colorado 32–35
  Aspen **33,** 34, **34**
  Boulder 34
  Colorado Springs 32, 33
  Denver **32,** 32–33
  Fort Collins 32, 33
  Great Sand Dunes NPP 35, **35**
  Mesa Verde NP 35
  road trips 34
  Rocky Mountain NP 34
  Telluride 35
  Vail 34

Connecticut 36–39
  Bridgeport 37
  Gillette Castle **38,** 39
  Greenwich 37
  Guilford 38
  Hartford 36, 37, **37**
  Mystic 38
  New Canaan 37–38
  New Haven 36
  Talcott Mountain SP 39
  Woodstock 38–39

D

Delaware 40–43
  Cape Henlopen SP 42–43
  Chateau Country 42, **42**
  Dover **40,** 40–42
  Fenwick Island 43, **43**
  New Castle 42
  Rehoboth Beach 40, **41,** 43
  Wilmington 40
  Winterthur Museum 42

District of Columbia 44–47
  Georgetown 46–47
  Martin Luther King, Jr. Memorial **47**
  National Mall 44–46
  Penn Quarter 47
  Rock Creek Park 47
  West Potomac Park 46

F

Florida 48–53
  Biscayne NP 48–49
  Cape Canaveral 52
  capitalism 49
  coasts **51,** 51–53, **53**
  Daytona International Speedway 52
  Disney World 49, **49**
  Everglades NP 51–52
  Florida Keys 52, **53**
  Florida Panhandle 53
  Fort Lauderdale 51, **51**
  Homestead 49
  Jacksonville 51
  Key Biscayne 48
  Key West 52, **52**
  Miami 48, **48, 50**
  Miami Beach 48
  Orlando 48, **49,** 51
  road trips 51
  Saint Augustine 48, 52, 53
  Sarasota 53
  Tampa–Saint Petersburg 51
  Tarpon Springs 53
  west coast 52–53

G

Georgia 54–57
  Atlanta **54,** 54–55, 57
  Augusta 57
  Blue Ridge 56–57
  McCaysville 56–57
  Plains 57
  road trips 56
  Savannah 54, **55,** 55–56, 57
  Sea Islands 57
  Stone Mountain Park 56, **56**
  Tybee Island **57**
  Warm Springs 57

H

Hawaii 58–61
  Hawaii (Big Island) 60, 61
  Hilo 60
  Honolulu **58**, 58–60
  islands 60–61
  Kauai 60, **60**, 61
  Lanai 61
  Maui **59**, 60–61
  Molokai 61
  road trips 59

I

Idaho 62–65
  Boise **62**, 62–63
  Bruneau Dunes SP 64–65
  Coeur d'Alene 62, 64
  Craters of the Moon Nat. Mon. &
    Preserve 65
  Hells Canyon NRA 64
  Idaho National Laboratory 65
  Jerome 65
  Lava Hot Springs 65
  Nez Perce NHP 64
  Pocatello 63
  Rocky Mountains **65**
  Sawtooth NRA **63**
  Shoshone Falls 65
  Smoky Mountains 64

Illinois 66–69
  Cahokia Mounds SHS **68**, 68–69
  Cairo 69
  Chicago **66**, 66–67, **67**
  Evanston 67
  Galena 68
  Metropolis 68
  Nauvee 68
  Oak Park 67
  Rockford 68, **69**
  Shawnee NF 69
  Springfield 66, 67–68

Indiana 70–73
  Angel Mounds 71
  Bloomington 72–73, **73**
  Corydon 71
  Evansville 71
  festivals 72
  Fort Wayne 70–71, 72
  George Rogers Clark NHP 73
  Hoosier NF 73
  Indiana Dunes National Lakeshore 72
  Indianapolis 70, **71**, 72
  South Bend **70**, 71–72

Iowa 74–77
  Amana Colonies 77
  amusement parks 77
  Backbone SP 76
  Cedar Rapids 75
  Davenport 77

Des Moines 74–75, **75**
Dubuque 74, 76–77
Herbert Hoover NHS 77, **77**
Iowa 80 Trucking Museum 77
Pikes Peak SP 76, **76**
Port of Dubuque 76–77
Sioux City 75–76
Waubonsie SP 77

K

Kansas 78–81
  Abilene 81
  Dodge City 81, **81**
  Fort Scott NHS 80–81
  Hutchinson 81
  Lawrence 78, 80
  Overland Park 79–80
  Tallgrass Prairie Nat. Pres. **80**, 81
  Topeka 78–79, **79**
  Wichita 78, **78**

Kentucky 82–85
  Bardstown 84, 85
  Bowling Green 85
  Cumberland Falls State Resort Park
    84
  Cumberland Gap 84, **85**
  Daniel Boone NF 84
  Danville 84–85
  festivals 84
  Fort Knox 85
  Harlan County 84
  Lexington 82, **82**, 83, 84
  Louisville 82–83, 84, 85
  Mammoth Cave **84**, 85
  Shaker Village of Pleasant Hill **83**, 84

L

Louisiana 86–89
  Baton Rouge 86–87
  bayou country 87, **89**
  Cane River National Heritage Area
    89
  Grand Isle 88
  Jean Lafitte NHP and Preserve 87–88
  Lafayette 88
  Lake Charles 88
  Mississippi Valley plantations **88**,
    88–89
  New Orleans 86, **86**, **87**

M

Maine 90–93
  Acadia NP 91–92
  Augusta 91
  Baxter SP **92**, 93
  Blue Hill 92
  Boothbay Harbor 92
  Bowdoin College 92
  Kennebunkport 93
  Portland 90–91, **91**
  road trips 93

Trenton 92
Wilderness Waterway 93

Manitoba, Canada 236–239
  Canadian Fossil Discovery Centre 239
  Churchill 236, 237–238, 239
  Hudson Bay **237**, 237–238
  International Peace Garden 157, 239
  Lake Winnipeg 238, **238**
  Mennonite Heritage Village 239
  The Pas 238–239
  Red River Valley 239
  Riding Mountain NP 239
  Wapusk NP 238
  Whiteshell PP 239
  Winnipeg **236**, 236–237, 239

Maryland 94–97
  Allegheny Mountains 96
  Annapolis 94, **95**, 95–96
  Assateague Island 97
  Baltimore **94**, 94–95, 97
  Catoctin Mountain Park **96**
  Chesapeake Bay **97**
  Eastern Shore 94, 97
  Frederick 96
  Piedmont region 96

Massachusetts 98–103
  Berkshires 103, **103**
  Boston **98**, 98–99, **99**, 101, **101**
  Cambridge 101
  Cape Cod **100**, 102, **102**
  Charlestown 101
  coast 101–103
  Gloucester 102
  Martha's Vineyard 102
  Minute Man NHP 103
  New Bedford 102
  Northampton 103
  Old Sturbridge Village 103
  Plymouth 98, 102
  Quincy 101–102
  Salem 98, 102–103
  Springfield 101
  Worcester 103

Michigan 104–107
  Ann Arbor **104**, 105
  Colonial Michilimackinac 106–107
  Dearborn 104–105
  Detroit 104, **105**
  Gold Coast 107
  Grand Rapids 105
  Holland 107, **107**
  Isle Royale 106
  Mackinac Island 106
  road trips 105
  Sault Sainte Marie 106
  Upper Peninsula 106, **106**

Minnesota 108–111
  Boundary Waters Canoe Area
    Wilderness 111

Brainerd 111
Duluth 108, 110
Ely 111
Hibbing 110, 111
Minneapolis 108, **108**
road trips 109
Saint Cloud 111
Saint Paul 108–110, **109**
Stillwater 111
Voyageurs NP 111, **111**

Mississippi 112–115
Biloxi 112, 113
Delta Blues Highway 114–115
Gulf Islands National Seashore 113
Jackson **112,** 112–113, **113**
Natchez 114, **114**
Ocean Springs 113–114
Oxford 115
road trips 114
Tupelo 115
Vicksburg 112, 114, 115, **115**

Missouri 116–119
Branson 119
Hannibal 118–119
Independence 118
Jefferson City 119
Kansas City 116, 117–118, **118,** 119
Ozarks 119, **119**
road trips 118
Saint Louis **116,** 116–117, **117,** 119
Springfield 119

Montana 120–123
Billings 120–121
Bozeman 120, **123**
Butte 120
Crow Indian Reservation 123
Flathead Valley 122
Fort Peck Reservoir 123
Glacier NP **120, 121,** 121–122
Great Falls 123
Great Plains 123
Helena 120, 121, **122**
Missoula 122
Missouri River 123
Rocky Mountains 121–123

N
Nebraska 124–127
"Carhenge" 126
Homestead Nat. Mon. of America 127
Lewis and Clark NHT 126
Lincoln 124, **125,** 125–126, 127
North Platte 126
Omaha **124,** 124–125
sandhill cranes **126,** 127
Sandhills 126
Scotts Bluff 126, **127**

Nevada 128–131
Black Canyon 130–131, **131**

Carson City 129–130
Elko 131
festivals 131
Hoover Dam 130, **131**
Lake Tahoe 128, **130,** 131
Las Vegas 128, **129**
Laughlin 131
Mojave Desert 131
Pyramid Lake 131
Reno 128–129
road trips 129
Valley of Fire SP **128**
Virginia City 130

New Brunswick, Canada 240–243
Bay of Fundy 242, **242, 243**
Cape Pelé **241**
Chaleur Bay 243
festivals 243
Fredericton 240, 242
Fundy NP 242
Hartland Bridge 243
Moncton 240, **240,** 241–242
road trips 242
Saint John 240–241
Shediac 243

New Hampshire 132–135
Concord 132–133, **133**
festivals 135
Franconia 134, 135
Isles of Shoals 135
Jefferson 134
Lake Winnipesaukee 134
Manchester 132
Mount Washington 133–134
North Conway 134
Portsmouth 132, **132,** 133, 135
Rocky Gorge **134**
Saint-Gaudens NHS 135
White Mountains 132, 133, **135**

New Jersey 136–139
Asbury Park 138
Atlantic City 136, **138,** 139
Cape May 136, 139, **139**
Hamilton 138
Jersey City 136, **136**
Jersey Shore **137,** 138–139
Long Branch 138
Morristown 137, 139
Newark 136–137
Ocean City 139
Sandy Hook 138
Trenton 138
West Orange 137

New Mexico 140–143
Abiquiú 142
Acoma Pueblo's Sky City 143
Albuquerque 2–3, 140, 141, **141,** 143
Bandelier Nat. Mon. 142
Carlsbad Caverns NP 143, **143**

Chaco Culture NHP 143
El Morro Nat. Mon. 143
festivals 143
Los Alamos 142–143
Santa Fe 140, **140,** 143
Shiprock 143
Taos 141–142, **142**
White Sands Nat. Mon. 143

New York 144–149
Adirondack Park 148
Albany 148
Buffalo 145, 147
Canandaigua 149
Catskill Mountains 148
Finger Lakes 144, 149
Hudson Valley 147–148
Hyde Park 148
Lake Champlain **148**
Long Island 147
New York City **144,** 144–146, **145, 146, 147,** 149
New York Harbor **9–10**
Niagara Falls 144, 149, **149**
road trips 148
Rochester 146–147, 149
Saratoga Springs 148
Syracuse 146
Thousand Islands region 144, 148–149
Watkins Glen 149

Newfoundland & Labrador, Canada 244–247
Avalon Peninsula 245–246
Burin Peninsula 246
Cape Bonavista 246
Cape Spear 245
Cupids 246
Gros Morne NP 246–247
Labrador 247
L'Anse aux Meadows NHS **246,** 247
Red Bay NHS 247
road trips 246
Saint John's **244,** 244–245, **245,** 247
Terra Nova NP 246
Torngat Mountains NP 247

North Carolina 150–153
Appalachian region 153
Asheville 150, 151, **151**
Chapel Hill 152
Charlotte **150,** 150–151
Chimney Rock SP **152,** 153
Durham 152
Great Smoky Mountains NP 153
Outer Banks 150, 152–153, **153**
Pisgah NF 153
Raleigh 151
road trips 152
Wilmington 150, 151–152

North Dakota 154–157
Bismarck 154, **154,** 155

capitalism 155
Cooperstown 157
Fargo 154–155, **156**
International Peace Garden 157, 239
Jamestown 156–157
Medora 156
Minot 156
North Dakota Lewis & Clark Interpretive Center 156
Theodore Roosevelt NP **155,** 155–156, **157**

Northwest Territories, Canada 248–251
Fort Providence 249–250
Fort Resolution 250
Fort Smith 248, 250
Great Slave Lake **248,** 249–250
Hay River 250
Inuvik 248, 251
Mackenzie Bison Sanctuary **251**
Mackenzie Highway 249
Mackenzie River 251
Norman Wells 251
northern lights **249**
road trips 250
Wood Buffalo NP 250–251
Yellowknife 248–249

Nova Scotia, Canada 252–255
Birchtown 254
Bras d'Or 254
Cabot Trail 253
Cape Breton Highlands NP 253
Cape Breton Island 252, 253–254, **255**
Cape Breton Miners' Museum 254
Grand-Pré NHS 255
Halifax **252,** 252–253
Lunenburg 254
Peggy's Point Lighthouse **253,** 254
Port-Royal 255
Ross Farm Museum 254
Sherbrooke Village 254
Yarmouth 254–255

Nunavut, Canada 256–259
Arviat 256, 258
Auyuittuq NP 258
Baffin Bay **257**
Baffin Island 258
Baker Lake 257
Bloody Falls TP 256
Cambridge Bay 256, **258,** 259
Ellesmere Island 258–259, **259**
festivals 258
Iqaluit 257, 258
King William Island 259
Kugluktuk 256, 258
Queen Maud Gulf Migratory Bird Sanctuary 256, **256**
Sirmilik NP 258
Thelon Wildlife Sanctuary 257
Ukkusiksalik NP 256–257

O

Ohio 158–161
Ashtabula County 159–160
Cedar Point 160
Cincinnati 158, **158,** 159, **159**
Cleveland 158
Columbus 158–159
Cuyahoga Valley NP 160, **161**
Dayton 161
Hocking Hills 161
Holmes County 161
Lake Erie Archipelago 160
lakeshore 159–160, **160**
Toledo 160, 161

Oklahoma 162–165
Black Kettle National Grassland 164
Chickasaw NRA 164
Fort Reno 164
Guthrie 163
Medicine Park 164
Native American heritage 164–165
Norman 162–163
Oklahoma City 162, **162,** 163
Route 66 164, **164**
Stafford Air & Space Museum 164
Tulsa 162, 163, **163**
Wichita Mountains 164, **165**
Will Rogers 165

Ontario, Canada 260–263
Hamilton 262
Lake Huron 262–263
Lake of the Woods 263
Lake Ontario **263**
Niagara Falls 260, 262
Ottawa 260, **260,** 261–262
Polar Bear PP 263
road trips 263
Thunder Bay 263
Toronto 260–261, **261, 262**

Oregon 166–169
Ashland 166, 169
Astoria 168
Bend 168, 169
Cannon Beach 169, **169**
Cascade Range 168
Columbia River 167–168
Crater Lake NP 168
Eugene 166, 167, **168**
Hells Canyon 168
Lewis and Clark NHP 168–169
Mount Hood **167,** 168
Newport 166, 169
Oregon Caves Nat. Mon. 169
Oregon Dunes NRA 169
Portland **166,** 166–167, **167,** 169
road trips 168

P

Pennsylvania 170–173
Fallingwater 172
Flight 93 Nat. Mem. 172
Gettysburg 172, 173
Harrisburg 171
Hershey 172–173
Johnstown Flood Nat. Mem. 172
Longwood Gardens 173
Penn State University 172
Pennsylvania Dutch 172, 173
Pennsylvania Wilds 172
Philadelphia **170,** 170–171, 173
Pittsburgh 170, 171, **171,** 173
Presque Isle SP 172
Valley Forge NHP **172,** 173

Prince Edward Island, Canada 264–267
Anne of Green Gables sites 265–266, **266**
Basin Head PP 266–267
Charlottetown **264,** 264–265, **265**
Confederation Bridge 266
Confederation Trail 267
North Cape 266
Points East Coastal Drive 266
Prince Edward Island NP 265–266
Summerside 266
Victoria-by-the-Sea 266
Wood Islands 264, 267

Q

Quebec, Canada 268–273
Gaspé Peninsula 273, **273**
Lake Saint-Jean 272
Laurentian Mountains 272
Mont-Tremblant NP 272, **272**
Montreal 268, **268, 270,** 271–272, 273
Quebec City 268–269, **269, 271**
Rimouski 273
Trois-Rivières 272–273

R

Rhode Island 174–177
Blackstone River Valley 176–177
Block Island 177
Bristol 174, 176
festivals 177
Narragansett Bay 176, **177**
Newport 174, **175,** 175–176, **176,** 177
Pawtucket 176
Providence **174,** 174–175, 177

S

Saskatchewan, Canada 274–277
Athabasca Sand Dunes PP 277
Batoche 276–277
Coronach 275–276
Cypress Hills 276, **277**
festivals 277
Grasslands NP 276

Great Sandhills 276
Moose Jaw 275, 277
North Battleford 276
Oakdale 276
Prince Albert NP **276,** 277
Regina 274, **274,** 275
Saskatoon 274–275, **275,** 277

South Carolina 178–181
Beaufort 181
Boone Hall Plantation **178**
Caesars Head SP 181
Charleston 178–179, **179,** 180
Columbia 179–180, **180**
Congaree NP 180–181
Hilton Head 178, 181
Low Country 180, 181
Myrtle Beach 178, 181, **181**

South Dakota 182–185
Badlands NP 185, **185**
Black Hills 182, 183
Crazy Horse Mem. 184
Custer SP 184
Deadwood **182,** 184–185
Hot Springs 184
Laura Ingalls Wilder sites 185
Minuteman Missile NHS 185
Mount Rushmore Nat. Mem. 183, **183**
Prairie Village 185
Rapid City 182–183
road trips 184
Sioux Falls 182
Sturgis **184,** 185
Wessington Springs 185

T
Tennessee 186–189
Chattanooga 188
festivals 188
Franklin 189
Great Smoky Mountains NP 189, **189**
Memphis 186, **187,** 188, 189
Nashville **186,** 186–188, 189
Oak Ridge Nat. Lab. 188
Pigeon Forge **188,** 188–189
road trips 187
Shiloh NMP 189

Texas 190–193
Austin 191, 192, 193
Big Bend NP 192, **193**
Dallas 190, **190**
El Paso 193
Fort Worth 190–191
Galveston 192
Guadalupe Mountains NP 192–193
Hill Country 192, 193
Houston 190, 191, 193
Hueco Tanks SP **192,** 193
Padre Island 192

Palo Duro Canyon 193
road trips 192
San Antonio 190, **191,** 191–192

U
Utah 194–197
Arches NP **194,** 196
Bryce Canyon NP **4,** 197
Canyonlands NP 196
Capitol Reef NP 197
Dinosaur Nat. Mon. 196
festivals 196
Glen Canyon NRA 196, **197**
Great Salt Lake 195
Moab 196
Navajo Nation 196
Park City 194, 195–196
Provo 194, 195
Salt Lake City 194–195, **195,** 196
Zion NP **196,** 196–197

V
Vermont 198–201
Barre 199
Bennington 201
Burlington 198
Connecticut River Valley 201
Green Mountains **200,** 200–201, **201**
Lake Champlain 198, **198,** 199–200
Manchester 201
Montpelier 198–199, **199**
Shelburne 200
Stowe 200

Virginia 202–207
Arlington 205
Arlington Nat. Cemetery 205, **205**
Blue Ridge Parkway **204,** 205–206
Charlottesville 206
Chincoteague Island 203, 207
Colonial Williamsburg 207, **207**
Douthat SP 206
festivals 203
Fredericksburg 206
Jamestown 207
Lexington 206
Mount Rogers NRA 206
Mount Vernon 206
Norfolk 202, 203
Quantico 206
Richmond **202,** 202–203, **203**
road trips 205
Shenandoah NP 205, 206
Tangier Island 207
Virginia Beach 202, 203, 205, **206**
Warm Springs 206
Yorktown 207

W
Washington 208–211
festivals 210
Mount Rainier 211, **211**

Mount Saint Helens 211
North Cascades NP 211
Olympic NP **6, 208, 210,** 211
road trips 209
San Juan Islands 211
Seattle 208–210, **209,** 211
Spokane 208, 210

Washington, D.C. *see* District of Columbia

West Virginia 212–215
Allegheny Mountains 214, **215**
Charleston 212, **212**
Cumberland Mountains 214–215
Harpers Ferry 212, 213–214
Huntington 212–213, **214**
Monongahela NF 214
Moundsville 215
road trips 214
Seneca Rocks **213**
Trans-Allegheny Lunatic Asylum 215

Wisconsin 216–219
Apostle Islands NL 219
Door Peninsula **218,** 218–219
Frank Lloyd Wright 219
Lake Michigan 217–218, **218**
Lake Superior 218
Madison 216, **216,** 217
Milwaukee 216–217, **217**
Mineral Point 219
road trips 219
Two Rivers 218
Wisconsin Dells 219

Wyoming 220–223
Casper 221
Cheyenne 220
Cody 223
Devils Tower 223
Flaming Gorge NRA 222–223
Grand Teton NP 222, **222**
Great Plains 223
Jackson Hole 220, 222
Laramie **220,** 220–221
road trips 222
Teton Range **221**
Thermopolis 223
Yellowstone NP 221–222, **223**

Y
Yukon, Canada 278–281
Carcross 278, 280, **281**
Coast Range 280
Dawson City **278,** 278–279, 281
festivals 281
Ivvavik NP 281
Kluane NPP **279,** 281
Tombstone TP **280**
Watson Lake 281
Whitehorse 278, 279–280, 281

50 STATES 5000 IDEAS

Since 1888, the National Geographic Society has funded more than 12,000 research, exploration, and preservation projects around the world. National Geographic Partners distributes a portion of the funds it receives from your purchase to National Geographic Society to support programs including the conservation of animals and their habitats.

National Geographic Partners
1145 17th Street NW
Washington, DC 20036-4688 USA

Become a member of National Geographic and activate your benefits today at natgeo.com/jointoday.

For information about special discounts for bulk purchases, please contact National Geographic Books Special Sales: specialsales@natgeo.com

For rights or permissions inquiries, please contact National Geographic Books Subsidiary Rights: bookrights@natgeo.com

Library of Congress Cataloging-in-Publication Data
Names: Yogerst, Joseph R., author.
Title: 50 states, 5,000 ideas : where to go, when to go, what to see, what to do / text by Joe Yogerst.
Other titles: Fifty states, five thousand ideas
Description: Washington, D.C. : National Geographic, 2017. | Includes index.
Identifiers: LCCN 2016028721 | ISBN 9781426216909 (paperback)
Subjects: LCSH: United States--Guidebooks. | United States--Description and travel. | BISAC: TRAVEL / United States / General. | TRAVEL / Canada /General. | TRAVEL / Reference.

Classification: LCC E158 .Y64 2017 | DDC 917.304--dc23
LC record available at https://urldefense.proofpoint.com/v2/url?u=https-3A__lccn.loc gov_2016028721&d=DQIFAg&c=uw6TLu4hwhHdiGJOgwcWD4AjKQx6zvFcGEsb-fiY9-EI&r=Ar3XRLWsOd9X4qagesooQpv_FSetDc1lkl9px-dILrhw&m=1vFNh9mDKXD2LKeOyNO9rzxsT0Tdg-CpN-IboTXGMHhg&s=h3o9mck4HX0TaoJtmHQceR-fH-STQZu_lBaWZQ3WgLmE&e=

ACKNOWLEDGMENTS

National Geographic Books would like to thank writer Joe Yogerst for drafting the detailed, insightful text for every state, province, and territory in this book. Thank you to art director Elisa Gibson for creating the book's design, designer Kay Hankins for laying out every page, and photo editor Uliana Bazar for researching hundreds of photographs. Thanks to Meg Weaver for fact-checking the copy and to Mary Norris for text editing the manuscript and writing captions. Many thanks to production editor Mike O'Connor for seeing the book through the final phases of editing, including copyediting by Jenny Miyasaki, proofreading by Mary Stephanos, and indexing by Connie Binder. Thanks also to production manager William Cline and manufacturing manager Jennifer Hoff. Finally, thanks to project managers Caroline Hickey and Olivia Garnett for shepherding the project through the editorial process to press.

Printed in China

16/RRDS/1